SPIRITED COMMITMENT

SPIRITED
COMMITMENT

The Samuel and Saidye Bronfman
Family Foundation, 1952–2007

RODERICK MacLEOD and ERIC JOHN ABRAHAMSON

Published for the Samuel and Saidye Bronfman Family Foundation by

McGill-Queen's University Press | Montreal & Kingston · London · Ithaca

ISBN 978-0-7735-3710-1

Legal deposit second quarter 2010
Bibliothèque nationale du Québec

Printed in Canada on acid-free paper that is 100% ancient forest free
(100% post-consumer recycled), processed chlorine free.

McGill-Queen's University Press acknowledges the support of the Canada Council for
the Arts for our publishing program. We also acknowledge the financial support of the
Government of Canada through the Book Publishing Industry Development Program
(BPIDP) for our publishing activities.

Library and Archives Canada Cataloguing in Publication

MacLeod, Roderick, 1961–
Spirited commitment : the Samuel and Saidye Bronfman Family
Foundation, 1952–2007 / Roderick MacLeod and Eric John Abrahamson.

Includes bibliographical references and index.
ISBN 978-0-7735-3710-1

1. Samuel and Saidye Bronfman Family Foundation–History. 2. Family
foundations–Canada–History. I. Abrahamson, Eric John II. Samuel and
Saidye Bronfman Family Foundation III. Title.

HV110.M65M34 2010   361.7'6320971   C2010-901191-0

This book was designed and typeset by studio oneonone in Sabon 10.3/15.3

Contents

FOREWORD

Why do philanthropists create foundations? And why does the decision to do so matter?

There are various motivations for engaging in philanthropy through a foundation: a wish for more personal involvement in the act of giving, the drive to involve family in a joint project, an appetite for risk-taking and innovation in social change. But the first reason most foundation creators give is their desire to give back to the community and to society. They feel that their personal wealth was earned with the support of the communities in which they live and work. They are fortunate to be able to make a significant gift that will benefit many others. Samuel and Saidye Bronfman and their descendants exemplify this spirit of altruism. Their decision to create a foundation at a relatively early stage in the growth of the Canadian family foundation sector was a remarkable demonstration of that spirit.

Yet what is it that makes a foundation more than an act of generosity with the added implication of longevity?· The answer is sustained impact – on people, on ideas, on communities, on societies. The story of the Samuel and Saidye Bronfman Family Foundation is a story of impact. As described in these pages, the choices of Samuel and Saidye Bronfman and those who guided their foundation were consistently strategic. They made thoughtful and significant investments in their community and society, with results that far outweighed the dollars spent.

The philanthropic strategies with the most impact begin with ideas, not money; they are outcome-driven; they are people-focused; they depend on building trust and new relationships; they develop aligned and influential partnerships; and they use multiple approaches.

All of these elements emerge in the story of the Samuel and Saidye Bronfman Family Foundation. It is valuable to know this story in detail. While no foundation is exactly like any other, much can be learned from the history of such a successful one. As the authors point out in their introduction, stories of the impact of foundations on our society are underrepresented in both the academic and the popular literature in Canada. This history is an important contribution to filling that gap.

The more than fifty-year period in which the Samuel and Saidye Bronfman Foundation was active was a critical period for modern Canada. Samuel and Saidye themselves could not have been expected to foresee the enormous changes in the country from the mid-1950s through the early 21st century. But the acts of creating the foundation, engaging their children and, very importantly, hiring people with vision to help them carry out their philanthropic work, enabled their impact to continue far beyond the years in which the foundation first began its work. Foundations that are prepared to be generous, vigilant, and encouraging over a sustained period are able to be more effective. The evidence of this can be seen over the decades the Bronfman Family Foundation was involved in major projects in the arts, including cultural management, in the heritage community, with seniors, and in the area of learning disabilities.

Foundation impact comes from staying the course vis-à-vis both policy making and the larger community. This is something the Bronfman Family Foundation also demonstrated in its engagement with decision-makers and policy leaders. The foundation, particularly under the leadership of John Hobday, did not hesitate to support the advocacy efforts of its grantees and to try to influence public policy to bring about lasting change for its beneficiaries.

Effective foundations will experiment with comprehensive long-term approaches, stay with initiatives for many years, and, ideally, engage with governments. Such foundations can take a lead in identifying problems and finding or experimenting with approaches that may be too risky for governments. In the following pages, the influence of the Samuel and Saidye Bronfman Family Foundation emerges in just this way, especially through the later decades of its work, when its programs were focused on five areas of long-term giving. As the authors note, the foundation chose to work with a handful of key organizations that it identified as "agents for change" in a specific arena of cultural or social policy. This was an unusual and creative strategy for a Canadian foundation and one that led to the development of national networks addressing learning disabilities, cultural management, and the needs of seniors.

The most engaged foundations want to learn from what they are doing. They bring people together and learn through evaluation. In the 1980s and 1990s, the foundation used the power of small grants to fund creative gatherings and exchanges of ideas with an extraordinary range of groups, from youth activists to urban mayors. It also used creative tools such as visioning workshops to help its clients build better common understanding of issues and to articulate new visions for themselves.

The Samuel and Saidye Bronfman Family Foundation is no longer in existence. But this history shows conclusively how it made a difference in people's lives. An answer to my opening question, "why does philanthropy matter?" can be found in this story. For the Bronfman family, as for so many other Canadian families, philanthropy is a way of making change. The impact of this leading Canadian family foundation, through succeeding generations of the Bronfman family and through the extraordinary individuals on its staff, is now well documented and well told, for the benefit of all those interested in the power of philanthropy to change the world for the better.

Hilary Pearson
President
Philanthropic Foundations Canada

Acknowledgments

This book has been a joint effort in more than the usual sense. Initially, the task of writing a commemorative fifty-year history of the Samuel and Saidye Bronfman Family Foundation was undertaken by Eric Abrahamson, who conducted a great deal of research and produced an admirable first draft. With Eric unable to continue the work for personal reasons, this draft eventually landed on my desk and I responded eagerly to the invitation to complete it. Curiously, by the time I was able to begin working on a second draft, the subject of this history had become even more interesting: not only had the SSBFF directors made the decision to wind down the foundation, but in doing so a number of programs and projects were concluded in unexpected ways, requiring additional material and to an extent recasting of some of the original material. It became a singular challenge for a historian (though of course hardly so for a journalist) to be writing about events that were currently the subject of media reports – to say nothing of interviewing people who were the active movers and shakers of the events in question.

And so, at the head of my list of people to thank must be Eric Abrahamson for leaving me with such a rewarding project as well as such a sturdy foundation, both in form and content, on which to proceed. Eric conducted most of the interviews that serve as important sources for this book, and on his behalf I must thank all of his subjects, both within the Bronfman family and without, for having contributed so much to his, and my, understanding of the SSBFF. For my part I am grateful for the informative talks I have had with Phyllis Lambert, John Hobday, Nancy Rosenfeld, and other members of the SSBFF/Claridge staff whose recollections and insights proved invaluable. Those three, along with several of the SSBFF directors and Eric himself, have read subsequent drafts of this manuscript and given me very helpful comments. All through this process, Jonathan Crago of McGill-Queen's Press has provided thoughtful advice about how to approach and present the material. The comments of the external readers, and of copy editor Elise Moser, have certainly made this a better book, and for that I am thankful.

On a more material level, Nancy Rosenfeld and the staff at Claridge did quite a lot of helpful legwork and went to great lengths to make an outsider to this busy world of philanthropy feel at home. Susan Spencer, Judy Strapp, and many others put in extra time hunting down often obscure information, but the hands-down tireless champion in that department is Carol-Ann Bray, without whose quiet and gracious efficiency I am quite sure the entire project would have unravelled. Of those helpful people outside the world of Claridge I would single out Shannon Hodge at the Jewish Public Library, and Janice Rosen and Hélène Vallée at the Canadian Jewish Congress Charities Committee National Archives. Finally, a big thanks to Heather Ungar of the Plum Coulee Community Foundation for providing a riveting private tour of the Saidye Rosner Bronfman Heritage Recreation Park; climbing a seventy-foot ladder to the top of a grain elevator was not something I had anticipated doing when I began working on this manuscript.

There is not much about whisky in this book. Nevertheless, I would like to raise a glass to Sam Bronfman, without whose efforts not only would there have been nothing to write about but also so much less pleasure taken in doing so.

Roderick MacLeod
Montreal

CHRONOLOGY

1847 First Hebrew Benevolent Society established in Montreal
1863 Young Men's Hebrew Benevolent Society established
      in Montreal
1891 Jewish Colonization Association established in London
      by Baron de Hirsch
1908 Young Men's Hebrew Association founded in Montreal
1917 Federation of Jewish Philanthropies (FJP) incorporated
      in Montreal
1919 Canadian Jewish Congress (CJC) established in Montreal
      Young Women's Hebrew Association founded in Montreal
1920 Jewish Immigrant Aid Society of Canada (JIAS) established
1922 Samuel Bronfman and Saidye Rosner marry (June)
      Quebec's Historic Monuments Commission established
1924 Distillers Corporation Ltd incorporated (May)
1925 Minda de Gunzburg (nee Bronfman) born
1927 Phyllis Lambert (nee Bronfman) born
1928 Samuel Bronfman purchases Joseph E. Seagram & Sons
1929 Seagram office building opens on Peel Street, Montreal
      Bronfman family moves to The Boulevard, Montreal, and
      names the house "Oaklands"

Edgar Bronfman born

Saidye Bronfman becomes president of the YWHA (to 1933)

1931 Samuel Bronfman becomes joint chair of the JIAS

Charles Bronfman born

1934 Samuel Bronfman elected chairman of the FJP (to 1950)

1937 J.W. McConnell Foundation established

1939 Samuel Bronfman becomes president of the CJC (to 1962)

1941 Combined Jewish Appeal (CJA) launched

1943 Saidye Bronfman is made an officer of the Order of Canada

1950 Dedication of new YM-YWHA in the Snowdon area of Montreal

1951 The Bronfmans establish CEMP (Charles, Edgar, Minda, Phyllis) Investments as a family trust

Massey-Lévesque Report on the arts and culture issued

Federation of Jewish Philanthropies becomes Federation of Jewish Community Services

1952 The Samuel and Saidye Bronfman Family Foundation (SSBFF) established (November)

1954 The Samuel Rosner Chair in Agronomy established at the University of Manitoba

1956 Samuel and Saidye's first visit to Israel

1957 Canada Council established

Canadian Association in Support of the Native Peoples founded

1959 McGill University Children's Learning Centre established

1963 Historic Monuments Act for Quebec passed

Bronfmans and the YMHA negotiate the creation of the Saidye Bronfman Centre

Canadian Association for Children with Learning Disabilities (CACLD) established

1965 Federation of Jewish Community Services becomes Allied Jewish Community Services

1967 The Six Day War in the Middle East

Canada's centenary

Saidye Bronfman Centre opens in Montreal (September)

1970 The Samuel Bronfman House built for the headquarters of the Canadian Jewish Congress

1971　The Samuel Bronfman Building built for the McGill Faculty
　　　of Management

　　　Sam Bronfman dies (July)

1972　Matthew Ram compiles a report on the Bronfman family's
　　　philanthropy

　　　Peter Swann becomes first Executive Director of the SSBFF

　　　First meeting of the board after Sam Bronfman's death

　　　Saidye Bronfman becomes president of the SSBFF (November)

　　　Bill 72 makes health and social services in Quebec a
　　　government responsibility

　　　Canadian Arctic Resources Committee (CARC) founded

　　　Cultural Properties Act for Quebec passed

1973　SSBFF directors decide on funding programs

　　　SSBFF headquarters is established on Tupper Street, Montreal

　　　Canada Business Corporations Act passed (July)

　　　Association of Canadian Foundations established

　　　Van Horne mansion destroyed in Montreal, galvanizing the
　　　heritage movement

　　　Heritage Canada Foundation established by the federal
　　　government

　　　Yiddish Theatre Company takes up residence at the Saidye
　　　Bronfman Centre

1974　Proposals for a new not-for-profit corporation law for Canada
　　　(June)

　　　Council for Business and the Arts in Canada (CBAC) founded

1975　SSBFF funds the creation of Heritage Montreal (October)

1976　SSBFF launches the Saidye Bronfman Award for Excellence
　　　in Crafts

1977　SSBFF provides direct funding to the McGill University
　　　Children's Learning Centre

1979　SSBFF launches funding program "Social Problems Concerned
　　　with the Elderly"

1980　Federal government establishes the National Advisory Council
　　　on Aging (NACA)

1982　John Hobday becomes director of corporate donations for
　　　Distillers Corporation–Seagrams Limited

1983 Peter Swann's last meeting as executive director of the SSBFF;
    John Hobday's first (May)
    SSBFF headquarters moves to the Seagram Building on
    Peel Street, Montreal
    Hobday submits "Toward Tomorrow" to the SSBFF board
1984 Canadian Association of Arts Administration Educators
    (CAAAE) formed
    Charles Bronfman's "Letter to Minda" (June)
    Reynold Levy report on the status of the Saidye Bronfman
    Centre submitted
    Arts Administration Specialization Program established at the
    University of Waterloo
1985 Renovations to the Saidye Bronfman Centre theatre and
    gallery begin
    Charles Bronfman establishes the CRB Foundation
    Heritage Montreal begins holding summer course in heritage
    conservation
    Phyllis Lambert becomes president of the SSBFF
    Minda de Gunzburg dies (July)
1986 CEMP dissolved
    SSBFF headquarters moves to Claridge offices, Peel Street,
    Montreal
    CACLD becomes the Learning Disabilities Association of
    Canada (LDAC)
    Seniors' national summit establishes One Voice as an
    organization for seniors
    Jean de Gunzburg joins the SSBFF board of directors
    (December)
1987 Cecil Rabinovitch becomes director of the Saidye Bronfman
    Centre
    Annex to the Saidye Bronfman Centre built (finished 1989)
    Saidye Rosner Bronfman chair in architecture established at
    McGill University
    Samuel Rosner Computer Assisted Learning and Farm
    Financial Management Program established at the University
    of Manitoba

Heritage Montreal and the Université de Montréal begin
   offering MA in Heritage Conservation
SSBFF forms Investment Committee (November)
Sale of Cadillac Fairview; Bronfman family makes endowment
   to SSBFF (November)

1988 Gisele Rucker hired as SSBFF programs officer (May)
Lon Dubinsky submits report on Bronfman family philanthropy
   (June)
"Masters of the Craft" exhibition at new Canadian Museum of
   Civilization, Hull, QC
Matthew Bronfman replaces his father Edgar on the SSBFF
   board   of directors
Hobday and Rucker submit "Preparing for the Nineties" to the
   SSBFF board of directors

1989 William J. Smith becomes director of the McGill University
   Children's Learning Centre
Official opening of the Canadian Centre for Architecture
   in Montreal
Centre for Cultural Management established at the University
   of Waterloo

1990 LDAC hosts a visioning workshop at Montebello, QC (April)
Community Foundations of Canada established
McGill University Children's Learning Centre becomes the
   Learning Centre of Quebec
Stephen Bronfman replaces his father Charles on the SSBFF
   board of directors
One Voice hosts a visioning workshop at Mont-Ste-Marie, QC
   (September)
SSBFF hosts a visioning workshop for heritage in North Hatley,
   QC (October)
Centre for Cultural Management hosts a visioning workshop
   at Elora, ON (November)

1991 SSBFF hosts a visioning workshop for craft in Banff, AB
Robert Vineberg and Robert Rabinovitch join the SSBFF board
   of directors
SSBFF ends core funding for Heritage Montreal

1992 Urban Issues program launched with a call for proposals
1993 SSBFF gradually ends funding to the LDAC
First annual meeting of the grantees of the Urban Issues
program in Montreal
1994 Federal Department of Canadian Heritage (PCH) created
SSBFF funds creation of the Canadian Arts Stabilization
Program (CASP)
1995 Saidye Bronfman dies; funeral at the Saidye Bronfman Centre
Second round of grants for Urban Issues announced
1997 SSBFF withdraws funding from One Voice
Allied Jewish Community Services becomes "Federation – CJA"
(Combined Jewish Appeal)
Peter Swann dies (December)
1998 Third round of grants for Urban Issues announced
Jean de Gunzburg becomes president of the SSBFF
1999 International Federation on Ageing Conference held
in Montreal
Cultural Management Institute (CMI) begins developing
a distance learning program
2000 SSBFF funds the National Arts and Youth Demonstration
Project
2001 Federal government announces national strategy for arts
stabilization (May)
Fourth round of grants for Urban Issues announced
Plum Coulee, Manitoba, celebrates centenary; SSBFF funds
heritage renovation proposals
2002 Plum Coulee Community Foundation incorporated (April)
2003 Hobday leaves the SSBFF to become head of the Canada
Council for the Arts
Gisele Rucker becomes interim executive director of the SSBFF
(January)
2004 SSBFF winds down its operations; Nancy Rosenfeld hired
as executive director
2005 Urban Issues program discontinued

2006 SSBFF reaches agreement with the Segal family over the Saidye
        Bronfman Centre
        Thirtieth Saidye Bronfman craft award celebrated at the
        Canadian Museum of Civilization
        Saidye Bronfman Award becomes a Governor General's Award
        SSBFF endows the John Hobday Award in Arts Management
        at the Canada Council for the Arts
2008 Saidye Rosner Bronfman Heritage and Recreational Park
        dedicated in Plum Coulee

Bronfman Family Tree

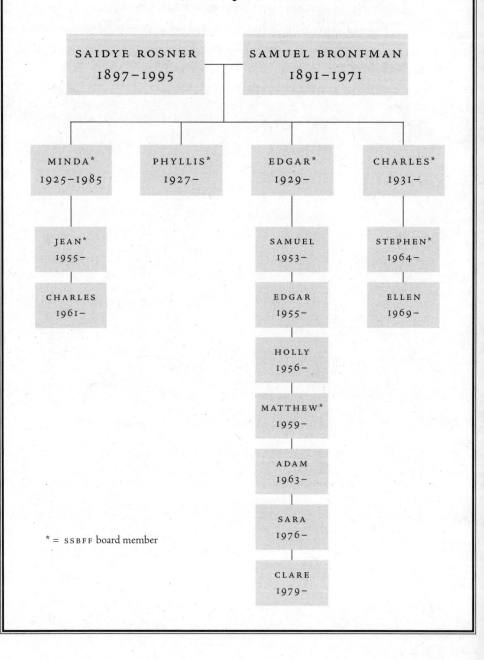

| SAIDYE ROSNER 1897–1995 | SAMUEL BRONFMAN 1891–1971 |

MINDA* 1925–1985

PHYLLIS* 1927–

EDGAR* 1929–

CHARLES* 1931–

JEAN* 1955–

SAMUEL 1953–

STEPHEN* 1964–

CHARLES 1961–

EDGAR 1955–

ELLEN 1969–

HOLLY 1956–

MATTHEW* 1959–

ADAM 1963–

SARA 1976–

* = SSBFF board member

CLARE 1979–

Samuel Bronfman and Saidye Rosner on their honeymoon,
1922 (Library and Archives Canada).

Main Street, Plum Coulee, c.1900
(Plum Coulee Community Foundation).

Interior of the Rosner store, Plum Coulee
(Plum Coulee Community Foundation).

Samuel and Priscilla Rosner on a formal occasion, c.1910
(Library and Archives Canada).

The Rosner family in Winnipeg. Saidye is second from the left
(Library and Archives Canada).

Former Seagram headquarters, Peel Street, Montreal (author photo).

Samuel Bronfman at a dinner party at Oaklands, December 1945
(Canadian Jewish Congress Charities Committee National Archives).

"Turning of the First Sod" – Saidye Bronfman at the site of the new YM-YWHA,
9 May 1948. Left to right: Boy Scout, Gerald Shalinsky, Saidye, Y Honorary Secretary
Zave Levinson, Rabbi Wilfred Shuchat, Y Honorary President Sol Kellert
(in morning coat and top hat) (Jewish Public Library).

Saidye Bronfman speaking at the dedication of the Snowdon YMHA, 1950 (Jewish Public Library).

Red Cross Sewing Club, 1940s. Saidye is seated at lower right
(Jewish Public Library).

"Rescue the Living" poster accompanying the CJC's 1945 campaign to raise funds for the United Jewish Refugee and War Relief Agencies (Jewish Public Library: Jewish Canadiana Collection, CJA).

The Bronfmans at the official opening of the Saidye Bronfman Centre, 1967.
Standing, left to right: Alain de Gunzburg, Ann Loeb Bronfman,
Edgar M. Bronfman, Barbara Baerwald Bronfman, Charles R. Bronfman.
Seated, left to right: Phyllis Lambert, Saidye Bronfman, Sam Bronfman,
Minda de Gunzburg (SSBFF collection).

Samuel Bronfman speaking at the Samuel Bronfman Dinner, Combined Jewish
Appeal / United Jewish Appeal, 1956. This annual event, named in honour
of the leading contributor, sought to raise funds for the support of Israel.
Campaign chairman Bernard Lande is seated at Sam's right
(Jewish Public Library).

Sam and Saidye at the 1956 testimonial dinner given by Canada-Israel Securities, of which Sam was the president. This event took place at Montreal's Windsor Hotel, which would become the headquarters of the SSBFF and other Bronfman organizations (Canadian Jewish Congress Charities Committee National Archives).

Turning the sod for the Samuel Bronfman House, new headquarters of the
Canadian Jewish Congress, 1970. The men with spades are CJC President
Monroe Abbey, Samuel Bronfman, and CJC Executive Vice-President Saul
Hayes. To Sam's right, in fur coat and hat, is Leo Kolber (Canadian Jewish
Congress Charities Committee National Archives).

אבן פינה
למוסיאון לארכיאולוניה ולמקרא
ע"ש שמואל ברונפמן
הונחה ביום כה תשרי תשכ"ו
במעמד משפחת ברונפמן
שרי מדינת ישראל ואורחים קרואים

Dedication of the Bronfman wing of the Israel Museum, Jerusalem, 1965.
Left to right: Barbara Baerwald Bronfman, Charles, Phyllis, Sam, Saidye,
Alain de Gunzburg, Minda (Canadian Jewish Congress Charities Committee
National Archives).

Peter Swann (photo courtesy of the estate of Peter Swann).

John Hobday (photo courtesy of John Hobday).

Head office of Claridge and the SSBFF from 1988: former Windsor Hotel, Peel Street, Montreal (author photo).

Spirited Commitment

ACORNS

When Samuel Bronfman prepared a company history of Seagram some years before his death, he called it *From Little Acorns*, which seemed to sum up the core principles of his life. The phrase was taken from a poem by David Everett, a late-eighteenth century New England schoolteacher, lawyer, and newspaper editor whose epigrammatic verse inspired generations with their homespun wisdom: "Large streams from little fountains flow / Tall oaks from little acorns grow." The notion that great achievements have small beginnings – alternatively, that small beginnings can lead to great things – seems to have had special meaning for Sam Bronfman, whose origins were truly humble yet who created what was then one of the world's largest industrial corporations.[1] The oak tree was the corporate symbol of CEMP, the business arm of the Bronfman family.[2] It was also used as a symbol of the Samuel and Saidye Bronfman Family Foundation (SSBFF), the philanthropic body that Sam and Saidye set up in the early 1950s and which their children, and later grandchildren, continued after their deaths. The foundation's website features an introductory page whose visual animation consists of an acorn falling to the ground and then sprouting into an oak. It is a telling metaphor for modern philanthropy, which is less about giving money away indiscriminately than it is about making strategic investments with an eye to creating healthy and independent organisms.

Of course, little acorns also grow from tall oaks, and the family behind this family foundation was certainly a tall oak, both within the Montreal Jewish community and within the international business world. The Bronfman name and the family's wealth presented a challenge to the second and third generations, who did not wish simply to dole out money to whichever worthy causes came calling, in the manner of a charitable trust whose main motive may have been to obtain tax relief. Sam and Saidye established the foundation in order to make investments in various community organizations, and arranged their business and personal holdings to maximize their philanthropic freedom. Many of their children and grandchildren also pursued philanthropic goals with their own money, often through their own foundations. But Minda, Phyllis, Edgar, and Charles, who were Sam and Saidye's children, and later on Minda's son Jean, Edgar's son Matthew, and Charles's son Stephen, wished to make the SSBFF an agent of real change within Canadian society. They wanted the dividends of family fortune to be reinvested in projects that would have lasting consequences. Through research, they identified the need for oaks and planted their acorns carefully.

It was not, of course, a straightforward matter to decide on the specific areas in which the foundation would seek to effect change. Sam and Saidye, a close couple with three decades of common interests behind them when they began the SSBFF, had no particular problems choosing what they wanted to focus on, but the members of the following generations were strong-minded individuals with different tastes and passions. Almost all the decisions made by the SSBFF board were coloured by the interplay of these personal differences. This factor is always present in the running of family foundations, although in the Bronfmans' case perhaps a little more so. These differences made for a very creative dynamic.

In determining the direction the foundation would take after Sam's death in 1971, his children opted to hire professionals who would manage the various funding programs. For the first ten years they employed Peter Swann, who worked with the SSBFF directors to identify key areas of interest and then judiciously responded to hundreds of requests for funding within these areas. For the next twenty years, the SSBFF executive director was John Hobday, who worked to consolidate these small grants into major support for larger organizations; his goal was always to create and nourish institutions with the capacity to operate on a national level, and so enable them to effect significant change within society. Hobday also initiated several new programs and hired Gisele Rucker as a grants officer; Rucker provided an empathic and very hands-on addition to the foundation, working for fifteen years under Hobday and then briefly as executive director in her own right. These individuals kept the foundation board members well briefed as to their activities, enabling them to make informed decisions. Although the directors regularly provided the impetus, most of the time they trusted the staff to proceed in the foundation's best interest. The SSBFF directors were part of a very successful family but they did not pretend to know everything, and wisely chose when and when not to interfere.[3]

The operative format adopted by the SSBFF – a board of directors composed of family members plus one or two financial or legal advisors and an executive director with support staff – is typical of family foundations, particularly following the death of the principal donor. That the directors created a number of specialized funding programs was by no means unusual, nor was the level of discussion and negotiation over the choice of these programs.[4] These features aside, however, it would be difficult to say what was typical about the SSBFF. Beyond basic format and procedure, every foundation is set up differently with different goals, and those who carry out the work have differing expectations and face different challenges; generalization is problematic. In other words, the story of the SSBFF is not presented here in order primarily to shed light on how family foundations operate, although of course much can be extrapolated from its particular experiences. It is not intended as a case study to form part of the larger theoretical literature on foundations exemplified by the work of Peter Frumkin, Peter Dobkin Hall, Ellen Condliffe Lagemann, George E. Marcus, Judith Sealander, and many others. This literature provides very useful background to any foundation history that acknowledges, as this one does, the importance of a context larger than the intricate details of individual funding projects.

Yet the emphasis here is on the general giving resonance to the specific, rather than having the specific flesh out (or, more accurately, help flesh out) the general.

This history does, we hope, contribute to the literature on Canadian philanthropy, although again not in a theoretical manner. In fact, not only is there little by way of a theory of Canadian philanthropy (outside the exploration of how the work of American foundations mirrors the branch-plant tendency of American industry[5]), but there is very little literature on the subject. Samuel Martin's *An Essential Grace* remains something of a classic in the field, limited as it is by a reliance on cultural generalizations. Needless to say, more work should be done on the history of the "private sector" in Canada, in part to offset the widespread notion that the Canadian state was always a major player in philanthropy. The works of Jeffrey Brison, Bernard Ostry, and Maria Tippett provide useful surveys of culture in Canada and how it was funded, distilled here by way of introduction to the SSBFF's involvement in this field. With luck there will soon be more detailed studies of major Canadian cultural institutions to render this sort of distillation superfluous.

This work is, in fact, an institutional history, its subject being one particular family foundation. For various reasons, the history of particular institutions – as opposed to the study of institutions within society – has met with disfavour in recent years as an academic genre. Some of this disfavour stems from an understandable aversion to dry commissioned histories, of which all too many are produced – although it is worth noting that there is no reason that such works must be dry other than that they are typically written by people with professional connections to an institution rather than by experienced researchers and writers. The bias against institutional and especially corporate history also harks back to a larger dissatisfaction within social history with biographical writing, which treats the subject as an end in itself rather than a means to a larger end; such dissatisfaction extends to corporate biographies, including the history of public bodies from planning commissions to parliamentary governments. It is good that scholars have moved history outside this particular box. At the same time, we do the discipline a disservice if we reject a subject as worthy of treatment simply because it does not obviously inform universal themes, or if we give it value only as a case study of something larger. Scholars should acknowledge the usefulness of an intimate study of a subject in providing a specialized set of information in a particular, perhaps unique, context whether or not it contributes to existing debates. Linking it to a larger context is certainly wise, as is the drawing of lessons, parallels, and other conclusions, but this should not imply that a story is necessarily better because it is typical.

The story of the SSBFF is unique on many levels. To begin with, the major players are the Bronfmans, historically one of the richest families in Canada and certainly one of the richest Jewish families in Canada. Members of this family are well known for being outspoken and engaged in a wide variety of causes both in Canada and around the world. An unusual amount has been written about them, some of it by family members themselves but much more by individual and corporate biographers such as Michael Marrus, Peter C. Newman, and Nicholas Faith. Bronfmans have also received mention with some frequency in the media, largely owing to the numerous projects in which they are involved, to say nothing of the interest surrounding the sale of Seagram in the early 2000s. The Bronfmans' fame makes for certain challenges in writing about them, from finding ground that has not already been covered to avoiding the temptation to take advantage of celebrity and cover the ground anyway. The focus of the current work is the Bronfmans' philanthropy, and more specifically one component of this philanthropy, the SSBFF – which is, significantly, one of the least known and understood of the family's achievements.

The strong personalities of the Bronfman family members are reflected in the wide diversity of their interests, and although they engaged in a process of negotiation over what the SSBFF would fund, the result was a wider range of programs than was usual in a family foundation of its size. Programs addressed such unrelated themes as the problems of senior citizens and of native peoples, arts and culture, heritage preservation, and the Jewish community – to say nothing of the dozens of

smaller projects covering an even wider range of topics. The members of
the foundation's board had an initial debate in the early 1970s over what
sorts of issues to fund – one that was informed by considerable study by
the executive director of what Canadians felt was needed – and this led
to a consensus on a small number of specialized programs. These programs represented areas that held specific interest for the individual
board members, matched broadly with a sense of what social problems
the foundation could reasonably expect to tackle. Unlike many foundations that are known primarily for their investment in education, health
or the arts, the SSBFF had a broader reach, with all the challenges that
implied. Consequently, a history of SSBFF programs must cover several
seemingly disparate themes, their diversity explained at least in part by
the nature of the family's consensus.

In the mid-1980s, the members of the foundation engaged in a deeper
debate over this consensus, largely regarding their commitment to the
Jewish community. Sam and Saidye had initiated an annual gift to the
Combined Jewish Appeal that typically represented around two-thirds of
their donations, and their children agreed to continue this after Sam's
death. The gift to what became the Federation CJA was never in doubt,
representing as it did the clearest expression of the SSBFF's adherence to
the wishes of the donor. The debate that preoccupied the Bronfman siblings during the middle years of the 1980s was over the SSBFF's priorities, or rather how the SSBFF fitted into the members' own priorities.
Was the foundation primarily a vehicle for contributing to the Federation
CJA (which now represented about three-quarters of its annual budget)
with a smaller set of social and cultural programs on the side, or was the
SSBFF a body that operated programs in the arts, heritage, etc., which
happened, as it were, to also make a huge annual contribution to the
Federation CJA? The debate was, of course, never presented in these
terms, but it did have the potential to cause tension as it hinged on the
emotional issue of loyalty to Sam's wishes.

In practice, the issue of Sam's wishes was not at all straightforward,
partly because he had always approached philanthropy in a creative
rather than a formal manner, and partly because his motives for giving

were complex. Sam and Saidye were from immigrant families, and as such the way they saw their community and country was different from the way a J.W. McConnell or a Hart Massey had done. Sam's philanthropy was, at some level, the product of a religious upbringing that saw a clear role for charity, but it was shaped more significantly by the experience of being a successful member of Montreal's Jewish community and its well-established business world. He and Saidye shared with many first-generation immigrants a desire to be accepted and respected, and came to espouse so-called British values (later Canadian values) as an answer to discrimination. But where Sam or Saidye's sense of Jewishness ended and where their sense of Britishness or Canadianness began is difficult to say, so to emphasize the one at the expense of the other is unjustified. It is hard, therefore, to say with certainty what the ssBFF's original mandate was; clearly there was a desire to help the Jewish community, but also interest in the arts and education. Sam's desire for recognition was met by the naming of two key buildings after him, one at the heart of the Jewish community and the other very much outside it.

This sort of ambiguity would also characterize the ssBFF and its programs after Sam's death, especially as Edgar and Charles became leaders of the Jewish community in their own rights (Charles in particular inherited Sam's mantle in Montreal) and as Minda and Phyllis moved away from this community. The resulting tension and how it played out is a significant theme of this history. At the same time, the main focus is clearly not on the donation to the Federation cja, despite its size and importance, but rather on the rest of the ssBFF's activities. (This is not to ignore the fact that the Federation and other major Jewish institutions in Canada merit more scholarly attention than they have so far received.) There is something of a paradox in presenting the history of a foundation that gave over $2 million annually to Jewish causes as though Jewishness was all but incidental to it, but such a paradox characterizes the ssBFF. The donation to the Federation cja was fixed, and required no significant administration on the foundation's part. By contrast, the activities involving the executive director (often referred to as the "executive director's program") took up a great deal of time for both board and staff.

Indeed, the diversity of these activities represented not only a variety of interests on the part of board members but a willingness to promote such interests within the funding programs and directly engage the client organizations. The SSBFF enjoyed a certain fame as a "hands-on" grantor, a reputation that was borne out by the level of personal commitment shown by the directors to the programs they created. Many other foundations provided grants and expected a report when the project was complete, but never engaged with grantees at a deeper level. By contrast, the SSBFF nurtured projects, often remaining engaged with grantees even after the financial contributions had ceased. SSBFF staff served on grantee boards and committees. Moreover, the SSBFF executive directors exhibited an unusual degree of skill at negotiating different interests and at building connections between groups and governments. John Hobday's drive to create organizations with the capacity for advocacy at the national level brought people together in particularly creative ways, although Peter Swann's populist empathy and Gisele Rucker's natural powers of observation also meant that potential grantees were assessed and nurtured as creative individuals rather than mere names on an application form.

The ambiguity over the mandate and the variety of approaches to funding makes for challenges in assessing the success of the SSBFF's philanthropy. At many stages in its development, and especially in the course of the seminal visioning workshops held in 1990–91, the foundation discussed the need to find a method for evaluating its various projects and even entire programs, several of which engaged only one or two client organizations. There was never real concern that funds would be misspent; even so, board and staff were well aware of the dangers in giving large amounts of money without adequate means of determining whether they were making a difference to people's lives. The SSBFF's policy of nurturing a number of key organizations did not mean that the directors wished to provide core funding indefinitely, but rather that initial funding would help an organization to develop its capacity and become self-sufficient. Even so, the nature of the various programs and projects meant that the SSBFF found itself having to approach each case on its own terms, and never managed to establish a universal set of criteria by which to judge success. Nevertheless, in an effort to bring continuity to the variety of themes covered, especially in the second half of the book, we have opted to address each program with a standard series of questions focusing on its ability to create dynamic and self-sufficient organizations which manage to effect social change.

Arguably, the soundest criterion for judging the success of a philanthropic foundation is that it consistently spends money to achieve results and manages to make a difference – although one should probably give high marks for foundations that make mistakes and learn from them. How much money is spent and how long a foundation lasts are not indications of success, as every foundation is set up differently with different goals, and those who carry out the work have different expectations and face different challenges. The SSBFF took risks with its money, met with some successes and some failures, and always strove to learn from its experiences.

This history of the SSBFF was gleaned from its own archive of records located at the foundation's Montreal offices, and also from interviews conducted with the principal players. Naturally, there are problems inherent in using the minutes of meetings and reports, beginning with their accuracy: even assuming that minutes present a faithful record of what was said at a meeting, this does not guarantee that everything that was said is fact. This problem can be countered effectively by critical reading and comparison to other sources. These records often provide a great deal of information on specialized subjects. In fact, the reports generated by SSBFF staff in preparation for board discussions contain material on client organizations that is not generally available elsewhere – although many of them may have their own internal records, which could (and in some cases should) be used to write their own histories. Interviews are useful ways to corroborate or nuance the information given in the written records; often the verbal pictures painted by an individual remembering an event allow for a much deeper understanding of what happened. Again, interviews must be conducted, and their transcripts read, critically in order for them to provide real insight; memories are often faulty, but impressions – rarely conveyed in written records – can be golden.

Given this book's heavy reliance on the testimonies and opinions of the players involved, it is important to address the question of editorial influence. This history was commissioned by the directors of the SSBFF in order to provide a comprehensive account of its work over more than half a century. As a commissioned history, it faces a number of dangers. One is the tendency to become a self-referential chronicle of achievements outside of any larger context, what Ellen Condliffe Lagemann describes as "boring to read and insignificant in the insight offered."[6] Increasing numbers of corporations, including the SSBFF, have opened their records to scrutiny by academic researchers in an attempt to produce corporate histories that resonate beyond their own experience by virtue of independent insight. Such insight does not, however, prevent a history from becoming hagiography, as John J. Miller's work on the John M. Olin foundation does, despite being a well-researched and entertaining read. One can, we hope, escape the charge of hagiography and yet fundamentally admire one's subject – indeed, it would be an unrewarding exercise to explore in great detail a subject one finds of little merit. If we have taken no special pains to find fault with the people involved in the SSBFF neither have we worked to present them in a glowing light. Furthermore, throughout this process the SSBFF board and staff have shown a remarkable appreciation for the demands of scholarship and a clear desire to produce a book that was not a mere vanity project.

Far from being a constraint on academic freedom, the participation of SSBFF board and staff in the research process has been most welcome. Their comments on earlier versions of the manuscript were invaluable, providing not only information and interpretation but also advice – above all, how best to draw the line between too little and too much personal detail. Again, as many of the individuals in question are well-known figures, there is the danger of shifting the focus away from the SSBFF and onto private matters. One reader felt our account was somewhat "bloodless," evidently remembering a good deal more spirit in many of the discussions than was suggested in the records and is described in the text; nevertheless, he agreed that to have underscored tension for its own sake would have been to lose sight of the SSBFF's efforts to effect change in Canadian society. Members of the Bronfman family and SSBFF staff made no objection to the inclusion of detail if it advanced the story of the foundation; on the few occasions when they pointed to elements that they felt did not pertain to the SSBFF, we tended to agree.

Although the Bronfman family is not the primary subject of this story, it is important nevertheless to understand the people who created the SSBFF. Accordingly, the book's first chapter presents the Bronfmans within the context of their social and religious background. Sam and Saidye grew up on the prairies of Manitoba in Jewish households and communities where religious and cultural traditions, as well as the experience of being immigrants, shaped their outlook and relationship to the world. Sam's business was also shaped by the prairies, but the couple settled in Montreal soon after their marriage and became deeply involved in the Jewish community there. In the late 1930s, Sam's community involvement put him on the national stage, and during the Second World War both he and Saidye spearheaded many patriotic initiatives which won them recognition from the broader community and the British Empire. Sam and Saidye's four children grew up in a household where philanthropy was an everyday event, involving support for Canada and Britain as much as for Jewish institutions.

Chapter 2 describes the establishment of the SSBFF in 1952 and explores the institutional context in which Sam and Saidye sought to contribute to many worthy causes. The background to the SSBFF includes the rise of scientific philanthropy and the establishment of philanthropic foundations since the late nineteenth century – or in the case of Canada, since the interwar period. Of particular interest is the somewhat checkered history of government involvement in the arts in Canada prior to the 1950s. While focused primarily on the needs of the Jewish community, both at home and in the nascent state of Israel, Sam and Saidye's philanthropy also embraced the arts, education, and even agricultural research. By the time of Sam's death in 1971, the SSBFF was the principal channel for the Bronfmans' funding of the Combined Jewish Appeal (CJA) as well as many other institutions of the Canadian Jewish community – including the arts centre in Montreal named after Saidye Bronfman.

From 1952 to 1971, the SSBFF had been characterized by an informal structure which had enabled Sam and Saidye to make donations as the need arose but did not involve specific funding programs. When the next generation took up the reins of the SSBFF, they had to work out how they would carry on its work and what exactly the foundation would do. After much discussion amongst themselves and with executive director Peter Swann, they agreed to focus on a number of key programs which suited the siblings' various interests and seemed to address needs within Canadian society. The transition from a family trust to a foundation dedicated to making grants within specific areas of interest and run by professional management is the subject of chapter 3.

Chapters 4 and 5 continue the story of the SSBFF's development into the 1990s, leaving the discussion of the evolution of specific programs to later chapters. A significant transition occurred with the arrival of John Hobday at the helm of the SSBFF in 1983 and the application of his more focused and strategic approach to the foundation's funding programs. Hobday's early years with the SSBFF coincided with serious soul-searching on the part of the directors as to their level of commitment to the foundation and the results they expected from it. Their thinking led to the critical decision to invest significantly in the SSBFF's endowment so that by the late 1980s the foundation could operate as a free-standing institution, its survival not reliant on periodic injections of cash from members of the Bronfman family. Chapter 4 takes the story to the creation of this free-standing institution, and chapter 5 carries it on through the early 1990s, a period that saw the funding of five visioning workshops designed to help the SSBFF's major client organizations focus on their goals and methods.

Chapters 6 through 11 mark a departure from the chronological sweep of the previous chapters and proceed thematically. Each is devoted to the history of the individual funding programs as they emerged over the course of the 1970s and 80s, and especially as they were shaped by the visioning workshops and their aftermath.

The subject of the first of these chapters is the Saidye Bronfman Centre. Although not technically one of the main funding programs, "the

Saidye" occupied a huge portion of the SSBFF's time, as this multi-purpose arts complex proved an unending series of challenges due to the expectations that the different parties involved – the foundation, the YM-YWHA, the Jewish community – had of each other. The story of this very particular legacy project raises some intriguing questions regarding what kind of responsibility donors have – especially living donors – to an institution that bears their name or the name of a family member.

Chapters 7 through 11 treat the SSBFF's major funding programs: (1) Learning Disabilities, a successful example of having nurtured two organizations towards autonomy; (2) One Voice, the national seniors' network, which proved a disappointment to the SSBFF but a useful lesson in managing an ambitious client organization; (3) Arts and Cultural Management, which involved the establishment of a very important centre for training in the management of arts organizations as well as a far-reaching program of arts stabilization bringing dozens of arts groups together with several levels of government; (4) Heritage, which saw the creation of the innovative Heritage Montreal at the crest of the 1970s heritage preservation movement, as well as such institutions as Heritage Canada, the Canadian Centre for Architecture, and the Saidye Rosner Bronfman Chair in Architectural History at McGill University, and which would eventually be recast as Urban Issues, which funded a great many community development projects across the country; and (5) the Saidye Bronfman Award for Excellence in the Crafts, which rewarded the work of an often overlooked genre and would help raise its profile to stand alongside the more established art forms recognized by the Canada Council.

The book's final chapter returns to the chronological survey of the SSBFF's inner workings, plus discussions of two projects begun after most others had wrapped up. A crucial issue was the commitment of family members to the foundation. By the beginning of the twenty-first century, with three generations of the family scattered around North America and Europe, the enthusiasm of the children and grandchildren of Sam and Saidye Bronfman toward the SSBFF as the principal agent of their philanthropic endeavours diminished. This reality, as well as financial circumstances, seemed to suggest that the foundation had come to a fundamental crossroads. In 2003, the directors chose to close the door to new grant applications and let the momentum of past funding commitments carry the foundation to its ultimate dissolution. Even while matters were slowly drawing to an end, the SSBFF found the time to carry out two timely projects: the National Arts and Youth Demonstration Project and the heritage restoration of Plum Coulee, Manitoba.

With the decision to wind down the foundation came a desire to take stock of what had been accomplished and even what had been learned from mistakes. This book is the result.

ONE

FAMILY FORTUNE,

PHILANTHROPIC TRADITION

Sam and Saidye Bronfman were the products of turn-of-the-century prairie upbringings, immigrants from Eastern Europe who moved from a rural to an urban setting, eventually crossing paths in Winnipeg's extensive Jewish community. Saidye's was the more genteel childhood, including exposure to music and studies; Sam's was rougher, and he cut his teeth on the challenges of the hotel business, then the liquor trade. Having made a fortune by the 1920s, with the family home and Seagram factory established in Montreal, Sam proceeded to devote considerable sums to philanthropic activities and to take part in the extensive Jewish community life there. Saidye was an important part of both. Sam and Saidye's attitude toward philanthropic giving was firmly rooted in Jewish tradition, but it was also shaped by their experience as newcomers to the complex world of Montreal's "third solitude," in which Sam would eventually become the prime mover and shaker. During the years of the Depression, and especially the Second World War, Sam and Saidye's public involvement moved beyond the Jewish community, and they began to see their philanthropic activities as having a potential impact on Canadian society as a whole, a vision that would later shape the work of the SSBFF.

Two Prairie Families

The Bronfmans and the Rosners came to Canada seeking freedom from Russian oppression. Following the assassination of Czar Alexander II in 1881, violence against Jews intensified in a wave of xenophobic hysteria which fuelled additional government persecution. Already legally bound to towns and *shtetls* in the Pale of Settlement, Jews suffered under laws that banned them from working at a multitude of occupations, owning land, and seeking an education. While the government accused them of being unwilling to work the land, state regulations wrecked the handful of Jewish agricultural colonies that were established. Quotas restricted Jewish enrolment in schools of higher learning. During the government pogroms, Jews were roused from their homes in the small hours of the morning, forced to show identification, robbed, extorted, or arrested. Boys and young men were conscripted for the Czar's army. In the face of this oppression, many Jewish families slipped deeper into poverty and hunger. Some survived only on the meagre subsistence provided by Jewish charities.[1]

The atmosphere of persecution pushed hundreds of thousands of Jews westward. Some fled to the cities of Western Europe; others sailed for North America. They left Russia at the rate of 50,000 to 60,000 a year; by the First World War nearly 2.5 million Jews had migrated from Eastern Europe.[2] Those opting for Canada arrived at Montreal and joined the small but flourishing Jewish communities there and in other eastern cities, but a movement also arose at this time to settle large numbers of Jews on the western prairies, which the federal government was in the process of opening as a homeland for immigrants. The most famous proponent of Jewish agricultural settlement was the Baron de Hirsch, a wealthy financier and philanthropist who first sought to relieve the plight of Jews in Russia by offering money to support Jewish institutions there, and then worked with the British government to help settle refugees in the colonies, including Canada.[3] Hirsch founded the Jewish Colonization Association (JCA) in 1891, which soon acquired a Montreal-based committee that orchestrated the settlement of several small Jewish communities on the Canadian prairies, beginning with the aptly named Hirsch.[4] British and especially Canadian officials were doubtful that Jews, who had not been permitted to own property in Russia, would make good farmers; some in fact believed that Jews were intrinsically non-agricultural.[5] Their fears seemed to be confirmed when many of the settlements failed after experiencing the harsh prairie winters, and Jewish colonization attempts never received the enthusiastic official backing that other immigrants received; nevertheless, a number of rural colonies succeeded, several of them persisting well into the twentieth century.

The Bronfmans had actually come to the Canadian west just prior to the establishment of the JCA, part of an earlier effort at Jewish colonization sponsored by various London-based Jewish philanthropists. One of these, Herman Landau, funded a settlement near Wapella in what is now Saskatchewan, as of 1886.[6] Yechiel and Mindel Bronfman left the southern part of Russia (Moldova) via Odessa on the Black Sea and sailed to Montreal by way of England, arriving mid-1889. They joined the Wapella colony and began the uphill struggle to establish a frontier homestead. In addition to being overwhelmed by back-breaking labour, Jewish immigrants were often homesick and suffered from terrible isolation.

Yechiel Bronfman gave up homesteading after one year and left his wife Mindel and children on the farm to go to town to find work in a sawmill.[7] Eventually he brought the whole family to the town of Brandon, Manitoba, where he tried his hand at commerce, selling fish and fuel, even wild horses, without great success. Yechiel had hoped for more for his sons in the New World, and decided to take greater risks. In 1903, he mortgaged his home and his team of horses to help his older sons Abe and Harry purchase a hotel in Emerson, Manitoba, on the border with the United States.[8] This venture turned the Bronfmans' fortunes around. The family soon owned a number of hotels across Manitoba and Saskatchewan, and after much hard work began to prosper. The hotel business provided an important training ground for Sam, Yechiel's third son, who at the age of fifteen began working as a bellboy at one family hotel; by the time he was twenty-three, he was the manager of the Bell Hotel in

Winnipeg. The family had moved to Winnipeg, the Prairies' one real metropolis, in 1906, and it became the home of the burgeoning Bronfman empire until the 1920s.[9]

It was in Winnipeg that Sam got to know Saidye Rosner. The couple first met in 1913, but she was six years younger and he hardly noticed her. He took much more interest in 1921 when a chance encounter in early spring led to a proper but affectionate courtship culminating in their engagement the following Valentine's Day. Saidye had studied for two years at the University of Manitoba and was currently working as a typist for the Red Rose Tea Company. She had an independent streak and was clearly something of a social butterfly. Sam, by then a successful businessman of thirty-three whose work took him across Canada and left little time for parties, must have seemed quite different from the sort of people she normally encountered. Despite the difference in their ages and temperament, the two seem to have quickly developed a romantic partnership as well as a close friendship that would last half a century.[10]

The Rosner family had settled in Plum Coulee, Manitoba, at about the same time that Yechiel and Mindel Bronfman began homesteading in the Wapella colony. In the 1890s, Plum Coulee was a thriving railway town boasting a number of businesses, including a *matzah* factory where Samuel Rosner was employed before opening a store in partnership with his nephew. Saidye grew up in relative comfort in a home known for its good food and generous hospitality, to say nothing of such startling modern features as a piano and a bathtub.[11] The synagogue was one of several places of worship in this immigrant community of Jews, Mennonites, and other European minority groups; walking down the wooden sidewalks of Plum Coulee's Main Avenue one would have heard more Yiddish, German, and Ukrainian than English. Despite this variety, there appears to have been a fair degree of social harmony and mutual tolerance; Rosner even served as mayor for a time. The inhabitants of Plum Coulee sought relief from hard agricultural work in common festivities related to the harvest or outdoor summer concerts held in the public square. As well as civilized pursuits such as music and studies, Saidye's childhood would have been marked by the lush surrounding landscape:

"wild plums, rich wetlands, majestic tall grass prairie, and groves of oak or aspen," according to one account. "Town elders tell stories of spectacular summer evenings swimming in the coulee to wash off the deep purple stains of the wild plums they had been enjoying all afternoon ..."[12]

In 1908 the Rosners moved to Winnipeg in order to enjoy the richer social and religious life of the large Jewish community there and to secure good educations as well as, they hoped, good husbands for their four daughters. Saidye clearly found both.[13] She and Sam Bronfman were married in June 1922 at the Shaarey Tzedek Synagogue in Winnipeg.[14] By that time, Sam's parents were dead, victims of the great influenza epidemic that had swept North America in the wake of the First World War, and he had begun to assume the role of head of the family business, despite the presence of two older brothers.

It had been Sam's passion for selling and sense of timing that had taken the family out of the hotel business at a time when wartime Prohibition undercut its major source of profit, alcohol,[15] and into the liquor trade – an occupation equally dependent on the whims of Prohibition but one that, with Sam's degree of skill, could prove lucrative. It was an exhausting game, however, constantly having to predict which provinces and states would declare themselves "dry," and when, and for how long. The ban on alcohol sales in Canada had ended after the war, but federal and provincial governments continued to make things difficult for importers and exporters. January 1920 had seen the implementation of the eighteenth amendment to the United States' constitution, which banned the sale, import, or transport of intoxicating liquors. The scarcity of alcohol that ensued created opportunities for suppliers such as the Bronfman brothers, but also dangers: in October 1922, Sam's brother-in-law, who had been dealing with some rum runners near the Saskatchewan border, was murdered.[16] Soon after, the brothers gathered in Winnipeg and agreed it was time to pull out of the liquor trade. With about $600,000 of accumulated capital, they established the Bronfman Family Trust and allocated shares.[17] Sam and Saidye, recently married, took the opportunity to set out on an extended tour of Canada and the United States, and by early 1924 decided to settle in Montreal.

ENTREPRENEURS IN SPIRITS

Because of its ongoing association with smuggling and gangsters, the liquor trade was the subject of widespread hostility in Canada, but manufacturing liquor remained the respectable part of the business. Accordingly, Sam became convinced that the family should open a distillery. While travelling with Saidye he had visited several distilleries, taking note of how they operated and if any looked promising for purchase. In the spring of 1923 he settled on the Greenbriar Distillery of Louisville, Kentucky, which he bought, dismantled, and moved to a new site in Lasalle, on the outskirts of Montreal.[18] This new venture was incorporated as Distillers Corporation Limited in May 1924. Four years later Sam purchased Joseph E. Seagram & Sons, a long-standing Ontario distilling company, now fallen on hard times but with a recognized name. Reincorporated as Distillers Corporation–Seagrams Limited, the Bronfman business now had two factories with ample warehouse space, an expanded inventory, and a name that helped put them on the map as reputable manufacturers of whisky.[19]

Reputation was important, as the anti-alcohol campaign continued to regard all aspects of the liquor industry as suspect. American Prohibition provided a curious business opportunity for Canadian alcohol producers such as Sam Bronfman. Although transactions required a deliberate lack of curiosity on the producers' parts as to where their products would end up, the act of selling liquor broke no laws. Even so, the 1926–27 Royal Commission on Customs and Excise allowed zealous investigators to hammer away for months at liquor suppliers in a desperate effort to uncover evidence of wrong-doing. Having weathered such attacks, Sam took pains to distance their operation from any taint of compromise, either in method or quality, associated with Prohibition trade. He correctly predicted that when Prohibition in the United States came to an end there would be a huge and sudden demand there for whisky. Domestic producers would need time to bring production facilities on line and they would not be able to properly age the product for the highest quality. As early as 1928, Sam began setting aside huge quantities of liquor to age for the American market.[20]

To reinforce a sense of respectability and reliability the Bronfmans built a striking new headquarters for Seagram in the heart of Montreal – a world away from the suburban distillery. Moreover, instead of a downtown location in the city's financial district, they chose a site on Peel Street in the more fashionable uptown commercial centre. The building, which opened in 1929, was a solid pastiche of Scottish baronial styles, complete with turrets, crenellations, and a spiked portcullis. As such, it resembled many of the great nineteenth-century mansions built nearby in Montreal's Golden Square Mile.

The castles that had impressed Sam and Saidye on their recent trips to Scotland were also appropriate inspirations for the headquarters of a whisky empire, given the centrality of that land to the industry. This connection would have been evident to the Bronfmans' Scottish counterparts with whom Sam went into partnership during the early days of Seagram's history.[21]

With the end of Prohibition in the United States, the Bronfmans launched a bold effort to become major players in the American market. They bought and built distilleries in the United States, including the Calvert distillery in Maryland, and then shipped their aged Canadian-made whisky to blend with the local product. In the free-for-all marketplace immediately following the end of Prohibition, Seagram distinguished itself by the quality of its products and a concerted advertising and sales strategy that appealed to more refined consumers, all the while stressing the values, and pleasure, of drinking in moderation.[22] Success came quickly. By 1936 Seagram sales in the United States reached $60 million, or six times the volume of the company's Canadian operations.[23] For years Sam spent most of every week in New York, working out of the Seagram office in the recently completed Chrysler Building.

The family's increasing involvement within Montreal's Jewish community and their extensive philanthropy, culminating in their active participation in the war effort, helped establish an image of the Bronfmans as good corporate citizens rather than mere liquor merchants. Restrictions on alcohol production during the Second World War did make for somewhat leaner years financially. Nevertheless, persistent in the pursuit

of quality products as well as in the advocacy of responsible social drinking, the Bronfmans gradually emerged as one of the most successful and
highly respected manufacturers of whisky across North America.

JEWISH MONTREAL

Since the nineteenth century, Montreal had been the commercial and
industrial capital of Canada, as well as its most cosmopolitan city. Like
New York for the United States, Montreal became the entry point for
all the nation's newcomers and, often, where they came to settle. Like
virtually all immigrant groups everywhere, Jews quickly established their
own institutions. Indeed, the city's first Jewish community formed a congregation as early as 1768, its synagogue having the distinction of being
the first non-Catholic place of worship in Quebec.[24] Subsequent generations of Jews, alongside the colony's rapidly growing Protestant population, continued to establish separate places of worship as well as
separate places of burial as each community claimed distinct spaces from
the Catholic majority. The ongoing cultural strength of this Catholic
majority combined with the political and economic strength of the substantial Protestant minority meant that Montreal's Jewish community
was obliged to support itself through its social institutions even more
determinedly than in other parts of North America. Montreal Jews were
often referred to as the "third solitude" – a reference to the polarization
of the city's Anglo-Protestant and French Catholic populations, in the
face of which the Jewish community represented an additional force.[25]

This third solitude became much more prominent after the rapid rise
of immigration in the latter part of the nineteenth century. Until that
time, the city's small Jewish population was relatively well-integrated –
geographically, at any rate – and disinclined to tout its cultural peculi-
arities. The oldest Jewish families had an affinity for, if not always
comfortable relations with, the Protestant establishment with whom they
shared the English language. At mid-century, Montreal Jews constituted
an ethnic grouping – never exactly defined and only superficially understood by outsiders – alongside the English, the Scots, the Irish, and the

French, or, in a different context, alongside the Anglicans, the Presbyterians, and the Methodists. The First Hebrew Philanthropic Society, for example, was founded in Montreal in 1847 as a kind of "national" society along the lines of the contemporary Scots' St Andrew's Society or the English St George's Society.[26] Like its Protestant counterparts, the Hebrew Society aimed to improve the lot of its own constituency, specifically to "alleviate the distress and satisfy the present wants of almost every Israelite, compelled by destitution to seek the charitable aid of their brethren."[27] In 1863, the organization was recast as the Young Men's Hebrew Benevolent Society in the belief that it was important for young, unmarried men to coordinate charitable work as part of their social maturation. A parallel society for young women was established in 1877.[28]

Such concern for the social aspect of charity was by no means unique to the Jewish community; most Protestant denominations placed as much importance on the social obligation to take part in charitable work as they did on the actual need to alleviate poverty. The religious foundation of charity, however, was significantly different for Jews than it was for Protestants, and for Catholics even more so. Protestantism had rejected the "salvation through good deeds" philosophy of traditional Catholicism, developing instead the belief that (depending on the denomination) prosperity was a sign of moral grace and that the prosperous had a duty to improve the morality of the poor, from which material improvement would flow. Protestant Victorian charity was notoriously moralistic and clinical, although by virtue of being administered by public bodies, including chartered philanthropic societies and municipal governments, it eventually allowed for the implementation of the notion of public welfare, just as it had for public education.[29]

In Jewish tradition, the merits of individuals are measured by their works on Earth – not that good deeds result in divine rewards so much as that they are evidence of striving for the betterment of the world.[30] The notion of *tikkun olam* (to repair the world) emerged as a response to the plight of Jews following the Diaspora, a context for charitable giving that focused on righting wrongs and restoring a balance; poverty and misery were clear signs of imbalance. For observant Jews, adherence to the *mitzvahs* (acts of kindness, including generosity toward fellow human beings) is a way to help put humanity back on the proper path. Similarly, by the doctrine of *tzedakah* (meaning righteousness or justice), Jews are expected to give to the poor – and not merely to relieve immediate misery but with the goal of making the poor self-sufficient.[31] By this doctrine, while the rich must obviously give more, it also falls to the poor to do what they can to help those who are even less fortunate than themselves. The act of charity ennobles the giver, which is his or her reward, while leaving the receiver of charity with a sense of dignity intact.[32]

By the 1880s, one of the greatest concerns of the Montreal Jewish community was the steadily worsening lot of Eastern European Jews, and promoting Jewish immigration to Canada became one of the Hebrew Society's major projects. In 1891 the Society changed its name to the Baron de Hirsch Institute in honour of the man whose philanthropy was allowing so many Jews to relocate to safer havens, including Montreal, where a major donation of money to the local organizers facilitated settlement. By the end of the First World War, the city's Jewish population had ballooned to 50,000, accounting for over 6 per cent of the total urban population and representing nearly 40 per cent of all the Jews in Canada. They were concentrated in one geographical area: St. Lawrence Boulevard, or "the Main," sometimes referred to as the "immigrant corridor," the street which in popular understanding divided the French and English portions of the city. The community's location "was symbolic of the precarious marginality of the Jewish presence in both communities."[33]

Helping significant numbers of suffering families improve their lives clearly righted a wrong and contributed to the repair of the world, but for the older generations of Montreal Jews the huge numbers of newcomers transformed Jewish life in the city. The new waves of immigrants were culturally distinct from them, and much less inclined to attempt to integrate with the mainstream population. Nine out of ten Montreal Jews listed Yiddish as their mother tongue in 1921, and most of them, unlike the more liberal established congregations, were Orthodox.[34] The cultural division did not fall precisely along class lines, but there was a clear tendency for the older families to join the ranks of the Anglo-

Protestant elite on the higher ground away from the Main, on the slopes of Mount Royal and Westmount. The topographical elevation of these neighbourhoods gave added meaning to the term "uptowners," which was increasingly used to refer to the older established minority as opposed to the less privileged and largely immigrant "downtowners" living on or near the Main. Over time, as a number of newer families achieved prosperity and moved to more fashionable neighbourhoods, the distinction between uptowners and downtowners became primarily a matter of class. In any event, the community remained prone to division over questions such as whether or not, or how much, to integrate with the mainstream (almost always with the English-speaking minority) and over institutional organization and party politics. Because of the "solitudes" in Quebec society, however, these divisions played themselves out in isolation, effectively uniting a community which at the end of the day had to look out for itself.[35]

A particularly grey area was education. In the nineteenth century, with virtually no institutions of learning of its own apart from the sporadically open synagogue schools, and given the absence of any legal provision in the province of Quebec for Jews to establish their own publicly funded system, the Jewish community turned to the city's Protestant school board, which operated mostly in English and resembled the public education system found elsewhere in North America. The Protestant board subsidized the synagogue schools as well as one based in the Baron de Hirsch Institute, and admitted increasing numbers of Jews into its own schools, particularly those near the Main. By the 1920s many of these schools had populations that were over 90 per cent Jewish.[36] Countering this trend, which some feared would lead to assimilation, religious Jews opened Talmud Torah schools as of 1896, while others opened the secular Peretz School in 1913 and the Jewish People's School the following year.[37] The Main's Protestant high school was the famous Baron Byng, whose student body was almost entirely Jewish (downtowners) from the years before the First World War through the 1930s. Uptowners were more likely to attend the High School of Montreal or one of the city's growing number of private schools. McGill University, where Hebrew literature was taught by a rabbi as early as 1853, attracted uptowners wishing to pursue higher education, and continued to do so even after the university placed a quota on the number of Jews admitted, out of the irrational fear that they would soon outnumber non-Jews.[38]

In matters of social welfare, Montreal's Jews were obliged to be entirely self-sufficient. In most parts of North America, civic-based poor relief and the rise of professional social work – despite their roots in Protestantism – gradually diminished the need for Jewish communities to maintain parallel institutions, albeit never absolutely. In Quebec, however, the responsibility for charity was jealously guarded by powerful Catholic religious orders on the one hand and the self-consciously Protestant organizations that had arisen as an alternative on the other. Such territoriality frustrated attempts to establish public welfare measures in Quebec at the time of the Great Depression and even in the wake of the Second World War. Only with the launch of the Quiet Revolution in the 1960s would the province see the gradual establishment of state control in such areas. Until that time, Montreal Jews developed an elaborate network of social welfare organizations and agencies that became the focus of much of the community's social and cultural life – even as its administration and overall direction remained subject to internal disputes.

Relieving the lot of the city's Jewish poor had became a critical issue at the beginning of the twentieth century as the needs of a rapidly expanding – and all too often impoverished – immigrant population overwhelmed the capacity of the existing charitable bodies. Although the Baron de Hirsch Institute remained the community's key charity organization, the extent and degree of poverty prompted the creation of more specialized agencies. Several prominent families – Davis, Jacobs, Vineberg, Goldstein – emerged as key philanthropists, supporting the establishment of the Montreal Hebrew Old People's Home, the Montreal Hebrew Sheltering Home, the Hebrew Orphans' Home, and others. In 1912, several prominent uptowners funded the Mount Sinai Sanitarium in the Laurentian Mountains north of Montreal for tuberculosis patients, and two years later a ladies' committee established the Hebrew Maternity Hospital in town.[39] Despite such philanthropic acts, Jewish charity in Montreal continued to depend to a large extent on foreign support, chiefly via the Jewish Colonization Association.[40]

During the First World War, with its universal mood of planning and cooperation, members of the Baron de Hirsch Institute spearheaded a drive to create an umbrella organization to coordinate fundraising for charitable activity within the Jewish community.[41] Although such federations had been appearing in many North American cities with sizable Jewish populations,[42] the need for one in Montreal was especially acute given the strength and territoriality of Catholic and Protestant institutions. In January 1917, twelve Jewish agencies, including the Baron de Hirsch Institute, formed the Federation of Jewish Philanthropies (FJP).[43] The Federation's goal was to create a modern, centrally organized fundraising body that would channel money where it was most needed. The virtues of such a body were soon demonstrated, when the initial campaign yielded $127,000 in only a few days – nearly twice the combined revenue of all the individual organizations for the previous year.[44] The Federation's first president was the lawyer Maxwell Goldstein, a respected civic leader and a vocal champion of the rights of Jews as citizens of Canada and the British Empire. Women were crucial to the Federation's success, a case in point being Esther Elkin who, in a manner that would seem to foreshadow the style of Sam Bronfman, urged her sisters to "wear last year's hat and give the cost of the new one to Federation," thereby shaming their husbands into writing generous cheques.[45]

Such involved charitable activity was clearly the preserve of the wealthiest members of the community who could be called upon to open their pocketbooks on a regular basis. Further down the social scale were those who lacked the time and resources to devote to charity in any significant way but who had clear social needs. In 1908, a group of such labourers and tradesmen formed the Young Men's Hebrew Association (YMHA), the counterpart to the Protestant YMCA which had had a branch in Montreal for over half a century. The Hebrew "Y" organized sports activities, classes, social events, and even theatre productions out of its headquarters in the Baron de Hirsch Institute building on downtown Sanguinet Street. It was only in the late 1920s that the YMHA acquired a home of its own on Mount Royal Avenue (around the corner from Baron Byng High School, the Jewish Public Library, and other key community institutions on or near the Main) thanks to the philanthropic intervention of Mortimer Barnett Davis.[46] The Young Women's Hebrew Association was formed by 1919 and was soon located in a building on St Urbain Street, where Saidye Bronfman joined it soon after her arrival in Montreal.[47] In addition to receiving direct funding from the Davis family and other philanthropists, the Ys came to rely on core operating grants from the FJP.

The Jewish community's first political organization was the Canadian Jewish Congress, founded in 1919, and although it took some time to be a truly effective body it did speak out about social and educational matters at home and the plight of Jews overseas. The wave of pogroms that year in Russia, as a consequence of the civil wars, prompted the CJC to form the Jewish Immigrant Aid Society (JIAS), which aimed to bring more refugees to Canada.[48] Members of this society, which comprised Romanian, Ukrainian, and Polish ethnic associations (*Verbands*), met boats at the docks and helped new arrivals adjust to life in Montreal.[49] Unlike the Jewish Colonization Association, which aimed to settle large numbers of immigrants on farms, the JIAS served as an advocate of immigrants' rights, especially with regard to the federal government.[50] The Jewish War Orphans Committee, also founded after the war, was led by Lillian Freiman, an Ottawa fundraiser and also a relative of the wife of Allan Bronfman, Sam's brother.[51] Throughout the 1920s these groups facilitated Jewish immigration to Montreal and elsewhere in Canada, and generally strove to improve the position of Jews within Canadian society. Their efforts were complicated mainly by the sorts of internal divisions that would soon seem much less important during the tumultuous 1930s and 40s: disputes between left and right, between secular and religious, between uptowners and downtowners, and between those committed to Zionism and those who preferred to focus on existence in Canada.

This was the community the Bronfmans joined.

The Bronfmans were clearly uptowners. Apart from their enthusiasm for Canada and the British Empire, which was typical of the uptowner outlook, their considerable wealth marked them as part of the Jewish elite. As of 1929 Sam and Saidye lived in a large house with extensive grounds on Belvedere Road in the very Anglo-Protestant municipality of Westmount. At the time they had two daughters: Minda, who was three, and Phyllis, who was one. Two sons soon followed: Edgar, born in 1929, and Charles, born 1931. The children attended private schools: The Study for the girls, Selwyn House for the boys, both quintessentially Anglo-Protestant institutions.[52] Sam and Saidye had the house remodelled with the help of the original architect, Robert Findley, and furnished in the manner of the European stately homes they had visited on their travels. It was staffed by as many as eight servants. Impressed by the surrounding trees on the property, the family dubbed the residence Oaklands, in keeping with the romantic monikers typically given to such estates. As well as being their home, Oaklands served the Bronfmans as a headquarters for their numerous philanthropic activities. Indeed, given the family's increasing prominence within the Jewish community and the lavish luncheons and dinner parties they held, it could be said that many key charitable undertakings had their origins at Oaklands.[53]

SAM AND SAIDYE'S CHARITY AND PUBLIC SERVICE

Sam Bronfman was the product of a Jewish upbringing with its focus on helping the poor and repairing the world, but he was also motivated by a need to cement a place for himself and his family in Montreal society. This meant winning over both the Jewish establishment and the larger business and social world. Like many successful Jews working in environments that were inhospitable or even hostile,[54] Sam would have been conscious of social status and understood that a strong record of philanthropy was one means of asserting it. This is not to suggest that the desire to improve the lot of the disadvantaged, to enhance the cultural life of the city, or to take on great patriotic causes were of lesser importance to Sam Bronfman than success in business. Indeed, the opposite could be argued: that acquiring wealth is essentially a means to position oneself to effect change in society and exert control over that change. Nevertheless, the reality for the Bronfmans was that business success required social acceptance, that public service was a crucial means to make valuable contacts, and that promoting philanthropic projects was a necessary part of achieving prominence within the Jewish community. Sam played many cards at once. Moreover, he was a skilful player and by all accounts derived considerable satisfaction from the results.

Charitable work came naturally to Sam and Saidye. Both grew up in households where community service was expected and revered. Despite the hardships of coming to Canada and settling on the prairies, Sam's father Yechiel gave away much of the cash he had brought in order to help his fellow immigrants. In their home in Brandon, the Bronfman family kept a *pischka*, a collection box for the poor. Yechiel made loans to poor Jewish immigrants, helped build a new orphanage for Jewish children, and sent money to Jews in Eastern Europe. He also helped organize the construction of a synagogue in Brandon, and served as its first president.[55] In Plum Coulee and Winnipeg, Sameul Rosner was a community leader, spearheading major charitable projects undertaken by the congregation. Only intermittently religious but an ardent Zionist, Saidye's father was a delegate to the first meeting of the Canadian Jewish Congress in 1917.[56]

After their father's death in 1919, Sam Bronfman and his brothers followed in his philanthropic footsteps – Allan especially, who became president of Brandon's Jewish orphanage. After joining Sam in Montreal, Allan was appointed chair of the campaign to raise funds for the construction of the Jewish General Hospital, and became its first president. Possibly the community's largest project to date, the hospital was intended to relieve the general shortage of beds in the city and, more specifically, to provide medical facilities for Jews and employment for Jewish doctors and nurses who often experienced discrimination elsewhere. The need for a separate institution was illustrated just prior to the opening of the Jewish General in 1934 when the staff at the Catholic Notre Dame Hospital went out on strike in protest at the hiring of a Jewish senior intern, Samuel Rabinovitch, who felt compelled to resign. Significantly, despite its name, the Jewish General was officially (and conspicuously) non-sectarian, its services available to all "irrespective of race, creed and religion."[57] This outlook mirrored that of Sam and Saidye and many other community leaders who strove for cultural inclusion even as they helped support institutions aimed predominantly at Jews.

Although it was Allan who officially led the hospital campaign, it was Sam who coordinated public relations for it, a role to which he was clearly suited. It was not long, however, before Sam began to make his own mark. In 1929, Sam joined the influential businessman's council of the Federation of Jewish Philanthropies (FJP), bringing him into direct contact with the major leaders of the community. Sam was a generous donor to any project (the hospital was a case in point) but it was not wealth that won him the respect of his fellow leaders; rather, it was his capacity for organization and stirring people to action. Sam's skills registered sufficiently within the FJP for him to be put in charge of their 1931 campaign.[58] That same year he was made joint chair of the Jewish Immigrant Aid Society of Canada, which gave him direct experience with the plight of Jews around the world and the politics of immigration. His co-chair was no less venerable a figure than Samuel Jacobs, civil rights lawyer, member of Parliament (the only Jew in Parliament for many years), and one of the original founders of the JIAS.[59] In 1934, Sam Bronfman took over as president of the FJP and remained in office for an unprecedented seventeen years. This record speaks both to his ability to raise funds on a large scale and to the community's acknowledgement of his prowess in this field. Within barely a decade of settling in Montreal, Sam had become the Jewish community's most influential figure.

Saidye played her part in this overlapping world of business and philanthropy by being a gracious hostess at Oaklands and coordinating "the wives," but she also had her own projects. Like her husband, Saidye willingly took on the responsibilities of office, which no doubt brought her personal satisfaction even as it forged additional contacts for the family. She joined the Young Women's Hebrew Association shortly after her arrival in Montreal and by 1929 had become president. Four years later when she stepped down from that position she was made honorary president for life. Saidye's passion for the women's association was expressed in an addendum to a budget report submitted to the Federation in 1933: "[It] serves a vital need in this community for the hundreds of women and girls whose lives are being demoralized by enforced leisure and all that this condition implies ... Just as men and boys receive Y training in social responsibility and Jewish duties, so must the women and girls of our community be given an instrument for similar purposes and for the development of a Jewish life that is richer and more permanent than that of the bridge table."[60] From the beginning Saidye spearheaded a campaign to move the organization from its "decrepit" headquarters on St Urbain Street to new facilities – a plan that was finally realized after the Second World War when the Federation of Jewish Philanthropies (of which, significantly, her husband was president) authorized the construction of a new YM-YWHA in the Snowdon area. On 9 May 1948, Saidye symbolically turned the sod on the site, in the company of Rabbi Wilfred Shuchet and other community leaders.

In their philanthropic activity, Sam and Saidye often worked in concert. In 1931, when Sam chaired the fundraising campaign for the FJP, Saidye helped establish a women's division of the campaign, and became its first chair. In this capacity she served a three-year term. (Sam only served one year as her counterpart, having other commitments and, possibly, his eye on the presidency of the Federation.) The creation of the women's division marked a change in women's visibility in Jewish philanthropy. For the first time, they made gifts in their own names rather than their husbands' or families', and they spoke out with a woman's perspective on issues. Saidye was a leader in this new women's movement and throughout the Depression was instrumental in improving the lives of urban Jewish women, who were often breadwinners in the retail trade or did piecework at home to supplement the family income.[61]

Fundraising was always a challenge but significantly more so with the advent of the Great Depression. Although as a cohort Montreal's Jewish community experienced a lower rate of unemployment than non-Jews owing to their high representation in the retail trades, large numbers of Jews counted among the city's destitute.[62] For them, the universal obligation to help repair the world was an impossible one. At the same time, the labour movement, which had always attracted large numbers of Jews, won additional converts during the hard years of the Depression; indeed, Fred Rose, the only Communist elected to Parliament in Canada, was Jewish. It could be argued that philanthropists at this time, within the Jewish community no less than outside it, operated with at least one eye on the spectre of socialism, which would have less appeal if the lot of the destitute could be improved by other means. That said, concern for the welfare of the poor was arguably no less genuine that it would have been had the Jewish community not been divided by political agendas or had the various levels of government moved more effectively to provide systematic relief measures. Whatever their motivations, the city's leading Jewish families were prepared to give generously to charity during the Depression and even more so afterwards – at least, if the intensity of Sam Bronfman's efforts was anything to go by.

Sam's favoured technique was to use a careful (if not always particularly subtle) blend of shame, guilt, and social one-upmanship. In the ballroom in the basement of Oaklands – known in philanthropic circles as "the sweatshop" – Sam and Saidye would hold lavish dinner parties, and when the guests were assembled Sam would outline the scope of a fundraising campaign for the JIAS or the FJP. He would announce how much he was going to contribute, delineating the percentage of increase over the previous year, and then say that he expected each of the men to make a contribution in proportion to their means.[63] Some no doubt found this intimidating, even distasteful. Sam and Saidye's daughter Phyllis recalled hating the social pressure that was put on people to give. She felt that the rare occasions when the family ate together were dominated by "all this talk about charity stuff," accompanied by discussions of who gave how much and whether they could have given more. It was not the cause she rejected, but the fact that the giving was socially driven. In retrospect, Phyllis did not believe her father gave money for this reason, however, even though he relied on the social anxieties of other civic leaders to achieve his ends. "I think he felt a big obligation. It was something he wanted to do, and he was very effective."[64]

The cause of helping out the Montreal community was eventually eclipsed by concern for the plight of Jews in Europe. The work of the JIAS was made much harder by the 1930s owing to a combination of xenophobia and economic protectionism that prevented Canada from taking in the tens of thousands of Jews it could have absorbed.[65] In 1931 the Canadian government closed its doors to new immigration, a measure born of desire not to increase the ranks of the unemployed at home, but with obvious ramifications for the Jewish community which had seen such a significant demographic rise over the course of the previous decades. This troubling political move became truly tragic with the rise of anti-Semitism overseas and the desperate need for refugees to find a haven. Because immigrants who settled on the land were technically exempt from the ban, some further attempt was made by the Jewish Colonization Association to bring Jewish refugees into Canada as farmers. Sam Bronfman, himself a product of the colonization movement, became active in the JCA in the later 1930s.[66] This movement was unable to make a significant difference, however, owing to the government's persistent belief – so persistent it strongly resembled an excuse – that Jews were intrinsically not an agricultural people.

This sort of frustrating prejudice was soon outclassed by the home-grown anti-Semitism of fascist sympathizers such as Adrien Arcand, who launched vitriolic attacks on Canada's Jews, even in the streets of Montreal. To respond to these attacks, Jewish leaders in 1934 decided to revive the Canadian Jewish Congress, which had faded through the 1920s owing to internal political and geographical disagreements.[67] Despite the renewed enthusiasm for the Congress as a political force in the face of rising fascism, it still held little appeal for many Jews – including Communists, who found it insufficiently radical, and the up-towners, who found it too working-class, Zionist, and Yiddish.[68] For years Sam Bronfman had dismissed Congress as a "useless organization … which was doing Canadian Jewry more harm than good."[69] As attacks on Jews in Germany increased, however, appeals to the government from Canadian Jews became increasingly urgent. Then, on 9 November 1938, Kristallnacht, Nazis attacked Jewish homes, businesses, and synagogues, destroying property and beating and killing Jewish men, women, and children. After Kristallnacht, leaders in the Canadian Jewish community felt they could no longer remain fragmented and ineffective. At the beginning of 1939, in the midst of international crisis, Sam agreed to become president of the Congress.

In this capacity he was a forceful voice of moderation. A less politically threatening figure than some earlier Congress leaders, Sam did much to raise the profile of Canada's Jews within government circles and fight for the admission of Jewish refugees. He was determined to turn

Congress from a socially isolationist and essentially downtowner organization into a respected and powerful voice on behalf of Canadian Jews.[70] He convened a meeting of leaders from various national Jewish organizations including B'nai Brith and the Zionists, and urged unity in the midst of the crisis. Sam agreed to chair a new Canadian Jewish Committee for Refugees (CJCR), which sponsored a nationwide campaign to raise awareness of German atrocities and the need to provide a refuge for European Jews.[71] Such efforts went up against hard-headed opposition to Jewish immigration – some of it clearly anti-Semitic – from within the federal government. As a result, very few refugees made their way to Canada during the course of the Second World War. Among the excluded were countless children who might have been expected to elicit a higher degree of sympathy from government officials.[72]

Sam's most significant contribution as Congress leader, however, was simply to lend the weight of office to important causes, notably social welfare and the war effort. Shortly after assuming the presidency he was invited to join the board of the influential Canadian Welfare Council, which advised the government and other organizations on relief measures. Ironically, the actual invitation came from Charlotte Whitton, the nation's leading social worker as well as a noted opponent of the liquor industry and of Jewish immigration; for Sam, the critical nature of the work superseded old enmities.[73] Congress declared its commitment to raising funds for the Red Cross, uniting labour and industry behind the war effort, and increasing military recruitment within the Jewish community.[74] The Bronfman family bought huge quantities of war bonds. Sam sat on two wartime committees which advised the government on several key issues: the Canadian War Production Board and the War Technical and Scientific Development Committee. He even donated a ship to the Canadian navy.[75]

Saidye was equally busy at war work, notably as president of the Montreal Jewish Branch of the Quebec Provincial Division of the Canadian Red Cross Society. Coordinating 7,000 women to knit, sew, and prepare packages for soldiers overseas became a full-time job for several years.[76] Her efforts on behalf of Canada did not go unrecognized. In 1943, Saidye Rosner Bronfman received the title of Officer of the Order of the British Empire (OBE), presented by the Governor General of Canada on behalf of King George VI.[77] Deserved though this honour was, some wondered why Sam had not received similar recognition. It is possible that the political pressure he exerted as Congress president hurt him personally even as it helped the Jewish community collectively: the Bronfmans still had enemies within government circles.[78] In any event, the family treated Saidye's achievement with all the excitement it was due, especially given that the award came from the head of the British Empire.

Saidye's recognition was the culmination of a decade or more of forging good relations with the world outside the Jewish community. On a business level, and on at least a superficial social level, this was not all that hard to achieve for someone like Sam Bronfman. From the early 1930s, Sam succeeded in winning the respect of Montreal's Anglo-Protestant establishment, not only as a businessman but as a promoter of numerous public events. Seagram sponsored a marathon snowshoe race between Montreal and Quebec City as well as boxing championships, swimming meets, and golf tournaments – sporting events that had direct appeal to all Canadians regardless of ethnicity.[79] This sense of civic pride would transcend both the Jewish community and Montreal as Sam and Saidye came to embrace and promote an idea of Canadian identity that included Jews and other groups under a common umbrella of British values and institutions.

Throughout the war Sam's emphatic patriotism underscored the Jewish community's fundamental loyalty to Canada and the Empire, something the Congress had never particularly expressed in the past.[80] The tone had been set during the 1939 Royal Visit, which saw Jews across the country cheering the King and Queen at every public appearance. Sam had taken the opportunity to present the monarchs with a sample of a new Seagram product, the aptly named Crown Royal, in honour of their visit.[81] In 1941 Sam commissioned McGill professor Stephen Leacock to write a patriotic history of Canada as a public morale builder– which he later had to turn over to his assistant, the poet A.M. Klein, to delete much of Leacock's jingoistic and even anti-Semitic content.[82] Over the next several years Sam took every opportunity in public speeches to extol the virtues of the Empire, notably its tolerance and sense of fair play; he also strove to instill this patriotic sense among his children. As his son Edgar put it, "He believed that Canada, the inheritor of British libertarianism, had made it possible for Jews to live as almost equal citizens under the Union Jack."[83] Given the degree of anti-Semitism that had always been present in Canada's treatment of its Jews, Sam's expressions of loyalty were remarkable. They were also consistent with the attitude of several generations of Montreal's uptowners, a group that had always striven to integrate socially and culturally with the mainstream. In the 1940s, even more than in the 1900s, it made sense to embrace broader definitions of commonality and citizenship than the one that saw people only in terms of "solitudes."

Many within the Jewish community were particularly puzzled by Sam's eagerness to support McGill University. Although it was clear that McGill was limiting its Jewish student population by means of a quota system, Sam and his brothers helped fund a branch of McGill's medical school in 1940. The following year, Montreal industrialist J.W. McConnell donated a mansion to house the School of Commerce and Sam, not to be outdone, promised to underwrite two professorships for five years.[84] Instead of protesting McGill's anti-Semitic policy, Sam appears to have opted to undermine it – by insisting on his right, as it were, to be on an equal footing with a donor such as the Anglo-Protestant McConnell. These efforts may well have done much to raise the Bronfman profile within the Canadian intellectual establishment and implicitly break down the old Anglo-Protestant character of such institutions. According to Seagram executive Leo Kolber, it was Sam who helped end the Jewish quota at McGill shortly after the war by inferring to Principal Cyril James that donations from the Jewish community would be much more forthcoming were it lifted – which eventually it was.[85]

None of this focus on empire and British values detracted from Sam and Saidye's principal focus on the Jewish community and its problems. In the summer of 1941, Sam called a meeting of various leaders representing the FJP, Congress, the Jewish General Hospital, and the refugee committee (now called the United Jewish Relief Agency) to establish the Combined Jewish Appeal. The CJA would raise funds more efficiently by cutting down the administrative costs incurred by each organization working independently, and by concentrating effort. Within a few months the Appeal had raised almost half a million dollars.[86] Sam used his usual technique of holding a reception at Oaklands and, with the heads of the most successful Jewish families assembled, lead off with his own pledge to set the standard for others. The Bronfman contribution frequently constituted "the largest annual gift made in North America to a charity."[87] A roll call would follow, each family offering its pledge. For the next three decades, regardless of who was actually chairing the campaign in any given year, Sam and Saidye would host the official launch of the Combined Jewish Appeal, in their home.

The end of the war brought the full horror of the Holocaust, and inspired the largest fundraising campaign to date within the Montreal Jewish community in an effort to "rescue the living" – as the 1945 campaign posters exhorted. If the world ever needed repairing, this was the moment. Volunteers went door to door, collecting from everyone in the community; the image of concentration camp survivors and even of displaced persons in general made any level of poverty in Montreal seem a blessing by comparison.[88] Over the next few years, the Combined Jewish Appeal earmarked refugees as the recipients of its efforts. Federation worked to open Canada's gates to survivors and to find a place for prospective refugees, including orphans. They succeeded in having Canada absorb over 11,000 Jews in the five years following the enactment of a new, more liberal immigration policy in 1947; two-thirds of these settled in Montreal, the city that would win the distinction of being home to the world's third largest population of Holocaust survivors.[89] To meet the needs of these new arrivals, the CJA launched ever-more ambitious campaigns – and usually succeeded, under Sam's persuasive gaze.

The other growing focus of fundraising efforts was the emerging Jewish homeland in Palestine. On this issue, Sam had to overlook the British Empire's lack of commitment to this cause since the end of the First World War. Sam had always endorsed the idea of a refuge for the Jews in Palestine, but he was guarded about supporting the Zionist campaign for a Jewish state. In 1936 he served as chairman for the United Palestine Appeal, an annual fundraising effort to raise money for Jewish settlement.[90] Towards the end of the Second World War, as the full extent of Nazi atrocities became clear, he grew more emphatic about the notion of a Jewish Homeland. In January 1945, in a speech to the Canadian Jewish Congress, he called for "a free and democratic Jewish commonwealth in Palestine."[91] Several months later, when the conference on the United Nations charter was hosted in San Francisco, Sam and Saidye travelled to California to monitor the discussions on the British mandate for Palestine and meet with other Jewish leaders.

After a United Nations report recommended partition in the fall of 1947, the Canadian Jewish Congress announced its support for this solution. As fighting broke out in the region between Arabs and Jews and attacks against British forces continued, Sam called for a peaceful solution to the conflict. After Jews declared the creation of the State of Israel, however, he led a delegation in June 1948 to appeal to the Canadian government to recognize the new state.[92] Sam was also active in the effort to provide for Israel's security. In 1950, Shimon Peres, then a senior official of the Israel Defense Forces, came to Canada seeking funds and materiel, and Sam personally helped him acquire artillery worth nearly $2 million.[93] He and Saidye would continue to invest in Israel for the rest of their lives, both directly and via donations to the Federation and the Combined Jewish Appeal.

THE NEXT BRONFMAN GENERATION

Sam and Saidye also thought about the role their children would play, both in the family business and in the world of philanthropy. The four children had grown up in the context of their parents' entrepreneurial drive and philanthropic zeal. According to Edgar, "there were always parties at the house. Either it was something mother was interested in, or father was interested in, and it was a fact of life."[94] Asked by Charles how he decided when to give money, Sam responded, "You learn." Charles and the other children came to learn too. As a teenager in the late 1940s, Charles went out with cards for people to fill out, pledging whatever amount they could afford. He was sometimes tempted to avoid the work of convincing his fellow students to pledge money by putting up ten or twenty dollars and filling in the cards himself, until he realized that giving was important to everyone, not just the wealthy. "That's not good enough," he remembered thinking as he rejected the shortcut approach. "I'd better go see these people because I knew the fifty cents meant a lot to them; a heck of a lot more to them than the ten or twenty dollars [to me]."[95]

In their twenties and thirties the Bronfman children moved away and focused on their own lives, but remained close to their parents. Minda, the oldest, was intelligent and attractive, and after graduating from Smith College and earning a Master's degree in history at Columbia University, she worked on Wall Street and at Time, Inc. In 1947 she met Baron Alain de Gunzburg, son of a French Jewish investment banker, who was studying business administration at Harvard. They were married in 1953 and established their life together in Paris. Minda became a patroness of the arts, promoting a cultural foundation called the *Association de soutien et de diffusion d'art* (ASDA), which was active in France, Canada, and the United States, and sponsored annual conferences for art historians.[96] They had two sons: Jean, born 1955, and Charles, born 1961.

Phyllis was two years younger than her sister. By the time she was ten she had developed a keen interest in art and form, and she later became a sculptor. She spent her first year in university at Cornell and then transferred to Vassar College, graduating in 1948. During her senior year, Phyllis met Jean Lambert, a French émigré who had come to the United States after fleeing Nazi-occupied France. They were married in 1949, but the marriage lasted only four years.[97] She was living in Paris, painting and sculpting, when her father began planning the construction of a new worldwide headquarters for Seagram in New York. When he sent her a sketch of the building, she intervened to persuade him to set the highest aesthetic standard. He gave her the job of selecting the architect. She chose Mies van der Rohe, and then continued as director of planning for the building. When the project was complete, she enrolled at Yale to study architecture. She moved to Chicago in 1960 to complete her Master's degree in architecture at the Illinois Institute of Technology, a world-famous campus designed by Mies.

A traditionalist when it came to gender roles, Sam Bronfman had assumed that his daughters would marry and avoid the business. He counted on his sons to take over Seagram. Edgar, the third of Sam and Saidye's children, was known for his rebellious nature. He entered Williams College in Massachusetts in 1946, but did not stay. Eventually he returned to Montreal to complete his degree at McGill University, graduating with honours in 1951. Two years later, he married Ann Loeb, a member of a prominent Wall Street banking family. Over the next decade, the couple would have five children: Samuel, Edgar Jr, Holly, Matthew, and Adam. After the birth of the two eldest sons, Edgar and Ann moved permanently to New York where Edgar would work in Seagram's executive offices. Even before Sam Bronfman died, it was understood within the family that Edgar would succeed his father as head of Distillers Corporation-Seagrams Ltd.[98] In 1957 Edgar became president of Seagram's American company, which opened its new corporate office building in New York the following year. He was deeply involved in Seagram's growth over the next decade. He also became interested in the entertainment business, for a time owning significant shares in MGM and later investing in several Broadway productions.[99]

Two years younger than his brother, Charles inherited his father's love for Canada. Unlike his siblings, he stayed in Montreal. He enrolled at McGill University, but left during his junior year to work for Seagram. In the mid-1950s he launched his own company, Thomas Adams, under the Distillers Corporation structure, to manufacture a new line of Canadian whisky.[100] In 1958 he took over responsibility for Seagram's operations in Canada, the Caribbean, and Israel. Charles married Barbara Baerwald of New York City in 1961, and the couple had two children: Stephen, born in 1963, and Ellen, born in 1969. Charles became increasingly involved in Montreal's civic affairs through the 1960s, and fulfilled a lifelong passion for baseball when he founded the Montreal Expos in 1968. Following Sam Bronfman's death, it was to Charles that the Jewish community looked to fill his father's shoes in Montreal.[101]

The division of the business empire into the more lucrative American section based in New York, led by Edgar, and the more historically significant Canadian section based in Montreal, led by Charles, was only one of the arrangements undertaken by the Bronfmans during the post-war period to ensure financial continuity beyond the lifetimes of Sam and Saidye. Another strategic one was the creation of trust funds for their four children, and the establishment by family lawyers Lazarus Phillips and Philip Vineberg of an investment company known as CEMP, an anagram based on the first letters of Charles, Edgar, Minda, and Phyllis. CEMP Investments Ltd became a highly successful corporation under the management of Leo Kolber, a friend of Charles's from university who had shown strong entrepreneurial skills in real estate and who became a source of sound business advice for many of the family's initiatives. By the early 1970s, CEMP's investments, largely through real estate development, were worth an estimated $300 million.[102]

CONCLUSION

By the end of the war, Sam Bronfman had become the undisputed leader of the Jewish community in Montreal, and he would retain this position for the rest of his life. "Nothing, but nothing, happened in the community, in terms of building buildings or taking positions, without having the agreement, the support of Sam Bronfman," according to Manuel "Manny" Batshaw, who grew up in the city and later directed the Allied Jewish Community Services, the successor to the Federation of Jewish Philanthropies. Batshaw's assessment of Sam would seem to be a typical one; people recall his often brusque and seemingly impulsive manner, his temper, and his uncompromising expectations, but they are also hard pressed not to admire his skills and achievements. Sam's presence did not always make people feel comfortable, and he tended not to brook much opposition or differences in opinion. "Fortunately," declared Batshaw, "his judgment was right most times."[103] Not everyone would have agreed. Nevertheless, Sam and Saidye's position within the community was such that, without them, the nature of Jewish philanthropy in Montreal, and beyond, would have been considerably different.

Although there was no written plan or statement of philosophy, the pattern of the Bronfmans' financial success and philanthropy had been established by the early 1950s. With the wealth generated by the growing Seagram empire, Sam and Saidye became the leaders of Jewish philanthropy in Montreal, and with Montreal the capital of Canadian Jewry this leadership led to an increasingly important role in Jewish philanthropy throughout Canada. They also gave to a host of non-Jewish projects and programs. These gifts were motivated by a variety of sentiments, including a desire to counter the gathering forces of anti-Semitism, the need to garner political and economic support for issues of concern to the Bronfman family, and a strong feeling of identity with the whole community of Montreal and the people of Canada. "He was a private guy," Phyllis said of her father. "Often it simply depended on who came to see him."[104]

It remained to formalize this pattern of giving through the creation of the Samuel and Saidye Bronfman Family Foundation.

TWO

SAM AND SAIDYE AND THE RISE

OF CANADIAN PHILANTHROPY

The rise of philanthropy in North America during the first half of the twentieth century, as well as the drive to identify and promote Canadian culture, formed the background to Sam and Saidye Bronfman's venture into the world of family foundations. The Depression and the war effort, the notion of scientific philanthropy, the efforts of an array of private donors and occasionally governments, and the involvement of major American foundations in the development of Canadian institutions all contributed, directly or indirectly, to the establishment of the Samuel and Saidye Bronfman Family Foundation in November 1952.[1] How the SSBFF fitted into this philanthropic history is as important as what it actually achieved over the course of its first two decades of existence, given that its strength as a family foundation eventually derived from the leverage it wielded as a major Canadian funding body.

The SSBFF was created as a vehicle to channel Sam and Saidye's considerable resources into support for charitable activities. In an age that saw both economic boom and increasingly interventionist governments, family trusts and investment corporations were useful tools to diminish the tax consequences of one's assets as well as to ensure that such assets could safely be transferred to the next generation. In the Bronfmans' case, the kind of fortune that Sam had put together by the 1950s translated into substantial donations to a variety of worthy causes. That the

SSBFF at this time could be described primarily as a device for estate planning does not take away from Sam and Saidye's commitment to philanthropy. Their involvement in the civic life of Montreal's Jewish community was clearly no longer part of a larger strategy that included making business and social contacts; this had been achieved. By the 1950s Sam and Saidye had identified a number of causes they wished to support and worked to maximize the resources they could regularly muster in order to continue supporting them. For the last two decades of Sam's life, the SSBFF represented the heart and soul of his and Saidye's philanthropy.

Up until the time of Sam's death in 1971, the Bronfmans made use of the SSBFF without overdue concern for process or policy. Compared to many other foundations – and to the SSBFF in later years – its management was informal and its funding patterns hardly strategic, much less scientific. For Sam and Saidye, there was little need or desire to establish formal funding programs; the SSBFF proved a useful tool for making the kinds of donations they felt were appropriate. Most of their philanthropy was directed at Jewish causes, consisting of regular support for established local institutions and occasional (though generous) support for emerging institutions in Israel. When it came to institutions outside the Jewish community, Sam and Saidye do seem to have made donations calculated to raise their prestige within a social world that had always kept them at arm's length as Jews, although this support clearly also reflected genuine long-held interests in areas such as the arts and scientific research. It was in making these donations that Sam and Saidye sowed the seeds of what would later become major funding programs for the SSBFF.

BRINGING BIG BUSINESS TECHNIQUES TO CHARITABLE GIVING

Before the First World War, only a handful of individuals across North America were wealthy enough to engage in philanthropy, in the sense of funding large-scale social or cultural projects such as museums, libraries, hospitals, and universities. The notion took root slowly over the course of the nineteenth century that such generosity should enjoy the privilege of tax-exemption that was normally granted to religious and other benevolent organizations. A landmark Massachusetts decision in 1874 recognized any institution as tax-exempt if it existed to advance educational goals, including "any antiquarian, historical, literary, scientific, medical, artistic, monumental, or musical" purpose; other states eventually followed suit.[2] That philanthropic foundations could have profound tax benefits for the rich was clearly a factor in their establishment; as taxes increased during the first decades of the twentieth century, the number of foundations rose in proportion.[3] Even so, most wealthy men who set up foundations saw them as a means to fund charitable causes. The classic foundations established by Andrew Carnegie in 1911 and John D. Rockefeller in 1913 served to formalize what both were already doing in a less organized manner: giving away large sums of money to recipients they deemed worthy.

The overarching desire to improve the lot of the less fortunate, or society in general, included a variety of complex motivations. Religious tradition was as strong a factor for Christians as it was for Jews. For the major American philanthropists of the early twentieth century, overwhelmingly Protestant as a cohort, the tendency to see wealth as a sign of divine favour was often mitigated by fear of excess; Carnegie, for instance, felt that after establishing a modest level of personal comfort, all surplus should be spent on the community.[4] These Protestant philanthropists expressed a desire to put things right in the world that recalls the Jewish notion of *tikkun olam*, but their motivations stemmed largely from a concern that what was causing grief in the world was the very thing that had made them rich. Industrial capitalism, by the end of the nineteenth century, had resulted in such discrepancies between the poor and the wealthy that the poor had little chance of escaping their predicament no matter how hard they worked or how moral their characters might be; it was the philanthropist's duty, therefore, to restore the balance.[5] Helping the disadvantaged by facilitating self-improvement was entirely consistent with Protestant tradition; so, too, was the disapproval of indiscriminate charity, which was seen as counterproductive, for it did not lead to true improvement and taught reliance on relief measures.[6] (In this respect also, the Protestant and Jewish traditions had much in common.) This preoccupation with self-improvement meant that much of the effort of early philanthropy went toward education. Indeed, prior to the Second World War, Carnegie was spending more on education nationally than the United States government.[7]

To get beyond simple acts of charity was a major rationale for creating foundations. The mandates of many foundations suggested lofty ambitions such as "the diffusion of knowledge" or to "promote the well-being of mankind."[8] The capacity to realize such ambitions was also much greater than it had once been, as the accumulation of vast wealth in the United States reached enormous proportions; the number of millionaires had risen from 100 in the late 1870s to more than 40,000 in 1916.[9] Individuals like Carnegie and Rockefeller amassed fortunes worth hundreds of millions of dollars; Rockefeller even complained that his money was coming in faster than he could give it away.[10] The philanthropic potential of fortunes on this scale was such that it required dedicated management, along with every other aspect of the business world. The private philanthropic foundation was born of a desire to make individual philanthropy run along scientific, managerial lines.[11]

"Scientific management," championed by Frederick Taylor in the late nineteenth century, was part of a major change in the approach to the structure and control of businesses and organizations. Seeking economies of scale in extraction and production, and encouraged by the process engineers who worked for these new industrial enterprises, professional managers promoted the development of systems for management. Scientific management took systems thinking to a new level, promoting efficiency and order in all of an organization's business processes. This new thinking soon affected all aspects of society, including what would become known as the public sector. The rise of national and international service organizations such as the Young Men's Christian Association encouraged the development of short-term fundraising campaigns that could be replicated from city to city.[12] During the First World War, governments adopted the strategies of YMCA campaigns as a model for efforts to rally the home front to provide financial and material support. The war thus drew all aspects of society into the effort to raise money, including businesses, labour unions, churches, and schools. After the war, these routines became embedded with the rise of the Community Chest movement in the 1920s. These organizations and movements reflected the tendency in urban industrial society to organize public and social services.[13]

By this time, some corporate leaders were beginning to introduce these ideas into their philanthropy. Proponents of what became known as scientific philanthropy were still in the minority in the 1920s, when most of the individuals who amassed great fortunes gave little during their lifetimes; those who did generally gave locally and responded to personal appeals. The advocates of scientific philanthropy, however, began to "seek causes and cures" for society's ills.[14] Led by Frederick Gates of the Rockefeller Foundation and Julius Rosenwald, the executive who had built Sears-Roebuck into a commercial empire, scientific philanthropy fomented a profound shift in the practice of charitable giving.[15] The movement had limited effect on philanthropy before the Second World War, however. By that time, only eight private foundations fully embraced the ideas of scientific philanthropy: those created by Carnegie, John D. Rockefeller Sr., John D. Rockefeller Jr., Edward Harkness, Olivia Sage, Julius Rosenwald, Elizabeth Milbank Anderson, and Edward Filene. Even so, the Rockefeller and Carnegie foundations dwarfed all the others by far and would have an enormous influence on the trajectory of philanthropy in the second half of the century.

Philanthropy took on additional significance after the Second World War. The war effort provided full employment, ending the crisis of the Great Depression when the ranks of the unemployed and disadvantaged swelled, draining the resources of traditional charitable organizations. Governments came to see the benefits of creating programs to alleviate poverty and improve citizens' health. The so-called Welfare State of the post-war period, coupled with an economic boom, relieved charitable organizations of many of their traditional responsibilities such as the sick and disabled, orphaned or troubled children, and the temporarily out-of-work. With prosperity at home, many charitable groups came to focus their efforts on causes in other parts of the world, such as Christian missions in developing countries and the emerging state of Israel.

Corporations also devoted increasing amounts of energy to philanthropic endeavours, following the pattern set before the war by the

Rockefeller Foundation and others. As government social programs expanded, corporations could respond to a wider variety of worthy causes, many of them cultural rather than charitable in nature. Corporations also came to see the importance of public relations, and understood that donating to charitable and other community undertakings marked them as good neighbours, or what came to be known as good corporate citizens. Increasingly, fledgling cultural or community-based organizations turned to corporations for assistance. By the end of the Second World War, corporate involvement had become critical to the success or failure of any fundraising campaign.[16] Governments made this process easier by offering tax incentives to anyone making charitable donations, and by registering organizations as having official charitable status. Given the increasing rate at which governments were taxing producers of wealth to pay for these social programs, it made sense to take advantage of such incentives.

Nevertheless, there was more at stake for donors than a tax break. Civic-minded concern for social welfare took on new meaning in the post-war period. The plight of refugees and the spectacle of bombed cities gave special impetus to people across North America to ease the burdens of victims of war. A spirit of rebirth, a sense that with effort and dedication a better world could be built, pervaded social and political thought in most Western countries; symbolic of this movement was the founding of the United Nations. A financial commitment from both government and the private sector would allow great improvements to be made in education, scientific research, and the arts – all the marks of great civilizations.

THE RISE OF CANADIAN PHILANTHROPY

Canada lagged behind the United States in the development of private philanthropy and in the ability of its government to provide services on a national level.[17] Its population was smaller, and until well into the twentieth century much of it was isolated with limited communication, especially in winter. Above all, its economy was dwarfed by that of its southern neighbour, as was the number of citizens who had achieved the level of wealth that permitted them to indulge in what was coming to be known as philanthropy. Although by the turn of the century Montreal, Toronto, and a few other cities had produced many wealthy families whose industrial and commercial enterprises drove the Canadian economy, there were none at the level of an Andrew Carnegie or a John D. Rockefeller, even relative to the local economic sphere.

The nineteenth century had seen plenty of benevolent societies formed to help the poor, often by groups based on national identity (the St Andrew's, the St Patrick's, and the St George's societies, to take the most famous), as well as voluntary corporations to fund and manage hospitals, cemeteries, schools, and museums. Very few individuals engaged in the direct patronage of institutions for the complex motivations that inspired the great American philanthropists: the desire to effect change, a sense of duty, the need for recognition. One who did was William Christopher Macdonald, the native of Prince Edward Island who became a tobacco manufacturer in Montreal and dedicated much of his income to improving McGill University (itself the result of a philanthropic donation by merchant James McGill in 1813), beginning with a series of scholarships in the 1870s and then in the 1890s a series of departmental chairs. Macdonald also funded the construction of a number of important academic buildings on the campus which would be named after him, and the creation of the huge Macdonald College to the west of the city which provided both agricultural training and a school for teachers. Macdonald's patronage extended to funding a seminal study of Quebec's public education system, the construction of consolidated schools across the country, and the creation of Canada's first crematorium, in Montreal. The zeal with which Macdonald made so many donations and undertook such grand projects did not come at the expense of his family, for he had none – a factor which, along with his personal austerity, may have greatly facilitated his decision to spend so much of his fortune rather than saving it for heirs or arranging for bequests after his death.

Macdonald established no foundations, however, although he did leave a number of bequests in his will which provided additional funding for institutions bearing his name.[18] The distinction of forming

Canada's first official foundation fell to the heirs of Hart Massey, the nineteenth-century businessman who had built his family's farm equipment manufactory into one of Canada's leading industries, based in Toronto. Having supported the arts and education throughout his life, Hart Massey stipulated in his will that the bulk of his estate be spent on various charities and institutions over a twenty year period.[19] His sons opted instead to create a philanthropic foundation, which would enable them to make strategic donations over a much longer period of time. This objective, and the decision to have family members sit on the foundation's board of trustees, marked this new body as the prototype of the family foundation in Canada.[20] Legal and political hurdles – inevitable, perhaps, given that such an arrangement had never been implemented in Canada – delayed the formal establishment of the Massey Foundation until 1918, although from the time of Hart's death in 1896 his sons had been supporting various causes in Toronto and beyond from the estate. The Massey Foundation's most entrepreneurial member, and its president as of 1926, was Hart's grandson Vincent, who funded the creation of several symphony orchestras and theatres across Canada, established the National Council of Education to promote Canadian identity and citizenship, and directly supported the National Gallery and the Dominion Drama Festival.[21] Although its vision of Canada was conservative and elitist – which is not to say this differed all that much from the outlook of many contemporary intellectuals – the Massey Foundation focused above all on the goal of creating a national culture.

The second private foundation formed in Canada was the first to be established by a philanthropist during his lifetime, and was in many ways the model for the SSBFF, which also saw its founder play a major role in grantmaking. John Wilson McConnell, a salesman from Ontario who had settled in Montreal at the turn of the century, had invested a small fortune in many of the city's businesses and utilities; it soon turned into a huge fortune. He then dedicated his wealth to a wide range of local causes, including benevolent and social organizations such as the Old Brewery Mission and the YMCA. Like the Massey family, McConnell was a Methodist, and shared Hart Massey's belief that the wealthy had a duty to relieve the destitute and improve their lives, mainly through the church and missionary work.[22] In 1937 he established the J.W. McConnell Foundation as a means of channelling his philanthropy, and managed the organization himself with the help of a secretary.[23] In addition to support for Montreal-based charities, whose operations were strained to the limit during the 1930s' Depression, the foundation continued to make major grants to the YMCA as well as to McGill University and the city's English-speaking hospitals. When McConnell died in 1963, his heirs continued his work as a board of trustees, renaming the organization the J.W. McConnell Family Foundation.

The poverty that so many Canadians experienced during the 1920s, and even more during the 1930s, was addressed only at the level of the community. Canada was constitutionally hampered from providing poor relief on a national scale, even had federal governments wished to do so. The burden fell on municipalities, which for the most part meant municipally-based charitable organizations, most of them connected to religious congregations. In many parts of the country, wealthy citizens – and some not-so-wealthy – supported charities with money and time. In Winnipeg, a civic-minded banker gave $100,000 in 1918 to what became known as the Winnipeg Foundation, and it soon attracted the generosity of others who felt the city in which they had made their fortunes should benefit from their success.[24] The notion of the community foundation built on recent developments in American cities – Cleveland, initially – whereby a variety of small and medium donors would contribute to a fund and act as, or elect, trustees to distribute the money locally.[25] Often community foundations were started by an enterprising individual, as in Winnipeg – or as in Vancouver a quarter century later when a secretary donated $1,000 she had carefully saved over many years to help homeless women, inspiring others to contribute and create the Vancouver Foundation, now one of the world's largest philanthropic organizations.[26]

In Quebec, language and religion fragmented efforts to provide welfare measures, but even so the need for institutions to become organized was keenly felt. The Montreal Council of Social Agencies, founded in 1921, was an early attempt to unite non-Catholic welfare organizations. The Federation of Jewish Philanthropies predated this association but shared the goal of providing assistance to people who did not fall under the charitable mandate of the Catholic Church. With the onset of the Depression, the inadequacy of traditional Catholic relief measures prompted the creation of two new organizations with principally lay leaderships. The Federation of Catholic Charities was founded in 1930 out of a fear that English-speaking Catholics were turning to Protestant charities – with the inherent moral dangers that implied – rather than to the largely francophone church and religious orders. In 1932 a group of French Canadian businessmen revived the Fédération des oeuvres de charité canadiennes-françaises, which had enjoyed a brief existence in the previous decade, in an effort to modernize relief measures for francophones, whose level of organization seemed to pale in comparison to that of Anglo-Protestants, and by implication that of Jews.[27]

Religious tradition and general altruism would appear to have been the motivation for most philanthropic activity in Canada prior to 1930. It was only in that year that the government passed the Income Tax Act which allowed individuals and corporations (including such institutions as the Winnipeg Foundation) to write off 10 per cent of their taxable income to charity.[28] Individuals gradually came to take advantage of this arrangement, but corporations were slow to do so; it was not really until the post-war period that the idea of corporate philanthropy took hold. In the 1940s, the bulk of charitable giving in Canada still came primarily from individuals. In 1945, individual donations comprised three quarters of the roughly $80 million that Canadians contributed to charity.[29] In 1949, individuals in Canada donated to charitable (including religious) institutions at a rate of 1.3 per cent of income per person. Although such individuals made relatively little use of the tax benefits available to them, in the long run the financial incentive to make large donations was crucial to the development of a culture of giving, especially for corporations.[30] It is likely that the 1930 Tax Act was part of what prompted J.W. McConnell to establish a formal foundation just a few years later. Certainly the number of Canadian foundations rose considerably over the course of the 1940s to the point where the SSBFF joined at least ten others that were not in existence a decade earlier.

SUPPORT FOR ARTS AND CULTURE
IN CANADA TO 1952

The Second World War brought a halt to much of the poverty and un-employment experienced during the Depression, and set the country on the road to establishing national relief measures that superseded Canada's constitutional logjam. One area of funding, however, in which the federal government was reluctant to become involved was arts and culture, despite constant lobbying from intellectuals and arts organiza-tions since at least the 1920s. Some government officials were against public investment in the arts on principle, believing it to be frivolous, or not part of British Protestant tradition, or the mark of – or at least the first step toward – a totalitarian regime; federal politicians also argued that culture was really part of education and therefore a provincial mat-ter.[31] Mackenzie King, who as prime minister throughout much of the 1920s, 30s, and 40s heard repeated requests for public support for arts and culture, especially in the wake of the Roosevelt administration's Federal Art Project, declared that this "mad desire to bring about State control" made him "shudder."[32]

Private patrons had been responsible for most arts-related funding since the nineteenth century. The Masseys, Macdonald, the CPR's Don-ald Smith (Lord Strathcona), the Bank of Commerce's Edmund Walker, and many others supported symphony orchestras across the country as well as the McGill and Toronto music conservatories. Wealthy Montreal families had been donating works of art to the Montreal Art Associa-tion since 1877 when a substantial bequest of art and land by merchant Benaiah Gibb had led to the opening of Canada's first fine art museum, later renamed the Montreal Museum of Fine Arts. Wealthy Toronto families did the same for the Toronto Art Museum (later the Art Gallery of Ontario) following historian Goldwin Smith's bequest of his house as permanent gallery space in 1910. Both institutions had art schools associated with them, and by the First World War there were art schools at Mount Allison University, in Winnipeg, Hamilton, and Vancouver. Other art galleries emerged thanks to philanthropic donations in such cities as Charlottetown and Regina. Montreal's Redpath family funded Canada's first natural history museum, while the McCord family provided the nucleus for a Museum of Canadian History, both at McGill University and both bearing the names of their funders. Edmund Walker and others contributed to the creation of a natural history and anthropological museum at the University of Toronto, later to become the Royal Ontario Museum. Newspaper magnate H.S. Southam gave crucial support to the Ottawa Drama League in 1915 (later the Ottawa Little Theatre) while the Masseys created the Hart House Theatre as part of the Hart House student centre at the University of Toronto.[33] Apart from providing direct financial aid, wealthy businessmen served on the boards of all major cultural institutions, often in the belief that their skill and experience were required to run a museum or orchestra, given that artists by temperament were not managers.[34] (This was an issue that the SSBFF would directly address with its Cultural Management program.) Women from wealthy families were even more involved, serving on fundraising committees, and even patronizing individual artists. Women were especially instrumental in reviving a widespread interest in crafts.[35]

Many of Canada's governors general were active patrons of the arts, beginning with the Earl of Dufferin and the Marquis of Lorne who promoted the Royal Canadian Academy of Arts (which led to the creation of the National Gallery) and the Royal Society of Canada (which led to the National Museum) in the 1870s and 80s. Canada's National Gallery, a rare case of a cultural institution that did receive government funding, found a home in Ottawa's Victoria Memorial Museum Building as of 1912, sharing space with the National Museum of natural history and anthropology; both received support from subsequent governors general and donations from philanthropists. By that time, Earl Grey had set up the Historic Landmarks Association to recognize historic sites, celebrated both the tercentenary of the founding of Quebec and the one hundred and fiftieth anniversary of the Battle of the Plains of Abraham, and presided over ceremonies giving national awards for excellence in drama and music. Subsequent governors general Bessborough and Willingdon promoted additional awards for the arts, including the one for best Canadian play given at the Dominion Drama Festival as of 1932. Four years later, Lord Tweedsmuir (himself a noted novelist) presided over the first Governor General's Literary Awards.[36]

These awards were judged by members of the Canadian Authors' Association, a lobby group established in 1921 for Canadian writers striving to protect their copyright. Other protective organizations also emerged during these years for performing artists, many of them calling themselves "national" so they could claim to speak for all Canadians and lobby the federal government. Achieving a truly pan-Canadian voice, even in one field, was difficult in practice; most such groups were based in Quebec and Ontario and reflected the problems and preoccupations of central Canada.[37]

Much of the drive for government support of the arts came from progressive movements critical of the traditional emphasis on British elite culture which permeated private patronage, especially that of the governors general. The social and intellectual elite tended to envisage Canadian culture as essentially British in nature and ignored the experiences of immigrants and the working classes.[38] During the Depression this criticism became more articulate as larger numbers of intellectuals joined left-wing political movements and pointed to the successes of Roosevelt's New Deal at giving work to artists and writers. In the absence of government funding, and disenchanted with private patronage, these intellectuals turned to American foundations for serious investment in education and culture. The directors of the Carnegie and Rockefeller foundations viewed this sort of investment as a way to build North American cultural networks, part of a larger desire to further integrate the two countries' economic and strategic interests.[39]

In the 1930s, American foundation money funded a wide variety of drama, film, and radio projects across Canada, helped establish fine arts programs in several Canadian universities and institutions (such as the Banff School of Fine Arts), and facilitated the creation of the Canadian Museums Committee as a national voice for museums and collections.[40] It also funded the McGill Social Science Project, whose findings would form the blueprint for Canada's post-war social welfare policies.[41] Further American funding for humanities and social science studies in Canada came during the war with the creation of the Canadian Social

Science Research Council and the Humanities Research Council of Canada, both of which would eventually lead to significant government funding for scholarship in these fields.

No corresponding arts council took shape at this time. Unlike the other two councils, there was no American model for such a body, nor a British precedent until the new Labour government created the British Arts Council in 1945. The Carnegie Corporation did fund the Conference of Canadian Artists at Kingston in June 1941, at which arts and culture representatives from across the country gathered to discuss common interests. The outcome was the formation of the Federation of Canadian Artists (FCA) as a lobby group striving to convince the federal government to fund arts and culture. Given that the FCA continued to receive funding from American foundations, it is no small irony that the drive for public support for the arts owes a great deal to private philanthropy.[42] At the end of the war, the FCA and several other arts organizations merged to form the Canadian Arts Council, which became the principal national voice for the rights of artists in the post-war period; after the creation of the Canada Council, it changed its name to the Canadian Conference of the Arts.[43]

Constant lobbying, along with the fear that the country's intellectual and artistic community would shift their vote to the left of the Liberal party, eventually convinced the Liberal government (led by Louis St Laurent after King's retirement) to establish the Royal Commission on National Development in the Arts, Letters and Sciences in 1949. Chaired by Vincent Massey, fresh from a term as Canada's High Commissioner in London and still titular head of the Massey Foundation, the Commission received briefs from the Canadian Arts Council and other key organizations. The report, published in June 1951, painted a woeful picture of the state of Canada's cultural scene – arguably much too woeful, given the country's long if limited tradition of art, music, theatre, writing, and research.[44] Overemphatic or not, the Massey Report made it clear that it was the federal government's duty to initiate public support for the arts as well as for major institutions such as museums, libraries, archives, universities, the Canadian Broadcasting Corporation, the National Film Board, and the Historic Sites and Monuments Board.[45] The government acted on many of the Report's recommendations, including the establishment of the Canada Council in March 1957 as an independent grant-making body. With its $100 million endowment from the federal government,[46] the Canada Council became a major funder of the arts and effectively one the country's leading philanthropic foundations.[47]

THE SSBFF, 1952–72

The Samuel and Saidye Bronfman Family Foundation came into existence in November 1952. In conformity with Canadian law, letters patent had been filed, and these designated Sam, Saidye, Edgar, Charles, Minda, and Phyllis as directors of the corporation. The foundation's stated purpose was for "carrying on ... without pecuniary gain to its members, objects of a national, patriotic, religious, philanthropic, charitable, scientific, artistic, social, professional or sporting character."[48] The directors were entitled "to receive funds and contributions, without any public appeal for funds, and to contribute to and assist charitable organizations and institutions" with the powers to borrow money and mortgage property, if required. In form and in spirit, the SSBFF resembled most foundations established by that time across North America. It had no significant assets, however. Funding for donations came from the family and its businesses and flowed through the charitable structure of the foundation to be distributed to recipients.[49]

The SSBFF's board of directors met for the first time at the end of January 1953 to acknowledge the letters patent and approve the bylaws. Sam Bronfman acted as chairman of the meeting and Edgar served as secretary, but there was no formal appointment of president or other officers; lawyer Philip Vineberg was also present as a legal advisor, and eventually served the board as its secretary.[50] During the first few decades of the foundation's existence, meetings were few and far between; essentially they served as formal occasions to deal with the organization's legal structure. Decisions about who would receive money and how much were essentially made by Sam and Saidye. They had no staff for charitable activities; Sam's secretary or an aide would log the contribution on a three-by-five index card for future reference.

Through their new foundation, Sam and Saidye made important donations to a variety of causes. They gave annually to the Canadian Cancer Society, and participated in the Federated Appeal of Greater Montreal, an amalgamation of Catholic Charities, the Protestant Red Feather campaign, and other local programs. Sam continued to support McGill University, which his two sons attended, and which remained the most prestigious institution of higher learning in the city, perhaps the country. Partly because of the quota regarding Jewish enrolment and partly because it was such a remarkable feather for a philanthropist's cap, McGill appears to have been something of an obsession for Sam Bronfman. A particular point of contention was that, despite his having given so generously since the late 1930s, McGill did not extend the honour of awarding him a seat on its board of governors, as it had often done with other philanthropists such as McConnell. Sam felt he was the victim of consistent opposition from within the McGill's establishment, either out of snobbery, jealousy, or anti-Semitism.[51] This honour only came to Sam in 1964, much to his satisfaction, however belated it may have been. When the crowded Faculty of Management (formerly the School of Commerce, which the Bronfmans had supported in the past) began to seek proper headquarters, Sam was willing to supply the funds for a new building, which was completed in 1971.[52]

Sam and Saidye's involvement in culture and heritage went back to Sam's passionate support for Canada and British values as leader of the CJC, but it was as one of Canada's major philanthropists that he was approached by the creators of the Canada Council to join its board of directors. Sam agreed to serve a term giving direction to this new body, joining nineteen other prominent citizens, many of whom were philan- thropists. Writing to his new colleagues in April 1957, Sam conveyed his enthusiasm for working with all of them "for the development of our national life and common heritage."[53]

Direct support for the arts was clearly Saidye's domain. In keeping with a certain tradition wherein arts patronage within a philanthropic family was a female prerogative, Saidye devoted much time to the cause of culture in Montreal. Her early love for music translated into pas- sionate support for the Montreal Symphony Orchestra, whose board she joined in the 1950s. Saidye was equally passionate about visual art, and supported the Montreal Museum of Fine Arts. Like many such institutions, much of the organizational work, including raising money for acquisitions, was done by a ladies' committee, comprising the wives of the city's business elite. Although this committee had no Jewish members, Saidye herself made annual contributions to the museum, especially to increase its collection of contemporary works. Eventually, the SSBFF began handling this donation; in 1963 it reached an agreement with the museum whereby it would give $10,000 a year for the acquisition of works of contemporary art, the intention being to increase the museum's collection while encouraging young artists. In 1981, the amount was increased to $15,000 per year; by this time, some 400 works of art had been acquired, half of which were drawings and prints.[54]

Saidye found she had much in common with her daughter Minda, the Paris-based art patron, and developed a particularly close relationship with Phyllis, who was both a sculptor and an architect. In recognition of Saidye's love of the arts (as well as her long involvement in the YW-YMHA) her children founded the Saidye Bronfman Centre in 1967 (the subject of Chapter 6) to honour her seventieth birthday, and the Saidye Bronfman Award for Excellence in Craft (the subject of Chapter 11) in 1977 to honour her eightieth.

Despite these sizable donations to general educational and cultural endeavours, Sam and Saidye's philanthropy continued to focus overwhelmingly on Jewish organizations. In addition to the annual contribution to the Combined Jewish Appeal, they gave to Jewish education and youth programs including summer camps and parochial schools. After working for many years to expand the Jewish General Hospital's facilities and services, Saidye was made vice-president and a life member of the hospital's Auxiliary. She also became a governor of the Jewish Public Library, another recipient of her and Sam's philanthropy.[55]

Sam retired as president of the Federation of Jewish Philanthropies in 1950, but remained head of the Canadian Jewish Congress until 1962. In the latter capacity he campaigned for the rights of Jews in Canada and for human rights in general around the world. In recognition of his

years of service, the CJC announced it would name its new national headquarters Samuel Bronfman House. The Congress acquired a prestigious
site on Côte-des-Neiges Road in downtown Montreal, amid the mansions of the Golden Square Mile, and commissioned Fred Lebensold (of
Affleck, Desbarats, Dimakopoulos, Lebensold and Sise, architects of
the National Arts Centre in Ottawa and Place des Arts in Montreal) to
design a striking building.[56] The SSBFF gave $150,000 to help pay for
construction, and before the decade was out it would contribute another
$400,000. In the spring of 1970 an ailing Sam was present at the open-
ing of Samuel Bronfman House, and gave one of his last public addresses
on the occasion, speaking of his years at the helm of the CJC.[57]

Israel

Sam and Saidye had always been keen supporters of Israel, but grew
even more enthusiastic in the wake of their first visit there in 1956, when
they were received by Prime Minister David Ben-Gurion and given tours
of key places. They were impressed by the young country's economic
and administrative achievements, and strove to do their best to help
strengthen it. Each year, Sam hosted the annual Guardian's Dinner
honouring those who had purchased $1,000 or more in Israeli Bonds. He
and Saidye supported the Israel Maritime League, an organization providing aid to seamen and sea cadets in Israel, beginning in 1958. The
family provided funds for the Jewish Institute for the Blind in Jerusalem,
and supported efforts to raise money for community development in
Israel by sponsoring the annual Negev Dinner, which honoured a prominent Montreal community leader and raised money for the development
of the Negev and the founders of the settlement of Eilat. The Bronfmans
were also involved in the Manufacturers Association of Israel. Sam's
parents were honoured in 1955 when the SSBFF provided for an annual
contribution to the Canadian Friends of the Hebrew University. These
donations funded the Yechiel and Mindel Bronfman Scholarship, a
Canadian award for overseas study.[58] In the late 1950s, Sam spearheaded

the move to combine the fundraising efforts of the Federation of Jewish Philanthropies and the United Israel Appeal, which were led by virtually the same individuals.[59] When war broke out over the Suez Crisis shortly after the Bronfmans' first visit to Israel, Sam worked to raise funds for the country's defence.[60] By nature a conciliator, Sam urged both sides to make peace, sensing a great deal of ambivalence on the part of the Canadian public towards the war. He also praised Canada's role as a peacekeeper in this conflict.[61]

The Six Day War, which erupted in the Middle East in June 1967, brought a dramatic shift in the Bronfmans' attention to Israel and elicited an enormous response from the Jewish community in Montreal.[62] For Jews in North America, the war was a turning point in their support for the state of Israel. The day after the war began, Sam Bronfman convened the leaders of the Jewish community at the Montefiore Club in Montreal. At that moment, no one knew how long the war would last or how deeply the crisis would be felt. Given the uncertainty, Bronfman announced that he planned to increase his contribution to the Combined Jewish Appeal by 300 per cent, and he expected everyone in the room to follow suit. There was some initial resistance, but in the end there came a "tidal wave" of support and Sam raised nearly $13 million.[63]

Arguably, the Six Day War and other threats to Israel in the late 1960s helped to complete a transformation in Jewish cultural identity. In the minds of many Canadian Jews, Israel had replaced Eastern Europe as the center of Jewish culture and identity.[64] For many Jews, as Edgar Bronfman has written, providing financial support for Israel at this time was one of the primary ways that they expressed their Jewishness.[65] Sam Bronfman reflected that transition in his work on behalf of Israel's defence. His children recognized his passion for Israel in the mid-1960s when they marked their father's seventieth birthday by donating $1 million to the Israel Museum to build an archaeology wing that would house some of the most precious artifacts of ancient Palestine.[66] They would also continue to honour his commitment to the Combined Jewish Appeal by maintaining the donation to the CJA as the SSBFF's largest single funding component.

NEW STRAINS OF GRAIN

The Bronfmans also supported scientific research, notably in agriculture – which, given the importance of grains to the production of whisky, was entirely appropriate.

In the post-war era, policymakers became increasingly concerned with the threat of overpopulation in less-developed nations and the potential for large-scale famine. In 1943, the Rockefeller Foundation had played a leading role in helping to found the Centro Internacional de Mejoramiento de Maiz y Trigo (CIMMYT) in Mexico, a scientific center for the development of hardier and more nutritious strains of maize and wheat.[67] Agricultural researchers had grown increasingly interested in this work by the early 1950s, but there was no endowed chair in Canada for agricultural research. In conversations with Edgar and Charles Bronfman, Dr A.H.S. Gillson, president of the University of Manitoba, suggested that the Bronfmans endow such a chair. Edgar told Dr Gillson that the family preferred not to donate a lump sum, but would be willing to support the salary of a full professor.[68] At the end of October 1953, Gillson submitted an outline for a program of fundamental research to be developed under the university's new head of the Department of Plant Science, Leonard Hylary Shebeski.[69]

The SSBFF provided funds for this chair, named Rosner after Saidye's family, from 1954 to 1973. This long-term support enabled Shebeski to design and implement a sustained research effort and attract other financial support. Over the next decade, researchers at the University of Manitoba developed a hybrid grain known as triticale through a process known as hybrid crossing. Work on triticale played a pivotal role in the development of the hardier and more nutritious grains that enabled the Green Revolution of the 1960s and 70s, saving millions of people from starvation. It also demonstrated to the Canadian philanthropic community the potential for strategic giving.

Triticale, a hybrid family of grains created by crossing wheat and rye, had been of interest to plant and agricultural researchers since the nineteenth century. By combining the high protein content of wheat with the high lysine content of rye, the grain offered an extremely nutritious food for humans and animals. Just as importantly, the plant offered the high yield of wheat but exhibited rye's ability to thrive in unfavourable climates and soils. Unfortunately, most first-generation plants were infertile.[70]

Work on triticale began in 1954 at the University of Manitoba when Burton Charles Jenkins was hired to fill the Rosner chair. Jenkins traveled the globe collecting specimens, cultivating them in test plots and saving the most promising examples for hybridization. In 1959, the Manitoba team began to improve these strains by cross-breeding successive generations. This time-consuming process was slowed even further when test plots were covered with snow. Hoping to accelerate their work, in 1963 the Manitoba researchers took strains of triticale to a winter nursery in Ciudad Obregón, Mexico. This move gave the researchers another growing cycle, and led to collaboration with researchers at the Rockefeller-funded CIMMYT. In 1965, CIMMYT launched a large-scale breeding program using the Manitoba strains of triticale.[71]

As early as 1961, the Manitoba researchers had begun to test their newly synthesized triticales against the yield and quality of long-established cereals in western Canada. The results exceeded expectations. Moreover, grain from these plants produced a higher quality animal feed than other cereals. These results brought increased financial support from industry and the government, and the research team expanded. By 1967 the Manitoba researchers had developed strains of triticale that produced yields as high as those of standard wheat in western Canada. In 1970 Canada's Department of Agriculture approved the first triticale variety for registration. Appropriately, it was named Rosner.[72]

International recognition of the importance of the research carried on by the University of Manitoba and CIMMYT exploded in the late 1960s. Efforts to cultivate the grain were launched in Kenya and Ethiopa. The Canadian International Development Agency and the International Development Research Centre in Ottawa increased their support for research. Popular reports that scientists had created a new "superfood" appeared in publications ranging from *Readers Digest* to the *Saturday Evening Post.* Norman E. Borlaug, who directed the research at CIMMYT, won the Nobel Peace Prize in 1970 for his fight against world hunger.[73] Most importantly, techniques learned through the development of triticale enabled improvements to other cereal crops that increased their productivity and resistance to disease.[74]

The success of the triticale program, summed up in a report completed by the University of Manitoba in 1974, prompted the SSBFF directors to continue to provide funding for the Rosner Chair in Agronomy for another three years. Apart from wishing to continue honouring Saidye's father, they felt strongly that the Rosner chair was "a source of very considerable prestige to the University" and had made "an important contribution to world agriculture."[75] Even after this period, the board continued to make annual grants to the University of Manitoba to maintain the chair, usually in the range of $35,000.[76] It was only in the mid-1980s that the directors began to think seriously of sponsoring another major project in the field of agriculture, the outcome of which is discussed in chapter 4.

Conclusion

Sam and Saidye's philanthropy was local, national, and international in scope, but it remained a product of their personal interests. The SSBFF was not unusual in this respect, as most foundations existed to provide funding to causes that their founders cared deeply about, although this was often a question of broadly helping educational and cultural programs or improving social welfare. Indeed, where the SSBFF differed from many contemporary private foundations was in having very specific areas of interest, although these were many and varied. Given their prominence as Jewish philanthropists, it is not surprising that Sam and Saidye devoted much of their energies to Jewish causes, both at home and abroad. The triticale project at the University of Manitoba was a natural offshoot of the family's links to the Canadian prairies and to grain products. More unusual, at least for the 1950s and early 1960s, was the SSBFF's support for arts and culture, which was a reflection of Sam's and especially Saidye's passion but also set the tone for the foundation's future involvement in this area.

The range of interests indicated by Sam and Saidye's philanthropy over two decades might suggest that donations were made in a spontaneous, even whimsical manner. Such a suggestion would seem to be in keeping with "Mr" Sam's personal approach to most aspects of his business. Arguably, it is also borne out in the functional nature of the SSBFF, which neither possessed permanent assets nor required much deliberation on the part of its board. However, rather than interpreting this pattern as spontaneous, it might be more helpful to see the SSBFF in the 1950s and 60s as an ideal vehicle for a wealthy family that desired a great deal of freedom in making philanthropic choices. The purpose of the foundation was evidently not to tie up resources in dedicated philanthropic programs but to enable Sam and Saidye to devote their wealth to important causes as they arose – always maximizing the amount of contribution they could muster and minimizing the tax consequences. Sam Bronfman's evolving career as a philanthropist may have remained deeply personal in the post-war era, but was hardly unfocused or undisciplined. Many of his donations outside the Jewish community seem to have been made, in part, from a desire to win respect, notably from an elite that had not always been welcoming. His generosity towards the Jewish community may also have been, in part, an effort to maintain connections with his cultural roots – not the same as, although perfectly consistent with, a concern for the welfare of the community. Sam also clearly understood, by virtue of his entrepreneurship, the power of systems embedded in the movement towards scientific philanthropy – even if he did not use the term. Improving one's community, one's country, and even one's world had always lain at the heart of the Bronfmans' philanthropy, even if it took time for this outlook to be transformed into something resembling policy.

THREE

Professional Management

Sam Bronfman's health declined rapidly around the time of his eightieth birthday in March 1971. Minda, Phyllis, Edgar, and Charles came from Paris, Chicago, New York, and Montreal to attend the elaborate party organized by Saidye at the Chateau Champlain hotel ballroom. The prospect of their father's death raised a host of conflicting emotions among them. It also made them more aware of his legacy to them, to the employees and shareholders of Seagram, and to the people of Montreal and Canada. One part of that legacy included Sam's well-recognized philanthropy, much of which he had pursued with Saidye in the form of the foundation that bore their names. When Sam died the following July, a portion of his estate passed to the Samuel and Saidye Bronfman Family Foundation as a permanent endowment.

For twenty years, the SSBFF had functioned as a vehicle for Sam and Saidye's personal philanthropic giving. Decisions about what to fund were based partly on a sense of community responsibility and partly on a desire to win the respect of certain institutions such as McGill or the Museum of Fine Arts, but mostly they were based on what Sam and Saidye found interesting. Sam's philanthropy revolved largely around educational and research institutions, while Saidye focused on the arts; both were passionate about local Jewish causes and Israel. There was enough consistency to suggest a pattern that subsequent directors of the foundation could follow, although it was equally possible to argue that the ssbff should depart in quite different directions. One crucial variable was the political and social climate, considerably different in the 1970s than it had been a decade or two earlier. A rapidly changing Canadian society required new approaches to the way the foundation conducted its business. Needs were different, with government social programs functioning to considerable capacity, and with new political and community forces on the scene. Methods, too, needed to be different, as the revolution in scientific philanthropy which had been brewing since before the war, had now been launched. There were many more foundations around and, as a result, applying for money had become complicated. Running a foundation had become even more complicated, typically requiring formal funding policies and even full-time staff.

Sam Bronfman's passing released and inspired his children to play a much larger role in civic affairs and to become promoters of cultural and social programs in Montreal, Canada, and the world. The next generation rose to the occasion, but they were also aware that they could not simply take over where Sam had left off. They agreed that a mechanism had to be introduced to effect a more reasoned way of investing. There were now four Bronfman siblings as well as Saidye involved on the board, each of them with a potentially different take on what the foundation's priorities should be. Establishing policies and guidelines was clearly the first order of business. Even so, more than mere consensus was required. Without departing from Sam's basic vision, or from their own passions and interests, the new directors worked to ensure that the ssbff would respond to real needs within Canadian society.

Canadian Society in Transition: Challenges for Private Philanthropy

Sam and Saidye's sense of Canadianness, which they earnestly espoused and promoted, was bound up in a sense of Britishness, shaped as much of it was by the wartime struggle in defence of Britain and the values it stood for. They were less familiar with a new notion of Canadianness that was gradually emerging in the post-war period, one that shed most of its ties to Britain and forged an independent position within the world. Along with a kind of nationalism (in Canada's case, arguably two nationalisms) came increased expectations of the state as a player in people's lives. The state would come to challenge the traditional role played by private philanthropy, not only by taking over many of its functions but also by setting limits to its powers. Sam and Saidye had a taste of this changing world in the 1960s, but it was the next Bronfman generation that would face, and eventually learn to work with, a more aggressive state and a much wider range of interest groups seeking funding.

Canadians had been exploring the question of who and what they were as a nation since before the First World War, but in the post-war period, and especially in the 1960s, the terms of the inquiry were changing. A huge influx of newcomers from all corners of the globe, first refugees and then immigrants, made it increasingly difficult to cast the Canadian identity in purely British terms, as generations had done despite the presence of a large French-Canadian minority and the claims of native peoples. In 1963, the federal government commissioned a study on bilingualism and biculturalism, which examined the situation of French-speaking Canadians not only in Quebec, where they were the majority, but across the country where communities continued to exist. The commission's findings led the government of Pierre Trudeau to recognize both English and French as Canada's official languages in 1969. The government also adopted a policy of multiculturalism in 1971, which recognized the ethnic diversity of Canadian society. By the 1970s many came to see this cultural mosaic as a defining quality of Canada, contrasting it with the United States which (so the argument went) had always encouraged cultural assimilation. One of the more glaring inconsistencies of the "mosaic" vision of Canada was the marginalized position of native peoples, an area that the SSBFF would later address.

Canadians also tended to feel pride in their arts and culture, especially in the degree to which their governments were – after resisting the idea for decades – willing to provide major support. The Canada Council dispensed an increasing number of grants over its first two decades, funding artists and arts groups across the country.[1] Canada's centenary in 1967 gave much impetus to the construction of bold new facilities for the arts. Theatre and symphony hall complexes appeared in Montreal (Place des Arts), Ottawa (National Arts Centre), Charlottetown (Confederation Centre), and Winnipeg (Manitoba Centennial Centre), largely the result of government arts spending. Governments invested as never before in education, enabling increasing numbers of Canadians to attend university, which required universities to expand their facilities. As the Bronfman family's experience at this time shows (the Saidye Bronfman Centre, the Canadian Jewish Congress headquarters, the McGill Faculty of Management), communities and institutions could and did turn to the private sector for funding. Private funding for the arts also increased in the 1970s, coalescing in 1974 with the founding of the Council for Business and the Arts in Canada (CBAC), an association of corporations interested in supporting the arts.[2] Even so, government funding deflected, or at any rate set much of the agenda for, traditional private philanthropy in the arts.

The 1960s and 70s also saw further advances by the Canadian welfare state, from the creation of a federal pension plan to national health insurance to the family allowance. In Quebec, the Catholic Church had always enjoyed a central role in the delivery of health and welfare services, as well as education. During the period known as the Quiet Revolution, the provincial government implemented a series of measures to secularize and bureaucratize such services. In the wake of major educational reforms, the government adopted Bill 65 in June 1972 to improve health and social conditions in the province. Such legislation marked a significant shift away from private, religious funding for hospitals and human services to state-run programs; Montreal's Jewish community expressed concern at the prospect of losing control over their institutions.[3] The increasing presence of the state in the realm of social welfare by no means obviated the need for private philanthropy, although organizations such as the SSBFF had to do careful groundwork to identify areas where the hand of government did not reach or where it lacked the interest or resources to go. This period clearly saw a decline in individual and corporate giving: in the late 1950s, private-sector donations equalled approximately 1 per cent of national income, whereas by the late 1970s that figure had fallen to 0.7 per cent.[4]

The Quiet Revolution and the Bilingualism and Biculturalism Commission also resulted in increased use of the French language in public life in Quebec. This meant that organizations based in Quebec that had always operated in English would find themselves having to interact with provincial and municipal governments and many other institutions in French, adding a level of complexity to public and private transactions, including the development of social and cultural programs. The official use of the French language, as well as the centralizing and bureaucratizing agenda of the Quiet Revolution, were entrenched by the Parti Québécois government, which won the 1976 provincial election with a mandate to take Quebec to a referendum on independence. While many in Quebec would find that a dynamic provincial government eager to promote social and cultural programs represented much-needed opportunities for innovation, others found themselves turning more than ever to the federal government for leadership in such areas. In the interest of promoting a pan-Canadian alternative to Quebec nationalism, federal governments would continue to encourage programs and institutions that were national (i.e., Canadian) in scope.

Despite the growth of the state – or perhaps because of it – the 1960s and 70s saw the rise of a new era in community activism. New cultural and neighbourhood-based organizations flourished separate from the traditional ethnic and religious institutions that had shaped local charities in an earlier era. Fledgling arts and cultural groups were examples of these organizations, as were those groups reacting to what they saw as the devastation of the urban environment by expressways and office towers. Responding to the needs of these groups and working with them to develop programs and projects would prove especially rewarding and challenging for the SSBFF.

Canadian philanthropists were conscious of the growing political challenges faced by their American counterparts during this period. Foundations came under increasing criticism in the United States by public officials concerned that tax policies and the rules governing foundations and non-profits provided too many opportunities for abuse. When

Republican members of the US Senate Finance Committee issued a report in 1959 recommending liberalization of tax code provisions affecting unlimited deductions for charitable contributions, a minority of Democratic senators on the committee charged that the recommendations would erode the tax base and harm society by leaving control of large fortunes in place for perpetuity. In part, the report reflected a political response to the remarkable growth of non-profits in the American economy. As the report noted, 87 per cent of the nation's 13,000 foundations had been created since 1940.[5]

Growing pressure to revise the laws affecting charitable contributions and the operation of non-profits led to a Treasury Department report in 1965 that recommended major changes in the rules governing foundations. The report called for "prohibitions on business dealings between donors and foundations, limits on foundation ownership of voting control of businesses, restrictions on the deductibility of donor-controlled gifts, and regulation of the number of years donors and their families could sit on governing boards."[6] Many in the United States feared that legislation based on this report would impose such limitations on foundations that philanthropists would scale back their programs and donations. In the end, however, the 1969 Tax Reform Act proved quite moderate in its terms, and served to reassure the public that the abuse they suspected within some philanthropic organizations would be curbed while the ability of other foundations to effect positive change would not.[7] Although it was not subject to the same degree of popular suspicion, Canadian philanthropy clearly needed to take stock of its own activities and its fiscal obligations to the public.

FAMILY FOUNDATIONS IN CANADA, 1972

Looking around at the Canadian foundations in existence at the time of Sam's death, the trustees of the SSBFF would have noted a great deal of money being spent on a wide variety of causes without very much attention given to being scientific and innovative. They might well have reached the same conclusion that Alan Arlett did a year or so later when researching his *Canadian Directory to Foundations*, published in 1973. According to Arlett, philanthropic investments in Canada tended to be conservative, directed towards well-established organizations and proven programs, and supporting the same areas of interest year after year. Because the majority of Canadian family foundations had been established since the end of the Second World War, many of the founders were still alive, exerting on their operations the sort of influence that Sam Bronfman did within the SSBFF. This situation meant that "Canadian foundations, in many cases, rather than reflecting a scientifically disciplined approach to philanthropy, tend to reflect the donor's personal philanthropic interests."[8] This is not to imply that such interests were of limited value to Canadians; far from it, as many philanthropic foundations specialized in key areas of health, welfare and education which answered clear social needs. For performing artists it was useful to know that the Floyd S. Chalmers Foundation, for example, gave grants in this area; equally, all manner of grant applicants in the region of London, Ontario, would have appreciated the two Ivey foundations which supported projects in that region. Even so, in such cases it was essentially serendipitous when a foundation's personal agenda and a potential grantee's needs proved a match. Few attempts were made to identify the directions in which entrepreneurial Canadians wished to go, and then supply the necessary funds in a strategic manner.

It was also far from easy for the Canadian public, or other foundations for that matter, to learn much about philanthropic organizations. Arlett's *Directory* was only the third incarnation of a guide of this sort, and by far the most useful. The first *Guide to Foundations and Granting Agencies* was published by the Association of Universities and Colleges of Canada in 1966, and a second version appeared three years later. In these volumes, foundations were included only if they volunteered information, and less than half of those contacted agreed to cooperate. As one fundraiser put it, most Canadian foundations "prefer to wrap themselves in substantial secrecy" and tended to shun publicity. No in-depth study of the activities, assets, and disbursements of Canada's foundations had ever been done. Guesses as to how many foundations existed in Canada in the late 1960s ranged from 200 to 1,400.[9]

Canada did little to offset the widespread sense of secrecy surrounding philanthropic organizations. Although the government published the names of new foundations when they applied for letters patent, it did not require them to issue an annual statement – in contrast to the tax codes of the United States. Fewer than a dozen Canadian foundations published reports on a regular basis, and only four provided financial details on assets and expenditures. In some ways, this secrecy was characteristic of the entire sector in North America. In the United States, for example, only 140 of the country's 22,000 foundations published an annual report in 1968.[10]

This lack of information hardly served the interests of foundations, nor did it help realize a genuine desire on the part of a large sector of society to improve social conditions. A 1972 public opinion survey conducted by Gallup for the Council on Foundations in the United States revealed that half of the American public believed that contributing to philanthropic causes was more important than it had been in the past. Three out of four said they thought that current income tax deductions for charitable and educational purposes should either be maintained or increased. Nevertheless, the role of grant-making organizations was somewhat obscure to the general public. Only one in three could actually name a grant-making foundation. One in three also agreed that "foundations are secretive about what they do" while only slightly over one in four disagreed and nearly 40 per cent said they had no opinion. The public, however, also seemed to understand that foundations played a key role in promoting innovation – two out of three people surveyed thought that "foundations are good because they give money to try out new ideas." Asked to identify their social priorities in 1972, people surveyed by Gallup reported that curbing drug abuse was number one, followed by support for hospitals and health clinics, and then finding ways to help older people.[11]

Canadian philanthropies would also have noted the growing criticism of American foundations by a public wary of secrecy and large institutions in the 1960s and early 70s, and they would have watched with interest the political response to such criticism that emerged over the following decade. In 1973 a Senate subcommittee began a series of discussions focused on the need for more public information on the scope and scale of foundation operations and finances.[12] In an effort to preserve their autonomy and defend their role in society, American foundations decided to organize. The Council on Foundations, the Foundation Center, and the National Council on Philanthropy formed a special committee led by John Gardner, the former secretary of the US Department of Health, Education and Welfare. After much study, the committee recommended changes in several areas, including increased support for independent research on foundations, the continuation and extension of library services to the general public, improved relations with government, the development of voluntary standards of good practice, and the creation of an information clearinghouse to improve communication among foundations. The Council on Foundations also moved from New York to Washington, DC, to improve its ability to articulate the concerns of its members to Congress and the Executive Branch of the government. Campaigning to build its membership and political clout, the Council on Foundations aimed to cultivate a culture of professionalism within the philanthropic community and to reposition foundations as public, rather than private, institutions.[13]

Seizing the policy initiative in 1973, the Rockefeller Foundation and other leaders of the US philanthropic community commissioned Harvard Professor Martin Feldstein to undertake a study of the economic effects of charitable contributions on tax policy and social welfare in the United States. Feldstein's report, issued at the end of the year, confirmed the long-held belief that by encouraging philanthropy, tax deductions produced far more dollars for social welfare programs than conventional government programs.[14] This was good news for philanthropic foundations, especially given the growing onus on professionalism and communications. Foundations that could marshal funds and ideas while retaining a high level of public accountability were in a position to effect real social change.

Canada responded to the question of public confidence in the work of private foundations by regulating their activities. In July 1973, Herb Gray, minister of Consumer and Corporate Affairs, tabled the Canada Business Corporations Act, designed to modernize corporate law in

Canada. The act's neglect of charitable organizations and non-profit corporations prompted Gray to commission a report addressing these
spheres. Entitled "Proposals for a New Not-for-Profit Corporations Law
for Canada," the report was released in June 1974 and led to legislation
later that year. The new law sought to simplify the administration of
non-profit corporations and clarify the definition of non-profit. Instead
of obliging public officials to exercise broad discretion, the new act
established rules that would respect the interests of managers, members
of corporations, and the public alike. It also dispelled confusion over
organizations that did at times generate a surplus: so long as such a surplus was used to advance the organization's mandate, and not to enrich
its members, it was clearly not "profit."[15] The effect of this legislation
was to increase public confidence in the non-profit sector: confidence
that such corporations were being run efficiently and not arbitrarily. For
foundations, it meant an increased sense of legitimacy and purpose.

In a further effort to ensure efficiency within Canadian non-profit
corporations, the federal government went on to amend the Income Tax
Act in 1976. This amendment required charities to spend certain minimum amounts on charitable activities. Foundations were required to disburse 90 per cent of their net income.[16] Although there was some concern
that this sort of government intervention in foundations' internal affairs
would mean that more time would have to be spent on accountability
and less on actual giving, such requirements did not cause problems for
most large charitable foundations. The directors of the SSBFF believed
that the provisions of the act were "reasonable and acceptable."[17]

Some Canadian foundations had also been taking steps to counter
the image that Arlett had drawn of them as conservative and out of
touch. In the late 1960s, the Donner Canadian Foundation undertook a
fundamental review of its programs to identify current needs in Canada.
Following the review, it announced that it would restructure to focus on
several key programs: legal and penal reform in Canada, Canadian foreign policy, educational research, French Canada, the native peoples of
Canada, the development of Canada's North, and the administration of
the arts in Canada.[18] Other foundations took note of Donner Canadian's
innovative approach. By the 1970s, Canadian foundations began to talk

to one another more frequently and look for opportunities to learn from one another. In 1973, the Association of Canadian Foundations was established with membership open to endowed institutions that did not depend on annual campaigns or fundraising for the majority of their funds.[19] With a government focused on providing social welfare measures and a public keen to see innovation in the arts, in education, in scientific research, and in human rights, it behooved philanthropic foundations to determine the best ways that they could effect significant social change.

SORTING THINGS OUT

In settling their father's estate, Sam Bronfman's children were confronted with a family foundation that now lacked leadership; their mother was not about to carry on the work of the SSBFF on her own.[20] Taking on the role of active directors of such a foundation cannot have been an entirely appealing prospect. For one thing, three of the siblings no longer lived in Canada: Minda was based in Paris and Edgar in New York, while Phyllis had been living in Chicago and other cities in the course of her work. Of the four, Phyllis was the least interested in being involved in the affairs of the Jewish community, having grown disenchanted as a child with the social pressures of fundraising, and having had this view confirmed as an adult: "I went to a Jewish philanthropy thing in New York and I thought it was so horrible I just never went to anything like that again," she recalled many years later.[21] By contrast, Charles had stayed in Montreal and was assuming his father's role as the leader of Jewish philanthropy there. Leaders of the Allied Jewish Community Services (the new name of the Federation of Jewish Philanthropies since 1965) noted various members of the Bronfman family – Sam's nieces and nephews as well as his children – leaving Montreal, and began to worry that Sam's habitual generosity toward local causes would dry up. Charles felt a particular obligation to reassure them, his motivations no doubt as complicated as Sam's had been several decades earlier. For Charles, the SSBFF represented an ideal channel through which the Combined Jewish

Appeal would continue to draw 10 per cent of its annual campaign from the Bronfman family.[22] Setting this goal was one thing, of course; it was quite another to take on the reins of a major foundation.

In the end it was the flexibility of the SSBFF as it existed at the time of Sam's death that made the prospect of a direct role in its governance more attractive. All four siblings could agree with Charles that it was important to respect "the donor's wishes" – meaning Sam – by continuing to make large regular donations to the Jewish community. At the same time, it became clear that the SSBFF could also be a vehicle for engaging in broader causes, outside the Jewish community and also outside the cultural and educational programs that Sam and Saidye had supported. As Charles put it, "we also thought we should start going afield, and start doing some things for the country."[23] It remained a point of contention exactly how much should be given to the Jewish community and how much would go towards doing things for the country, but the idea that both objectives could be met brought all four of Sam's children, plus Saidye, into the SSBFF as directors of a modern family foundation. "We found that ... the Canadian aspect of doing something broadly and generally ... was good," Phyllis recalled. "My [interests] were very focused, and Charles's became somewhat a Canadian thing, too – Canadian and Israel eventually – and Minda was in the arts, so I think we all thought it was a good thing to do, as a family that had developed in Canada."[24] Significantly, Phyllis would move back to Montreal within a few years of her father's death, in large part because of her growing involvement in preserving the city's built heritage – a cause in which the SSBFF would soon become a major player.

Never having been involved in a systematic way in the SSBFF's management – in Minda's and Phyllis's case, never having been consulted – the siblings had no very clear idea how to proceed. They were aware that Canada's needs were changing, and that a new corporate environment was changing the rules by which foundations operated. They decided to approach the challenge ahead as systematically and as scientifically as possible. It was important to understand the current financial situation and discern the pattern and character of the foundation's gifts over the previous several years. As much of the value of Sam's remaining estate was to be transferred to the SSBFF to provide a corpus for annual grants and donations, the foundation would become a repository of funds with a principal to invest and interest to distribute. The Bronfmans had in Leo Kolber an expert in profitable investment, but there remained the question of how to dispense the interest. When it came to developing programs and criteria for making regular grants and donations, the directors had to determine exactly what had been established practice and where there was room and need for innovation.

To understand the foundation's practices in relation to grants, Kolber suggested turning to Matthew Ram, a social worker and fundraiser who had worked for many Jewish institutions in Montreal – the Zionist Organization of Canada, Maimonides Hospital, Miriam Home of Montreal – and was director of Community Services for the Canadian Jewish Congress.[25] Kolber asked Ram to prepare an analysis of the Bronfman family's charitable involvement, including Seagram's programs in both Canada and the United States; the study proved helpful to Kolber in advising the family on many fronts, not merely the SSBFF.[26] Ram's preliminary report, submitted at the beginning of 1972, was followed three months later with his outline for a new donations program for the SSBFF and Distillers Corporation Seagram's Limited.

When it came to charitable giving in Canada, Ram noted considerable overlap and lack of consistent policy. For years, these philanthropic entities had given to a wide range of worthy and deserving programs and services "across the length and breadth of Canada in the fields of health, education, welfare, civic culture and recreation." Criteria had never been developed, however, to explain why gifts came from one entity rather than another. "Corporate giving and personal giving are not always synonymous," he reported, "and some broad policy should be set for the future." He also noted the lack of an annual budget for giving. Analyzing the years between 1967 and 1971, Ram reported that giving varied widely from year to year. The Bronfmans and Seagram had given to 570 different organizations in five years. Many of these organizations received annual contributions, and just under half received $250 or less. Ram described this giving as "charity" (which he defined as giving in order to meet an immediate need) rather than "philanthropy" (giving as part of a sustained policy). In other words, it was hardly strategic. Total giving to date by the SSBFF amounted to approximately $10 million, of which 68 per cent had gone to Jewish organizations and institutions.[27]

Ram's report suggested that with Sam's departure, the SSBFF should carry the weight of the family's charitable giving in the future. In keeping with modern scientific philanthropy, the foundation should support programs "that reflect the needs of the times" and not be locked into the priorities of the past. It should provide "risk capital" for innovative social projects that have yet to prove themselves to private or government funders. Furthermore, the growing volume of requests for funding demanded a more effective evaluation procedure to ensure that funds were being spent wisely and effectively. To achieve all this, a professional experienced in community work, rather than a corporate executive, should be recruited to "to centralize and coordinate the donations program of both the Family Foundation (SSBFF) and the Distillers Corporation."[28]

The professional the trustees eventually hired was Peter Swann.

THE EXECUTIVE DIRECTOR

Peter Swann was born in London in 1921 and grew up in a working class neighbourhood. His father, a decorated veteran of the trenches of the First World War, abandoned the family when Peter was seven. For the most important lessons in life Swann always credited school, where he learned to box, and the streets of London, where he learned to fight. His mother eventually got a job in the welfare office to support Peter and his sister. According to Swann, his mother had "a magnificent soprano voice and might have become an operatic star," but her father refused to let her perform on stage. "The destruction of her dream," wrote Swann, "made her determined to give me every chance to fulfill mine."[29]

In 1942 he joined the Navy and, after a fourteen-month intensive course in Japanese, served in the Combined Chiefs of Staff Intelligence Service. After the war, continuing his education in Chinese language and culture, he completed a BA at the University of London and took an MA degree in Chinese art and culture. A collector of Chinese art since he was a teenager, Swann became keeper of the Department of Oriental Art at the Ashmolean Museum at Oxford in 1950, and over the next sixteen years he completely redesigned and rebuilt the Oriental Art galleries. In 1966, he was asked to become the director of the Royal Ontario Museum in Toronto. Swann swept "the cobwebs" from the institution, developed exhibits with popular appeal, and worked to attract younger audiences "without any denigration of the research function of that venerable institution."[30] Under his leadership, the ROM's membership grew from several hundred to several thousand and the museum emerged as a nationally acclaimed educational centre with greater independence from the University of Toronto.

Swann's populist convictions and his sometimes imperious manner precipitated a clash with his board of directors over contract issues. On 1 June 1972 the board gave him an ultimatum: resign or be fired. Swann refused to resign. News of Swann's firing brought a groundswell of support. More than 1,000 people rallied at one meeting. Supporters argued that the museum's board was an anachronism, citing a 1971 study by Price Waterhouse that reached the same conclusion. In the past, when contributions from wealthy patrons provided most of the support for institutions like the ROM, their positions as trustees were appropriate. In the post-war era, as state support and broad-based membership programs expanded and private funding decreased, critics argued that trustees should be accountable to the public. The Price Waterhouse report had recommended that a majority of the museum's trustees be elected by the museum's membership rather than appointed by the government. The conflict between Swann and the museum board reflected not only the social and ideological turmoil of the times, but also the transition from personal patronage to professional management that was taking place in the non-profit world. Unfortunately, neither the report nor the groundswell of support prevented Swann's firing.[31]

Charles Bronfman had met Swann through Charles's wife's uncle and aunt, who were avid collectors of Chinese art, and the two men remained friends throughout Swann's tenure at the ROM. After Charles purchased the Expos baseball team for Montreal in 1968, the two men had a joking competition over who would draw a greater attendance each year, the Expos or the ROM. Shortly after Swann's dismissal, Charles called him and asked if he would be interested in taking over the management of the SSBFF as well as Seagram's corporate giving in Canada. Swann was unsure at first whether he had the appropriate talents for the job, but Charles knew that "when you're starting up something like [the SSBFF] you need an entrepreneur, and Peter was an entrepreneur." Charles characterized Swann's presence within the foundation as "a very, very happy relationship."[32]

Swann was formally welcomed to the foundation at the board's November 1972 meeting, and given the title of executive director.[33] This was the first meeting since Sam's death, the first formal occasion for the trustees to sit down and make decisions as a board. Charles presided as chair and Philip Vineberg served as secretary, although one of the chief items of business was the appointment of new officers. Saidye became president, Charles vice-president, Vineberg secretary, and Phyllis treasurer. For several years, until her health began to decline, Saidye ran the meetings, which took place at her home on Belvedere Road, although much of the time it was Charles and later Phyllis who did the principal steering of the SSBFF.[34] Vineberg and others from outside the family would regularly sit on the board, but they were not generally considered trustees or directors of the foundation; normally it was the family members on the board that voted as directors. This working balance of family members and close advisors on a board was quite typical of family foundations in Canada, although each foundation had its own rules about who could vote and of course its own internal dynamics.[35]

At the November meeting, the board also asked Swann "to prepare a record of the proceedings in a greater detail apart from those which required formal resolutions."[36] By this request, the operations of the board symbolically passed beyond the mere formality of occasional meetings of family members with titular executive positions. Having a professional staff person taking notes and preparing reports for the directors marked the board as a functioning governing body for the foundation. From this point on, the board's minutes contain a variety of critical items and reflect detailed and thoughtful discussion, rather than a bare record of resolutions passed to fine tune the foundation's bylaws. The presence of an experienced executive director, combined with a dynamic board newly awakened to the foundation's potential, set the stage for a highly creative period of focused activity.

Swann Goes to Work

The November 1972 meeting marked the birth of the Samuel and Saidye Bronfman Family Foundation as an institution separate from the personal philanthropy of Samuel and Saidye Bronfman. Minda, Phyllis, Edgar, and Charles, who had in the past been minimally involved at best, now had to understand the scope of the foundation's giving and shape their own vision of its future. They drew on Matthew Ram's analysis. Philip Vineberg summarized the restrictions imposed on the foundation by Canadian law. Charles outlined an effort, already underway and led by Peter Swann, to "rationalize the Distillers-Seagrams' donation policy and those of the foundation and the individual members of the family."[37]

At one point the board considered the idea that all Jewish requests would be handled by the SSBFF and Seagram would manage everything else, but this option was rejected. Clearly, Sam and Saidye's children wanted to shift from a passive, reactive role to a position in which the foundation could decide for itself what it wanted to accomplish and pursue those goals. Charles then suggested that Seagram should handle "traditional" giving while the foundation focused on "innovative giving." According to Arnold Ludwick, a long-time financial advisor to the family, "traditional giving meant answering appeals. Innovative giving was defining, ourselves, the need we wanted to go after, and designing a program to take care of that need. It also meant appealing to others to join us."[38] It was important to develop a focused plan for giving: requests for grants were increasing every year and it was tough for anyone to "play God" every time an appeal came in.[39] After a great deal of debate, the directors decided to fix the SSBFF's annual contribution to the Allied Jewish Community Services at around $2 million, which after administrative costs left about half a million dollars a year that Swann could invest in what became known as the Executive Director's Program.[40] Phyllis and Minda might have been happier to have seen a larger percentage go to non-Jewish programs, but conceded the point that "this is what Father wanted."[41]

To give the foundation an identity separate from Seagram, Peter Swann insisted on offices that were not in the company's Montreal building. He wanted a headquarters that would not intimidate potential grantees and a process that was not bureaucratic and that stayed close to the recipients. The SSBFF's small staff moved to an office within Swann's own house on Tupper Street, in a quiet neighbourhood just west of downtown. From this venue Swann set to work identifying needs within Canadian society and designing funding programs to meet those needs.

Swann began by canvassing the SSBFF directors themselves. He asked them to highlight important characteristics of the programs they wanted to support as well as categories of problems they wanted to work on. Not surprisingly, he received a variety of responses. There was general agreement that SSBFF programs should demonstrate a high degree of originality and social innovation, and that they should enhance a sense of Canadian identity; Saidye believed her husband would have wanted the foundation to adopt a pan-Canadian focus, rather than merely Montreal.[42] The directors were keen to encourage communities to identify and evaluate their own needs rather than have the foundation or others impose ideas from above.

At the same time, the directors clearly had their own views as to what they felt the SSBFF should be doing – views that might have seemed to Swann to belie the desire for the foundation to be community-driven. Phyllis, Minda, and Edgar expressed a strong preference for focusing on problems of the urban environment and for helping with the conservation and adaptation of old buildings; Saidye, Charles, and Philip Vineberg were far less keen to pursue this sort of program. Edgar and Charles placed a high priority on gifts to educational institutions, while Saidye, Minda, and Phyllis did not.[43] Minda and Edgar felt that Canada, with an aging population, needed to do more for its elderly. Phyllis expressed the opinion that many Canadians were not aware of the cultural and social contributions and problems of the North, especially Canada's northern native peoples. Charles argued that people with learning disabilities needed help.[44] There was general agreement that illegal drugs had become a major social problem, but the linkages between drug and alcohol abuse made this a sensitive subject for a foundation so closely identified with Seagram. Moreover, the challenges of drug abuse suggested that the problem should be addressed on a local, rather than national, basis.

Swann even offered his own priorities on the assumption that "since it will be my task to administrate the program I thought Directors might expect me to state my preferences …" Not surprisingly, given his background, Swann felt it was important to support the arts. Although there were private foundations across the country dedicated to the arts, few that were based in Quebec provided very much in this area.[45] Even the McConnell Family Foundation had only devoted 1 per cent of its donations to the arts – and although that still represented a considerable sum of money, most of it had gone to fund the recent construction of Montreal's Place des Arts complex.[46] Swann felt it was particularly important that the SSBFF provide funding in the graphic and performing arts rather than for traditional university education. He also wanted to pursue programs that would "span the gap" between what he characterized as "the material and cultural outlooks" – meaning that the world of business and the world of the arts should be brought together for their mutual advantage.[47]

Eventually, Swann proposed several broad areas of funding over which all the directors seemed ready to agree: programs to highlight Canadian achievements; community activities at the grassroots level; the Canadian North; and culture, including graphic and performing arts.[48] Swann was eager to move ahead by publishing a brochure and soliciting applications in these areas, but the directors wanted to give more thought to the programs. Minda reminded Swann that Sam Bronfman had generally made unilateral decisions about what should be funded. In their new role as active directors, she and her siblings wanted more information about past as well as prospective grantees before embarking on new projects. The SSBFF's programs should be anchored in solid research, and not simply emulate the work of other foundations.[49] Phyllis suggested that Swann travel across Canada "to confirm or repudiate our hunches" about what was important, and to give the issues substance.[50] At their May 1973 meeting, the board agreed with this view and authorized Swann to tour the country.[51]

Swann spent the summer of 1973 on the road. He was struck by the great diversity among communities in Canada, yet noted that all parts of the country struggled with some common problems. He was touched by his encounters with the youth of the Baby Boom generation who "were prepared to give their time and efforts to correct social and economic inequalities and improve the 'quality of life.'" He was struck by the flow of government funds into certain arenas of public life. He also noted a deep desire among people for Canadian cultural identity. There was a clear absence of trained leadership: "Ideas proliferate and enthusiasm is widespread but the means, both human and economic, are lacking."[52]

Travelling and talking to people made Swann feel more personally connected to the struggles of potential grantees. He suggested that "the Executive Director should travel as much as possible and be in close personal contact with the foundation projects." Most foundations, he suggested, made a mistake in only sending a cheque. "Advice is always welcomed," he wrote, "and, if it is accompanied by financial help, it is doubly welcome ... A foundation can thus be personal rather than bureaucratic and this Foundation should try always to be personal and human." Swann also noted a universal request from potential grantees for flexibility and timely action. "I would like to see the foundation gain the reputation for speed and effectiveness to match say the business decision-making of CEMP."[53]

When he reported back to the board in the fall, Swann summarized what he had learned about Canada during his travels and presented a more focused recommendation for new programs. His suggestions were based on a combination of factors: what the directors had suggested they would be willing to fund, what Canadians seemed to need, and what in his opinion would result in feasible projects. He proposed four funding programs: 1) learning disabilities; 2) culture, including heritage and crafts; 3) the North, with a special focus on native peoples; and 4) educational and/or community television. Each program would have a budget of $75,000. A fifth program, called "Added Dimensions," with a budget of $50,000, would provide seed money to promising projects which did not fit into one of the other categories. The board was pleased with Swann's distillation of conversations and travels, and budgeted a total of $345,000 for his five categories. They also authorized him to develop a brochure advertising the foundation's new programs.[54]

Having agreed on these programs, the directors gave Swann wide discretionary powers in allotting funds. Throughout his tenure as the director of the SSBFF, Swann sought to professionalize the operations of the foundation, which meant streamlining decision-making so that the board could respond quickly to requests for support. It meant cultivating and sustaining relationships with people in the field in order to determine real needs and to provide follow-up to grants. An outspoken leader with populist sympathies, Swann believed in making a difference by helping as many projects as possible, investing small amounts widely. Added Dimensions was intended as a miscellaneous category, but within each of the others the list of recipients was long, individual grants often ranging from $1,000 to $5,000.[55] As part of the Culture program, for example, Swann gave out thirty scholarships of $500 each "to enable advanced students to be employed in cultural and artistic enterprises to give them practical experience."[56] The Visual Arts Centre in Westmount, Quebec, was given $9,000 over a three-year period, which inspired other funders to contribute to its program, enabling the Centre to raise $150,000 by 1974.[57] This kind of investment did give the foundation broader insights into the social and cultural needs of communities throughout Canada and allowed it to leverage other philanthropic and governmental resources.

Over time, however, it became clear to the SSBFF that some programs were not adequately tapping their budgets, and potential new categories were emerging from Added Dimensions.[58] In 1975 the SSBFF discontinued Educational Television, which did not seem to be moving in any concrete direction, and created a new program for Heritage, into which a number of recent miscellaneous grants could be grouped.[59] By 1979 Swann reported that appeals to the Culture program had "dwindled almost to zero" as a result of "the provision of bursaries for the support staff of cultural agencies" by governments. The SSBFF was not directly supporting arts organizations through the Culture program, but rather attempting to improve the training of arts managers; they would have much better success a decade later with the Cultural Management program. Another highly successful arts-related project, but not part of the Culture program, was the Saidye Bronfman Award for Excellence in the Crafts, which Swann had spearheaded in 1977 (and which forms the subject of chapter 11). Although Swann had argued for a well-funded Culture program, the SSBFF had obviously not found the appropriate niche, and he proposed cancelling it. At a previous meeting, Minda had asked Swann whether there were other categories of projects that could be separated from Added Dimensions, and he had mentioned "the elderly," which had been a theme raised at the board's initial sessions. In November 1979, the directors voted to replace Culture with a new program, Social Problems Concerned with the Elderly, which was given an annual budget of $82,500.[60]

The seniors' program, like Learning Disabilities, took time to develop and eventually became a major concern for the SSBFF – and will be discussed later in separate chapters. The North had a shorter but significant life as a program that proved early on to be far too ambitious for the SSBFF's scope.

CANADA'S NORTHERN NATIVE PEOPLES

As natives attest, and historians and royal commissions confirm, Canada's aboriginal peoples had long suffered from official policies of assimilation – a glaring limitation to the notion of Canada as a cultural mosaic. Attempts to undermine their cultural identities and political coherence presumed that natives were inferior, unable to govern themselves in their own best interests. These policies dismissed the substance and spirit of treaties concluded in the colonial era that recognized the sovereignty of native tribes. They also assumed that the European approach to social and political organization, to technology and economics, was inherently good for aboriginal people.[61] When the federal government under Trudeau released a white paper in 1969 proposing to assimilate native people and end their special status within the state, aboriginal groups protested vehemently. Although the government withdrew its proposals, the episode focused overdue attention on the status and condition of native people and their communities in Canada.[62] In the 1970s, Canada's First Nations launched a series of court cases aimed at reclaiming land and rights lost over the course of the previous decades. As this political and cultural movement gained strength, non-Aboriginal people in Canada witnessed a growing debate over the identity and place of the First Nations within Canadian society.

The SSBFF's interest in the problems of Canada's Inuit and other northern native peoples was logical in the early 1970s, given the widespread sympathy for aboriginals, their threatened situation, and the fragile environment of the north. More specifically, Phyllis, having returned to Canada from the USA, had joined the Canadian Arctic Resources Committee (CARC) in 1974 on the suggestion of a family friend, Maxwell Cohen, dean of the Law Faculty at McGill University. CARC was formed in the wake of the 1972 decision by the federal government to permit the construction of a huge oil and gas pipeline to run the length of the Mackenzie River valley in the Northwest Territories. Within a short time, a number of court cases had been decided in favour of native groups on the question of land claims, enough for the government to postpone the pipeline project until after the findings of a royal commission on the subject. Thomas Berger, chair of the commission, proved willing and eager to hear briefs from hundreds of individuals and interest groups, including CARC, whose efforts the SSBFF decided to fund. The foundation granted the committee $80,000 over a period of two years, believing that the pipeline posed a serious threat to the environment and that CARC was well-positioned to articulate opposition to the government's plan.[63] Berger's report, issued in 1977, recommended against building the pipeline, its text reflecting the conviction of natives and their supporters that the North was intimately linked with aboriginal culture and that a threat to the northern environment was an affront to that culture.[64]

Another group that the SSBFF decided to fund was the Canadian Association in Support of the Native Peoples, a non-native organization which had been in existence since the 1950s to study the problems of aboriginals. In the previous few years it had begun to work more closely with native groups themselves, agreeing to act as their advisors and supporters rather than their principal interlocutors with the government. Despite the useful work it did, this was an organization in need of modernization. The SSBFF provided a small grant to fund a management training workshop for the association, believing that an improved administration would enable it to do better work.[65]

Peter Swann spent considerable time looking into the condition of the country's Northern peoples in an effort to determine how best the foundation could serve their interests. The extent of social problems facing native peoples meant that much of the program's budget over the initial decade was devoted to small, one-time grants to drug abuse programs, resource centres, arts and crafts societies, and outdoor education programs.[66] Swann concluded early on that the native cause, however sympathetic, was not easy to assist by means of small grants or support for one or two interest groups. The Inuit and many Status Indian communities, he felt, were receiving liberal assistance from the government, although the Metis needed help.[67]

The foundation increased the annual budget for the Canadian North program to $100,000 in 1977 and to $110,000 two years later. By 1980, however, interest was waning, especially in light of rising inflation and a sense that it was more appropriate for native peoples to make arrangements with the federal government than with private foundations; Charles suggested that this program should be trimmed.[68] Swann continued to monitor events surrounding native peoples, however, feeling that the foundation had to be sure that its efforts were addressing the right needs. Countless social problems persisted, as well as the ongoing issue of land claims, issues which seemed outside the powers of a private foundation to resolve. There was also a growing trend for native groups to ask for funding for a small number of much larger projects, grants for which might conceivably yield greater results.[69] Swann reiterated his frustration in 1982, noting that the overall atmosphere in the native community was "somewhat confusing." The response by native groups to the settling of land claims, and the consequent decline in direct government support, was varied: some moved towards greater self-reliance, others to increased militancy. "At the same time, old expectations die hard and requests from some of the better organized native groups are often unrealistically large – ranging from $500,000 to $1,500,000."[70]

The SSBFF gradually diminished its support for their program on the North over the course of the early 1980s, realizing that the problems of Canada's native peoples were too great for a single funding program to handle. After a series of discussions with a number of organizations, it was determined that the SSBFF could not oversee programs sufficiently to be effective "unless we were prepared to spend hundreds of thousands of dollars on monitoring and helping to develop expertise."[71] John Hobday, Swann's successor as SSBFF executive director, was particularly struck by how difficult it was to evaluate the success of their northern funding program, given the cultural differences between funder and recipient: "how difficult it must be for Inuit and Indian people ... with the constant expectation that in order to qualify for support they should behave in our world as we see fit, not as they are."[72] For a while the directors considered a number of projects "aimed at improving awareness and understanding of Indian and Inuit concerns by all Canadians, including natives."[73] Two in particular seemed promising: a university scholarship program of the Association of Canadian Universities for Northern Studies, and an Indian History Film Project at the University of Regina. In the end, however, the program was cancelled. This was an important lesson: it was possible to achieve good things with a small amount of leverage, but difficult to achieve great things unless a foundation were prepared to invest a great deal of money, and even then it was hard to ensure a successful outcome. The SSBFF was realizing the importance of choosing its objectives carefully, of basing decisions less on the enormity of the problem than on the likelihood of achieving results.[74]

OTHER SSBFF PROGRAMS

Swann's job also involved handling projects that had begun long before his tenure, and this often meant having to decide whether to continue them or not. Like many foundations in the 1970s, the SSBFF had grantees that had gotten used to their annual cheques. These funds were put to good use in many cases, but in others one suspected they were absorbed by organizations that were no longer producing desired results. Under the new regime, as Swann told many long-time grantees, the foundation's role was to provide initial support and then, once the project seemed to have gotten off the ground, turn the grantees over "to more traditional sources of funding."[75]

One relationship from the past that left much to be desired was the annual $10,000 donation to the Montreal Museum of Fine Arts for the acquisition of contemporary works. Although the work of young artists was dear to Saidye's heart, her money did not seem very high on the museum's radar. Eventually, museum officials contacted the SSBFF with a request to increase the donation to $20,000, citing the provincial government's recent support for the Musée d'art contemporain, which enjoyed a yearly acquisitions budget of $300,000, as opposed to the MMFA's $180,000, which had to cover all its acquisitions. Costs of artworks had also skyrocketed, and it was hard to find something appropriate for only $10,000.[76] Saidye replied that she did not wish the money to go "into the general purchase fund but rather to be accumulated until there is enough money to purchase a specific object to fill a gap in the Museum's collection." She also wished to be notified of the museum's intentions before it made a purchase. The SSBFF voted to raise the annual grant to $15,000.[77] The museum accepted this compromise but made no particular effort to keep its donor abreast of its decisions. By 1985 Saidye agreed to the SSBFF's suggestion that the donation be discontinued.[78]

While Swann strove to rationalize the foundation's giving, the SSBFF also reflected the Bronfmans' personal and familial concerns. Honouring Sam Bronfman's priorities in life, the SSBFF continued to provide the largest single contribution each year to the Combined Jewish Appeal (CJA) in Montreal. A major part of the funds raised by the CJA financed the work of AJCS in Montreal which organized camps for families and children, provided services to seniors, offered classes and programs in Jewish education and culture, and operated clinics to meet the health needs of the community.[79]

The commitment to the CJA, although granted by the foundation, was essentially outside the purview of the executive director. Inheriting the expectations of the community for other gifts, Charles and Edgar also asked for the creation of what became known as the Plus program, a pool of funds available to make grants to institutions that Charles and Edgar were particularly interested in, largely relating to the Jewish communities that each was a part of. In a sense, the Plus program continued the pattern of personal philanthropy that characterized Sam and Saidye's era and blurred the transition to professional management under Swann.[80]

The pursuit of individual projects led to tensions within the foundation. To a large extent tension was a natural and inevitable feature of family foundations, given that each brought to the table a point of view shaped by his or her own passions and experiences. At the same time, much of the division within the SSBFF resulted from the directors still not having agreed on the SSBFF's overall priorities. Programs such as Plus ran the risk of becoming the bailiwick of certain members and could potentially conflict with the foundation's other objectives. Admittedly, Charles and Edgar had the additional burden of carrying the family name – a burden in that it was harder for them to separate what they did as Bronfmans from what they did as members of the SSBFF. Phyllis and Minda were also much less involved in the family business, and identified less strongly with the Montreal Jewish community; it was clearly their preference that the SSBFF, apart from its donation to the CJA, should focus on matters such as culture and heritage.[81] These tensions would be resolved over the course of the 1980s as the SSBFF acquired a stronger focus to its programs and greater efficiency in the management of its resources.

CONCLUSION

By 1980, the SSBFF was ranked twentieth among Canada's foundations according to assets and twelfth in terms of total grants. That year, the foundation had $19 million in assets and gave away $2.5 million.[82] It had clearly succeeded in funding a wide array of projects, and specialized in a number of areas such as learning disabilities, heritage preservation, and native rights. Swann remained concerned, however, that the SSBFF was not making a significant difference in these areas, despite the many recipients of grants who seemed to be achieving good things. As so many of these grants were relatively small and the applicants' objectives limited, it had never seemed necessary to devise a formal evaluation system to help quantify success. What was needed was more ambitious investment in larger projects which could be expected to effect real change; the SSBFF could then play a more complex role, working with grantees and evaluating their achievements over time. This required greater planning and coordination.[83] In expressing his concerns Swann seems to have been reflecting his own tendency to jump into interesting projects rather than concentrate on the method of selecting them.

As he closed his annual report to the board in 1982, Swann acknowledged that his ten years with the foundation had been "happy and productive." To be sure, it had not always been easy. And sometimes it was hard for a man like Swann to stand back and enable others to be a part of the action. "Though the satisfactions of this kind of work are sometimes vicarious," he wrote, "they are nevertheless very real. It is by no means the least of these satisfactions to know that the foundation has become a visible, effective and respected force in the country."[84]

FOUR

HOBDAY AND THE YEARS

OF TRANSITION

The middle years of the 1980s constituted a period of transition for the SSBFF, not only in terms of its managerial style but also in its operating philosophy. The first decade since Sam Bronfman's death had seen the SSBFF consolidate its philanthropy along a number of specific lines, agreed upon after much discussion by board members and research by the executive director. Under Swann, the SSBFF's approach to philanthropy reflected an entrepreneurial bent, providing seed money for a variety of projects, hoping that funding at an early stage would promote innovation. By temperament, Swann looked to support the underdog, an approach that gave great satisfaction when funding proved successful but frustrating when recipients were clearly unable to manage the seed money and the foundation's efforts seemed wasted. By the end of this period the SSBFF could look with satisfaction on the great number of small projects it had made possible, but Swann felt that it could do more.[1] Swann's successor at the foundation's helm, John Hobday, was to take a very different tack by striving to create or encourage larger client organizations who would then become agents of social change. Swann was about initiative, Hobday about strategy.

On another level, the SSBFF directors themselves were grappling with issues that had gone unresolved since the days of Sam's death, and which had always caused certain tensions within the family. What was the foundation's overarching purpose — to continue Sam and Saidye's philanthropy, or to break new ground by funding innovative projects? Or, if both, where should the emphasis lie? In resolving these issues, the directors had to think carefully about their own lives and personal interests, as well as their long-term commitment to the SSBFF. After much soul-searching, various members of the Bronfman family would reaffirm the importance of Sam and Saidye's foundation and enable it to continue and expand its philanthropic work for another two decades.

SWANN BOWS OUT

One of the Bronfman projects that most appealed to Swann was the idea for a museum devoted to Seagram. Charles and Edgar had been discussing the idea for some time as part of a campaign to educate the public in the history and science of distilling, using their own company as a model. The public appetite for museums displaying technical processes and linking industry to local history was growing. Charles and Swann visited the Corning Museum in upstate New York and were very impressed with the way that the history of glassmaking was depicted in an attractive and informative manner. They discussed possible sites for the Seagram Museum: sentiment suggested Montreal where the distillery was located, but prudence favoured Toronto where the economy was better. In the end they settled on the Waterloo, Ontario, home of the Joseph E. Seagram Company's 1857 factory.[2]

Plans to build the new museum were announced in 1981. The proposed complex would feature a state-of-the-art museum devoted to all aspects of the industry: the process of distillation from the science to the machinery; the history of the alcohol trade in Canada; the social history of alcohol consumption, including the temperance movement which had once caused so many headaches for Sam and his brothers; and the history of the Seagram company itself. This, "the world's only integrated museum devoted to the history and technology of wine and spirits" would draw visitors from across the country, elementary and high school students on educational tours, and scholars researching the history of the industry and the history of drink.[3]

In the early 1980s, Swann's attention was increasingly directed toward the museum, an enterprise that could absorb his passion in a way that the complexities of the SSBFF could not. In August 1982 Swann's job as executive director of corporate donations for both the SSBFF and Seagram was divided in two, the latter position going to John Hobday, long-time director of the Canadian Conference for the Arts, who Swann felt would do an excellent job managing a philanthropic organization. The following year, Swann stepped down as director of the SSBFF in order to head the Seagram Museum, leaving Hobday to assume both roles, as Swann had recommended. Not willing to lose Swann's expertise in the field of museum management and the arts, the SSBFF invited him to remain as a member of the board, in which capacity he continued to be involved in the foundation's business until his death in 1997. Swann's last meeting as executive director, and Hobday's first, came in May 1983. Phyllis summed up the board's feeling that Swann's leadership over ten years had been "superb."[4]

HOBDAY AND SEAGRAM

John Hobday was born in 1937 in Richmond-upon-Thames near London and grew up in Redhill, Surrey. His family, as he put it, "had often been in either colonial administration or missionary work" throughout the British Empire. What he took from this heritage was a sense of public service but, he later confessed wryly, no direct experience in the arts; that would come from a kindergarten teacher who had worked with the BBC and instilled a passion for the theatre in her young pupils, and at a Devonshire boarding school where he was sent during the war to escape the bombs falling on London. In addition to acting in school plays, Hobday acquired a love for radio drama, what was often referred to as the "theatre of the imagination."[5]

In October 1952, after his parents divorced, Hobday immigrated to Canada with his mother and older brother, bringing only £100 with them because of currency restrictions. They landed in Halifax, where his mother had gone to school as a child while her father was stationed there with the British Navy shortly before the First World War. Hobday took a job in a bank to help support the family, but through friends got involved in amateur theatre, and eventually work with the CBC, first in administration and then for seven years as a producer of radio drama, where he won several awards. The experience at the CBC's Halifax offices, one of five regional centres, gave Hobday an "intense, intense education in practically everything," from political coverage to rock and roll shows, and Shakespeare.[6] When the CBC began to squeeze out radio drama in favour of television, Hobday went freelance, and eventually moved back to England at the end of 1964 to do celebrity interviews, trade reports, and radio drama for the BBC as well as television mini-documentaries for the sinisterly named Central Office of Information.

In 1966 he was approached to run the theatre at the new Confederation Centre in Charlottetown, Prince Edward Island, which brought very useful experience in marketing and programming for diverse audiences; Hobday's most memorable achievement was booking country music stars Hank Snow and Wilf Carter for back-to-back concerts, which then allowed the theatre to invite the McGill Chamber Orchestra two days later, even though it only attracted an audience of one hundred. Hobday's flair for negotiation was developed further in raising funds from local businesses and ultimately securing a bailout from the federal government, which wanted to encourage centennial projects. He returned to Halifax in January 1968 to run the Neptune Theatre, which proved another struggle, working with a sixty-member board and a theatre that was barely filling a third of its 525-seat capacity. Along with artistic director Heinar Pillar, Hobday achieved considerable success, but the effort required was excessive. He was quick to accept an offer to become national director of the Canadian Conference of the Arts, the major advocacy body for the arts set up at the end of the Second World War. After ten years building up the membership of the Conference, however, Hobday felt frustrated at its inability to produce a significant breakthrough in the federal government's commitment to funding the arts. He was ready for a change. "By chance, the Seagram Company was looking for someone to handle their corporate donations. Peter Swann suggested me."[7]

As director of Corporate Donations for Seagram Canada, Hobday was asked to implement a new corporate vision for philanthropy. He built on an initiative already undertaken by Charles Bronfman, who was seeking to establish his own approach to business in the wake of his father's death. Charles, head of the company's Canadian wing, had articulated this vision in a 1981 speech to the Montreal Chamber of Commerce, entitled "Corporations and the Community." Charles compared the perspectives on corporate giving offered by economist Milton Friedman and futurist Alvin Toffler. Friedman believed that corporate managers had one job only – to maximize profits for shareholders. Addressing social concerns through corporate giving, he said, misappropriated shareholder resources and encroached on the proper role of government. Toffler, on the other hand, suggested that business institutions were evolving in a changing society; they no longer served only a "specialized economic function" but instead were becoming multipurpose institutions. Charles clearly favoured Toffler's point of view. He quoted his father Sam, who had written early in the 1940s that "The horizon of industry, surely, does not terminate at the boundary lines of its plans: It has a broader horizon, a further view."[8] Charles noted that "businesses that do well for their communities tend to do well for themselves." He offered his personal theory about why this was so. The word company, he noted, came from the Latin meaning "a group sharing bread." "Thus, a corporation seen in this light is surely defined by – and draws its real meaning from – the activities and values of its people." The corporate contribution to community development came from a sense of entrepreneurship and an "innovative urge to build."[9]

Hobday proceeded to rationalize the company's donations program. He discovered that the level of Seagram's donations put the company ahead of the average for American food, tobacco, and beverage companies, and far above most Canadian companies, which at that time tended to give somewhere between 0.5 and 1 per cent of their pre-tax profits to charity.[10] Seagram gave $4.6 million (US) in corporate donations in 1982, $3.9 million in the United States and $700,000 in Canada. This was a lot of money, but it was Hobday's view that the company gave to too many organizations to make a significant difference. In the spring of 1983 he restructured the Seagram donations program to support a number of corporate goals. Instead of giving to communities all over Canada, Seagram would target those where the company had plants or a large number of employees. In focusing the program, the company would de-emphasize brick-and-mortar projects. "Our new philosophy is more people oriented," Hobday told employees. The company adopted key areas of focused giving: amateur sports, music, crafts, and the tourism and hospitality industry.[11]

In explaining the revamped donations program to employees, Hobday balanced a variety of concerns. To those oriented towards sales and the bottom line, he acknowledged that donations would not sell cases of whisky. Corporate gifts, particularly for health and welfare organizations, reflected a genuine desire to help improve the quality of life in a community. "But a company does have a right to expect some visibility and recognition in the community for its generosity," Hobday wrote, and he predicted that a more focused corporate donations program would bring higher visibility that would, in turn, produce "more favourable attitudes towards our Company."[12]

In making this transition, Seagram was in line with changes taking place among many of the leading companies in Canada. In the face of a recession in the early 1980s, corporations were under pressure to show a stronger link between donations and the bottom line. As a consequence, themed sponsorships became more important and marketing departments played a bigger role in supporting arts and cultural organizations.[13]

Carrying forward Swann's idea that Seagram needed to articulate a clear philosophy for its donations program, Hobday helped develop a new mission statement which asserted the company's desire to help Canadians "lead healthy, active, productive lives." The emphasis on a healthy lifestyle was significant given that the company's chief product was a drink that all too many individuals used in ways that were decidedly not healthy. The public relations benefits derived from emphasizing the need for good health echoed Sam Bronfman's campaigns to encourage responsible drinking since the 1930s. From a public relations perspective, the new mission statement made it easier for Seagram to fund medical research or to make grants to hospitals.[14]

Hobday would apply many of the techniques used in rationalizing Seagram's donation program, as well as the philosophy of concentrating resources for maximum leverage, to his work at the SSBFF.

HOBDAY TAKES THE REINS AT THE SSBFF

With Seagram's corporate donations program restructured by the summer of 1983, Hobday was ready to take on the additional role of executive director of the SSBFF. His first request was to move the SSBFF offices back to Peel Street. Although Swann was no longer living in the Tupper Street building, Hobday still found it preferable to be closer to Seagram and its top management. Phyllis remembered Peter Swann's arguments about the need for separation, but the prospect of lower overhead was attractive. In addition, the Seagram headquarters on Peel Street would provide greater security; the Tupper Street offices had been broken into twice in recent months.[15]

At the time that Hobday became executive director, the SSBFF ranked eleventh among Canadian foundations in terms of assets (up from twentieth place in 1980) and twelfth in terms of total grants ($3.2 million, some $700,000 more than in 1980) according to the Canadian Centre for Philanthropy. The value of the SSBFF's portfolio had recently increased from $21.4 million to $27.8 million, thanks to a donation of $6.5 million from CEMP. Over half the total grant money continued to go to Jewish philanthropy, with around $800,000 going to the Executive Director's Program.[16]

Having additional funds to spend did not mean launching into a new round of small, scattered grants. This was not Hobday's style, but furthermore, times had changed. The 1970s had been a period of enterprise and innovation, even at the grassroots level, but by the early 1980s the days of social experimentation were on the wane. As the economy worsened and unemployment rose, Canadians were more likely to worry about making money than their counterparts of ten or twenty years earlier. Instead of trying out new fields, most students strove to develop skills that would land them good jobs. The general focus on achieving results had its effect on both government programs and corporate donations. Wary of making investments that would yield little in the way of social dividends, funders spent increasing amounts of their time and budgets on monitoring the progress of their investments and assessing the outcomes. Swann had noted these "tendencies toward retrenchment" in his annual report to the Board at the end of 1981. In hard economic times, he suggested, non-profits had a tendency to focus on survival. As a result, fewer new initiatives were developed and the number of innovative proposals submitted to the foundation declined.[17]

As he had done for Seagram, Hobday began by defining a new strategic vision for the SSBFF. At his first board meeting in May 1983 (and Swann's last), the directors asked the two men to collaborate on a review of all of the SSBFF's existing programs and to recommend changes. Having secured Swann's input, Hobday decided to recruit someone to do field work in order to assess the impact of the foundation's past giving and to discern the needs and concerns of non-profit organizations across the country. He hired Ivan Hale, a man who would later play a role in a number of SSBFF projects.

Ivan Hale had been an activist since his teenage years in Toronto. He had founded a student exchange program, Education Canada, while still in high school, and later served as Director of Educational Exchanges for the Canadian Bureau for International Education (CBIE).[18] After leaving the CBIE in 1981, Hale was invited by Edgar Bronfman to run a project which aimed to bring communities together by getting anglophone and francophone junior baseball teams to play one another. Teams were accepted into the program not on the basis of their competitive skills but rather on their local commitment to a cultural exchange. Encouraged and supported by the Montreal Expos, the project gave some teams a prized opportunity to play games under the lights in the Olympic Stadium. The Sports Exchange was created and funded by Edgar to honour his brother Charles on the occasion of his fiftieth birthday.

Hale's research proved very useful to Hobday in making his recommendations to the board. The report, a seminal document entitled

"Towards Tomorrow," was both a review of existing programs and a declaration of Hobday's approach to running philanthropic foundations. In his view, the needs of the non-profit sector were huge and a foundation had to be strategic and develop a policy. By concentrating on several major objectives and making a more substantial investment, the impact could be greater. In most program areas, the report called for continued funding but with a new emphasis on the development of national and provincial organizations to serve as advocacy groups for a particular cause.[19]

Hobday's impulse to promote national associations derived from his work with the Canadian Conference for the Arts, but it also reflected a growing trend in North America towards what some have called "social movement philanthropy." Designed "to organize or represent the interests of a previously unorganized or politically excluded group," social movement philanthropy developed in the Civil Rights era in the United States. It surged in the 1970s in response to a wave of urban violence and grassroots organizing. The trend gained legitimacy in philanthropic circles when some of the largest North American foundations warmed to it, including the Ford Foundation, the Carnegie Corporation, the Rockefeller Foundation, the Sloan Foundation, and the Lily Endowment.[20] In these instances, and others, foundation funding played a key role in professionalizing grassroots organizations and "thus channelling movements into institutionalized actions" which capitalized on the movement's legal and political gains. Hobday hoped that SSBFF funding to programs such as Learning Disabilities and Seniors would create new institutions able to permanently influence the policymaking environment on behalf of their respective constituencies.

As for Native Peoples and the North, Hobday was no more optimistic than Swann had been when making his own assessment a few years earlier. He did suggest a modest increase in funding for Heritage projects, and proposed establishing a significant source of funds for the development of professional management training in the arts. The SSBFF's original arts program had been cancelled in 1979, but Hobday felt it was time to create a new program called "Development of the Arts and Culture in Canada." This program, with a proposed budget of $130,000, would fund the Saidye Bronfman Award for Excellence in Crafts, a cultural management training program (to fill a need for well-trained leaders for arts organizations), and the development of cultural archives with national inventories and professional training. The Added Dimensions budget, which Hobday recommended be renamed Special Initiatives, should be scaled back considerably from its current $275,000 to a manageable $85,000, and continue to provide seed money to "exciting new and innovative projects across Canada."[21]

Finally, Hobday proposed to launch a new program called Canadian Understanding designed to promote an awareness of Canadian identity. He suggested sponsoring a series of televised debates, either between Canadian universities or between American and Canadian universities, to discuss focal issues; other suggestions included the production of cultural vignettes to appear on commercial radio (a wider audience than public radio), travelling lectures on Canadian topics, and scholarships for Canadian Studies programs.[22]

Hobday also encouraged the board to adopt an overall statement of purpose that would help the foundation define its program for potential applicants. The imminent publication of a new edition of The Canadian Directory of Foundations made this need even more immediate. As foundations came under increased public scrutiny and at the same time more non-profit organizations began to seek foundation support, the amount of public information about foundations increased, as did the pressure to provide even more detail. With the federal government's adoption of the Freedom of Information Act, outsiders now had a better sense of a foundation's resources and the size of grant they could expect to receive.[23] If the SSBFF focused its areas of interest and put more emphasis on larger grants, it was doubly important for applicants to understand what the foundation would fund and what it would not.

The SSBFF directors discussed Hobday's Towards Tomorrow report at its board meeting in November 1983. They agreed with the idea that the SSBFF should be more strategic in its approach to philanthropy, and they approved the plan to focus on a more limited number of projects in order to have a greater impact. They were ready to accept most of Hobday's recommendations for the funding programs; the only major one they voted to drop, after considerable reflection, was Canadian Under-standing, which they had difficulty imagining as a workable program. They also preferred not to scale back Special Initiatives to the extent that Hobday had suggested, opting to peg its budget at $150,000. This pro-gram, they asserted, enabled the foundation "to respond creatively to new innovative projects anywhere in Canada" that showed potential for lasting value.[24] One of the SSBFF's greatest strengths was the ability to respond rapidly to community needs and its support of new and innovative projects.

Towards Tomorrow also inspired the directors to give serious thought to their long-term goals for the foundation. By this time, over a decade after taking on the SSBFF as a significant family project, the Bronfman siblings were becoming aware that the foundation meant different things to each one. Although variety of perspective made for a creative dynamic, it was perhaps time to agree on a basic vision. A key issue was the degree to which the SSBFF's funding agenda should conform to the pattern set by Sam Bronfman, above all how much the foundation should focus on concerns of the Jewish community and how much on larger social and cultural problems.[25] This issue would be addressed and resolved over the next few years against a backdrop of radical changes in the directors' lives and their personal projects; the board's composition would also change with the arrival of new members, notably Minda's son Jean de Gunzburg and Edgar's son Matthew Bronfman.

INDEPENDENT PROJECTS

Over the course of the 1980s, many of the SSBFF directors developed their own projects largely outside the parameters of the foundation. To an extent, this involvement reflected dissatisfaction with the SSBFF in its present form, or at any rate a recognition that the SSBFF was only a small part of the directors' increasingly complex spheres of interest. For Edgar and Minda, the foundation's activities also took place far away from their lives. By that time, Edgar had spent nearly three decades in New York and had become an American citizen; it was natural for him to channel his own philanthropic energies into such causes as the Samuel Bronfman Foundation, which had been established in the United States at almost the same time as his arrival there.[26] Minda, in Paris, had her own interests that she developed through *L'Association de soutien et de diffusion d'art* in France and the United States. In Montreal, Phyllis spent increasing amounts of time developing the Canadian Centre for Architecture – which was funded in small part by the SSBFF and so will be discussed in chapter 10. For her part, Saidye had her own foundation which supported the fine arts and crafts.

Charles seems to have felt particularly that the SSBFF, though an important part of Sam and Saidye's legacy, was not sufficient for his own philanthropic needs. In 1985 he created the Charles R. Bronfman Foundation with an initial contribution of $50 million, subsequently raised to $100 million, which made it the third largest foundation in Canada, behind only the McConnell and the Vancouver Foundations. The new institution had two primary purposes: to promote "the unity of the Jewish people, whose soul is in Jerusalem" and to contribute to "the enhancement of Canadianism."[27] Charles's sense of the importance of Canadianism had been underscored by his induction as an officer of the Order of Canada in 1981 (in 1992 he was promoted to companion of the Order of Canada). It was also born of ongoing worries about Quebec separation despite the federalist victory in the 1980 referendum and the return of the provincial Liberal party to power in 1985.[28] One of the CRB Foundation's major efforts initially was to produce a series of one-minute television/film segments on Canadian history designed to kindle Canadians' interest in their own past by highlighting ordinary people in heroic moments. Charles hoped this effort would strengthen Canadians' "emotional and intellectual bonds to their country."[29]

Although it was not part of the Executive Director's Program, the SSBFF continued its earlier commitment to agriculture research at the University of Manitoba, largely because it was a legacy project for Saidye's father, Samuel Rosner.[30] For a time, the directors considered a project to study "the use of biotechnology in conjunction with the development of canola," but in the end settled on a project that would fill a need and likely achieve results within a short period.[31] In late 1986 they received a proposal from Dr Daryl Kraft of the University of Manitoba to develop computer resources for Canada's farmers, a great number of whom needed to become much more proficient in order to manage the modern farm. At their December meeting, the directors approved a grant of $235,000 over five years toward what was to be called the "Samuel Rosner Computer Assisted Learning and Farm Financial Management Program." Three years later, the program produced a learning package which could be distributed and operated using computer diskettes. Declaring themselves satisfied with this research, the directors opted not to continue to make regular grants to the University of Manitoba.[32]

The ssbff also made direct contributions to the Jewish community, quite apart from its annual commitment to the Combined Jewish Appeal. In addition to funding the Jewish People's Schools, the ssbff had pledged capital dollars to a number of brick-and-mortar projects in Israel including the Weizmann Institute, the Canadian Technion Society, and the Israel Museum, although in an effort not to commit themselves to endless donations they put a cap on this sort of support overseas. Over the course of the later 1980s the directors began to wind some of these projects down, making their final payment on a $70,000 commitment to the Jewish People's Schools in 1985, followed by the completion of a $375,000 commitment to the Weizmann Institute; the following year, a $50,000 payment ended a multi-year grant to Canadian Technion.[33] In 1989 the Israel Museum came to Charles looking for funding for a new air conditioning system for the building's Bronfman Wing. As was the case with the Saidye Bronfman Centre, the family had to wrestle with the question of whether it was willing to let conditions deteriorate in a facility that bore the Bronfman name. By this time, however, the directors' commitment to the discipline of the ssbff mission statement and the focus of its programs weighed more heavily than legacy obligations. They concluded that a donation to the museum would not be relevant to the mission statement or the foundation's long-term plan.[34]

This withdrawal from the direct funding of projects relating to the Jewish community was the result of much prolonged discussion on the

directors' parts. This discussion was opened when Charles sent a letter
to Minda in the summer of 1984 outlining matters for her to think over
while she was on a holiday cruise in the Mediterranean.

THE LETTER TO MINDA

Charles's letter outlined conversations he had been having recently with
his brother Edgar on the subject of the SSBFF.[35] They recognized a growing tension between the brothers on the one hand, increasingly focused
on providing support for institutions in Israel through the Plus program,
and Minda and Phyllis on the other, who placed a higher priority on cultural institutions. Edgar also confessed to having little interest in the
SSBFF, and Charles acknowledged his own preference was to develop
the CRB foundation. It was also clear that Phyllis was deeply devoted to
the Canadian Centre for Architecture and that Minda had her own commitments in Paris. There was no question for anyone of discontinuing
the SSBFF, but it did not seem practical to use it as a vehicle for various
personal projects when there were other options. Perhaps it would be
better for the Bronfman siblings to agree on funding the Executive
Director's Program and the CJA, and each go their separate way with
personal projects.

Charles included with his letter some suggestions as to how such an
arrangement might play out financially given the foundation's current
commitments. The special projects should be gradually phased out or
undertaken outside the SSBFF. The foundation's annual commitment
to the CJA should be fixed at $2.6 million. The remaining budget, after
operating expenses, would go to the Executive Director's Program,
which ought to amount to around $895,000. This was a recipe for
consolidating the SSBFF's administration and the impact of its funding
programs, to the mutual satisfaction of the four siblings.[36] Charles's
letter provoked much reflection on the part of the Bronfman siblings;
however, personal and financial issues arising at this time added to the
complexity of the situation.

Minda's health proved one such issue. At the time of Charles's letter she had been diagnosed with cancer of the liver, information she shared only with Leo Kolber and Philip Vineberg so that they could rearrange her affairs to minimize the taxes on her estate.[37] For some time, the extended family was spared knowledge of her suffering, but eventually they too were told. She died on 1 July 1985. At that time, Minda's husband, Alain, was chairman of G.H. Mumm & Co. and a member of the board of Seagram. Their eldest son, Jean, had completed his doctorate in molecular biology at the University of Paris. The younger son, Charles, was living in the United States, having earned his BA at Dartmouth College. In Minda's memory, the de Gunzburg family gave $10 million to Harvard University to renovate Adolphus Busch Hall as a home for the Minda de Gunzburg Center for European Studies, a tribute that acknowledged the bridges she crossed between North America and Europe throughout her life.[38]

Jean de Gunzburg took his mother's place on the SSBFF board, attending his first meeting in December 1986.[39] By that time, Edgar was hoping that one of his own sons would replace him on the board. The problem was that all four had been born and raised in the United States and felt only a tenuous connection to Canada. Matthew remembered how strange it felt coming to Montreal to visit his grandparents. "I loved going to Montreal, but it was a little weird because in New York we were totally anonymous. In Montreal we were all of a sudden plunked into this town where we were almost royalty. It was very disconcerting as a kid."[40] Matthew's sense of being "royalty" was of course not all that far off the mark, although the crown had clearly passed to his uncle Charles, and would soon pass in turn to his cousin Stephen, as leader of Jewish philanthropy in the city – a title that held little significance for Edgar's branch of the family.

Even so, loyalty to his parents' commitment to Montreal prompted Edgar to encourage whatever feelings his own sons had towards Canada.[41] Samuel, Edgar's oldest, lived in California where he was busy running Seagram's wine business; moreover, Sam's wife, Melanie, had been recently diagnosed with breast cancer and he was focused on her care.[42] Edgar Jr was on a rapid ascent up the corporate ladder at Seagram in New York; in his mid-thirties, he was executive vice president for Seagram's American operations, heir apparent to succeed his father as CEO. Matthew, the third child born to Edgar and Ann Loeb, had graduated from Williams College and completed an MBA at Harvard before going to work for Cadillac Fairview for two years. Because of his business training and having spent time living and working in Canada, Matthew seemed the likeliest candidate of the three to take a seat on the board. In 1987 Charles and Phyllis pushed him along this path by asking him to be part of an investment committee evaluating the SSBFF's financial situation.[43]

At this time, the Bronfman siblings were in the process of dissolving CEMP, the investment company that Sam Bronfman had created for his four children and through which they had been able to inject money into the SSBFF and other causes of common interest. Given their disparate interests, and especially in the wake of Minda's death, it made sense for the siblings to go their separate financial ways. When the dissolution was completed, Charles created Claridge Inc. as a holding company for himself and his own children, and asked Leo Kolber to serve as its chairman. He arranged for Claridge to continue to provide in-house financial services for the SSBFF and pay the management fees for its portfolio.[44] Charles also decided he wanted to put his business and his own philanthropic activities together under one roof with the SSBFF. Accordingly, Claridge, the CRB Foundation, and the SSBFF moved into the top three floors of the former Windsor Hotel, now renovated as luxury office space, situated a few blocks down Peel Street from the old Seagram Headquarters. Charles hoped that the "money-makers" and the "money-givers" would learn from one another. Kolber was skeptical: "You had foundation people giving away money in space that was costing $35 per square foot ... They should have been in a loft somewhere uptown."[45] Charles's view was that family foundations associated with great wealth are often expected to reflect the trappings of power; besides, when Claridge managed a multi-billion dollar portfolio, the cost of office space was not an issue.[46] The advantages of having common office space would be enhanced in the 1990s when the foundation converted to a new networked database that allowed employees to link all the "philanthropic pockets" at Claridge.[47]

The breakup of CEMP meant that no common family capital could be used to fund the foundation. Any new injections of capital would have to come from each family individually – an arrangement not likely to lead to constructive decision-making with each of the siblings engaged more than ever in individual projects. An endowment from the family as a whole, however, would provide for the SSBFF in perpetuity and leave each member to move on.[48] The impending sale of Cadillac Fairview, CEMP's major asset, provided the opportunity to make such an endowment. After making spectacular profits in the 1970s, the value of this real estate conglomerate diminished considerably with the economic downturn of the early 80s, and Kolber struggled for several years to bring it back up again.[49] By 1986, the value of Cadillac Fairview had risen from $5 to $18 a share, and Kolber decided that the time was right to sell. A buyer was found, and the deal was completed by November 1987; the Bronfman family's share of the proceeds totalled $1.2 billion.[50]

Charles's 1984 letter to Minda had anticipated the will to dissolve CEMP, and the sale of Cadillac Fairview provided the opportunity to create a sizeable endowment for the SSBFF, but it remained for the Bronfman siblings and their extended families to agree to make this injection of funds. Unfortunately, Charles's financial projections had not accurately predicted what the SSBFF's situation would be three years later. By the summer of 1987 the Claridge financial advisors had worked out that the SSBFF was in much worse shape than the letter to Minda had anticipated. Charles's calculations had not factored in the cost of investment management fees and other administrative costs related to accounting and tax compliance, nor had it calculated the effects of inflation on administrative costs. Decisions to expand the program had added to the overall budget, above all the donation to the CJA which had since been fixed at $2,775,000 and not $2.6 million. The foundation also had a number of significant ongoing commitments which could not easily be wrapped up: $600,000 over four years to fund the Saidye Rosner Bronfman Chair in Architectural History and Theory at McGill (see chapter 10); $230,000 over two years to pay for special renovations

to the Samuel Bronfman House (owned by the Canadian Jewish Con-
gress); $250,000 over five years to the capital campaign of the Canadian
Centre for Architecture, $235,000 over five years to help fund the new
Samuel Rosner Farm Management Programme at the University of
Manitoba, and a few others.[51]

Financial advisors Arnold Ludwick and Michel Boucher predicted
that if all remained unchanged, the SSBFF would soon be eating into its
capital; as a result, their assets would diminish to the point where all
funding programs would have to be eliminated. Within ten years, they
said, the SSBFF capital would yield only enough to cover the donation
to CJA.[52] At the board meeting in August 1987, the directors were presented with some grim choices. They could choose to endow the foundation at a level that would allow it to expand its current programs.
They could try to determine what amount would be necessary to sustain its current program into the distant future without needing a fresh
infusion of capital. Or they could choose to begin winding the institution
down, spending the endowment over a number of years.

Phyllis, Jean, and Charles agreed that they wanted the SSBFF to
continue with the various programs and funding commitments they had
agreed to over the last few years.[53] To do so, new capital would have to
be injected. Two issues, therefore, needed to be resolved. How much
would it take? And who should give? The first question was relatively
straightforward and could be based on simple extrapolations from
previous budgets accounting for inflation. The amount of capital required to produce a reasonable amount for sustained programs was $50
million. The simplest solution to the second question was for each wing
of the family to contribute an amount equivalent to the percentage of
CEMP each sibling had been allotted; this was the pitch that the SSBFF
directors made to the extended family in the autumn of 1987, hoping
they could count on a sympathetic understanding of the foundation's
work and its importance as a legacy to Sam and Saidye.[54]

Charles articulated his own feelings about the foundation and its
significance to the family. Philosophically, he asserted, he and Phyllis
were on the same page. They looked upon "the SSBFF as a reminder
to all of us of whence our roots stem." The foundation, he asserted,

"should reflect not only the immediate philanthropic desires of the founders, but some of the broader aspects of life in the country in which they spent their lives." In other words, as a legacy to Sam and Saidye, the foundation should continue their pattern of giving, but it should also be sensitive to the current needs of the Canadian people. Charles pointed out that the contributions to the CJA and the Saidye Bronfman Centre had been effectively taken care of or set aside. Any further contributions, he wrote, "that are not within the scope of the SSBFF will be addressed personally by whoever is interested in that aspect of life." Charles then explained the strengths of the Executive Director's Program under Hobday's management. In closing, he conceded that, "I well realize that you and probably your children are, and will be, Americans ... Nonetheless, it does seem to me that something meaningful in Granny and Papa's name is important not only for my generation and yours, but those that follow us."[55]

The greater issue for each of Sam and Saidye's children and grandchildren was the future of the foundation and their relationship to it. By this time, each of the families was engaged in enormously significant philanthropic activities of their own. The financial situation challenged each family first to decide if they wanted to continue the pattern of giving that Sam and Saidye had established as a legacy – in particular giving to the CJA. Secondly, the families had to assess the meaning and significance of the Executive Director's Program and determine whether its projects were valuable as a philanthropic legacy to Canada worthy of their grandparents' memory. Emotionally, the issue was complicated and there was a sense among many of the members of the family that if they agreed to the contribution they wanted to make sure that the plan for self-sufficiency with this added infusion of capital would work. Having to face this decision over and over down the road was not something anyone looked forward to.

In November 1987 the board established an Investment Committee composed of Jean, Matthew, and Philip Vineberg; Arnold Ludwick and Robert Rabinovitch acted as secretaries. The Board wanted to make the SSBFF "free-standing," supported by its own permanent endowment without expectations of annual or further contributions from the family.

The Investment Committee was asked to determine how the foundation's assets should be managed to achieve this goal. A number of key questions were raised. Should funds for the CJA be nominally segregated from the other assets of the foundation? Should the foundation's assets continue to be managed by Claridge or should they be invested by outside money managers? If Claridge managed some or all of the portfolio, what kind of management fee should it charge? In some ways, these questions were long overdue.[56]

Nearly fifteen years after Sam Bronfman's death, the close relationship between Seagram donations and the foundation was still evident in the day-to-day operations of the two organizations. Hobday estimated that he spent two-thirds of his time working on foundation initiatives and one-third on Seagram grants. His staff divided their time between the two entities in various ways.[57] The foundation "owned" the filing cabinets and three secretarial chairs while Seagram "owned" the desks, the sofa, and the three chairs in the executive director's office. Seagram paid for heat, lights, and telephone lines – even the foundation's number – but the foundation paid for the office coffee.[58] Going forward, there needed to be a clearer understanding of which entities would contribute to which activities and operations.

The Investment Committee moved quickly to create a professional separation between the foundation and the management of the endowment. In December 1987 it put the management contract out to bid, with Claridge having the opportunity to bid along with others. The committee also agreed that the foundation should ask Claridge to propose an annual fee to cover the cost of providing all other services (excluding investment management) in two categories: accounting and general office management.[59]

In March 1988 they interviewed a number of prospective teams. All of the advisors noted the high expectations of the foundation. Budgets were based on a 9 per cent annual return or better. To hit that mark year-over-year in the short run would be difficult. Their ability to invest for the long term would be constrained. As a result, growth would be slow in the first couple of years.[60]

While the Investment Committee deliberated over the mechanics, Sam and Saidye's children considered how committed they were to the SSBFF. Of the three, Phyllis was the most passionate about the need to stabilize the finances and continue the work begun in the Director's Programs. In her view, the question was not whether the family would reinvest in the foundation, but how.[61] Charles had worked hard for the SSBFF, but his interests had been taking him elsewhere and he was spending more and more time away from Montreal, in New York, Palm Beach, and Israel. Edgar had very little interest in taking part in the foundation, but he proved willing enough to keep it running by making a sizeable injection of money. In the end, the family came through with sufficient funds to bring the SSBFF's endowment to well over $50 million – thanks in large part to the sale of Cadillac Fairview.[62] Having made his own contribution – out of a sense of obligation as much as anything, his son felt – Edgar withdrew from the board, leaving his branch of the family to be represented by Matthew.[63]

Charles and Phyllis continued working to bring the next generation into the governance of the SSBFF; Phyllis even wrote personally to her nephews and nieces, inviting them to attend board meetings.[64] In the early 1990s, Charles formally withdrew from the board, and his son Stephen took his place.[65] Stephen found himself stepping into his father's shoes, not only within the foundation but in terms of his social and business commitments. Like his cousins Jean and Matthew, Stephen Bronfman had grown up in a household where philanthropy was a major activity. "There were always fundraising parties," he remembers, "and as a kid, sort of looking over the rail in your pyjamas, you would see hundreds of people dressed up downstairs." Unlike Phyllis, who had been sensitive as a child to the social pressures on people to give, Stephen's childhood memories were dominated by a sense of pride and honour. He remembered being impressed by the medals hanging in his grandparents' house and asking his father Charles if they were from a war. Charles said no, they were for humanitarian purposes, for his grandparents' philanthropy. "I grew up feeling that my grandparents were heroes," he says.[66]

At the end of 1987, the board lost another long-time member when the family's legal advisor, Philip Vineberg, passed away. Early the following year, Arnold Ludwick, who had served in recent years as the board's treasurer, submitted his resignation. The subject of board composition took up much time at the directors' April 1988 meeting. It was acknowledged that there was some ambiguity as to whether the offices of secretary and treasurer necessarily constituted directorships of the foundation. Having appointed as the new treasurer Robert Rabinovitch, a vice-president at Claridge and a member of the CRB foundation board, the question arose whether he should be considered a SSBFF director. Equally, an obvious candidate to succeed Philip Vineberg as secretary was his son, Robert, whom the board proceeded to appoint without having entirely resolved the issue of creating new directorships.[67] Although there would have been clear advantages to having several experienced outsiders serving on the board, this would have significantly changed the board's dynamic and represented an abandonment of the concept of a family foundation. Family members were unwilling to go this route, however difficult it was for them at times to attend meetings in Montreal from different parts of the globe.[68] The problem was underscored at the next board meeting in December 1988 when both Vineberg and Rabinovitch were present but only three directors – Phyllis, Charles, and Peter Swann – leaving the meeting without quorum. Although the quorum issue was resolved by having all decisions ratified subsequently, a solution to the question of the board's size was not found until 1991 when the number of directors was expanded to include Vineberg and Rabinovitch alongside Phyllis, Charles, Jean, Matthew, and Swann.[69]

Saidye had formally resigned from her position as president at the time of Minda's death, when she herself was eighty-eight. At its June 1985 meeting the board unanimously declared Saidye the SSBFF's honorary president.[70] Phyllis formally took over as president at this time, and continued to serve in that capacity for another thirteen years. Saidye gradually withdrew from public life as her health declined, but she continued to live at Oaklands until her death at ninety-eight in 1995. Throughout her last years she remained close to all her children and interested in the activities of the SSBFF, even if she could no longer take part.

CONCLUSION

The arrival of John Hobday at the SSBFF marked a decided shift from an entrepreneurial to a more strategic approach to creating and managing funding programs. It also coincided with an intense period of introspection on the part of the directors and their families as to the long-term direction the foundation would take. After much negotiation over levels of emotional and financial commitment, the extended family of Sam and Saidye Bronfman decided to make a substantial investment in the SSBFF so that it could operate as a free-standing institution with a major endowment from which to make grants. This period also saw the departure of Saidye and two of her children as directors of the foundation, and the arrival of Jean and Matthew as representatives of the third generation. By 1988, with a reaffirmation of purpose and a renewed commitment of the family, John Hobday now had to devise a plan for the foundation's program of giving that could operate within this new financial arrangement. Devising that plan also provided an opportunity to rethink and refocus the foundation's approach to philanthropy.

FIVE

A Free-Standing Institution

Before starting his day at the foundation, John Hobday often met Lon Dubinsky, an old friend and colleague, for breakfast. Over coffee, they talked about the state of the arts in Canada and the world of philanthropy. They also wrestled with the future of the SSBFF. Dubinsky offered an interesting point of view, having worked as a researcher for a government commission created to stimulate private sector funding for the arts; for this he had prepared case studies of various leading foundations in Canada and the United States, including the SSBFF.[1] Given this history, Dubinsky struck Hobday as an ideal person to carry out a formal study of the foundation within the context of Bronfman philanthropy and to make recommendations regarding its potential as a promoter of innovative projects. In the spring of 1988, Dubinsky set to work. His findings would form the basis for a new strategic orientation for the SSBFF. Hobday would implement Dubinsky's recommendations, beginning with the hiring of specialized staff and culminating in a series of visioning workshops to help give each of the foundation's five key client organizations a new direction for the 1990s, focusing above all on making them effective national institutions. This overhaul of the SSBFF's operations would launch it on a solid course for the next decade and a half, a period that would prove the most creative of its history.

Unlike Peter Swann, whose approach emphasized the sowing of seed money without ensuring a clear mechanism for reaping the results, Hobday saw the big picture and prepared for a long commitment. His efforts were rooted in a profound belief in the benefits of acting strategically. He also saw the need to work with governments; his sense was that only national or at least provincial organizations had the capacity to influence governments and the highest levels of business. The SSBFF had a great deal of potential, Hobday concluded after much analysis; it had a track record that suggested it could be a leader in difficult times. By focusing on innovative programs for people rather than bricks and mortar, by consulting widely and studying the issues before launching a program, and by working closely with grant recipients, setting high expectations but helping them to prove themselves, the foundation could make great strides in a number of vital areas. The SSBFF was well positioned, "plugged in" to the "real needs of Canadian society." Furthermore, by showing the way for other funders to contribute to a project, the SSBFF exerted a degree of leverage that exceeded its own financial resources. Overall, Hobday characterized the foundation's activities as "professional," by which he meant that "ideas are managed, not merely funded."[2]

With a more substantial endowment, and a board of directors that included members who were further removed from the world of Sam and Saidye Bronfman, the SSBFF was in a better position than ever to focus on a series of innovative programs geared to the needs of late-twentieth-century Canadian society. The tensions that had emerged among Sam and Saidye's children over the fundamental purpose of the SSBFF had often proved creative and had resulted in funding projects of a diverse nature – learning disabilities, native peoples, the arts, heritage conservation, and above all Canada's Jewish community – but after the soul-searching and negotiations of the mid-1980s the board now had a common (though still diverse) agenda. Although still linked on many levels to the Bronfman business enterprise and its offshoots (Claridge, for instance), the SSBFF was no longer dependent on the Bronfman family to provide resources for its philanthropy. In effect, the directors had become trustees of a modern foundation who happened to have personal connections with Sam and Saidye, as opposed to members of the Bronfman family who happened to sit on a particular foundation. By focusing less on the legacy of the donor and more on the needs of society, the ssbff had matured as a philanthropic organization.

DUBINSKY'S REPORT ON THE SSBFF

Hobday's first step toward drafting a new operations plan for the foundation was to give serious thought to how the ssbff could best fill needs within contemporary Canadian society. Government cutbacks had created "serious holes in the social safety net," he wrote to the board in April 1988.[3] Longstanding programs and institutions faced termination. Despite some improvements in the economy, corporate giving remained frozen or increased only marginally. "There is mounting frustration as governments try to turn over responsibilities to a private sector which is seemingly not yet willing to contribute more." Straining resources even further, a decline in voluntarism and individual giving was reflected in recent studies.[4] Concern over this decline had led the Canadian Centre for Philanthropy to develop a public relations campaign entitled IMAGINE to promote philanthropy and voluntarism.[5] The ssbff helped fund this campaign, but Hobday also believed the foundation had a direct role to play.

Lon Dubinsky's study, presented in June 1988, helped to sharpen the focus of Bronfman philanthropy in Canada and continue the movement toward strategic intervention in a limited number of issue areas.[6] Dubinsky began his study by analyzing the interrelationships between the ssbff, Seagram and Claridge's charitable programs, and the CRB Foundation, in order to understand the overall impact of Bronfman philanthropy across various institutions. He put his findings within the context of changes taking place in North American philanthropy. In 1987, the top fifty charitable foundations in Canada had assets totalling more than $1.5 billion, which constituted 80 per cent of all the foundations' assets in the country. They granted more than $108 million a year. Most of these foundations continued a traditional pattern of giving established by the founders, usually limited more by geography than specific fields of interest. Fewer than 9,000 grants exceeded $500 each. Grants for education and health care accounted for more than half of all grants, followed by social services. Arts and culture ranked fourth, receiving 13 per cent of the foundation monies granted – an improvement over the situation fifteen years earlier. Of Canada's biggest and best-known foundations, family foundations accounted for more than 80 per cent of the total number of institutions. The J.W. McConnell Foundation was the largest of these entities with more than $280 million in assets.[7]

Among all these foundations, the SSBFF distinguished itself by the number of grants it made. Although it ranked eighth among Canada's top fifty foundations in terms of assets, it gave money to 168 entities, far more than the wealthier McConnell's 56. This discrepancy confirmed Hobday's sense that the SSBFF was spreading itself too thin. Even so, Dubinsky praised the Bronfman organizations for their increasing commitment to giving that was strategic, based on a careful analysis of issues and a deep understanding of the grantees and their communities.[8] He found the SSBFF to be one of the most proactive among the country's philanthropic organizations, its executive director and board of directors spending an atypical amount of time exploring ways to address social and cultural issues, and guiding their client organizations through the process of undertaking a project.[9]

According to Dubinsky, the foundation's success raised a new set of organizational challenges. How should it structure its relationship with maturing programs, cultivate new fields of endeavour, and at the same time manage a growing tide of requests for support? All of these challenges had to be considered in the context of a basic set of questions. How should programs and recipients be evaluated? What kind of information did the foundation need to achieve its goals? What areas of giving could be eliminated from consideration to streamline the foundation's work and focus its operations? How important were partnerships or the geographical reach of the foundation's programs? Finally, how and to what degree could the Bronfmans' philanthropies exercise leverage?[10] Underlying all these questions was an understanding that strategic giving depended on intelligence, and that the gathering of that intelligence was the main work of the foundation's staff.

Considering the evolution of each of these Bronfman philanthropies, Dubinsky outlined the challenges ahead. The CRB Foundation, for example, was still "in an early stage of development," experimenting, and looking to sharpen its focus before expanding, modifying, or terminating its initial programs. Seagram's philanthropy seemed generally unfocused, as it gave many small grants to various educational, welfare, health, and cultural organizations, as well as much solid support to symphony orchestras and, more recently, to Montreal universities. Claridge did not have a donations program comparable to either the CRB or Seagram. Clearly, the SSBFF had the most mature and disciplined program, with five key areas as well as the flexibility provided by Special Initiatives. The foundation's sustained commitment to the core program areas, and its determination to continue these through 1991, provided an opportunity for a handful of key grantees to "attain greater maturity."[11]

Dubinsky concluded that by 1988 the SSBFF had developed and implemented what was in many ways a highly rationalized system of philanthropy. Through Special Initiatives the foundation conducted research and development, scanning the horizon of needs and opportunities, evaluating patterns and trends in a wide variety of social arenas. At the same time, John Hobday worked to increase his networking with other foundations and corporate donations officers. As he had recently informed the board, "Through these informal 'networks,' it is often possible to assist claimant groups to match or better the SSBFF 'seed' money.'"[12] By virtue of their active involvement in a variety of related philanthropic endeavours, Board members were able to constructively test and challenge the conclusions that Hobday drew from his interactions with others. Out of this process, consensus emerged on particular areas for focused giving.

In Hobday's reorganization of the SSBFF's programs, these areas of focused giving would come under the name Transitions, the rationale being that these were programs "which can effect 'transitions' in Canadian society" given sustained funding over five or ten years or more. They included five major funding arenas which had already achieved significant results: Persons with Learning Disabilities, Seniors Participation, Arts Management Training, Conservation of the Canadian Heritage, and the Saidye Bronfman Crafts Award.[13] (See chapters 7 through 11 for the histories of these programs.) Under Hobday's leadership these core parts of the Executive Director's Program would become associated with certain characteristics. All were intimately connected to the development of a single client organization: One Voice for seniors, the Learning Disabilities Association of Canada, Heritage Montreal, and the Centre for Cultural Management at the University of Waterloo. These organizations had demonstrated their potential to act as "agents of change."[14] As Hobday defined it, these organizations offered new approaches to issues, promoted heightened public awareness of their interest areas, and realized projects that had the potential to shape public policy.[15] The SSBFF provided these organizations with financial resources and collaborative consulting on a wide range of issues related to organizational development.

According to Dubinsky, all of these programs were "maturing" by 1988. By this he did not mean to suggest that these were middle-aged organizations growing grey around the temples and entering a period of wisdom. Indeed, they were more like teenagers, increasingly intelligent, independent, and capable in the world, but still absolutely dependent on the foundation for guidance, resources, and structure. Like teenagers, they would soon reach an age when they would have to sink or swim on their own. Indeed, in 1988, the board and the executive director had determined that these organizations had three years to complete their coming of age.

Hobday proposed redefining the Special Initiatives funds as Futures, by way of contrast with Transitions. Futures would continue the practice of providing small grants which would give the foundation information about innovative activities taking place in a variety of social arenas and feed the development of new programs. In effect, Futures was not unlike the efforts of a large established corporation to remain innovative by providing small amounts of capital to a variety of entrepreneurial firms hoping that one or more of these businesses might eventually develop a product or service that could be acquired by the corporation and matured within its own structure.

As the foundation looked beyond the three-year horizon, it needed to begin testing the waters in various parts of the country to identify the leverage points for new programs. In addition to Transitions and Futures, Hobday recognized a third category of giving that he dubbed Special Interests, which included the family legacy programs of the SSBFF including the Combined Jewish Appeal, the CCA, the Samuel Rosner program in farm management, and the Saidye Bronfman Centre.[16]

PREPARING FOR THE NINETIES

A more disciplined operation would, of course, place additional strains on the foundation's human resources. In late 1986 John Hobday had reported that he received an average of twenty inquires a week from organizations wanting to know what the foundation did and how to apply for funding. The following year, he reported that the growing adoption of the personal computer and increasing professionalization among grantee managers had increased the volume of well-organized and targeted appeals. These demands also put a premium on Hobday's time.[17] In early 1988 the SSBFF decided to look for an experienced grants officer.

Gisele Rucker came to the foundation with a different sort of background, one that was tuned to the perspective of the Jewish community in Montreal and highly sensitive to the needs of the poorest members of Canadian society.[18] Born in France to Polish Jews who had immigrated to Paris before the Second World War, Rucker was a kindergartener in the 1950s when her father, a furrier and leather worker by trade, decided to bring the family to Canada, hoping for a better life. Following the path of many Jewish immigrants, the family lived first in Mile End, then Snowdon, and finally in Côte St-Luc, a rural area that was being developed as a bungalow suburb for Jewish families. She went to school in English even though she spoke French; Montreal's Protestant public school system accommodated almost all of the city's Jews at this time. After graduating from McGill in the mid-1970s with a degree in art history, Rucker married and had a child, but remained interested in the controversies surrounding the city's architectural heritage, especially the Milton-Park affair. Years later, she remembered being impressed by a newspaper article she read during that time about Phyllis Lambert and her efforts to preserve Montreal's historic structures and communities. Caught up in the demands of a young family, Rucker admired and even envied Phyllis's drive and passion. After her marriage had ended and she became a single mother, Rucker landed a job in Ottawa at the Canada Council. She and her son moved into mixed-income housing where Rucker saw first-hand the effects of poverty on families and individuals. Working her way up at the Canada Council, she became a grants officer for the Explorations program, designed to give established artists the opportunity to try their hands in a different medium. Frustrated by the glass ceiling, however, she went back to school, taking business classes at the University of Western Ontario.

Returning to Montreal with her son, Rucker looked for a job. Her background and disposition favored something in the arts, and when she saw an ad for a position at the Saidye Bronfman Centre, she applied.[19] She began as an assistant to director Harry Gulkin in the mid-1980s, and after he left became director of administration. Frustrated in this position, Rucker responded eagerly to the SSBFF's advertisement.

When she began work in May 1988, Rucker was keen to understand the differences between Seagram's donation program and the SSBFF's. She brought with her the memories of her experiences at the Saidye. "Seagram was a corporate program," she concluded, "and everything depended on how well the corporation would look by the donations that it gave." By contrast, the SSBFF was the "embodiment, the intellectual and moral conscience, of the Bronfman family. It was their private investment in the public realm."[20] Rucker's assessment underscores the change that had taken place in the SSBFF since the days before Sam's death. Sam and Saidye may have donated in part out of a need to win broad respect and to play the part of good corporate citizens – both motivations that still seemed to apply to Seagram in its corporate philanthropy. The SSBFF, however, although clearly sensitive to its need to be a respected and effective foundation, operated from a desire to effect social change – as did, presumably, its directors. This was its essential role as a family foundation.

In her new job, Rucker was asked to track the grants given through the Special Initiatives program and to evaluate the emerging trends in requests for assistance. As these trends became apparent, she would suggest arenas of activity to Hobday, who acted as gatekeeper to the board. "John was the keel and he would more or less say, look this is not for them or this is for them," Rucker recalled. Some issue areas appealed to the Bronfmans' concern for community. Other issues – violence in society, for example – he did not push forward.[20] Rucker particularly assisted Hobday in drawing up the new strategic plan which they called "Preparing for the Nineties." The plan reiterated and sharpened the foundation's sense of its own core competencies, and made recommendations for future programming. The document pushed the foundation one step further along the path of professionalization by articulating a mission statement and a clear discipline for getting the work done.

In articulating how the organization would work, "Preparing for the Nineties" provided the best summary of the foundation's learning to date and its ideas for how to build on its experience. Many of the ideas about the organization's core competencies were drawn from Hobday's earlier document, but the new plan put a priority on "creating a better climate for major clients." In other words, Hobday saw an opportunity to play an active role in cultivating the networks of stakeholders on behalf of the foundation's key clients in each of the program areas. He and Rucker believed they could do this by creating a forum for the discussion of important and emerging issues in the appropriate policy arenas. "Preparing for the Nineties" also acknowledged the growing importance of the SSBFF's role as a "guarantor." By endorsing projects at an early stage of development, underscoring their viability, the foundation hoped to facilitate negotiations between its clients and other funding sources. These activities would leverage the return on even modest grants from the SSBFF. Finally, "Preparing for the Nineties" also called for a renewed effort to improve public awareness of the work of the SSBFF. Greater awareness would attract better applications related to the foundation's philanthropic goals.[21]

Programmatically, "Preparing for the Nineties" adopted Hobday's earlier proposal to organize all programs under three categories: Special Interests, Transitions, and Futures. The last of these was modified somewhat: rather than serve as a conduit for small one-time grants to organizations as a way to do good work and keep an ear to the ground, Hobday and Rucker now proposed that Futures help organizations that "require incubation in the form of more financial and professional support before tangible results could be expected." Hobday and Rucker proposed that instead of limiting grants to $5,000, "leading edge" projects could receive up to $30,000 a year for not more than three years.[22]

Hobday presented "Preparing for the Nineties" to the board in December 1988 at a meeting held at the CCA. Unfortunately, the board, which only met twice a year, had no quorum. Robert Vineberg suggested that those present could still make decisions and have them ratified later by those directors who were not present, but Phyllis replied "I don't want to make decisions! I want to have a discussion!"[23] Those members who were present did have a discussion. Charles, Phyllis, and Peter Swann praised the document and at the end of the meeting Phyllis agreed to contact those who had been unable to make the meeting to get their approval. In the interim, Hobday was instructed to move forward with the plan.[24]

SSBFF PHILANTHROPY IN THE LATE 1980S

Formally and informally, the Bronfmans had always remained open to new and interesting projects. Special Initiatives money, roughly $200,000 a year in the mid-1980s, allowed the foundation "to respond creatively to innovative projects anywhere in Canada which show potential lasting value." With an average contribution of two to three thousand dollars, these grants allowed Hobday and the directors to stay close to new and developing projects. These projects were particularly attractive because they often represented the most creative or cutting edge solutions to problems.[25] They also offered opportunities for the foundation to remain in the public eye.

In 1987, for example, the SSBFF helped publish the findings of the Centre for the Great Lakes, a bi-national independent body, on the economy and environment of the St. Lawrence River. It subsidized the work of four teenage filmmakers in Montreal who organized Children for

Peace and conducted a Youth Nuclear Disarmament Tour that reached 200,000 young people in fifty cities across Canada. To evaluate the opportunities for nationwide networking among organizations focused on children and youth, the foundation gave support to the Canadian Council on Children and Youth to begin a long-range planning process for forty-nine national voluntary organizations dealing with young people.[26] The following year, the SSBFF sponsored the Bronfman Guest Lecture Series at the University of Toronto and at Confederation College in Thunder Bay, Ontario; the lectures featured executives from various cultural organizations talking about their institutions and the environment surrounding arts administration.[27]

In 1989, under Futures, the foundation provided support for the West Coast Community Leadership Training Society, an organization directed by Bruce Fraser that sought to enable urban leaders to develop the skills and knowledge they needed to be effective. The BC group organized a "Mayors' Institute for Community Development," bringing twenty mayors together with business leaders to explore "traditional and non-traditional ways to engender new economic activity." The SSBFF helped the society expand its reach and enable other Mayors' Institutes to take place, bringing urban leaders into contact with experts in a wide variety of fields.[28]

The foundation also provided a grant to Project Focus, a Toronto-based group dedicated to developing and implementing environmental education programs for students of all ages. The grant funded the development, production, and distribution of focus group kits for Ontario high school students and their teachers participating in a pilot project titled Visions 2020. The project introduced students to concepts of sustainable development.[29] Gisele Rucker worked closely with Project Focus's executive director, Steve Smith, providing contacts and ideas and suggesting additional possible funders. These efforts aggregated funds from a variety of sources including various ministries in the provincial government; businesses such as Abitibi-Price, Ontario Hydro, and Canadian Pacific Forest Products, Ltd.; and foundations such as the Helen McCrea Peacock Foundation and the Laidlaw Foundation. The SSBFF's $10,875 contribution helped leverage a program budget of more than

$162,000.[30] Visions 2020 was so successful that it became a national venture the following year, supported by an additional $34,000 grant from the SSBFF.[31]

While Project Focus sought to cultivate environmental ethics among a new generation of Canadians, the SSBFF's board was not comfortable venturing into the field of medical ethics. In 1990, Gisele Rucker presented a proposal from a foundation hoping to organize a series of community-based seminars titled Ethics, Power and Change on issues in contemporary medical ethics. Jean de Gunzburg, who was a leading cancer researcher in France, firmly opposed this project. The scientific community was unable to reach consensus on many of these issues, he said, and the foundation would be ill-advised to venture into these waters.[32]

THE VISIONING WORKSHOPS

When it came to the core programs, Transitions, the SSBFF's goal was to build on its achievements. Through the 1980s, the foundation had changed its approach in two fundamental ways: it had broadened its scope to the whole of Canada, and it had actively sought to invest money and ideas to develop a handful of key organizations that could effect change in a specific arena of social or cultural policy. The foundation had brought the players together and supported the creation of national networks for learning disabilities, cultural management, and seniors. Now, it began to work with these players to develop a strategic vision that would drive the work of multiple organizations in many different environments toward a common set of goals.

This vision was shaped largely by a series of workshops which the SSBFF funded and helped organize over the course of 1990 and 1991. Inspiration came when Gisele Rucker had a telephone conversation with Donna Cardinal, the director of arts and multiculturalism in the city of Edmonton. Cardinal was working with futurist Warren Ziegler on a community-based process to craft a new cultural policy framework for the city. Ziegler called his process "Envisioning," although it was often referred to simply as "visioning." This was a grassroots, networked

approach that brought people together from different backgrounds, constituencies, and institutions and challenged them to develop a coherent
and collective vision. They then worked backwards to articulate the steps
needed to achieve that vision.[33] Rucker was intrigued, and shared this
information with Ivan Hale and John Hobday, and they agreed that the
SSBFF should look into this visioning process.[34]

Initially, the process seemed best suited as an exercise for Heritage
Montreal, but it soon developed into a wider initiative. For two days,
Rucker met with Ziegler to understand his process. When she presented
it to Hobday, he quickly realized that it could benefit the grantees in all
of the foundation's major program areas. In November 1989 Hobday
presented a plan to the board to hold five workshops focused on the
future of each of the foundation's major areas of interest – seniors, learning disabilities, cultural management, heritage, and crafts.

Having moved far beyond the world of passive responses to appeals
for funds, the SSBFF organized a meeting in Montreal of its primary
clients. Ivan Hale represented the seniors organization One Voice, Bill
Poole came from the Centre for Cultural Management, Isabel Corral
came from the CCA, June Bourgeau came from the Learning Disabilities
Association, and Peter Weinrich came from the Canadian Crafts Council.
As the SSBFF staff outlined the concept to the foundation's clients, they
underscored the fact that while the workshops would help to develop a
common vision among stakeholders in a given program area, the opportunity to host such a major think tank project would help to position
each organization as a leader in its field.[35] As Hobday later told the
board, he and Rucker also hoped that the workshops would cause a
"ripple effect by engaging the involvement of players currently outside
our clients' organizations," thereby giving the foundation greater leverage in the program area.[36] Each of the organizations agreed to proceed,
and pledged to identify and invite twenty creative individuals to a three-
day retreat. The foundation committed $25,000 per organization to
finance each workshop.[37]

Seeking a facilitator for the workshops, the foundation issued a call
for proposals to twenty-two consulting firms in Canada and the United

States. Four finalists were selected from the responses, and on 9 February 1990, the foundation assembled the leadership from each of its client organizations to interview the prospective consultants. The group chose Victoria, BC-based Salasan Associates, headed by Dr Bruce Fraser, who was head of the West Coast Community Leadership Training Society, had worked with One Voice on the Habitat project in 1989, and had briefly consulted for the foundation with the Learning Disabilities Association of Canada.[38] "They were much quieter and West Coast," Rucker remembers, characteristics that seemed to fit the group.[39]

The foundation asked Salasan to facilitate the actual workshops, but to make the process productive. Salasan began working with the participants well in advance of the meeting. People were suggested by the SSBFF's client organizations and those people, in turn, recommended others. For the participants, the program was attractive. It offered an opportunity "to retreat from the 'how-to's' of today to the 'what-if's' of tomorrow and offered a forum for creative visionary people to discuss, with other extraordinary minds, new paths to accomplish positive change in areas which deeply involve them."[40] Fraser and his team did advance interviews to allow participants to state their expectations for the workshop, highlight their personal views of the outlook for the field, and identify the major themes they believed were important. Prior to the workshop, participants prepared personal statements articulating their visions of the future of their fields. Salasan then compiled the agenda for the workshop based on the views articulated by the participants. The agenda, however, was not set in stone; the participants, not the facilitators, were in control. Over the course of the three-day workshop, the facilitators worked with the participants to develop a shared view of the future. After each day, Fraser and his collaborator, Ed Sutherland, compiled a written synthesis of the day's discussions. At the end of each workshop, the facilitators presented a draft report for final review by the participants.[41]

Each of these workshops sought to survey the road to the future. Fraser and his team provided a final consultant's report soon after the workshop was completed. Whether or not a coherent and powerful vision was articulated in the long run, the workshops provided participants with an extraordinary opportunity to share ideas and network. Active participation by the foundation's staff led to a stronger common understanding of issues and practices between grantor and grantee.[42] It also led to even closer involvement by foundation staff "in our clients' affairs." Through each of the workshops, the theme of community was echoed over and over. For the foundation staff, this theme embraced the greater circle of philanthropy in Canada and led Hobday to explore closer collaborative relationships with other foundations.[43]

The workshops were crucial to the establishment of foundation policy over the next decade or more. The ability of funded organizations to live up to the vision expressed at the workshops, or in some cases to articulate a vision that had been only partly shaped during workshop discussions, determined to a large extent their long term success. Their success, of course, ultimately represented success for the foundation as a force for positive change in Canadian society. Ten years later, members of the board could look back at some of their projects and claim real achievement; in other cases, they had to content themselves with learning from their mistakes.

The foundation was also keen to develop a process by which the programs could be evaluated along with the organizations they supported. The directors did not want their funds to be wasted, but they were also keen to nurture organizations, especially fledgling ones, beyond the stage where they depended on the foundation for their existence. All along, the risk in the SSBFF's approach to philanthropy had been that in becoming so close to its client organizations it would not be able to exit from active support. There were two threats here: first, that the clients would never achieve independence, and second, that these entities would simply become operating arms of the SSBFF. To curb any tendencies in this direction, the foundation asked for performance reviews to be conducted in two years' time for each of their grantees.

It was one thing to call for evaluations and another to establish the exact criteria for determining a program's success. The SSBFF directors acknowledged a certain tendency in some funding circles to measure success by the attention that it brought to a foundation or the family behind it. From this point of view, the SSBFF's Saidye Bronfman Award for Excellence in the Crafts would have to be considered its most successful program, even though the award's actual impact on the arts community as a whole was not as significant as the foundation's ambitious program for cultural management. It was Phyllis's view, however, that the SSBFF was not interested in simply promoting its name; it existed to help in areas that otherwise would not be supported.[11] (This view echoed Rucker's impression of what motivated the foundation.) As such, the obvious criterion for success was whether or not an organization made the transition from client to autonomous and self-funding entity. But was it reasonable to expect all organizations to make this transition in the same way and at the same time? This gave rise to a new series of questions regarding the sort of "model development cycle" that the foundation should pursue. In other words, how long should it allow for a program or organization to get off the ground? What was the right pace and scale of funding? Should funding be minimal in the early experimental years? Should it increase as an organization hit its stride? At what point should an organization be expected to develop independent means of support?

In the end, the directors did not reach a firm decision and did not establish clear criteria for success; they would come back to these issues over and over again as they struggled to find the best model for a funder-client relationship. Even so, it is possible to apply a standard set of criteria to each of the five programs supported by the SSBFF after 1990 in order to assess their achievements: 1) Did the organization make the transition from client to autonomous entity? 2) How effectively did the SSBFF allocate funds in order to ensure a sufficient rate of growth? 3) Did the program make a difference? Of course, any quantitative analysis cannot take into consideration the many variations within each program or the circumstances in which each client organization had to operate. Nevertheless, it is important to address these questions systematically in order to arrive at a clearer sense of the SSBFF's success as a funding agency. This will be done in each of the following six chapters.

CHALLENGES

The SSBFF's funding programs would be implemented against a particular political and social background. The 1990s would bring significant challenges for Canadian society, which in turn would have consequences for philanthropy. Having established a policy and administrative structure for the foundation, the board now had to address some fundamental questions regarding its role as both supporter of key institutions and promoter of risky innovation. As it had done in the wake of 1960s enthusiasm and government largesse, and again in the early 1980s with the advent of serious government withdrawal from public programs, the SSBFF needed to adjust its approach to meet changing needs.

The political situation gave much impetus to designing and supporting programs with a national scope. The failure of the 1980 referendum on Quebec sovereignty and Quebec's refusal to sign the 1982 Constitutional Accord had resulted in a long federal campaign by the Conservative government under Brian Mulroney to provide a constitutional solution to Canada's internal divisions. The ultimate failure of this campaign led to the return to power of the Parti Québécois in 1994 and to a second referendum on Quebec sovereignty that was lost by only a tiny margin. Sensitive to accusations that it had not done enough to keep Canada united, the new Liberal federal government under Jean Chrétien promoted Canadian federalism with renewed enthusiasm, creating a department of Canadian Heritage (known by the acronym PCH, the "P" standing for "patrimoine") to oversee all aspects of culture in Canada, and investing substantially in programs reflecting the country's linguistic duality. In this environment, non-profit organizations strove to develop programs that were national in character, rather than merely local or regional. The SSBFF under Hobday had anticipated this national focus by some years, although the directors had always been keen to promote activities that touched all parts of Canada. In late 1984 Phyllis had noted that Ontario received a far higher percentage of grants than any other province, and Hobday conceded that the West (with the exception of Vancouver and Winnipeg) and the Atlantic provinces did not submit very many proposals.[45] Wanting to ensure that its programs were as effective as possible, the SSBFF strove to make them known across the country and be relevant to all regions.

Running somewhat contrary to the Chrétien government's willingness to invest in national heritage programs was its determination to be even more fiscally draconian than its predecessor to bring down the deficit. The recession that began across North America in 1989 brought a decline in tax revenue, resulting in ever-deepening federal debt, which the government aimed to escape by means of massive cutbacks to public programs. These cutbacks put new pressure on philanthropic giving. Hobday reported to the foundation board in the spring of 1990 that the number of appeals had risen sharply, and predicted that this trend would continue.[46] Did this mean that private foundations should step in and offer the kind of social services formerly provided by government? Clearly it would be impractical, even irresponsible, to do so. Arguably, the approach foundations were adopting represented a more effective way to tackle problems than the cyclical pattern of doling out largesse in good times and starving clients in lean years; organizations that had come to rely on government funding were discovering the drawbacks of such reliance, and private foundations were wary of finding themselves playing a similar role. Instead of ambitious schemes to solve huge social problems – poverty, discrimination, or the welfare of children – foundations opted to look at problems holistically. This meant locating points for intervention where an investment could leverage a chain reaction of changes.[47] Often this meant taking a risk with an untested grassroots organization.

One of the promising developments on the philanthropic horizon was the expansion of community foundations across Canada. Community foundations began in the 1920s and sprang from the same civic spirit that produced community chests and other public charitable bodies. Leaving money to a community foundation was a good way to ensure that it would be put to good use within the local community. Despite much enthusiasm, however, by the 1980s only the Vancouver and Winnipeg Foundations had built any significant assets ($260 million and $40 million respectively). In recent years, however, the community foundation concept caught on throughout North America, and by 1991 there were fifty-four such institutions operating in all of the nation's largest cities save for Montreal, Quebec City, and Halifax.[48]

The SSBFF could take some credit for helping to bring about this dramatic change. In April 1990, community foundations from across the country sent representatives to an Ottawa conference, where they decided that there was a need for a national association. The conference was organized by Alistair Gamble of the Ottawa-Carleton Community Foundation, who would be named national coordinator for the fledgling association. After a meeting with Hobday, Gamble submitted a proposal to the SSBFF for a grant to get Community Foundations of Canada started.[49] The SSBFF provided the CFC with $25,000 a year for the first three years to help it get a strong start, thereby helping establish an organization capable of managing the nearly half a billion dollars in capital funds that the various member community foundations represented.[50]

The SSBFF also helped the Canadian Centre for Philanthropy study the attitudes of people in Quebec towards philanthropy. What they found in 1993 was that, even with the economic downturn, nearly three out of four individuals made charitable contributions, and more people than not had increased their giving during the recession. Most made modest contributions, however, and did not ask for receipts for tax purposes. Their contributions were generally spontaneous; less than 15 per cent of those surveyed actually sat down and planned how they would give in a particular year. Those who gave to charitable organizations also tended to be volunteers and believed that donating money was a good way to get involved in their community. Among those surveyed, nearly two-thirds of those who gave, gave to fight diseases.[51] The study clearly revealed that foundations such as the SSBFF had a role to play, particularly given the political climate of austerity. In December 1993, Hobday gave his assessment of the situation. With increased government funding unlikely, and with the business sector "unable or unwilling to play a larger role," and with individuals increasingly overburdened by taxes, only foundations had the discretionary money to give to good causes. Hobday asserted that "a complete transformation" in funding for the non-profit sector was underway. "Canadian foundations, while generally ill-equipped to take on a larger funding role, *can* use their special status to demonstrate leadership."[52]

CONCLUSION

The SSBFF's ability to demonstrate leadership was substantial in 1993, but not unlimited. With its capital fund now at about $59 million, the foundation anticipated that it could invest about $4.8 million a year in programs and operations. Of this $4.8 million, $2.675 million was committed annually to the Combined Jewish Appeal and approximately $818,000 was spent to cover operating expenses, the investment managers, and the shared costs with Seagram Donations. This left $1.2 million to be invested in the foundation's other programs.[53] With this sum, the SSBFF sought to effect change by supporting the projects it had helped launch over the course of the 1980s and which had been given new focus and direction thanks to the visioning workshops. This support was not unconditional, however. Part of the challenge was to ensure that these projects did not become dependent on the foundation. The question of when to nurture a promising organization, when to hold the course, and when to pull the plug, became a great preoccupation for the board over the next decade.

Saidye's eighty-fifth birthday, 1982. Standing, left to right: Samuel Bronfman II,
Matthew Bronfman, Charles de Gunzburg, Jean de Gunzburg, Charles R. Bronfman,
Stephen R. Bronfman, Edgar Bronfman Jr, Alain de Gunzburg. Sitting, left to right:
Andrea Bronfman (Charles' second wife), Ellen Bronfman, Edgar M. Bronfman,
Saidye Bronfman, Minda de Gunzburg, Holly Bronfman (SSBFF).

Maquette of the Saidye Bronfman Centre
(Jewish Public Library: photo by Bomac Photo Studio).

Interior space, Saidye Bronfman Centre. The low-rise
apartment buildings visible out the window suggest how
striking the new arts complex originally appeared in its
suburban setting (Jewish Public Library).

Theatre rehearsal, Saidye Bronfman Centre, 1969. The modernist structure with glass-wall windows was an unorthodox arrangement for a theatre, which usually involves a stage that can be "blacked out" when required. Another unorthodox arrangement was that the audience entered the theatre from the side, near the stage (Jewish Public Library: photo by Dick Nickle).

Saidye Bronfman Centre: gallery space (Canadian Jewish Congress
Charities Committee National Archives).

Samuel and Saidye Bronfman at the dedication of the Saidye Bronfman
Centre, September 1967. The speaker is Dr A.W. Trueman, former
president of the universities of New Brunswick and Manitoba. Next
to Saidye is YM-YWHA president Samuel Godinsky (Canadian Jewish
Congress Charities Committee National Archives).

Painting class, Saidye Bronfman Centre (Jewish Public
Library: photo by Jack Markow & Co. Ltd.).

Saidye visits the Saidye, September 1992. Left to right:
Dora Wasserman, John Hobday, Saidye Bronfman,
Alain Dancyger (photo courtesy of John Hobday).

McGill-Children's Hospital Learning
Centre brochure (SSBFF files).

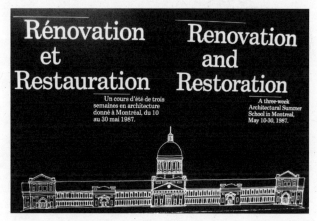

Heritage Montreal brochure for the summer course in
heritage conservation, 1985 (SSBFF Files).

Canadian Centre for Architecture with the Shaughnessy House, Montreal
(Canadian Centre for Architecture).

Brochure for Urban Issues (SSBFF files).

Urban Issues college of collaborators meeting, Montreal, 1993. John Hobday and Phyllis Lambert are at the lower right; Dinu Bumbaru is in the centre (SSBFF collection).

Thirtieth Saidye Bronfman Award presentation, Canadian Museum of Civilization, Gatineau, October 2006. Stephen Bronfman is at the podium (SSBFF collection).

Thirtieth Saidye Bronfman Award gala, October 2006.
Left to right: Nancy Rosenfeld, Stephen, Charles, Phyllis,
Governor General Michaëlle Jean (SSBFF collection).

Thirtieth Saidye Bronfman Award gala, October 2006. Left to right: award winner Peter Powning, museum Director Victor Rabinovitch, Stephen Bronfman (SSBFF collection).

Jean de Gunzburg (SSBFF collection).

Stephen R. Bronfman (SSBFF collection).

Plum Coulee Agricore Grain Elevator, Plum Coulee. The Saidye Rosner Bronfman Heritage Recreation Park is at rear left (author photo).

Hobday's television interview in front of the Agricore Grain
Elevator, Plum Coulee (photo courtesy of John Hobday).

The Saidye Rosner Bronfman Heritage Recreation Park,
Plum Coulee (author photo).

New Beach, Plum Coulee (author photo).

Unveiling the plaque for the Saidye Rosner Bronfman Heritage Recreation Park, Plum Coulee, August 2008. Left to right: Phyllis Lambert, Rick Rempel (deputy mayor, Plum Coulee), Heather Ungar (president, Plum Coulee Community Foundation) (SSBFF collection).

Plum Coulee: plaque listing the names of local contributors to the heritage restoration project (SSBFF collection].

Phyllis Lambert at the dedication of the Saidye Rosner Bronfman Heritage Recreation Park, Plum Coulee, August 2008 (SSBFF collection).

THE SAIDYE BRONFMAN CENTRE

The art and theatre complex that the Bronfman children founded in their mother's name had never been intended as a SSBFF project, but it remained a preoccupation for the foundation throughout its existence. Indeed, at the beginning it was financed by the family as a special donation to honour Saidye, like the ones made to establish the McGill Faculty of Management and the Canadian Jewish Congress headquarters to honour Sam. However, because of the centre's administrative structure, worked out in connection with the YMHA, and the lack of a permanent endowment, the SSBFF found itself regularly having to make additional financial contributions as well as becoming embroiled in larger operational decisions regarding the Centre's role and vision. The question of when to keep funding a project and when to pull out would be a constant source of concern for the SSBFF, but the Saidye Bronfman Centre proved a challenge of a more painful, and complex, variety.

It also brought heartache. For the Bronfman siblings, naming the centre they founded after Saidye was "a gift to their mother," and one that by all accounts she valued greatly.[1] The centre itself, however, was a gift to the Jewish community, and that community did not always seem to value it. Because the centre bore Saidye's name, the community seemed to expect the family to pay for its upkeep – that is, on the occasions when it noticed that upkeep was needed. Again, because the centre bore Saidye's name, the family did not wish to see it decline and came to its rescue even when a dispassionate observer might well have advised them to pull out. Arguably, when it came to the Saidye Bronfman Centre, the directors of the SSBFF, motivated by sentiment, put aside their usual commitment to fiscal responsibility. At the same time, there was every reason to support the centre, which was for most of its history one of Canada's, and certainly one of Montreal's, leading cultural institutions. Furthermore, it was an institution that for complex reasons most key public and private funding agencies – with the notable exception of the SSBFF, of course – would not support.[2] At no other point in the SSBFF's history – indeed, arguably in the history of any public institution of this importance in Canada – did a project provoke such a sense of obligation, combined with resentment, frustration, and guilt on the founders' part. It was also the project that most profoundly underscored the "family" element within the workings of a family foundation.

ORIGINS

Early in the 1960s, with Saidye Bronfman's seventieth birthday approaching, Minda, Phyllis, Edgar, and Charles began to discuss ways in which they could honour their mother for the work she had done to enhance the community life of Montreal. One of Saidye's strongest commitments for years had been to the "Y" – the Young Men's, and especially the Young Women's (of which she had been the president for many years) Hebrew Association of Montreal. Harvey Golden, the Y's director, suggested that Montreal's Jewish community had very well-established social institutions to care for the poor and the elderly, and even had a good library, but lacked a facility for the arts.[3] Golden himself had been involved in theatre within the Y movement, and felt that the Montreal Y should provide a permanent home for the arts as well as for athletics. This idea dovetailed with Phyllis's own conviction, articulated in her master's thesis, that community centres should be designed to bring "jocks and artists together."⁴ Charles was intrigued with Golden's proposal and promoted it within the family as a legacy project for Saidye, who of course had also been a patron of the arts. He suggested that Phyllis should be the one to design the new building, given her interests, her talents, and her particularly close relationship with her mother.⁵

Sam, Saidye, Phyllis, and Charles met with Golden in March 1963 to discuss the arrangements.⁶ The family was prepared to create a major institution to cater to the community's cultural life, providing a theatre, an art gallery, and studios for a fine arts school. It was their intention to fund the construction of the centre, which would be built on land already owned by the Y, adjacent to its main complex on Westbury Avenue in the neighbourhood known as Snowdon. This area was by that time home to most of Montreal's "downtowners," who had been moving there since the war, and so the new arts centre, like the Y itself, would be convenient to the Jewish community. Indeed, the land in question was a corner lot, and the new building would front on Côte-Ste-Catherine Road, a major artery running across the northern part of the city. All aspects of the construction process, including the selection of the architect and the approval of the design, would be overseen by a planning committee including representatives from the family and the Y.

The contractual agreement signed between CEMP and the Y on 10 September 1964, spelled out what each party was expected to contribute to the new Centre.⁷ CEMP would pay the sum required to construct a building that met the approved specifications; the building would be "known in perpetuity as 'The Saidye Bronfman Centre'" and would be referred to as such even within the context of the Y's larger structure. Title to the building would be vested in the Y, which would sign all required contracts relating to the construction. CEMP would pay for any "furniture, fixtures, equipment and accessories" as would be initially required. Once the building was completed and all related expenses paid, however, it would be the Y's responsibility to cover any costs relating to "heating, maintenance, repair, reconstruction, replacement and recon- stitution of the building, taxes, if any, and replacement of the original furniture, fixtures, equipment and accessories ... without any responsi- bility whatsoever to CEMP." Moreover, the Y's responsibility would be applied to "any extensions, additions, or replacements thereto however and whenever made." Unfortunately, it was not then understood by CEMP or the Y that a good part of these functions ought to be covered by an endowment. Knowing that it might take time for the centre to get established, the family did agree that CEMP would provide funds to ensure "adequate programming in its formative years." For a period of six years following the beginning of operations, CEMP would offset any deficits, up to $25,000 in any one year and not to exceed $100,000 over-all. Beyond this period, it was up to the Y to make the centre work.

The agreement also spelled out the governance structure for the centre. Overall management, both structural and cultural, would be placed in the hands of the Y's Metropolitan Board. In this task, the board, which of course had a great many other responsibilities, would be guided by an advisory council for the centre, to be largely appointed by the Y but with some representation from CEMP. Apart from this nominal representation on an advisory council with no decision-making powers, the family had no say in the running of the new centre. This was very much their intention: the centre was meant to be a gift to the community, and the advisory council intended to "provide a link between outstanding citizens of different cultural backgrounds interested in promotion of cultural development within the community." Although the purpose of the centre was to enrich a "cultural, spiritual, intellectual, historical, literary, artistic and dramatic heritage" that was clearly Jewish, it was the family's hope that these activities would foster "mutual respect, understanding and appreciation between the different cultural traditions which make up our great cosmopolitan community."[8] This was a broad vision, but one that was in keeping with the spirit of the times; the centre's construction coincided with that of Expo '67, the world's fair held in Montreal that depicted a cultural mosaic within a single Canadian identity.

Indeed, the building that soon rose on Côte-Ste-Catherine Road seemed to personify the growing emphasis on Canada's multicultural heritage and its enthusiasm for bold new design. Phyllis seized the opportunity presented to her and, fresh from completing her Master of Science in Architecture from the Illinois Institute of Technology, conceived a structure that drew significantly from the seminal work of her mentor, Mies van der Rohe.[9] The centre's clean lines and smooth glass-and-steel walls presented a striking contrast to the suburban duplexes and modest post-war apartment buildings nearby. Architecturally, the building was also a clear departure from the traditional brick of the Y behind it, which now seemed to pale in significance along a side street. Despite this contrast to its surroundings – or perhaps because of it – the centre's overall effect was one of unity; it provided a visual focus for the entire area in keeping with its function as a civic and cultural nucleus. Its uncompromising modernism also linked it to the confidence and optimism of its time.

Montreal had never had a professional English-language theatre company, although until the 1950s theatre-goers were used to seeing major travelling productions from Broadway or London's West End, most of them staged at His Majesty's (Her Majesty's after 1952) Theatre on Guy Street.[10] Such productions grew increasingly expensive to mount and saw falling attendance, especially with the advent of television; symbolically, the year the Bronfman siblings signed the agreement with the Y (1964) was the one that saw the demolition of an outdated Her Majesty's Theatre. The same period had seen a similar decline in community theatre, which had enjoyed a long tradition throughout Canada and especially in Montreal.[11] The founding of the Montreal Repertory Theatre in 1929 had marked the beginning of a golden age of community theatre in the city. Run by Martha Allan, daughter of one of Canada's wealthiest families, who had trained in the United States, the MRT attracted some of Montreal's best talent and produced actors who would gain international fame. The same was true for the McGill Shakespeare Society, the YMHA's Little Theatre, and the Negro Theatre Guild – whose efforts famously won them the top prize at the 1947 Dominion Drama Festival.[12] By the late 1950s, most of these troupes had folded, the talent moving directly to Stratford or Toronto or Broadway.

A theatre space was sorely needed, but Saidye Bronfman's devotion to fine art and crafts made it equally important for the new centre to feature an art school and exhibition space. The school was a natural offshoot of the Y, which had given courses in painting and drawing for many years. Many Jewish artists had received their first exposure to art

at the Y, and then went on to perfect their techniques at the Art Association of Montreal, the city's main art school, and its only one prior to
the opening of the École des Beaux Arts in 1922.[13] The Art Association
and the École trained a number of leading Jewish artists, including Louis
Muhlstock and Ernst Neumann; as the Jewish community moved to the
Snowdon area, however, a younger generation of aspiring painters and
sculptors seemed to feel more comfortable at the Y. The Art Association
also exhibited contemporary artists' works in their annual Spring Exhibition. In the 1940s these shows were dominated by young avant-garde
artists, many of whom were Jewish, but by the more radical 1960s the
avant-garde had left the Art Association (now the Museum of Fine Arts)
for more fashionable private galleries.[14] For its part, the Y had often held
art exhibitions, although the facilities at the new centre came as a welcome improvement over the crowded halls next door.

The Saidye Bronfman Centre for the Arts – or "the Saidye," as it
would be known – opened on 24 September 1967, the year that Canadians celebrated their nation's centenary (and, symbolically, the year of
the last Spring Exhibition at the Museum of Fine Arts). The dedication
address was delivered by Dr A.W. Trueman, former president of the
Universities of New Brunswick and Manitoba as well as former director
of the Canada Council and Chairman of the National Film Board.[15] The
Saidye's launch left no doubt that this was an institution conceived on a
national, even international, scale in the service of Montreal's lovers of
the arts, both within and beyond the Jewish community.

By this time, the advisory council and the Y had put together committees to advance the centre's various departments. The Performing Arts
Committee was first off the mark with a proposal to create a professional theatre company, arguing that "theatre was the dominant physical feature of the facility."[16] Within a year such a company was installed
and moving in a direction that worried the members of the advisory
council, who felt that the space should be available to community theatre and not principally to a professional company.[17] The council (which
at this time rarely included anyone representing the Bronfman family)
was already articulating an ambiguity about who "owned" the Saidye
that would continue to complicate the centre's existence over the following four decades.

From the beginning, the Saidye was anything but a mere showcase for local talent. Its first artistic director was Marion Andre, a Holocaust survivor and playwright who was determined to stage theatre that would have contemporary relevance and put the Saidye on the artistic map. Unfortunately, Andre's four-year tenure at the centre ended in tension. In 1972 the staging he proposed for Robert Shaw's *The Man in the Glass Booth* proved offensive to a group of Holocaust survivors who complained to the Y. Fearing a controversy, the Y then instructed the centre to withdraw the play. Andre was furious at this interference in artistic decisions, and resigned.[18] Quite apart from an example of the sort of clash between artist and managers that never bodes well for a theatrical company, Andre's experience illustrates the increasingly strained relations between the Y and the centre, and the chronic lack of clarity as to who was really in charge of the Saidye.

Over the course of the 1970s the theatre program became less controversial but won critical respect and popular support. Andre's successor, Muriel Gold, selected plays with more general appeal in an effort to maintain high levels of attendance. In this she succeeded, doubling the number of season subscriptions from 2,000 to 4,000 in only one season.[19] Gold also scored a hit by inviting Dora Wasserman's Yiddish Theatre Company to take up permanent residence at the centre. Wasserman, who had studied theatre in Russia in the 1930s and emigrated to Canada after the war, had founded North America's only permanent Yiddish theatre company in the 1950s. A big draw for the Jewish community in Montreal and from further afield, this organization would flourish at the Saidye under Wasserman's direction for another quarter century.[20] The centre's art gallery also won acclaim for its celebration of contemporary artists and the fine arts school proved popular with students from across the city.

Throughout this period the family continued to help maintain the Saidye's financial solvency, but they did so largely through the SSBFF. Saidye herself made additional annual donations to the centre which bore her name, through her own personal foundation, typically in the range of $30,000 but on occasion as much as $70,000.[21] The SSBFF provided yearly grants to offset deficits for the six-year period stipulated in the agreement with the Y, and did so again in 1974. By the following

year, in light of Saidye's generosity and sensing that the centre seemed to
be on sound footing, the directors decided that unless they had funds
available at the end of the season "it will not be necessary to contribute
to the Saidye Bronfman Centre."[22] It seemed the original gift had now
been paid for. Within two years, however, they would once again receive
requests for money to help with the centre's maintenance.[23]

DEPENDENCE

When the Bronfman children first conceived of honouring their mother
with the construction of the Saidye Bronfman Centre, they could hardly
have imagined that they would soon be struggling with the complex
responsibilities and emotions that parents enjoy and endure on the road
to raising their offspring. As is always the case, even if children are raised
to be independent, their actions reflect on their parents, and even if parents wash their hands of responsibility, a sense of expectation remains.
Although the 1964 agreement had been clear that the family's role would
be limited to the original construction and furnishing costs and possible
financial assistance for six years, the Y and the Jewish community knew
that the Bronfman family had resources and a personal connection with
the centre. In many ways this expectation lay at the core of the Saidye's
problem: the Bronfman name had been prominently inscribed in gran-
ite on one of the centre's retaining walls, suggesting that the family could
be relied upon to provide financial help. As a result the Jewish community, and certainly the Y, did not develop a strong sense of responsibility
for their possession.[24]

For their part, the family clearly retained an emotional attachment to
this institution that bore their mother's name – not to mention the name
of the SSBFF's current president. Because they continued to be active
public figures, the Bronfmans were closely identified with the buildings
and organizations named after them in way that the city's earlier, long
deceased patrons and donors – McGill, McCord, Macdonald – were not.
Decisions taken regarding the Saidye had potential consequences for the
family, particularly when it came to the centre's appearance and the qual-

ity of its programs. This concern lay behind the SSBFF's willingness to support the Saidye with residual funds even after the six-year commitment had ended. At the same time, the foundation was growing increasingly disenchanted with the Y, which seemed to be giving the Saidye far less importance than it deserved. Peter Swann also became critical of the Y's top-heavy bureaucratic structure, and on one occasion complained to Charles Bronfman that if much of its management were removed many additional resources could be devoted to the Saidye and other Y programs.[25]

The foundation had reason to resent being asked to continue funding the Saidye. The SSBFF already provided indirect financial support through their substantial annual commitment to the Allied Jewish Community Services (AJCS), which in turn gave funds to the Y, which was supposed to manage the centre. For most of the 1970s the Saidye also received as much as $400,000 annually from the federal and provincial governments, although this amount barely served to underwrite its performing arts programs.[26] Nevertheless, when the Y began to plan an expansion of the centre's exhibition space in the late 1970s, it sought financial assistance from the SSBFF.

The proposed expansion of the gallery was a result of its success attracting high-calibre exhibitions. At the same time, the possibilities for hosting travelling exhibitions were limited by the gallery's size and technical specifications, originally conceived on a modest scale. The SSBFF directors acknowledged that it was "essential to increase and improve the exhibition space in such a way that it meets the requirements of the National Museums," an action that would also enable the centre to qualify for government grants for travelling exhibitions.[27] In order to preserve the spirit of the original design, Phyllis herself drew up plans for a modified gallery. The expansion would take over the section of the building currently occupied by offices, and so new quarters for the Saidye's staff had to be found; Charles Bronfman offered to confront the Y with this situation and attempt to secure some space within the Westbury Avenue building. The long-term solution to the problem of inadequate space was the construction of an annex, but at the moment the board voted to endorse Phyllis's plan and contribute to the cost of the gallery expansion.[28]

The gallery area was enlarged and improved, but no space could be found in the Y building and the Saidye's staff took up temporary accommodation in the centre's basement. The SSBFF gave $80,000 for these renovations in 1979, $25,000 the following year, and for some time after that made annual contributions of $50,000 to support the Saidye's activities.[29] This regular income, along with the Saidye Bronfman Foundation's annual $40,000, meant that the centre did not have to feel quite so dependent on the Y for its operating funds. The result, unfortunately, was to enhance the Y's impression that the Saidye was the wealthy child of the Bronfman family and did not require additional support.[30] When the centre ran into financial difficulties, as multi-use arts complexes almost always do, the Y showed little sympathy. Some observers, such as *The Montreal Gazette*'s theatre critic Marianne Ackerman, attributed the Y's attitude to a scant regard for the arts in general: "Used to dealing with sport and social service events," she wrote, "the central board [took] a dim view of the risk and work involved in making cultural programs a success."[31] The situation worsened in the early 1980s as government budget cuts took their toll. In 1982, when the Saidye's English-language theatre company revealed a projected deficit of $115,000, the Y's board of directors decided to shut down the program.[32]

This unilateral decision was naturally distressing to the SSBFF and seemed to confirm Swann's low opinion of the Y's management. Frustrated by the endless squabbling among the multiple governing bodies, Swann had tended to avoid getting involved in the running of the Saidye and rarely attended meetings of the advisory council on which he had a seat as a representative of the family as per the terms of the 1964 agreement; he advised his successor Hobday to steer clear as well.[33] For his part, Hobday did not consider the Saidye as a specific concern of the SSBFF, making little mention of it in his "Towards Tomorrow" report. Early in 1984, he did accompany Charles and Phyllis to a meeting with Manny Batshaw, a former director of the AJCS and now a trusted advisor to Charles on Jewish community issues, to discuss how to improve the Saidye's situation "which has reached a serious low."[34] Batshaw suggested that the SSBFF commission an independent study of the Saidye to see what could be done to improve its administrative structure.

The study was undertaken by Dr Reynold Levy, the former executive director of the 92nd Street Y in New York City, at a cost of $41,000.[35] Completed in May 1984, Levy's report called for "a radical change" in the Saidye's governance and operations, suggesting that the centre would only raise its profile by increasing the scope and quality of what it offered. According to Levy's vision, the Saidye would not only provide cultural and art programs to the Jewish community but become "a cultural centre for the City of Montreal."[36] The price tag for this change was high, involving considerable renovation as well as the hiring of additional staff for fundraising and marketing: the report proposed an increase in the centre's annual operating budget from the current $790,000 to $1,760,000 by the following year. Most importantly, under the Levy plan, the Saidye would be given independent non-profit status.

The SSBFF realized it would be expected to supply a sizeable portion of the increased costs and decided it would do so only on certain conditions. The directors "would need to be satisfied that there was a new relationship established with the YMHA and the establishment of a new board for the centre with much greater autonomy than in the past. This new board would have clear responsibility for fund raising to ensure that there were adequate funds for an enriched program of activities."[37] They also awaited evidence from the Y of a willingness to collaborate, and from the federal and provincial governments of forthcoming funds.

The Y's collaboration came in the form of a joint committee composed of representatives from both the Y and the advisory council. Although the Y's directors were sceptical that the Saidye could function independently, they understood that the Levy report provided a way forward. Through the late summer and early fall of 1984 the committee "sought a middle road" that would give the Saidye "a degree of autonomy while, at the same time, maintaining the necessary controls of the Association" and, most importantly, keeping the centre firmly within the multiplicity of institutions identified with the Jewish community in Montreal.[38] While still subservient to the Y, the Saidye's board would become the front-line decision-making body for the centre, guided by a president who would serve as its official head. In an effort to bring together a wealth of experience from across the community, the board would comprise what one commentator called "a whopping thirty-eight members."[39] The committee made a point of reserving two seats on this board for Batshaw and Hobday to represent the interests of the Bronfman family. With some misgivings, remembering Swann's warnings, Hobday agreed to attend these meetings in the hope that "the centre will [now] be much more firmly rooted as a community responsibility and ... have a far greater degree of autonomy."[40]

By November the SSBFF was sufficiently impressed with the growing spirit of cooperation for the directors to decide to "contribute towards the start-up costs for the re-vitalization of the centre."[41] This meant that instead of $90,000 (the combined total from the SSBFF and Saidye's foundation) the SSBFF would now give the Saidye an annual grant of $250,000. The necessary capital was made possible thanks to an injection of funds from CEMP; Charles also provided the Saidye with a special grant of $142,000.[42] Conscious that generosity had previously given the wrong impression, the SSBFF put pressure on the Saidye's new board to get serious about its own efforts to raise money: the promised funds came with the expectation that the Saidye would raise at least $150,000 a year on its own.[43]

By this time, the centre had a new slate of staff members in place, beginning with Harry Gulkin, its executive and artistic director. At fifty-eight, Gulkin was a leading figure in the arts. After careers as a merchant seaman, a trade union organizer, and a top aide to grocery magnate Sam Steinberg, Gulkin had turned to filmmaking in the 1970s and produced one of Canada's best-loved movies, *Lies My Father Told Me*, about Jewish life in Montreal during the Great Depression.[44] Looking for a new challenge in the 1980s, Gulkin agreed to lead the Saidye through its transformation. The Saidye's board also hired a director of development, a director of marketing, a director of administration, and an executive assistant – the latter being Gisele Rucker, who would later work for the SSBFF.[45]

Gulkin put together a new mission statement for the Saidye in collaboration with Hobday and an outside consultant. Gulkin's vision was
bold and ambitious, not least in that he attempted to reconcile the ambiguity over whether the Saidye served the Jewish or a wider community.
It was, he argued, "a window into and out of the Jewish community."
Although it presented "the best in Jewish art" and promoted "those
aspects of its program that have a particular relevance for Jews," the
centre clearly had a mandate to expand beyond the community's cultural boundaries.[46] Instead of offering classes in Hebrew language and
in Jewish heritage to Jews, the centre must broaden its focus to appeal
to that segment of the greater public that was interested in Jewish heritage, as well as to what Gulkin referred to as "the 'unaffiliated' Jew."
After the anticipated renovation and expansion of the Saidye, Gulkin
proposed some key changes intended to make the programs more successful: for example, have the art school offer more flexible workshops
rather than courses which followed the academic year.[47] Gulkin also
proposed holding yearly festivals with contributions from each of the
centre's programs: for example, a festival entitled "How Montreal
Jewish Artists Saw the World in the Thirties" would include a thematic
exhibition ("Jewish Painters & Modernity: Montreal 1930–1945") and
a musical revue ("We Beg to Differ") originally produced in 1938 by
Montreal's New Theatre Group. Such ideas promised to put the Saidye
on the artistic and cultural map.[48]

Of course, these plans also depended on having the necessary space
and a sufficient budget. For some time, the foundation held off making
decisions about contributing to the cost of the renovations proposed by
the Levy report, which included building an annex to contain new offices
and a new space for the art studios. Finally, in March 1985, word came
that the federal government would provide $870,000 to the Y for this
purpose.[49] At its June meeting, the foundation agreed to put an additional $550,000 towards the renovations, hoping that the Saidye could
raise a matching amount.[50] Their calculations were based upon a projected overall cost of roughly $1.8 million; unfortunately, by the end of
the year the projections had been revised and costs were now estimated

at $3.4 million. Undaunted, the Saidye's board got to work raising funds through a variety of methods, including a special gala presentation of the film *Shoah* which alone brought in $93,000.[51] The SSBFF directors even considered underwriting a mortgage as a form of guarantee should construction take significantly longer; they wished to reassure the presidents of the Y and the Saidye that the SSBFF was committed to the centre's expansion.[52]

Phyllis recommended that another architect, Peter Lanken, be chosen to design the annex and carry out the renovation work on the theatre and the gallery. Over the latter part of 1985, Lanken's plans were reviewed by a committee consisting of Phyllis, Hobday, and Batshaw, to make sure that what was proposed remained conceptually true to the original design.[53] Phyllis was understandably sensitive to the substantial changes proposed for the theatre and gallery, but Hobday convinced her that this was a time when aesthetics had to be sacrificed for practicality: the theatre had an elegant lobby but it obliged patrons to enter the house from the side, a problem for latecomers wishing to gain their seats unobtrusively; equally, the gallery had striking windows but they let in too much light for certain exhibitions.[54] These were not easy concessions for Phyllis to make, both because the original design had been hers and because it had been conceived as a gift to her mother, but she understood that the Saidye had to adapt to changing needs.[55]

Obtaining planning permission for the annex proved more complicated than expected. The Y objected that the new building would partially obstruct the view from the Y itself, requiring much negotiation between the two parties and with the city's planning department. In the end the city decided that the building's proposed height was not a problem, but that it would have to be situated further away from the Y.[56] This issue was not resolved until the summer of 1986, by which time other problems had raised their heads.

Because of these delays over the annex, the refurbishment of the theatre became the first phase of the project. By the spring of 1986, Jane Needles, director of administration at the Saidye, sent a very encouraging report to Hobday. "The stairs are installed as are the balconies, and the ventilation and mechanical areas are almost complete as well. The next step is to install the electrical, replace the ceiling, hang the lighting grid and wire the stage lighting system." She assured him that the summer would see the construction of the stage floor and the installation of seating and carpeting.[57] The seating was the most visible change to the whole renovation of the theatre, increasing its capacity from 270 to 390. Based on this optimistic report, the SSBFF board authorized the release of the second half of the $550,000 grant, which was dependent upon good results.[58]

Needles predicted that the theatre would be "back in our hands" by September, and Gulkin issued a press release announcing an exciting upcoming season. The expanded facility, he told one reporter, symbolized "a turnaround for Anglophone culture." Given the lack of facilities for English-language theatre, he hoped the Saidye would "have a kind of catalyzing effect" on the community and would serve as "the creative laboratory for new projects in Montreal." Emphasizing its support for Canadian work, the Saidye's first season in the renovated facility would feature only Canadian plays, several by Montreal writers. The twenty-nine-year-old Yiddish Theatre troupe, a mainstay at the Saidye, also welcomed the expanded space. The season would also feature the Saidye's first dance performance series, chamber music concerts, jazz, films, and lectures.[59] Theatre critic Marianne Ackerman embraced the Saidye's new direction, saying that the entire multi-art season "could establish SBC as a real force in the Anglo arts community and turn the complex into an important civic cultural address on the European model."[60]

The theatre was not entirely finished by the autumn, but the work that remained did not impede the launching of the season. Gulkin's grand words, however, belied an overall lack of preparedness. A successful theatre season depended on advance subscribers, but the task of selling subscriptions had somehow fallen by the wayside. Part of the problem was that the staff was still working in highly inadequate conditions in the basement of a building that was undergoing major renovations. It was Rucker who, at the last minute, took on the job of advertising subscriptions, and built up a database with over a thousand names; unfortunately, it was too late to help the first season.[61] The new in-house, English-language company, Encore Theatre, was obliged to fold, and this served to discourage the government funding agencies from continuing their support for the Saidye's program of renewal.[62] Renovations to the gallery were far from completed by the end of 1986, and there were currently no funds with which to begin construction of the annex. Batshaw's assessment of the situation was that the renovations had begun prematurely; the Saidye had imprudently moved ahead on the basis of "enthusiastic reports" about prospective donors rather than firm commitments.[63]

At their December 1986 meeting the SSBFF expressed deep concern over the situation at the Saidye. Hobday underscored the seriousness of the Canada Council and the Quebec Ministry of Culture and Communication having pulled out of the funding process. What was needed, he suggested, was to restore general confidence in the Saidye, and the key to doing this was to put together a board of directors with proven experience as fundraisers, "people who can plan and lead as well as give and get." The board's current chair, Ed Spiegel, had shown "effective, bridge-building leadership," but had not managed to recruit sufficiently high-profile board members. It was Hobday's hope that an improvement in the Saidye's financial situation would convince such people to take part.[64] Spiegel had requested an immediate injection of $240,413 to complete the work on the theatre and gallery, and added that construction of the annex could not be delayed for long given the complaints from the staff and art school. The only solution would be for the SSBFF to provide $1.8 million to fund the annex, or else make a mortgage available which the Saidye could pay off when it had acquired additional sponsors. Significantly, he added, three potential sponsors had expressed some interest in having the theatre, gallery, and fine arts building named after them, but had since declined, feeling that "their own names cannot compete and will be submerged" by "the overpowering name of Saidye Bronfman."[65]

Unwilling to make a multi-million dollar investment in the annex, the foundation did release the $240,413 for work to continue on the theatre and gallery. After a disastrous season, the fate of the theatre remained uncertain, but the gallery was refurbished in time to mount the anticipated "Jewish Painters and Modernity" exhibition which capped the much-touted 1986–87 "Arts Showcase."[66] The exhibition highlighted the work of many artists whose vision was a clear departure from that of previous generations; instead of painting the Canadian wilderness, they focused on urban poverty and unemployment during the Depression and on industrialization and the war effort in the early 1940s. After several weeks at the Saidye, the exhibition moved to Sherbrooke and Joliette (Quebec), Toronto and Saskatoon, finishing in Edmonton in the spring of 1989.

Gulkin's resignation in the summer of 1987 added to the climate of uncertainty at the Saidye. Hobday attempted to help work out a solution to the mounting crisis, and was often called in four times a week to help resolve disputes within the Saidye board or negotiate with the Y. Phyllis recalled him taking this work very much to heart, reporting on the frequent crisis meetings at the Saidye with his head in his hands and groaning in despair: "Oh, Phyllis, oh." Finally Hobday decided that the time had come to be blunt with the family. He went to Charles and said: "You've got two choices. Either you take Mother's name off the door, or you fix it. It boils down to that."[67]

After much soul-searching, Charles decided to fix the Saidye, but not to burden the SSBFF with a request for a major commitment of funds. He hired the consulting firm of Richter Usher and Vineberg to conduct a detailed study of the operations at the Saidye, and based on their assessment had an agreement drawn up whereby nearly $6 million would be transferred to the centre.[68] This agreement stipulated that $2,225,000 would pay for the completion of the restoration at the centre and the construction of the Fine Arts and Administration Building. Another $250,000 would cover transition costs. The remaining $3.5 million would go towards establishing a permanent endowment fund for the Saidye, to ensure "that the SBC's annual financial requirements will be fully satisfied without further funding by the undersigned" – meaning that the family would not be expected to bail the centre out again. Significantly, the endowment would be entrusted with, and be the responsibility of, the AJCS, rather than the Y; the hope was that this arrangement would give the Jewish community a sense of ownership. For its part, the AJCS had to honour its commitment to the Y, as well as acknowledge that "Jewish Cultural programming is important to maintain the quality of life of the Montreal Jewish Community" and that "the SBC is a significant community resource for the provision of cultural services." In turn, the Y would maintain the centre, and ensure that its programs enhance "the opportunities for the Jewish community to appreciate its cultural, spiritual, intellectual, historical, literary, artistic and dramatic heritage and creativity."[69]

The agreement was signed between Charles and Hobday (representing the SSBFF and the Saidye Bronfman Foundation, of which he was also executive director) and representatives of the Y and AJCS on 23 June 1987. Soon after, work began on the annex and continued throughout most of the following year. A dedication ceremony took place in January 1989 at which the six new fine arts studios and a floor of modern offices were unveiled. That year, the School of Fine Arts offered 115 courses over three semesters, and the new public affairs programs drew thousands of Montrealers to the Saidye to attend lectures on focal issues and a special panel on the environment. Dora Wasserman's Yiddish Theatre continued to flourish, and a new director of performing arts, Andrés Hausmann, was appointed to develop the English theatre season.[70] The crisis appeared to be over.

OWNERSHIP

Much of the credit for putting the Saidye back on track in the late 1980s and early 90s belonged to Cecil Rabinovitch, who became executive director in May 1988. Hobday and the SSBFF directors knew of Rabinovitch through her husband, Robert, who was the foundation board's treasurer and a financial advisor at Claridge as well as a former senior public servant with much experience in the field of communications. Cecil Rabinovitch was, in her own right, a promoter of the arts, with twenty years' experience as a public servant with a focus on culture, as well as an officer of the Canada Council.[71] As such she was a logical choice to run the Saidye at a time when it had to raise its profile within the corporate world to maximize its fundraising potential. Hobday also recognized Rabinovitch as "fiercely determined, very well organized," and a "straight shooter" at a time when the Saidye's governance structure was characterized by rivalry and suspicion.[72]

Rabinovitch applied herself at once to the Saidye's two key challenges, which were interrelated: how to raise revenue from within the community, and how to give the community a sense that the centre was theirs and not simply the Bronfmans'. She introduced the notion of "Friends of the Saidye" which allowed an individual to become a member of the institution for $150. While not a huge source of income, the "Friends" campaign did develop a base of support which could then be tapped for sponsorship and fundraising.[73] Gradually, more high-profile people from across the community agreed to sit on the Saidye's board, and this made it all the easier to create publicity for shows and events. During this period the family and the SSBFF remained at arm's length from the Saidye's operations, not wanting to appear to be interfering – nor for that matter particularly wanting to interfere. By 1991, however, Stephen began to show a particular interest in the Saidye and it was decided that he would take a seat on its board. To Hobday, this was a sensible move: "Our strategy ... to try to distance the family from the SBC, in order to send a signal that the community should start to claim 'ownership', may have been interpreted as indifference," he wrote to Charles. "This can be overcome if Stephen is able to play a more active high profile role."[74]

Cecil Rabinovitch was certainly keen to have Stephen on the board, and spoke to him about intervening with the rest of the family to get them to make additional gifts to the Saidye.[75] Aware that interest rates had been steadily falling while the funding from the Y had been frozen at an annual $115,000 since the mid-1980s, Rabinovitch anticipated that they would soon have to begin eating into the endowment in order to maintain the full slate of programs offered in recent years. The Saidye's twenty-fifth anniversary in 1992 seemed the perfect occasion to launch a large-scale fundraising campaign as part of a year-round celebration; she targeted $4 million in sponsorship, the bulk of which would come from finding patrons for the theatre, gallery, and arts studio willing to have these institutions named after them under the umbrella of the Saidye Bronfman Centre. In November 1991 she met with Charles and his wife, Andrea, to explain the financial situation and propose that the family make a further substantial gift to honour Saidye on the occasion of her ninety-fifth year.[76]

This issue was brought up at the SSBFF board meeting held a few days later, and led to a long discussion of the relationships between the various institutions concerned with the Saidye, and even of the future of Montreal's Jewish community.[77] A decision about another major gift was of course up to the family, but the foundation agreed to commit $30,000 towards the twenty-fifth anniversary special programming. Stephen and Robert Rabinovitch offered to approach the Federation CJA (as the AJCS was now called) regarding an increase of funding to the Y. At a meeting in April 1992 with the president, Harvey Wolfe, they convinced him to increase the Y's allocation so that it could, in turn, increase the Saidye's program budget from $115,000 to $150,000 annually. As a mark of improving relations, Wolfe also agreed that a representative from the Saidye should sit ex officio on both the Federation's board and the Y's executive committee.[78]

The Saidye's anniversary celebrations began in February with a fundraising gala, and special activities were held throughout the centre over the following months, but the culmination of the festivities was a special exhibition featuring the Claridge art collection, its grand opening coinciding with the Saidye's actual anniversary in September.[79] Bronfman family members attended various events throughout the year, but Hobday realized that the lady in whose name everything took place was conspicuous by her absence. At ninety-five, Saidye was alert but physically fragile and confined to her house on Belvedere Road, attended night and day by resident nurses who Hobday described as "fiercely protective." Clearly Saidye could not attend an event, even were the nurses to permit it, but Hobday knew that a visit to the centre would mean a great deal to her and to the staff who worked very hard with only the vaguest sense of who she was. Despite considerable misgivings, the nurses agreed to let Saidye have an afternoon out. She was driven down the hill, helped into a wheelchair, and given a tour of the centre that bore her name. Impressed with the structural changes of the past decade and the excitement surrounding the special exhibitions, Saidye was particularly delighted to meet and chat with all the current staff members, who were visibly moved by the encounter. The nurses feared the experience had been "so exhausting" for Saidye; Hobday concurred, but knew that "what she did that afternoon touched a lot of lives."[80]

The anniversary year was an overall success and clearly raised the Saidye's profile, but the expected revenue from sponsorship did not materialize. Rabinovitch acknowledged the need for a more systematic approach to marketing, communication, and fundraising, and drew up a proposal for the SSBFF to consider. The directors were impressed with the detail in the proposal, which outlined what would be achieved in each of the next five years and how results would be evaluated. Rabinovitch's idea was that the foundation would provide $150,000 for years 1 and 2, which would cover an assistant director's salary, consultants' work, and a full communications and publicity strategy; year 3 would cost $100,000 and the last two $50,000 each, the gradual scaling back reflecting a diminishing need for additional income when the earlier investments began to bear fruit. The directors could see that Rabinovitch's proposal addressed crucial strategic needs and represented a worthwhile investment; they authorized the allocation of $500,000 for the implementation of what was in effect a five-year plan.[81]

In the first year of the new Marketing, Communications, and Fundraising Strategy, Rabinovitch hired a consultant from Saine Marketing to advise her how best to spend the money directed at publicity. Accordingly, $5,000 of the budget went to promote the gallery and its exhibitions; $10,000 went to advertise the School of Fine Arts, especially within the city's francophone community, which was as yet an untapped source of potential students; $25,000 increased awareness of the theatre, both the English and Yiddish programs. Saine Marketing also felt that the Saidye needed to direct much more energy into engaging the youth of the community in the arts; $10,000 was spent to this end. In addition to a publicity consultant, Rabinovitch hired an assistant director, Alain Dancyger, who sought out government funding contacts, and a director of Marketing and Development, Derek Jessop. In the spring of 1993, Rabinovitch reported on a varied and profitable year in all sectors within the Saidye, and concluded that "the SSBFF grant has given the centre a real lift!"[82] A final recommendation from Saine Marketing was that the Saidye's name be officially changed to 'The Saidye Bronfman Centre for the Arts' to emphasize its function within the community rather than the family name.[83]

The first year was in fact so successful that it generated a surplus. Although good news, this development provoked unexpected antagonism between the Saidye and the Y. According to standard practice in the Y, surpluses in the operating divisions were returned to the central organization to help balance the budget. Understandably, the Saidye objected to having to surrender the money, on two counts: that it was desperately needed by the centre as a cushion for any less fortunate years to come, and that the money had specifically been given to the Saidye as a grant from the SSBFF and could not really be claimed by the Y. Reluctantly, the Y's board agreed not to pursue the matter: "We feel that an exception is to be made for the Saidye Bronfman Centre," wrote Y president Barry Silverman, "given that it would not seem fair or financially prudent to take away the end profits of a significant investment on behalf of the [SSBFF] towards future development of the centre."[84] It was clear, however, that the Y felt this arrangement was unfair, and continued to believe there was a special relationship between the centre and the Bronfmans.

Having overseen the Saidye's transition from crisis to stability and then from stability to growth, Cecil Rabinovitch announced her decision to step down as director of the centre in the summer of 1993. Hobday was active in the search for a replacement, and eventually recommended the assistant director Alain Dancyger, who had been well-trained by his former boss.[85] Even so, Stephen and others worried that Dancyger, although talented, might not be ready for the job, an impression that seemed confirmed by the end of Year Two of the Marketing, Communications, and Fundraising Strategy, when it was clear that the Saidye had "been through a rough time."[86] Nevertheless, Hobday felt that Dancyger was new and should be given the benefit of the doubt, especially given how challenging this job undoubtedly was. It did not help that the Y appeared to be going through a rough time of its own: Nancy Rosen-feld, the Y's executive director who had worked hard to build bridges between the two organizations, resigned early in 1994 along with three key board members. It seemed that for all the achievements since the late 1980s the Saidye was not to have an easy ride.[87]

The centre enjoyed a good year, however, and the SSBFF directors felt more optimistic when they met in May 1995. They were even willing to make a special contribution to some renovations at the Saidye, conscious as they did so that more were to come and that they had no real way to ensure that any structural changes would conform to the original design concept.[88] The import of the initial gift took on added significance later that year when Saidye Bronfman died at the age of ninety-eight. As a special acknowledgement of the institution that had borne her name for three decades, her funeral was held in the theatre and adjacent auditoriums at the Saidye Bronfman Centre. Over 2,000 people, including Prime Minister Jean Chrétien, crowded into these spaces to hear tributes to a remarkable lifetime of achievement; these were given by Phyllis, by Minda's son Charles de Gunzburg, and by Charles Bronfman's daughter Ellen Bronfman Hauptman.[89] If the family had been entertaining any doubts that the struggles of the previous thirty years had not been worth it, this was the kind of event to dispel them.

In advance of the funeral, the family set up a Saidye Bronfman Memorial Fund to direct donations into the centre, with the intention of targeting some special project in Saidye's name that would "help the place stay fresh," as Stephen later put it.[90] By the following spring, over $100,000 had been collected. A similar amount was added to the fund when the Saidye decided to devote the proceeds from its 1996 gala fundraiser to this end. What remained of the Saidye Bronfman Foundation was largely rolled into the fund as well. The total sum was invested and the interest used to create a Saidye Rosner Bronfman Youth Institute designed to help develop a youth market for the centre.[91] Ari Cohen, hired as the Institute's director, soon "launched a dynamic program which is helping to draw new audiences (age 15-35) to performances and exhibitions, both at the centre and at other important arts organizations in the Montreal area."[92]

At about the same time, an endowment fund was established in the name of Dora Wasserman to support the Yiddish theatre in anticipation of the upcoming launch of a trilingual publication, "A Hundred Years of Yiddish Theatre in Montreal." This campaign was spearheaded by Manny Batshaw and Alvin and Leanor Segal, two of a newer generation of Montreal philanthropists who were keen to support components of the Saidye Bronfman Centre.[93] This was not a memorial fund: Dora Wasserman, although elderly, was as much of a creative powerhouse as ever: "Impossible, brilliant, implausible," Hobday recalled emphatically, but still "one of those special characters that emerges from time to time." If working with her was not always the smoothest of experiences, Hobday conceded that the Yiddish Theatre was "the heart and the soul and the guts of everything. There was so much spirit in there."[94] Hobday valued the theatre as a unique institution – and an enjoyable one, thanks to the technology of simultaneous translation. Stephen, who had been brought up in Montreal learning at best a few Yiddish slang words, confessed to being surprised at how much he enjoyed listening to the original: "I was having a blast because I knew half the words. I just never knew what they were or what context." As a result, he felt Wasserman's theatre had a real impact on all generations; even the young had "a place to feel like they're at home."[95]

A new generation was also drawn to the Yiddish theatre as Bryna Wasserman, Dora's daughter, took on a larger role, eventually becoming artistic director of the program despite her mother's continuing presence within the centre. Dora Wasserman officially retired in 1998 and was lauded throughout the community. In May, the Académie québecoise du théatre presented her with a lifetime achievement award at their annual Masques award ceremony, and a month later the Saidye itself hosted a fortieth anniversary tribute evening for the Yiddish Theatre, with Wasserman as a guest of honour. In September, a special celebration of the Dora Wasserman Endowment for Jewish Culture was held at the Saidye, on which occasion Leanor and Alvin Segal presented the endowment with $100,000 to bring it up to $1 million. In gratitude, the Saidye's theatre was officially named after them.[96]

The Segals' enthusiasm for the Saidye appeared to have a parallel within the larger community. Just a few years earlier, Dancyger had reported how difficult it was to interest the Jewish community in Yiddish theatre, and by extension other programs offered by the centre: "As you know at the moment culture is low on Federation CJA's list of priorities."[97] After Saidye Bronfman's death, however, Federation CJA announced it was willing to participate in a plan to replenish the centre's main endowment fund, promising an annual injection of between $17,000 and $21,500.[98] As the SSBFF began to frame a renewal of its 1992 five-year grant to the Saidye, it convinced the Federation CJA to add to the centre's main endowment. David Moss, who had replaced Dancyger as the Saidye's director in 1997 when the latter left to head up Les Grands Ballets Canadiens, announced that revenue from the endowment would decrease from $313,000 to $234,000 within two years.[99] After some negotiation, the Federation CJA agreed to increase its allotment to the Y so that an additional $50,000 could go to the centre's operating budget. Although less than he had hoped for, Moss declared that the Federation's commitment "certainly does display good faith on the part of the community."[100]

The SSBFF remained concerned about the centre itself, and especially how to ensure high standards for any renovations. The answer was for the Saidye to establish a Properties Committee, modelled on the similar body at the Y, to oversee any changes to the physical plant. The committee's policies and guidelines were worked out between the centre and the SSBFF and signed early in 1997. Peter Lanken, the architect of the annex and the 1986 renovations, would sit on the committee in an advisory capacity to "ensure the retention of the integrity of the original design of the building." Furthermore, it was understood that the committee "will consult the original architect whenever any proposed work is required involving significant changes in the architecture and aesthetics of the buildings: specifically, changes to lighting systems, ceiling systems, wall configurations, flooring, and fixtures."[101] The "original architect" was, of course, Phyllis, who continued to worry that the Saidye's administration, and in particular the Y to which it was still subordinate, did not respect the building's unique aesthetic quality.[102] When the SSBFF debated what form its ongoing commitment to the Saidye would take, Phyllis felt they should not give in to the understandable temptation to fund programming. It was easier for others to donate to programming, she argued, but that "people do not wish to contribute to maintenance costs."[103] Although it had never promised to do so, it seemed it was the SSBFF's lot to maintain the Saidye.

The SSBFF agreed to continue supporting the Saidye for an additional five-year period to the end of 2002, essentially targeting maintenance. During this time, the centre appeared to flourish. Hobday referred to the 1998-99 season as "the most successful ... ever."[104] In 1999 the centre's main lobby was remodelled in a manner that met with Phyllis's approval.[105] Moss continued to be enthusiastic in his reports, his only caveat being that the budget was always "under a certain amount of pressure" due to the high costs of theatre productions, leaving "little margin for error in the centre's programs."[106] The Saidye suffered financially in the aftermath of the events of 11 September 2001; in order to balance the budget the English theatre program had to be reduced somewhat.[107] In 2002, reminiscent of the decision made three decades earlier to cancel *The Man in the Glass Booth*, the Saidye withdrew its planned production of *A View From the Bridge* in an effort not to cause offence in the emotionally charged climate post-9/11 – although Moss admitted they were also motivated by a desire not to lose money on a controversial play.[108] Such disappointments notwithstanding, the Saidye was clearly in no worse a financial situation than one might expect of an arts centre in difficult times.

Even so, the Saidye hoped that the SSBFF's five-year grant would be renewed; indeed, it hoped for an increase of the maintenance allocation, from $100,000 per year to $150,000.[109] Phyllis was in favour of this; a few years earlier she had expressed surprise that their contribution "did not seem to cover maintenance costs."[110] Now, as the family contemplated winding down the foundation, and planned its long-term budget, Phyllis suggested that the annual grant to the Saidye be gradually increased to $250,000 by 2018.[111] For the next five years, however, the foundation was happy to provide an annual $150,000, directed at maintenance and equipment. At the board meeting held on 23 May 2003, the directors approved the contribution agreement to be signed with the Y, noting particularly the clause that stated: "It is the Y's responsibility which the Y accepts, to maintain the building and equipment of the SBC in a first class condition ... and that the Y will undertake to ensure that all required and preventative maintenance with respect to the building and the equipment will be effected in a timely and workmanlike manner with a view to maintaining the functionality of the building and its equipment at the level for which it was designed."[112]

A few days after the board meeting, Phyllis went to the centre with a friend and toured the building she had designed nearly forty years earlier.[113] She immediately sent an email to the other members of the SSBFF informing them that there was no way the foundation could sign the agreement. "The SBC is at risk," she wrote. "It is a slum. The lower floor is filthy, water damage has occurred here and there, floor tiles are rotting, ceiling tiles have not been replaced, there is not one room that is not thoroughly junked up ... Although the beautiful 'bones' are still there, at the rate of deterioration it will soon be irreparable and the building trashed. A contract to maintain the building in first class condition is a joke." Her assessment of the cause of the problem summed up the difficulties experienced by the family since the Saidye's birth: "I can only assume that those who protect our built heritage would have protested its condition, had they not assumed that I was protecting it." She called for a meeting with Stephen, Leo Kolber, and Robert Rabinovitch to evaluate the situation and decided what could be done. Although she confessed to having despaired at first, Phyllis announced she was ready to take the active role in the Saidye's physical fabric that she had refrained from for so long in an effort to give the community a sense of ownership. "The SBC is the only testimony to Saidye in Montreal," she concluded. "We must find a way of making the testimony endure honorably."[114]

It was Gisele Rucker's view that the SSBFF had in recent years developed a kind of blind faith that all was well at the Saidye, having lived so long with frustration.[115] Certainly they had never wanted to micromanage the centre or become involved in its day-to-day operations. At any rate, whether or not the SSBFF should have seen these troubles coming was now a moot point; there was a great deal of work to be done if the Saidye was ever to regain its former glory. The family hired architect Vianney Bélanger of the firm COPRIM to inspect the centre and make recommendations. His report, submitted in November 2003, was not encouraging: not only was the original building's condition poor, but the annex was in danger of early degeneration as much of it had been used for storage. A substantial injection of money was needed, not merely for physical repairs but also to develop the administrative and managerial skills to ensure against a repetition of such neglect.[116] In reviewing the report, Phyllis echoed Hobday's previous advice to Charles: either the family should pay or remove Saidye's name from where it had been inscribed. After much discussion it was agreed that, for the time being, the foundation would fund a further study to see just how much it would cost to restore the centre.[117]

A key problem was a lack of leadership at the Saidye. David Moss had resigned the previous spring to take up the position of executive director of l'Opéra de Montréal, and it was several months before a replacement was found. Moss's successor lasted only a few months, and the Saidye's board decided not to replace him; instead, it would "engage a consultant to help with the reorientation of its operations." In the meantime, the centre would be administered by the Y's executive director Linda Kislowicz.[118] By June 2004, Jean de Gunzburg predicted that if the Saidye did not acquire proper leadership soon, it would be "dead in the water."[119]

Bélanger's report had put a price tag of $400,000 on what it would take to bring the centre architecturally up to code as well as professional and consulting costs for long-term planning. On top of that, the Saidye needed $250,000 to pay off its current deficit. The SSBFF directors gave the situation much thought and decided: "No." "Not a cent," was how Charles put it.[120] The family continued to care deeply about the fate of the Saidye, but with no one at the helm and a long history of disappointment, they were no longer willing to come to its rescue.

Alvin and Leanor Segal did come to its rescue. Having agreed to sit on a task force with representation from the Saidye, the Federation CJA, the Y, and the SSBFF, the Segals came forward with the required $250,000 to stabilize the 2004-05 budget and promised to offset any losses incurred by the theatre over the following two years.[121] Even so, no work was carried out on the centre until the spring of 2005 when the annex roof started to leak and needed emergency attention; Bélanger undertook the necessary repairs.[122] No executive director was hired and the Saidye continued to be run by Kislowicz. The task force did commission consultants Gail Lord and Associates to undertake a strategic planning process. To represent the Bronfman family interests in this process, Charles asked John Hobday to come out of retirement, which he did early in 2006. The Y management then asked Hobday to become interim executive director, hoping that at last the situation could be resolved. This was a role he took on with understandable misgiving, but also with some confidence that there were not many who could pretend to have the necessary experience.[123]

Hobday, the consultants, and members of the task force got to work over the latter part of 2006 and worked out a plan to breathe new life into the centre. The Bronfman family collaborated closely with the Segals throughout this process, sensing a solution was in sight. Although the Saidye continued to produce successful plays, mount innovative exhibitions, and attract students to the fine arts school, there was a consensus that the centre's focus had to be narrowed. The Segals were prepared to invest up to $20 million or more in the centre's "programmatic and physical renewal," but preferred to concentrate on the theatre they were already supporting.[124] This meant that the art school and the gallery would close. In their place would appear a multi-purpose space available for presenting lectures or films, an academy of performing arts, and a second stage to give separate accommodation for the English and Yiddish theatre programs.[125] When news of these changes began to leak, many in the community protested that the gallery and art school did not deserve to disappear; others, however, recognized that to be reborn on very different terms was perhaps the only way for the centre to survive.[126]

In many ways the most significant change of all would be the separation of the centre from the Y's control and its establishment at long last as an independent institution. The Bronfmans could hardly object to this

arrangement given their long frustration with the Y, although of course
the intention had originally been to honour the organization that Saidye
had supported throughout her life. Overall, the family were pleased that
centre they had kept alive for so long would have another chance at success.[127] When asked if they would consider making a special donation or
investment in the new centre, however, the extended family politely
refused.[128] Even so, the centre had been saved and Saidye's name did not
have to be removed. By way of a curious but reverent compromise, the
institution's new title would be "The Segal Centre for Performing Arts
at the Saidye."

CONCLUSION

The question remains whether the SSBFF would have given so much time
and money to the Saidye over the years had the centre not borne the
name that it did. Clearly, the Saidye Bronfman Centre cannot be evaluated the same way as other funding programs, for it was intended essentially as a one-time gift that would always be part of the Y. Furthermore,
although the success of its programs depended on its having sufficient
operating funds, the needs of a theatre company, a gallery, and an art
school are quite different from those of a network or advocacy group.
Even so, the level of repeated funding and the many large grants given
by the Bronfmans to the Saidye made the so-called "gift to their mother"
a very expensive gift indeed. It would be far too simple, however, to
argue that the Saidye would never have survived had the Bronfmans not
been there to keep it going. The thousand natural shocks that arts organizations are heir to notwithstanding, the Saidye clearly suffered from a
too-complex chain of command and too many involved parties, each of
whom had specific and conflicting expectations of the others. Had the
Bronfmans and the SSBFF not been around to provide emergency funding, it is likely that these forces would have continued to cross swords
and the Saidye would have suffered. At the same time, it is possible that
without the reliance on the Bronfmans other forces within the community might have been marshalled earlier. This, however, would be to

blame the Bronfmans for having been around and for caring about the centre. From the perspective of philanthropy, the story of the Saidye Bronfman Centre is a fascinating example of how an act of great generosity, presented in the form of a legacy project, can result in enormous headaches and heartaches for the donor over a protracted length of time.

Even so, for all the headache and heartache, no one connected with the SSBFF had any regrets about having supported the Saidye for so long, nor doubts that it had achieved great things. "It was a hell of a gift, and I'm very happy we did it," Charles declared, and Phyllis concurred: "It's been very important to the cultural life of Montreal, not just the Jewish community." [129] Stephen echoed Phyllis's belief that the centre did a great service for "Jews and non-Jews alike. It's a wonderful arts centre, but it's a battle, and it always is ... a struggle, to keep polished, to keep the programs fresh, to keep money coming." When asked what he had learned from his own involvement with the Saidye, Stephen replied simply: "I don't ever want to have my name on a building." [130]

SEVEN

LEARNING DISABILITIES

At the board's seminal May 1973 meeting Charles brought up the issue of children with learning disabilities, arguing that it was an area the foundation should consider funding. He noted that in October 1971 the Quebec Association for Children with Learning Disabilities had asked Seagram for a grant of $40,000 over three years to finance a number of projects, and had been turned down.[1] The following month, Alan Edwards, head of the McGill Learning Centre's joint management committee, had written to Charles regarding efforts to raise money for the centre.[2] Charles had met with Edwards early in 1972 and had agreed to bring the matter up with the SSBFF, which he did the following winter in a memo to Peter Swann. Charles reported that through his work with AJCS and his social contacts he had become aware that "one of the grave problems that exists in Montreal is that of children with learning disabilities."[3]

From this observation developed one of the SSBFF's main funding programs, one of four that the board had identified and agreed upon by the end of 1973. Unlike the SSBFF's arts and heritage programs, however, Learning Disabilities took some time to get off the ground, despite the apparent urgency of the matter and despite the presence of organizations ready and willing to tackle the problem. Part of the difficulty may have been that research on learning disabilities was already being carried out at hospitals and university psychology departments, and the SSBFF hoped to be able to do more than simply fund continuing research, important though that was. They preferred to develop a community group, or find one in need of assistance, that would play a role in the delivery of services or in the dissemination of information.

In time, the foundation discovered suitable candidates for its program, and scored a number of modest successes. One of these client organizations was the Children's Learning Centre at McGill University which, in addition to conducting research, provided services to the community and worked with school boards to identify and help children at risk. The SSBFF's other main client within this program, the Learning Disability Association of Canada, would host one of the SSBFF-funded visioning workshops in 1990. The association would also prove successful enough for the foundation to withdraw its funding, confident that the organization would continue to thrive on its own. Although it was not perhaps as ambitious as some of the other programs, Learning Disabilities represents a sterling example of the SSBFF making an impact without its clients becoming dependent on it for core funding.

THE CHILDREN'S LEARNING CENTRE

As Swann tested various program options during his travels in 1973, he confirmed the need for resources to help the learning disabled and their families. Since the early 1960s parents and researchers had begun to realize that many of the learning problems children experienced were not due to their being lazy or stupid or to poor parenting or poor teaching, but rather resulted from dysfunction of the central nervous system, often caused before and during birth. In addition to finding medical solutions to such conditions, much attention needed to be given to relieving children of the social stigma associated with having these sorts of difficulties. Low self-esteem and poor understanding of the situation exacerbated a child's chances of coping with a disability, as did society's obsession with applying standardized tests to determine intelligence and aptitude.[4] Swann sensed that the time was ripe for investment in a field that seemed poised to move in innovative directions.

Swann suggested that the foundation work with Dr Samuel Rabinovitch at McGill University, who was generally considered Canada's leading researcher into children's learning disabilities and a believer in the importance of being sensitive to the needs and feelings of children.[5] His work at the Learning Centre was regarded by many as a pioneering holistic approach, one that linked intervention to children's specific abilities rather than apply standardized treatments.[6] Rabinovitch and others had established the Learning Centre in 1959 at the dawn of public awareness of learning disabilities. The rationale for its creation was a sense that medical professionals had insufficient knowledge of the causes of such problems to prescribe proper treatment.[7] The Learning Centre was administered by a joint management committee with representatives from the Montreal Children's Hospital and McGill. It worked with the hospital and with the Protestant School Board of Greater Montreal, bringing together experts in child psychology and neuropsychology, special education teachers, social workers, speech therapists, and art therapists to create a professional staff and a focused environment in which children diagnosed with learning disabilities could master crucial skills. In the process, research could be made in identifying and diagnosing disabilities, and these findings were transmitted with the help of presentations and workshops to wide audiences.[8]

In order to set the groundwork for creating an effective funding program, Swann searched for a project idea that was both manageable and indicative of the scope of the problem. Rabinovitch proposed carrying out a needs assessment of the Atlantic Provinces, an area where learning disabilities had received less attention than in the urban areas of central Canada. The report generated by this assessment "would be of great value to other provinces," Swann concluded, and would suggest appropriate paths for expansion of the foundation's efforts.[9] The SSBFF decided to make a three-year investment of $50,000 in Rabinovitch's work, half payable in 1974, $15,000 the following year, and $10,000 in 1976.[10] Rabinovitch's premature death in 1977 presented a considerable setback for the project. Although the Atlantic Provinces study suggested that an enormous amount of work had to be done across the country to provide children with adequate help, the SSBFF directors concluded that the best thing they could do was to help advance the research being done at McGill. By making a five-year pledge to contribute a total of $250,000 to the Samuel Rabinovitch Memorial Fund, the foundation provided direct funding to the McGill University Children's Learning Centre and allowed it to continue its pioneering work.[11]

John Hobday wrote approvingly of the centre's achievements in his 1983 report to the board, "Towards Tomorrow." He made no specific recommendation that the board continue to fund the centre, preferring to devote the foundation's resources to developing national organizations. The directors were concerned for the Learning Centre's future, however, sensing that despite their investment it was not on solid financial footing. As a result, they authorized a special contribution of $50,000 "to assist with their immediate needs" and to develop "a long-range plan to ensure the Centre's financial stability."[12] Equally important, they argued, was to encourage awareness of other research into learning disabilities and of networks for information and support. The 1984 budget included $10,000 to develop Friends of the Learning Centre, a volunteer organization with the mandate to raise funds and awareness of the centre's work.[13]

The Learning Centre embarked on a five-year program to revitalize its approach, its staff, and its finances, hiring a new director – child psychologist Gerry Taylor – and embarking on a major $5 million capital campaign. The SSBFF continued to provide core funding for three years, hoping the centre would become self-sufficient. By 1986 the last payment had been made and the SSBFF withdrew. Over the course of 1987, however, it became clear that the goals of the capital campaign would not be met, and the foundation felt obliged to make another contribution so the centre would not have to eat into the money raised so far merely to meet operational expenses.[14] Furthermore, the new provincial government had concluded that the centre did not meet the criteria of a public educational establishment and had withdrawn the subsidy it had previously made to the school board to offset the costs of having the centre educate public school children.[15] In January 1988, Taylor announced that the centre could not continue without receiving an additional $400,000 and so would be obliged to radically reduce its clinical services.[16]

While government, university, and school board officials debated the best course of action, the SSBFF decided to intervene once more. In early March the foundation provided a grant – not, significantly, to keep the institution going for a few more months until the next crisis, but to pay for consultants to assess its long-term viability. The study, carried out by Touche Ross, specialist consultants in health care management, found that the problem was largely administrative and recommended a new governance structure, including a new board of directors.[17] In May, weary of the administrative burden that the centre had become, Taylor resigned to take up a university research position in the United States. Hobday joined a search committee to find a director for the new centre, following the Touche Ross recommendation that a new executive position be created. During this time, the centre was administered directly by the Children's Hospital, as a provisional board was not installed until the spring of 1989.[18]

An executive director was hired in January: William J. Smith, an expert in Quebec's education system, both its legal and pedagogical aspects, whose understanding of the local situation gave him an advantage over his American predecessor. Smith and the provisional board worked with the SSBFF and the MCH Foundation to develop an action plan. The plan, promulgated in July 1989 under the title "Learning for Life," called for the Learning Centre to be restructured as an independent organization with strong ties to a wide network of institutions, francophone as well as anglophone. Smith also conducted a needs assessment, which identified opportunities for the Learning Centre to provide contracted services to local school boards for fees that would provide between 25 and 35 per cent of the Centre's annual financial needs.[19] Smith developed a financial management system for the centre, negotiated contracts with school boards, and made contact with French-speaking groups across the province.[20]

As a result of Smith's efforts and Hobday's skills connecting people and resources, the Learning Centre gradually emerged from its crisis. In the summer of 1989, the provincial government decided it would provide the centre with yearly operating grants of $150,000.[21] At the end of year, the centre made a proposal to the SSBFF for assistance on two levels: the creation of a development office for fundraising, and the presence of John Hobday on a critical ad hoc fundraising committee. The foundation approved an immediate grant of $50,000 to this end and a subsequent, similar grant the following spring upon receipt and approval of the Centre's fundraising plan.[22] There was no objection to Hobday sitting on the committee; indeed, when the centre's permanent board was formed in the spring of 1990 Hobday accepted to serve on it as well. His involvement was an effective way to facilitate the centre's transition to independence, and to maintain close links with a key client.[23]

The centre was reborn in the spring of 1990 as Le centre d'apprentissage du Québec / The Learning Centre of Quebec, an incorporated body distinct from McGill and the Children's Hospital but affiliated with both, as it was with Concordia University, l'Université de Montréal, l'Université du Québec à Montréal, and l'Hôpital Sainte-Justine.[24] Its mission incorporated the legacies of the past as well as a vision of the future. It was "devoted to the advancement of knowledge concerning the nature, causes, assessment and remediation of learning disabilities" and to the dissemination of this knowledge to both practitioners and researchers in the field.[25] The new fundraising policy brought in sufficient revenue for the SSBFF not to renew its grant in 1991, although Hobday would continue to monitor the centre's financial health from his position on the board.[26] By the following year, it was felt that the centre was stable enough to no longer require Hobday's direct involvement.

LEARNING DISABILITIES ASSOCIATION OF CANADA

Having begun to develop the Children's Hospital Learning Centre as its major client in the 1970s, the SSBFF continued to seek out worthy recipients of program money. In 1981, it awarded grants to the Centres Offering Independent Lifestyles in Saint John, New Brunswick, to develop a summer project that would provide psycho-educational diag-

noses for children experiencing learning problems. The foundation also
extended assistance to Children at Risk, an Ottawa-based group operating a preschool centre for children suffering from autism and similar
communication-disabling conditions.[27] Grants were given to other
university-based research projects into a variety of disabilities, from
hearing impairment to autism to aphasia.[28] All of these donations
represented a way for the foundation to make a difference with a sector
of the population that seemed neglected by other funders and public
programs. They also gave the foundation a way to learn more about the
needs of people with learning disabilities.

In reviewing this program's achievements at the beginning of his
tenure as executive director of the SSBFF, Hobday acknowledged the
difficulty of directly meeting the needs of local organizations, whose
numbers were rapidly increasing. The variety of projects and participants
made it difficult to coordinate and supervise the overall implementation
of grant money. In the Learning Disabilities program, as it would do
later with its program for the elderly, the foundation had chosen a
decidedly grassroots approach that required considerable staff time and
effort. Again Hobday sought additional help and again he turned to Ivan
Hale, whom he hired to work with the various groups involved in the
learning disabilities program.[29] Hale's presence made it possible to
undertake a more detailed analysis of requests for funding and to take a
more hands-on approach to the development of major projects.

Having begun to make contact with provincial and national organizations for children with learning disabilities, Hobday suggested that
this be the way to proceed, rather than spread the foundation's resources
too thin. Of the program's $115,000 budget, he recommended using
$35,000 to fund provincial groups and another $35,000 to provide
core funding for the Canadian Association for Children with Learning
Disabilities (CACLD).[30]

The association had been established in 1963 to provide a voice for
people with learning disabilities at the national level and to raise awareness of the nature and impact of such disabilities. It had a board of
directors representing Canada's provinces and territories and a national
headquarters in Ottawa.[31] As a result of the investment by the SSBFF, the

association was able to improve the capacity of its member groups to raise awareness of learning disabilities and of their own efforts; such publicity took the form of radio and television commercials, brochures, posters, and displays.[32] With SSBFF funding, the association held a "chapter development workshop" in Charlottetown for representatives of the four Atlantic provinces to learn how to advance their local groups. In Quebec, where the provincial association was already well-established, funds from the SSBFF helped pay for a newsletter for parents and association members.[33] SSBFF funding also "lent weighty credibility to CACLD in the eyes of its affiliates" and "enhanced its position vis-à-vis the Federal Government ... in obtaining project funding."[34]

In the spring of 1984, the association approached the SSBFF with a proposal entitled Positive Options, Productive Choices which sought to reduce the number of young people with learning disabilities whose behaviour led to incarceration, an experience all the more debilitating for individuals already suffering from low self-esteem and poor social skills. The project coordinator would work with judges and lawyers to help them recognize the problems associated with learning disabilities and adjust their sentences accordingly so that young offenders could be more easily rehabilitated. The foundation was pleased to contribute $30,000 to this project, and watched its progress with some enthusiasm over several years.[35]

By 1986 the association had succeeded in getting various regional groups to approve and adopt a national logo, which paved the way to having such groups become provincial affiliates of the national organization. With financial help from the SSBFF, the association formally changed its name to the Learning Disabilities Association of Canada (LDAC), and its provincial counterparts also adopted titles which began with "learning disabilities," thereby making them easier to locate in telephone directories.[36] The SSBFF encouraged the new organization further by helping develop a direct mail fundraising campaign to centralize and streamline the appeal, the proceeds of which would then be distributed to groups across the country.[37]

The relationship between learning disabilities and the growing problem of illiteracy was underscored in 1987 when Southam Press released

198 · SPIRITED COMMITMENT

a study that revealed that nearly five million Canadians were illiterate, many because of learning disabilities.[38] As a result of this study, the federal government began to take a serious interest in the work of the LDAC, and increased its annual grant to $120,000. The executive director, June Bourgeau, attributed this success directly to the SSBFF's enthusiastic support over the years.[39] The LDAC would proceed to undertake numerous literacy projects for which it was able to tap into various levels of government funding, building on the considerable success of the Young Offenders project (Positive Options, Productive Choices).[40]

In 1990, LDAC was host to the first of the visioning workshops that the SSBFF funded. Twenty-one participants gathered at Montebello, Quebec, in April 1990. In the course of their time together, the group compiled a series of core ambitions including a desire to cultivate public understanding of the diversity of human capabilities, promote early assessment and diagnosis, make access to remedial services universal, ensure that solid science underlay every treatment strategy and device, involve persons with learning disabilities in the development of their own strategies for coping, create a safe environment, and provide opportunities for lifelong learning. The group also imagined a Canada where the workplace was tailored to enhance the productivity of every employee according to their personal capabilities, and create a system of justice that would assess offenders with learning disabilities to understand the challenges they might have faced in childhood.[41]

The LDAC workshop culminated in a plan to launch three long-term initiatives.[42] The first was to establish centres of excellence focusing on research, treatment, education, and services on behalf of persons with learning disabilities. The second sought to strengthen the legal rights of persons with learning disabilities to obtain social, educational, judicial, and related services appropriate to their individual needs. The third intended to improve access to services for persons with learning disabilities. To launch these initiatives, the LDAC would need to analyze and identify current priorities in the research community, consider the Education Acts in existence in each of the provinces, gather information about similar service models already in existence, and "most importantly" survey persons with learning disabilities to understand what their needs were.[43] In November 1990, Hobday recommended that the SSBFF continue funding the LDAC to enable it to carry out its plan, and the board agreed.[44]

June Bourgeau, the LDAC's executive director, and others within the organization worked to establish the centres of excellence by means of a steering committee, and study the legal rights situation via a task force; access to services was deemed more ambitious and so deferred for the time being.[45] The task force was quickly put together under the chairmanship of Winnipeg lawyer Yude Henteleff and began meeting in the spring of 1991; by early 1993 it had produced and published a report entitled "Making the Most of the Law" targeted at both parents and lawyers.[46] The steering committee proved harder to organize owing to the extremely democratic nature of the organization, which resulted in lengthy consultation throughout the national and provincial networks. Hobday decided an organizational review of the LDAC was required – not to undermine the democratic structure but to strengthen the national leadership. This was particularly timely given June Bourgeau's expected retirement in the summer of 1992 after twenty years at the organization's helm.[47]

The organizational review was carried out by means of a workshop held in November 1991 as part of the LDAC's annual conference. As a result of the thorough discussions, it was generally agreed that the success of the organization depended on forceful leadership that could be trusted by the extensive membership to carry out the LDAC's mandate. This agreement, and the consequent modified job description, greatly facilitated the process of searching for Bourgeau's replacement.[48] Confident that their client was on the right track, the SSBFF worked out a gradual phasing-out of its support, to which the LDAC agreed.[49]

In 1993, the last year of SSBFF funding, the LDAC launched one significant initiative. The new executive director, Juli Voyer, secured an additional $25,000 to launch a new public project: Support for Families with Children at Risk for Having Learning Disabilities. The project aimed to produce a manual for community leaders to give to parents with children at risk between the ages of four and seven years; it also planned to create a series of regional workshops for parents. Hobday was particularly pleased to see that even as the SSBFF gradually reduced its funding to the LDAC, its research and publications programs remained strong, signalling its commitment to intellectual leadership in the field.[50] In making this grant the SSBFF showed its confidence in the LDAC and its new executive director. Having attached no conditions to the execution of the project, Hobday and the directors had no doubts that the grant money would go to improving awareness of children with learning disabilities and making the lives of their families easier.[51]

CONCLUSION

After two decades, the Learning Disabilities program proved a success for the SSBFF. Both the LDAC and the Learning Centre had been provided with sufficient funding to get organized and carry out a variety of projects. In the case of the Learning Centre, the foundation had been directly responsible for rescuing its client from near financial disaster and for helping it restructure itself. The foundation also left the LDAC in good hands, not only with an experienced executive director but also a governing structure that strove to become increasingly sensitive to the needs of the broader membership. From early 1993 on, the LDAC worked to bring more individuals with learning disabilities onto its board, allowing for greater insight into the challenges facing people served by the association.[51]

The Learning Disabilities program remained small, however, and involved two organizations that were already established at the time the SSBFF was ready to begin funding. Neither was nurtured to independence, but both were left by the SSBFF in a good state of health. The Learning Centre did go through a rough period during the course of which the foundation might have been expected to withdraw funding, sensing dysfunction; instead, they persevered, assisting in what was arguably the most useful way by first funding a viability study which enabled the organization to identify its weaknesses, and then supporting it on its road to recovery. The SSBFF's involvement with LDAC was more straightforward, although the latter's participation in the visioning workshop exercise proved integral to its long-term success. Both organizations continue to function and do work that is widely recognized in the field; as such, their story serves as a good example of the kind of investment in people and institutions that the foundation set out to make. Even so, the success of the Learning Disabilities program at nurturing and then easily withdrawing from a client organization would not be reproduced in other, more ambitious funding programs.

EIGHT

ONE VOICE: A NATIONAL

ASSOCIATION FOR CANADA'S SENIORS

In developing its program to meet the needs of the elderly, the foundation sought to make its biggest contribution in the arena of public policy. By rights it should have succeeded. It identified a clear need within Canadian society, and enabled an organization to answer that need, through substantial core funding and much additional support. In the end, however, the organization failed to thrive, and the foundation was left asking itself painful questions. Had it completely misread the situation from the beginning? Should it have stopped funding the organization earlier? When should a funder remain loyal to a client organization despite some evidence that things are not going well? These sorts of questions are crucial ones for a philanthropic foundation, especially one like the SSBFF that wanted to make a difference in people's lives beyond mere day-to-day support. The foundation's experience with One Voice becomes a good case study of the problems inherent in trying to make a difference in a strategic and cost-effective manner.

NEEDS OF THE ELDERLY

Despite having secured a national pension plan in the 1960s, Canada's retired people were hit badly by the high inflation encountered throughout the 1970s and the accompanying rises in levels of taxation. Demographics had a particularly serious impact on seniors. Government pension programs had been relatively easy to introduce when the vast majority of the population was steadily employed; the low number of retirees relative to workers had made pay-as-you-go programs affordable. By the late 1970s, however, the senior population was growing in absolute numbers relative to the overall population. Longer life expectancies and declining fertility rates contributed to this changing balance. Long-term projections for baby-boom retirement looked especially troubling.[1] Government pension programs also faced rising costs due to inflation. As benefits were tied to cost-of-living increases, high inflation produced sharp rises in payouts. Moreover, high unemployment contributed to a loss of government revenues for the program. The situation left Canada's seniors very worried for the future.

Canadians had been aware of a growing crisis for some time. In 1973, a government-sponsored survey had reported that "All the speeches, reports, documents and theories – and there are plenty of them – have not helped to dispel the conviction of a great number of senior citizens that they are the forgotten people of Canadian society."[2] In social policy circles, however, some experts pointed to the declining population of dependent children and argued that public funds would increasingly be shifted from schools to long-term care facilities.[3] By the end of the decade there was much less optimism. The federal government recognized the growing need for programs and policies for the elderly when it created the National Advisory Council on Aging (NACA) in May 1980. Eighteen months later, NACA issued its *Priorities for Action*, a blueprint for policy initiatives designed to meet the needs of Canada's growing elderly population.[4] Across the globe, policymakers and social activists were focusing attention on issues affecting the elderly. In the summer of 1982, the First World Congress on Aging was held in Vienna.[5]

In November 1979, six months prior to the founding of NACA, the SSBFF launched its seniors program, called "Social Problems Concerned with the Elderly," and allocated $82,500.[6] As was typical of programs under Peter Swann, this money was distributed to a wide variety of projects: building renovations, recreation activity programs, newsletters, and even the purchase of buses. One larger donation of $50,000 over three years was made to support a professorship in gerontology at St Thomas University in Fredericton, New Brunswick.[7] On a broader level, the SSBFF aimed to improve the public's perception of elderly people by providing funding to NACA to develop short television programs that were aired all across the country, using puppets to depict healthy aging.[8]

The foundation's efforts were frustrated at first by the lack of capacity in the sector that the program was trying to help. As Swann told the board in the fall of 1981, "The groups who work in this area seem far less aware of and unsophisticated in approaching funding sources for help than many other types of organizations." He suggested that perhaps their generation was simply "more self-reliant."[9] Nevertheless, he advised the foundation to stay the course for another two to three years to allow the program "to become well-known throughout the country" and for seniors' organizations to become better organized.[10]

Hobday decided that the program should be more focused. Until that time, too much attention had been paid to small local projects and not enough to establishing national and provincial organizations. The working philosophy had been one of "try us," and, as a result, funds had been too widely distributed. Hobday's 1983 "Towards Tomorrow" report recommended that the foundation support projects "concerned with the overall physical and mental health of our senior citizens" and "which promote and result in active participation and self-help by elderly people." It should also adopt a clear mission statement for the program, and apply it systematically. Above all, it should concentrate on assisting the formation of larger associations with the potential "to serve as strong advocacy groups able to influence governments and private sector policies."[11]

BUILDING A NATIONAL ORGANIZATION

In early 1984, the SSBFF began the process of establishing a framework for a national seniors' organization. Working with St Thomas University, the foundation began discussions with the New Brunswick Senior Citizens' Federation with an eye to addressing the concerns of seniors in the four Atlantic Provinces. In March, the university hosted an exploratory meeting, with representatives from British Columbia, Saskatchewan, and Manitoba as well as New Brunswick. The group agreed to push ahead with the idea to create a national coalition. In May, the university and the New Brunswick federation submitted a joint proposal for a "national consultation on networking for seniors in Canada."[12] This emphasis on consultation reflected Hobday's view that successful groups had to come from the grassroots, however much a body such as the SSBFF might facilitate the process. Grassroots organizing gave an institution the weight and legitimacy it needed in order to become a national body.

Two-thirds of the 100 delegates to the consultation were to be senior citizens representing each of the provinces and territories in Canada. The other third would be professionals and government officials. Major topics of discussion would include networking, community development, public relations, advocacy, fundraising, and self-help. "The eventual outcome of this Consultation," the applicants wrote, "will be one strong voice for seniors on all major issues." They hoped that by 1985 the group would be able to open a national office in Ottawa.[13] At their June 1984 meeting, the SSBFF board supported Hobday's recommendation to invest $53,000 in a national steering committee with a mandate to develop the consultation.[14]

Unfortunately, the consultation was delayed as seniors' groups debated how their interests would be represented and how they would be served by a national organization. Despite much involvement at the local level, many elderly people had difficulty appreciating the purpose and function of a national body. As Hobday remarked, "Our involvement in this area continued to pose many challenges – the seniors challenging us and us challenging them!"[15] He remained convinced, however, that a national network would prove the only effective way to capture the attention of either governments or the private sector. The SSBFF continued to promote the idea of a consultation, meeting with various provincial federations and with Canadian Pensioners Concerned, an organization with a national scope but whose members came mostly from Ontario. Ivan Hale, who had been helping coordinate the SSBFF's Learning Disabilities program, also spent long hours negotiating with seniors organizations. Establishing these sorts of relationships, Hobday noted, was far more effective than simply providing money.[16]

The attention of seniors across the country was immediately riveted in the summer of 1985 when the federal government announced it planned to de-index old-age pensions. With no real history of collective political agitation behind them, seniors voiced their protest loudly and clearly, much to the surprise of nearly everyone, including the seniors themselves. As a result of this clamour, the government backed down. The protest had the effect of raising seniors' political consciousness and sense of themselves as a potential powerful lobby group. The SSBFF produced audio-visual materials highlighting the experiences of seniors who were active in provincial organizations, and identified people to conduct workshops and seminars on networking. Hobday noted that the federal government appeared ready to work with a national seniors' network, and in particular that Health and Welfare Canada seemed willing to spend $250,000 on such an organization.[17]

In September 1986 the long-anticipated summit meeting was convened in Hull, Quebec, just across the river from Ottawa. At this summit, leaders in the seniors' movement across Canada agreed to form a new organization to be called One Voice-La Voix.[18] This organization, with offices in Ottawa, would serve as an information clearing house, researching national issues and policies from a senior perspective, and highlighting concerns for both lawmakers and the general public. The committee chose Jerry Holland, a long-time seniors advocate from Nova Scotia, as acting chairman of the One Voice pro tem committee.

As Hobday reported on these events to the board he made an analogy to the American Association of Retired Persons (AARP) in the United States, which by that time had several million members.[19] The powerful AARP began as a service organization in 1958 and gradually accumulated its political clout. Founded by Dr Ethel Percy Andrus, a retired high school principal, the AARP evolved from the National Retired Teachers Association (NRTA) founded eleven years earlier. NRTA's primary focus was on "productive aging" and, in an age before federal Medicare, providing health insurance to elderly teachers. The organization's insurance programs and its discount mail order pharmacy service attracted thousands of individuals who were not teachers and could not obtain insurance. Andrus organized the AARP as an umbrella organization with the NRTA as a subsidiary.[20] "The American Association," Hobday wrote, "provides an incredibly powerful and highly respected voice in Washington, plus it offers a tremendous range of programs and services. One Voice will become the Canadian equivalent."

"Naturally," he continued, "One Voice will take several years to become self-financing." But already other funding agencies, private and public, were showing interest in the project.[21]

ONE VOICE: GETTING STARTED

One Voice was officially organized in March 1987, with Jerry Holland elected president. As part of its ongoing support for the new organization, the foundation provided the services of Ivan Hale, who became One Voice's national secretary, his salary paid directly by the SSBFF in order not to burden the new organization with the obligation to pay a senior staff salary. One Voice hired a part-time editor and a full-time projects officer. Yhetta Gold, former executive director of the Winnipeg Volunteer Centre and president of the National Advisory Council on Aging, served as a consultant.[22] Once it was formally launched, One Voice began issuing memberships to seniors across the country, leaving it up to individuals to decide if they were old enough to be eligible. Symbolically, the first membership was issued to Saidye Bronfman.[23]

The challenges facing One Voice were formidable, beginning with the problem of how to organize the elderly as a political community. Some research found that seniors tended to feel less optimistic than others in society about prospects for political change; as a result, they felt little motivation to participate in the political process and were inclined to disengage from society and lose interest in the issues of the day. Other studies, however, showed the opposite pattern, that the elderly actually were becoming more engaged as child-rearing and job-related preoccupations diminished with retirement.[24] In any case, this kind of information gave Hobday, Gold, and others involved with the project hope that the organization could become a powerful voice for the country's growing population of seniors.

In the fall of 1988, with federal elections looming, One Voice committed itself to supporting three major political goals: 1) restoration of the New Horizons for Seniors program, a federal government initiative that had recently become the victim of cutbacks;[25] 2) greater input by seniors in the formulation of national housing policies; and 3) consideration of a national guaranteed annual income policy for all Canadians.[26] One Voice also published the *Seniors' Election Handbook*, designed to help seniors engage in the election process. According to Thelma Scambler, who had succeeded Jerry Holland as president earlier that year, the handbook "generated enormous response and recognition of the emerging power of the seniors' vote."[27]

Governments proved willing to listen to this new group. In April 1989 the federal minister of Finance invited the president of One Voice to participate in pre-budget consultations. Ivan Hale was asked to address the New Democratic Party during platform development talks. One Voice represented the interests of disabled seniors to the National Transportation Agency and argued for accessibility. The organization was also represented on government consumer products committees. According to Hobday, these consultations reflected the first time that seniors had had an early voice in policymaking circles. As policymakers turned to the organization, however, it was important that it have carefully considered policies and approaches of its own. Clearly, the directors needed to have the staff and resources to research and write about the issues. Seeing the potential for the organization, Ivan Hale planned a trip to Washington, DC to learn how the powerful AARP had developed its political reach.[28]

Hobday believed that One Voice needed stable core funding and management expertise to develop its policy positions on key issues, expand its membership, and broaden its base of financial support.[29] To further these goals, the SSBFF decided in 1988 to commit virtually all its budget for the Seniors program ($240,000) to One Voice.[30]

The foundation's support gave the organization running room for advocacy and helped attract government funding. In 1988, One Voice received just over $300,000 from the government for a program called HABITAT. Under this program, One Voice organized six regional workshops on Housing for Seniors in Yellowknife, Edmonton, Toronto, Winnipeg, Montreal, and Halifax.[31] The success of these workshops in 1988 prompted the government to solicit a proposal from One Voice for HABITAT 2.[32] With additional funds from the Canada Mortgage and Housing Corporation, One Voice held additional workshops in every province and territory to focus on appropriate housing for seniors. In the spring of 1990, after a systematic assessment of the nation's elderly, One Voice sponsored a national conference on literacy and older adults called "Learning – That's Life" to address the needs of the nearly 40 per cent of Canada's seniors who were illiterate. This advocacy and close cooperation with government agencies helped convince the minister of National Health and Welfare in 1990 to approve a sustaining grant to the organization of $35,000 a year for five years.[33]

This was good news for the foundation, whose hope it was that One Voice would become self-sufficient and not continue to depend on the SSBFF. The real path to self-sufficiency, however, was through an expanded membership, and in its first year One Voice had only recruited 700, a disappointment to the directors and a source of worry to the foundation. Still, more than 90 per cent of these members renewed in their second year, which was a positive sign. Thelma Scambler declared she was "optimistic that a broad funding base can be established within three to five years."[34]

Unfortunately, Scambler did not live to pursue this objective. Her sudden death in October 1988 underscored one of the key challenges facing a senior's organization: the susceptibility of its leadership, and indeed of its members, to growing infirmity and decline, and even death. Many who were involved in the organization were energetic and dedicated, but many others had the will but lacked the facility. Because of this problem, it was vital for a seniors' association to be run from the grassroots; seniors were not simply to be the beneficiaries of such an organization but the principal players in its overall vision.[35]

VISIONING SENIORS

The SSBFF-sponsored planning workshop for seniors convened in September 1990 at Mont Ste Marie, Quebec. Entitled "Visions of the Future for Older Canadians," the conference brought together nearly a dozen senior advocates, government policy advisors, and academics. The group included Kevin Donnellan, legislative counsel for the American Association of Retired Persons, as well as Dr Giff Gifford, the author of *Canada's Fighting Seniors*. Thelma Chalifoux represented the Aboriginal Veterans' Association and the Métis Elders' Senate.[36]

The outcome of the discussions was a carefully articulated vision of society, a future state, it was hoped, towards which all generations had to strive. In this vision, seniors would live within the community, contributing their lifetimes of experience to address a multiplicity of issues, and not just those related to a narrow definition of their own welfare. Seniors' issues would be seen as society's issues, quality of life would be a lifelong matter, and seniors would have the ability to manage their lives independently as long as possible. There would be no discrimination by gender, race, or ethnicity; intergenerational communication and cooperation would be everyday occurrences and individuality and cultural differences would be respected. Transportation would be universally accessible and housing would be designed with accessibility, affordability, and energy conservation in mind. Family would be redefined so that it could include support networks beyond those conceived as falling within traditional kinship. It was agreed that One Voice would be responsible for leading this effort.[37]

With the report of the visioning workshop in hand, One Voice sought to continue its expansion and influence. Unfortunately, having built its strategy for growth on the idea that it would be a service and lobbying organization with strong government support, One Voice suddenly confronted governments reeling from the onset of a national recession. The organization had enjoyed significant financial support between 1987 and 1991, having received over $1 million from various government ministries, but now felt the impact of government cuts. An application for $85,000 in sustaining support filed in 1990 was unfunded as of May

1991, while the promise of $35,000 in 1990 had only been 25 per cent fulfilled by that time. [38]

John Hobday tried to put a good face on the situation, saying that any money received at all offered "evidence that One Voice has not been cut off the Health and Welfare list, as so many non-profit organizations expect to be in this recessionary period." [39] With these cutbacks, however, One Voice was once again more or less dependent on the SSBFF for funding. The board of One Voice concluded that it would have to focus its fundraising on individuals and community groups. As President Jean Woodsworth wrote to Hobday in April 1991, "We believe the key to long term financial health for the organization rests in having a large donor and member base." [40] While this effort was underway, SSBFF contributions to One Voice totalled $385,000 in 1992, surpassing donations to any of the other director's programs by almost 50 per cent. [41]

One Voice's funding difficulties were obscured by its considerable success on another level. Having positioned itself as a voice for seniors in Canada, the organization was increasingly invited to participate in conferences and projects with other groups. With the Canadian Dietetics Association and Mead Johnson Canada it co-sponsored a national workshop on seniors and nutrition. One Voice collaborated with the Canadian parks service to undertake a consultation with seniors on issues and concerns relating to national parks. With the New Brunswick Senior Citizens' Federation, One Voice organized a national conference entitled "Planning Today for Good Age Tomorrow." One Voice representatives served on a seniors' advisory committee created by Revenue Canada. It spent two years developing a "National Literacy Strategy for Older Canadians." It sought to raise awareness of seniors' issues with the United Way and Centraide. It lobbied the government on issues related to public access and disabilities. [42] Ivan Hale also began working on the international front. At the International Federation on Ageing's annual meeting in India in August 1992 he convinced that organization to move its headquarters from Washington, DC to Ottawa. [43] All of these developments combined to give One Voice prominent standing within policymaking circles.

The SSBFF was pleased by the attention One Voice was receiving, but it continued to insist that the organization strive for independence. In

1992 the SSBFF told One Voice that it would diminish its grants over a five-year period and cease funding altogether in 1997.[44]

ADVOCACY VERSUS FUNDRAISING

Salasan's evaluation of One Voice in 1992 was mixed. It highlighted the organization's "important role," the quality of its products and research, its outstanding track record, and the respect shown to the staff and director. At the same time, One Voice lacked a central focus; it was not clear what immediate benefit members derived or how closely they identified with its policies and activities. Salasan recommended a strategic planning initiative to help One Voice identify particular constituencies likely to benefit from its program and services. For example, One Voice could do more for francophone communities. Administratively, it suffered from an "organizational bottleneck" in that all decisions came to rest on the national secretary's desk, even though the nature of his job demanded that he travel frequently to visit constituent organizations in the provinces. Salasan recommended adding staff for administration and outreach, an expense that would prove worthwhile in the long run as One Voice grew more efficient. The board of One Voice should also be strengthened, by bringing in new members with particular areas of expertise, and by instilling in all board members a sense of the importance of their roles as national advocates and spokespersons.[45]

Salasan encouraged the SSBFF gradually to withdraw its core funding and concentrate resources on strategies to make the organization independent. Instead of spending money entirely on salaries and overhead, the SSBFF should assist with member recruitment and fundraising. It should certainly stop paying Ivan Hale's salary directly, as this distorted the picture of One Voice's financial situation and was an expense that the organization must learn to cover.[46]

Ivan Hale and the board of One Voice took these recommendations to heart and redoubled their efforts at membership development and fundraising.[47] In January 1993 the board established a goal of financial self-sufficiency by 1999. To reach that goal they hoped to have a donor base of 4,000 individuals and entities by 1996, with donations rising from $100,000 in fiscal year 1992/93 to $350,000 by 1994/95. To hit these targets, they planned to undertake a country-wide membership drive including advertisements in community newspapers in every province.[48] They understood that long-term viability depended on taking the route of the AARP in the United States by offering direct services and benefits to members.[49]

It was clear, however, that the passion of the organization lay in advocacy, not in building membership or revenues. Each year One Voice submitted its recommendations to the minister of Finance as the government began preparation of the federal budget. In 1993, its report was entitled "No More Cuts: Fair Taxation for Deficit Reduction," and argued that budget cuts had caused "a steady erosion of the fundamental values we believe our country has always espoused." The tax system was increasingly skewed to favour the interests of business and the wealthy "at extreme cost to average and vulnerable Canadians." The report also challenged exemptions for capital gains and provisions for tax deferrals for private family trusts, and chastised the government for allowing corporations to write off a "deluxe box at the Skydome, drinks and all, while an unemployed worker runs out of UI (unemployment insurance) benefits." The situation "caused hardship and despair in a country which possesses the resources to prevent such needless suffering." In fact, according to One Voice, the government's cuts represented a pattern of "persistent destruction of our social heritage to the advantage of the few." Despite this egalitarianism, One Voice also opposed the government's proposal for a "claw back" provision that would reduce retirement benefits to more affluent seniors.[50]

Efforts were made to address administrative issues. In May 1993, One Voice decided to establish a Task Force on Future Development, which would create a business plan to ensure long-term financial viability – in effect, a strategy for attracting and retaining paid members who would provide a base of funding to the organization. Putting together the actual task force proved a challenge, however, with time and resources occupied with lobbying during that year's federal election. One Voice published an election guide encouraging seniors to challenge candidates on issues of concern to the elderly, notably stronger government action against elder abuse. Ivan Hale also began planning a major conference on Healthy Aging to take place in Montreal in collaboration with the International Federation on Ageing; Hale even became one of the federation's vice-presidents.[51] Against this busy backdrop, efforts to focus on the future of the organization stumbled.

Eventually, under pressure from the foundation, the One Voice board instructed Hale to make funding his top priority and he promised to have a solid business plan in place by May 1994. When the SSBFF directors met in December 1993, they voted not to provide additional funding until the business plan had been received. Hobday was still optimistic that the transition to independence would be smooth and that One Voice would be left in good condition.[52] There were some indications of growing self-sufficiency. The government did provide nearly $200,000 to mount the conference on Healthy Aging, and nearly $100,000 to hold consultations on the Future Direction of Seniors Employment Bureau. Smaller government grants financed a pilot project in Ottawa on Police Response to Seniors, a bilingualism program, and the secretariat functions of the Canadian Coalition on Medication Use and Seniors. Apart from a $35,000 sustaining grant from Health and Welfare Canada, however, government money did not help finance basic overhead and operations.

Failing to find government support, One Voice turned to the corporate world. Seniors represented a substantial and important market for a number of industries, especially those in health care and pharmaceuticals. One Voice reasonably hoped that by offering a conduit to this marketplace it could attract corporate support in return. In 1994, the organization appealed to nearly 200 major corporations for support for operations. Twenty of these companies had declared an interest in funding aging-related issues, so the staff and board at One Voice hoped for the best. But the response was disappointing.[53] The SSBFF also tried to help One Voice win support from other Canadian foundations – only twenty of which gave to seniors organizations in 1994.[54] Again the results were disappointing.

If One Voice could not attract sustained support from the government or the corporate sector, then it had to turn to its own constituency. After all, the organization had been created in the 1980s, in part to play the same political and social role in Canada that the AARP carried in the United States. The American organization had grown on the strength of the services and products it offered to its membership. Hobday encouraged One Voice to follow the AARP's example and provide insurance and travel benefits for members, or else seek an alliance with the American behemoth that would generate revenue in Canada where the AARP already had 40,000 members. [55] Unfortunately, efforts to build such a partnership did not succeed, nor did attempts to connect with the Canadian Association of Retired Peoples. CARP was modelled closely on its American counterpart and was primarily focused on providing discounts and services to seniors. Although it purported to do lobbying and policy work, it spent very little time on such matters and so One Voice did not appear very interesting. For their part, neither Hobday nor the Canadian government felt that CARP represented a real force for effecting change – hence the ongoing need for One Voice. [56] Even so, the existence of such parallel organizations made it harder for One Voice to establish credibility within the senior population.

Over the next two years, One Voice did achieve some limited success in expanding its membership, but policy debates and international developments continued to demand the organization's attention. In the fall of 1995 Parliament debated a major pension reform initiative, and One Voice was careful to make its stance known. Ivan Hale travelled to Jerusalem for the International Federation on Ageing Conference and lobbied for One Voice to host the fourth global conference in 1999 in Montreal. These efforts seemed to pay off financially late in 1995 when Human Resources Development Canada approved the organization's proposal for a two-year, $900,000 project to set up and activate an employment network for older (age forty-five and up) workers. But this project did not address the organization's immediate needs for funding for operations, and even as it extended this project envelope the federal government announced that it did not intend to renew One Voice's

$35,000 sustaining grant. The government suggested that with major funding from the SSBFF, One Voice did not need public funding. With this news, staff was cut back to three days a week at the end of November, with more drastic cuts on the horizon.[57]

ONE VOICE IN CRISIS

One Voice retained a consultant to develop a business plan and established a Revenue Generating committee, with both Hobday and Rucker serving as members. It sent an appeal to its members citing the urgency of the pension reform initiative as a reason to help the organization stay afloat. One in four members responded with a donation.[58] Meanwhile, to make its intentions clear, the foundation reduced its funding to One Voice from $300,000 in 1995 to $250,000 in 1996.

One Voice was still in crisis by late 1996, but apparently getting its house in order. Corporate and individual support were both up. Membership increased 6 per cent. The organization had eliminated many unfunded projects and spending on fundraising and membership recruitment had tripled. The loss of government support for overhead, however, continued to weigh on the organization. In 1995–96 restricted government funds represented 15 per cent of total revenue. In 1996–97, however, these encumbered funds accounted for 53 per cent of the total. To try to match spending to revenue, One Voice had trimmed its expenses for general administration from 66 per cent in 1995–96 to 21 per cent in 1996–97.[59] Despite these improvements, the organization still failed to seriously address the basic core of its financial needs. At the end of 1996, Hale reported to the foundation that One Voice would hire a development director.

In his end-of-the-year report to the directors of the foundation, Hobday noted that "One Voice had not developed the leadership that would ensure its survival." It had not been able to attract a high-profile individual to serve as president. The realization that One Voice might not survive provoked frustration among the SSBFF's board members. Phyllis suggested that the foundation should have addressed this problem earlier by going to "specific high-profile people to tell them about One Voice." Hobday conceded that perhaps the foundation could have done more in 1992 after receiving Salasan's evaluation, but also suggested that "this kind of direct intervention is a fine line to cross."[60] Indeed, One Voice represented all the risks inherent in the SSBFF's hands-on approach to philanthropy, whereby the client organization was nurtured towards independence, often with considerably high levels of funding in hopes of long-term social dividends. In this case, it was looking as though the financial investment and hard work were not going to pay off.

By 1997 accumulated frustration and disappointment with One Voice had reached the breaking point. As Hobday told the board, One Voice had strayed from its original mandate to serve as an advocate and network for seniors, and become "an organization primarily devoted to providing services to some government departments." The board of directors had not provided strong leadership and the commitment of the staff was weak. As a result, the SSBFF now faced a tough choice. It could walk away from the project and risk weakening the foundation's reputation. It could withhold further funding until the management issues were addressed. Or it could turn over the remaining funding, with or without conditions, and hope for the best. In June 1997 the board agreed to wait until the new development officer at One Voice had created a plan, but time was running out.[61]

Although the government had been supportive of One Voice in the past, senior officials in the Division of Aging and Seniors at Health Canada now told Hobday that they too were concerned about One Voice's viability. After meeting with officials in Ottawa, Hobday suggested to Phyllis that the foundation "work with the government so that our exit strategy leads to the maintenance of One Voice – but at the same time, [pressures] the organization to make significant changes in the way it is governed, managed and financed."[62]

In September, Hobday told the president of One Voice that the SSBFF had come to the end of its patience. It was the foundation's belief that "international involvements" had come "at the expense of working on behalf of Canadian seniors on Canadian issues."[63] Hobday was also dubious about One Voice's ability to manage budgets, and announced that the ssbff would withhold a promised $170,000 in funding pending the outcome of an independent assessment undertaken by "a respected and knowledgeable authority on national not-for-profit organizations.[64] Hobday hired ARA Consulting to evaluate One Voice's organizational strengths and weaknesses and to offer suggestions for the future.

The ARA report confirmed the ssbff's impression that, after ten years, "the network is either very weak or does not exist." The consultants conceded that it may have been unrealistic to expect seniors' organizations, "which are often small and run by volunteers, to make communication with One Voice a priority;" at the same time, One Voice failed to build that network, perhaps because it got distracted by its desire to become a player on an international stage. Hale's success at bringing the Federation on Ageing conference to Montreal helped to raise the profile of One Voice internationally, but it represented "a divergence from the mission." One Voice had waited too long to build its membership and its own source of revenue, and now was hit by substantial cutbacks in government funding to social service organizations. Furthermore, the staff had lost faith in the leadership: the board of directors was out of touch and had not provided Hale with the governance, supervision, or support needed to ensure the success of the organization.[65]

The need for a national organization of seniors, however, was still real and immediate. As the consultants reported, stakeholders in the senior community and in government believed "that if One Voice did not exist, it would have to be reinvented. Potential funders, especially the federal government, require a non-governmental organization to take on programs, and policy and decision makers need such a group for thoughtful advice on issues facing seniors." Despite its problems, One Voice had a sound reputation among policymakers, and it remained "a valuable organization" with "tremendous potential." The consultants offered two options for the ssbff to consider at their November 1997 meeting: continue funding One Voice with the proviso that it refocus on the mission, or merge it with another national seniors' group "with an interest in advocacy and the financial and human resources to support federal initiatives and advocacy efforts."[66]

Having invested over two million dollars in the creation of One Voice, the directors of the SSBFF were doubtful that continued investment would produce success. At the same time, cutting ties to One Voice completely had risks. Failure might suggest that the funds invested in the organization had been wasted. In the business world, failure is never welcomed, but it is understood as an important element of risk. In the world of policymaking where foundation money is perceived to be public money, the tolerance for failure is much lower. Hobday and Phyllis still looked for a way to save One Voice, but Jean de Gunzburg expressed his frustration that the organization did not seem to be willing to change. "You cannot make them succeed if they do not want to," he said. In the end, the board agreed to release the remaining funds for 1997, but to end support for One Voice at the end of the fiscal year. The directors reflected that they had learned a lesson. As Phyllis put it, "when an organization is hand-fed, it never comes out of it."[67]

When the SSBFF terminated its funding, One Voice tried to continue on by reducing staff and moving to a smaller space, but these reductions in overhead failed to create a stable platform for operations. Within a year, the organization closed its doors. From Ivan Hale's point of view, no senior organization emerged to play the same thoughtful role in the policy arena.[68]

CONCLUSION

The failure of One Voice prompted a lot of soul-searching within the SSBFF and beyond, not only in accounting for what had gone wrong but in assessing the foundation's role as a funder. Had it done the right thing by holding the course for so long, or ought it to have been firmer sooner? The result was an organization that neither achieved independence nor, despite Ivan Hale's lobbying and networking efforts, really made a significant difference. Hale believed there had been conceptual problems from the start, that the foundation and One Voice had embraced the wrong business model to sustain the organization. "It was very idealistic," he says, "to believe that we would have a huge constituency of members. When you have to sustain a membership organization the sheer costs of organizational overhead are substantial."[69] Others saw the One Voice failure in a different light, suggesting that the organization never had the right leadership to fit a membership organization. Hale had come from the world of consulting, not from the arena of grassroots organizing. At times, the organization's overhead had been out of proportion to its character and purpose. It had been hard to build a committed board of directors with the vision appropriate for the beginning of the twenty-first century. In addition, provincial rivalries in the senior community had made it hard to build a national coalition. In the end, as Jean de Gunzburg suggests, One Voice's failure may have signalled the fact that seniors in Canada simply did not feel they derived sufficient benefit from the organization to sustain it.[70]

From another point of view, the One Voice case speaks to the discipline of the SSBFF's approach to philanthropy. Organizations that hope to take risks and be innovative must have the ability to acknowledge failure and move on. This is a painful process. In business or in the world of social policy one can always second-guess and imagine that with a few more resources the enterprise might have hit its stride and become sustainable. At a certain point, managers and boards have to be able to draw the line. The SSBFF poured money into One Voice even after the evaluation from Salasan raised red flags in 1992, but in the end the foundation stood by its stated intention to move on. For the directors, One Voice represented a painful, but profound lesson. Even in the world of philanthropy, innovation has its price.

Even so, over the course of barely a decade – a short time when it comes to attitudinal change – One Voice helped make politicians and bureaucrats aware that seniors, organized or not, were a force to be reckoned with and wanted to have more say in decisions affecting their lives.

NINE

CULTURAL MANAGEMENT
AND ARTS STABILIZATION

Both Peter Swann and John Hobday had backgrounds in the arts, and both were keen for the SSBFF to invest in this area. Although the Saidye Bronfman Centre and the Saidye Bronfman Award for Excellence in the Crafts were ongoing concerns for the foundation, it was generally felt that a major contribution could still be made to the arts in Canada beyond what the Canada Council was prepared to fund. The foundation's first success in this area was in nurturing university and college programs in arts management, followed by the creation of a university-based centre for cultural management at Waterloo and the development of a network of these programs called the Canadian Association of Arts Administration Educators (CAAAE). An equally significant achievement was in helping establish arts stabilization programs across the country, requiring a great deal of patient negotiation and political sensitivity on the part of Hobday and the SSBFF directors.

The SSBFF's efforts in arts and culture highlight the ongoing concern to provide enough funding for a project to get off the ground and be able to function on a long-term basis without locking the foundation into an unending commitment. Although the SSBFF did provide small one-time grants to various arts groups through its Futures program, its main contribution was to enable organizations to become self-sustaining and for the arts in general to become less dependent on governments, whose funding outlook could change overnight.

ORGANIZING ARTS ADMINISTRATORS

As leaders among the country's arts and cultural managers, Hobday and Swann had known each other for a number of years and shared a frustration with the government's approach to cultural policy. Relatively generous programs in the 1960s and early 70s had made life easier for many cultural organizations, but little attention had been paid to their management. With cutbacks in funding since the late 1970s, institutions suffered from both dwindling resources and a lack of professional training. When he was director of the Canadian Conference for the Arts, Hobday worked to convince the federal government to empanel a royal commission of "three wise persons, maybe four" to conduct a thorough review of government policy in the arts.[1] What the government finally established, in August 1980, was the Federal Cultural Policy Review Committee, co-chaired by Louis Applebaum and Jacques Hébert, but consisting of as many as twenty members by the time it wrapped up. Instead of a tight coherent report with a clear message like the Massey Royal Commission of 1951, the Applebaum-Hébert Report of 1982 "kind of fell with a dull thud," as Hobday put it.[2] On the crucial question of management training for arts organizations, the report acknowledged that more was necessary, but provided no real solution as to how managers should acquire such training.[3]

Up to that time, managers of arts and cultural organizations in Canada generally learned on the job. They were subject-matter experts in art or history who found themselves increasingly challenged with executive responsibilities. A growing appreciation of the need to provide administrative training in the arts led to the development of a university-level curriculum in 1970 when the University of California, Los Angeles, appointed the first professor of arts administration in North

America. The first Canadian university training in arts administration came later that same year when York University admitted the first student to its new program. The following year, the Banff School of Fine Arts launched its own program in arts administration.⁴ Several community colleges also offered one- and two-year training programs. But by the early 1980s, most of the existing programs in arts administration were directed at entry-level personnel or took the form of in-service training. Managers and would be managers in arts and cultural organizations needed a comprehensive professional program.

Too often the prevailing view was that the arts should not be sullied with business. Business was something other people did, people who had no understanding of how to run an art gallery, a ballet school, or a theatre. People who ran such organizations had to be artists or dancers or actors; it went with one's artistic vocation and could not be learned. Hobday remembered being told to "work your way up through the ranks," however long it took, but this made no sense to him. "No, no, no, no," he kept telling the leaders of the arts community, "I don't believe that. You can teach me. First of all, I have to have a passion for the art. That's where you've got to start. You need that. The rest you can teach me. You can teach me marketing. I don't love marketing; I pick it up … Teach me accounting. Amazing, amazing what I can learn, okay? But I'm not going to learn it by sweeping the stage."⁵ To Hobday and Swann arts management was a profession and would-be professionals needed to be trained, including such prosaic skills as administration and handling money.

While he was head of the Royal Ontario Museum, Swann had fought for the professional integrity and autonomy of museum and cultural directors, and continued to do so afterwards. In 1976 he helped organize the Association of Cultural Executives, a network of professionals who wished to share experiences and best practices.⁶ The association could promote the idea of creating a cultural management program, but lacked resources. It was clear, too, that little could be expected from the government. In November 1980, Phyllis reported to the SSBFF board on her recent meeting with federal Minister of Communications Francis Fox and Minister of the Environment John Roberts, who made it clear to her that there would be no increase in funding to arts and cultural organizations for the next three years. In light of this news, Phyllis suggested that the SSBFF board find a way to make a greater investment in cultural programs.[7]

The opportunity came as institutions across the country appeared willing to form a national organization to promote cultural management. In March 1983, the Canada Council sponsored a conference at the Banff Centre to explore the state of arts administration in Canada. Nine educational institutions offering various arts administration programs attended the meeting, along with fourteen representatives of arts organizations who employed administrators, and representatives from funding agencies.[8] From this meeting, collaboration between the educational institutions began. To keep the momentum going, the SSBFF decided to help fund a follow-up meeting a year later, which took the form of a retreat held at Stanley House on the south shore of Quebec's Gaspé Peninsula. A former governor general's summer home that had been left to the Canada Council, Stanley House was an ideal setting for gatherings of this sort: in elegant surroundings on an isolated point of land, participants were able to resolve their many differences and agree to form the Canadian Association of Arts Administration Educators (CAAAE).[9]

In June 1984, the SSBFF decided to devote an annual $130,000 to its arts program, following on the proposal Hobday had made in "Towards Tomorrow." Over half this amount would go to support the CAAAE's activities.[10] The association hired management consultant Marion Paquet to undertake a study of the challenges facing arts administrators and the resources available to them. As a result of Paquet's findings, the CAAAE launched an effort to identify and organize bibliographies of research and learning materials on arts administration education.[11] But Paquet's report also highlighted the need to improve the state of governance in most cultural organizations.[12] This was a long-time grievance of Peter Swann, who tended to put the blame for the problems of arts organizations on inexperienced and bureaucratically minded boards of trustees.[13] Whether or not this assessment was entirely fair to most trustees, it was agreed that what was needed was some sort of handbook on governance.

Accordingly, the SSBFF sponsored the preparation of *A Handbook for Cultural Trustees*, written by Paquet, Donna Cardinal, an arts administration educator from Edmonton, and Rory Ralston, founder of the Institute for New Interpretive Creative Activity which conducted research and policy development. The handbook was published in 1986 by the University of Waterloo Press in both English and French versions and had a significant impact on arts and cultural organizations, whose leaders appreciated its emphasis on management as a complex process involving every player within a group, not merely one coordinator in an office.[14] The handbook sold quickly and required a second printing to meet the demand even from beyond the arts community; it was picked up by all kinds of non-profit organizations, including native groups, thereby raising the profile of the SSBFF. As a dividend, the foundation decided that organizations that sold copies would be allowed to keep the profits for themselves.[15]

The University of Waterloo was also site of the November 1985 Cultural Imperative Conference, partly sponsored by the SSBFF. This was one of the first conferences to involve trustees in the broad discussion of arts management issues, and those who attended felt it was a watershed event: "It helped focus attention on issues related to governance and board and management relations."[16] Three years later, the SSBFF co-hosted a meeting on board development, also at the University of Waterloo, which was attended by representatives of arts, heritage, and cultural organizations from across the country eager to find ways to improve governance.[17] The choice of Waterloo as the site for these events was not surprising, given that the university offered one of Canada's few arts administration programs. The presence of Peter Swann at the Seagram Museum nearby was also a factor in the foundation's ongoing support for the University of Waterloo. One of the country's leading arts executives, Swann continued to play a key role in helping to organize museum administrators in Canada. As a member of the National Museums Task Force, which sought to advise the government on its museums policy, Swann spoke openly about the need for better training for managers in all the arts.[18]

These concerns were echoed in *The Report of the Task Force on Funding of the Arts*, co-chaired by Edmund Bovey and Joan Chalmers, which was published in 1986. The report identified three factors contributing to cultural management problems in Canada: weak governing boards; insufficient and poorly trained management staff; and funding agencies with insufficient interest in management evaluation and progress.[19] That same year, the CAAAE published its *Final Report of the Study of Management Development Needs of Publicly Funded Not-for-Profit Arts and Heritage Organizations in Canada* which provided the foundation and other funders with a blueprint for the development of arts management programs.[20] Also written by Marion Paquet, the report identified the crucial need for training, education, and research, and also called for a labour market study to be sure that the provision of managers would be linked to the demand.[21]

Despite these numerous discussions and publications, no concerted national effort emerged to implement cultural management training. Hobday felt there was little interest from within established cultural institutions, including the Canada Council who did not seem to understand why he was "bothering" them with talk of training managers, even when he pointed out that 80 per cent of the Council's budget went to arts organizations (as opposed to individuals) whose financial health was surely of interest to their funders.[22] Furthermore, it was evident early on that the CAAAE was not the body to administer a plan for management training, even though the foundation continued to provide funding for the association until the spring of 1995.[23] The CAAAE was divided by strong personalities with conflicting agendas; one ongoing and seemingly irresolvable debate was whether management training programs should be the preserve of universities or community colleges.[24] In order to advance the cause of cultural management, the SSBFF would clearly have to play a more direct role.

Cultural Management at the University of Waterloo

The issue of developing managers in cultural institutions was important in an era of diminishing public resources, not least because it would enable such institutions to be independent. When it came to museums,

Phyllis and Swann both argued that government largesse in the 1960s and early 70s had had the unfortunate effect of diminishing the capacity of arts organizations to be resourceful. In a letter to Swann, Phyllis asserted that "the museums in Canada are too dependent on government (one could say that they are colonized by government). Because of this, they tend to wait for government funding" and fail to make a case to their own communities and constituencies. Phyllis wanted the government "to establish attractive tax structures that would permit a broader participation of the public in funding." Phyllis favoured greater autonomy for museum directors, particularly within the structure of the National Museums.[25] As a member of the Visiting Committee of the National Gallery of Canada she had seen that too many levels of bureaucracy, manifested in the creation of the Museums Corporation as a super-museum to govern all the parts, weakened the management of each individual institution. In summary, she wrote, "The goal is to strengthen museums by *allowing* them to govern themselves ... Dependency breeds dependency; independence breeds ingenuity and toughness."[26] This view was equally applicable to other aspects of the arts.

In June 1984 the SSBFF decided to invest directly in a small number of institutions offering arts management training, notably the University of Waterloo, Confederation College in Thunder Bay, and the École des hautes études commerciales (HEC) in Montreal.[27] The Waterloo program was the most ambitious and received the largest portion of funding, $45,000 a year. The program was enthusiastically endorsed by Douglas Wright, president of the university and former deputy minister of both Education and Culture in the Ontario government, who was looking for ways "to put ... a human face on this technological university."[28] The Arts Administration Specialization Program was part of the Faculty of Arts and was run by John Stubbs, associate dean of Arts; as such it was fundamentally different from its counterpart at York University in Toronto, which was a specialization within the MBA program. Mavor Moore, whom Hobday regarded as an esteemed mentor who was currently teaching at York, advised against going the MBA route, predicting that graduates would simply be lured away by the prospect of more money working at IBM or the Royal Bank, thereby defeating the purpose of training arts managers.[29]

The Waterloo undergraduate program was the first of its kind in Canada. In keeping with the university's tradition of cooperative education, students alternated study terms with work placements, gaining them valuable practical experience. The ssBFF's annual $45,000 enabled students to work for the Royal Winnipeg Ballet, Harbourfront, the Vancouver Arts Club, the McMichael Gallery, Edmonton's Fringe Festival, Opera Hamilton, Toronto Independent Dance Enterprises, and many other institutions.[30] In May 1987, the first four students in the program received their degrees and were promptly employed in key positions, including some for which they had interned. This was naturally welcome news for the ssBFF, and prompted the university to renew its commitment to the program. As discussions ensued, two primary goals became evident: the existing arts administration specialization needed to be strengthened and effort had to be taken to spark major inter-faculty collaboration in cultural management research and graduate education. To achieve both of these goals would require the creation of a new institution: the Centre for Cultural Management. Developers at the University of Waterloo estimated that a new centre and its related activities would need $1.5 million in funding over five years.[31]

In March 1988, the new associate dean Michael McDonald sent a detailed proposal to the ssBFF and other funding agencies requesting grants to help create this Centre for Cultural Management (CCM). Hobday began a series of conversations with the administration at the University of Waterloo to assess the level of commitment that the university might bring to an expanded program as well as its potential to attract other funders. He became convinced not only that the CCM would be of crucial benefit to the arts in Canada, but that the University of Waterloo was the institution to develop it. The university had one of the largest and most successful cooperative education programs in the world, a program that gave real-world experience to students even as they learned the theory behind their work. It also had the most extensive existing program in arts administration.[32]

Hobday told the ssBFF directors that "dramatic changes could take place over the next decade" if investments were made by both government and the private sector in cultural management.[33] At their April

1988 board meeting, the directors agreed that it was appropriate to provide major support to a single institution with demonstrated leadership in cultural management training, rather than dilute their support among a number of different organizations;[34] accordingly, the foundation's commitments to the Haute études commerciales program would be brought to an end by 1990.[35] The directors also agreed that the University of Waterloo should be the recipient of their support, although they had some reservations about making a sizeable grant for the creation of a new centre. They wanted to know if the centre would be back in five years for more money. Would the undergraduate program be significant enough to be recognized by employers in the cultural industry, or would the program have to expand to offer a master's degree? Would the creation of the centre help spark other cultural administration programs around the country? A major concern was the low number of students in the existing Arts Administration specialization: four years after its launch, only eleven students were enrolled.[36] Hobday had to go back to the university for clarification before the board would approve the five-year, $775,000 grant to create the CCM.

For Hobday, the way to increase enrolment was the same as attracting diversifying funding sources: build credibility. He felt that the SSBFF, whom he referred to as the CCM's "founding funders," had "already demonstrated a long term commitment to the arts in Canada." Its presence would add credibility, bring in government support, and highlight "the importance which the private sector attaches to the improvement of arts management."[37] Marion Paquet helped officials at the university fine-tune their proposal to other potential funders so that the SSBFF's involvement was evident.

These efforts soon paid off. Mobil Canada pledged $100,000 over five years beginning in 1988, as did the Richard Ivey Foundation and the McLean Foundation.[38] By 1989, the Floyd S. Chalmers Foundation had given $650,000 to provide scholarships to students in Arts Administration programs, and Imperial Oil committed $100,000 to fund what became known as the Arts Administrator Distance Learning Project (AADLP), a kind of correspondence course for parts of the CCM curriculum.[39] Over the following two years, the J.W. McConnell Family

Foundation awarded a $500,000 gift to the AADLP and the federal departments of Employment and Immigration contributed $422,000 towards the CCM's operations.[40] This was the kind of leverage or catalytic support that the SSBFF looked to provide in all its programs.

In its agreement with the University of Waterloo, the SSBFF also stipulated that a review should be conducted after three years to assess the CCM's national placement rate for its graduates, the profile of the program in Canada, the performance of the centre's director, the commitment of the university to administration, the materials and documents generated, and the CCM's influence on similar programs at other institutions.[41] The review process was important, not only because the directors wished to have an account of moneys spent, but because they hoped to justify their decision to invest in the development of a national centre housed by one university. Other institutions around the country had hoped to receive funds from the SSBFF to develop their own programs in arts and cultural management and were now left feeling their needs would not be heard. These expectations put a great deal of pressure on the CCM's new director, William Poole, who arrived at the University of Waterloo in January 1990.[42]

Poole came from the National Ballet School in Toronto, where an eight-year term as administrative director capped a seventeen-year career in arts administration. He was familiar with the program at Waterloo, having been invited by John Stubbs to serve on its advisory board along with Hobday. At the Ballet School, Poole had employed some of the students from Waterloo, and he understood the potential benefits of the program to both future arts managers and arts organizations. He also understood the challenge that lay ahead, although the full force of that challenge hit Poole after the opening ceremonies were over and he walked into his new, empty office. He realized that funding for this new institution was in place for four or five years, but after that the future was entirely uncertain. Using the CAAAE report prepared by Marion Paquet as a roadmap, he focused on building a service organization. Travelling across Canada to meet with the directors of other arts administration programs, he tried to put to rest institutional rivalries and develop his own sense of priorities.[43]

Poole got some sense of the fractious nature of the arts community when the SSBFF and the CCM convened the workshop entitled "2020 Vision – Cultural Management in Thirty Years" at Elora, Ontario in November 1990. The thirty-one participants represented opera companies, museums, festivals, dance troupes, the theatre, private industry, and academe. Asked to envision the future, participants had no difficulty imagining the role of the arts within Canadian society, but when it came to the role of the cultural manager they had difficulty. They wondered, for example, whether the job of a cultural manager was fundamentally different from the work of a manager of any other kind of organization. They also gave advice to Poole as he worked to shape the CCM, and there were plenty of opinions as to what its priorities should be.[44]

If the vision of cultural management remained vague, there was general agreement as to the shape that arts and culture should take. Traditionally, or at least since the Massey-Lévesque Commission era of the 1950s, the realm of arts and culture had been defined by a relatively small number of institutions and elites generating cultural "products" for a large number of consumers. According to the participants at the Elora workshop, the future would be defined by community-based organizations or even informal associations. A huge variety of producers would be organized to reach smaller, but more specific, audiences. Increasingly, these audiences would be more engaged with the processes of production. This transition would be driven by the growing cultural assertiveness of Canada's First Nations, francophones, and new immigrants. This vision became known as the "Elora Model."[45]

The Elora Model provided a philosophical underpinning to the CCM's curriculum, and the program's graduates carried these ideas into their careers.[46] Student numbers did rise as the CCM gained credibility, especially after the visioning workshop and the numerous funders taking interest. By the spring of 1996 there were thirty-five graduates, and all reportedly found appropriate jobs in their fields – welcome news to the SSBFF directors.[47] The scheduled review, which was conducted over the course of 1992 by independent evaluators, was favourable, although it was still early to assess its long-term prospects. The evaluators predicted that success would depend on the university's active effort to support

the CCM. In the short run, core staffing for the program could be provided by making cross-appointments from within the Faculty of Arts,
but the university eventually needed to appoint a full-time faculty position. Eventually, the CCM would have to generate significant research
that would provide tangible benefits to the field. The evaluators also suggested that the university, rather than the director of the centre, ensure
that the co-op program provide placements and counselling to students
as part of its overall commitment. By securing a solid and respected place
within the University of Waterloo, the CCM would establish itself as a
"catalytic" institution within the field of arts and culture in Canada.[48]

After receiving what was on the whole a positive evaluation, the
SSBFF opted to provide a long-term funding commitment to the CCM:
$100,000 per year for five years, beginning in 1994. Noting the evalua-
tors' recommendation that it show support for the centre, the University
of Waterloo announced it would match the SSBFF's $100,000 for the
current year.[49] The foundation was encouraged to see matching grants,
never wishing it to be assumed that a client organization could resort
exclusively to one source for core funding, but some directors were concerned that the university might not continue its commitment, especially
over five years. It was decided to phrase an appreciative letter in such a
way that it would be clear to Waterloo that the SSBFF assumed it would
repeat the matching grant for the duration, rather than leave the matter
unresolved and hope for the best.[50] In his discussions with the university administrators Hobday could never be sure how committed they
were to the program, although the matching grant did always come
through, albeit at the last minute in the manner of large institutions with
complex budgets.[51]

The SSBFF also gave money to special projects initiated by the CCM.
In an effort to improve its curriculum, the centre put together a "Cultural
Management Learning Strategy" by late 1995, building on earlier efforts
to fine-tune its courses to meet the needs of students and markets.[52] The
CCM's increasing use of the internet as an information tool suggested
that the Arts Administrator Distance Learning Project could be even
more useful if put on-line. Poole conceived of this service as a marvellous
way to take the CCM's expertise to people who had no means or oppor-

tunity to study full time at the University of Waterloo.[53] A new website was launched in the summer of 1997, but much work lay ahead to develop appropriate content. The CCM also made overtures to the HEC in Montreal, hoping they could be brought into the project to provide a French-language component. In the university's proposal to the SSBFF for additional funding (in which matching funds were promised), president James Downey declared that the CCM "is positioning itself to be an international leader in the field of cultural management development."[54]

The directors liked the principle of long-distance learning, although some felt that a price tag of $100,000 seemed high for developing a website. They requested a better description of how the course modules would work, how they would be developed, and how exactly students would receive accreditation on-line.[55] Poole responded by inviting members of the foundation to a demonstration of materials already being developed. In early February 1999, Hobday and Robert Rabinovitch travelled to Waterloo and, along with other selected arts managers and government representatives, were shown the CCM's first learning module, "Toward Greater Self-Reliance."[56] Poole then presented his plan "to create twenty new Interactive Learning Modules" over the next five years "for delivery to Canadian cultural managers via the World Wide Web." The objective was for the website "to become the single most indispensable tool for working cultural managers; to create a 'level playing field' and equal access to professional development for all cultural managers, trustees and other volunteers in Canada ...; to be the premier Canadian source of capacity building in cultural organizations; to add French-language access to the CCM website through [HEC]." The website would "overcome all of the traditional barriers to professional development in the sector – time, money and geography." It also had "the potential to transform the way in which cultural organizations are run in Canada."[57]

This ambitious agenda convinced the SSBFF directors that the CCM would have no difficulty spending $100,000 a year for the next five years. If anything, they worried that the CCM was launching a major initiative without sufficient planning or funding prospects. Robert Vineberg wondered if the CCM had considered the project's "possible commercial implications" and called for the preparation of a business plan which could then be independently evaluated.[58] The CCM obliged by preparing an impressive business plan which the board reviewed at their June 1999 meeting. Stephen felt that this project, now referred to as the Cultural Management Institute (CMI), was unprecedented and could be marketed around the world. Hobday agreed, noting that the students of the CMI would be employable in many countries, particularly England where there was "a chronic shortage of trained people."[59] With this end in view, Poole had collaborated with David Barr, the president of Distributed Educational Systems, to write a paper entitled "Online Professional Development for Cultural Managers," which the two men presented that same month at the Fifth International Conference on Arts and Cultural Management, held in Helsinki, Finland.[60]

The independent evaluation of the proposal was "very positive" and the SSBFF agreed to contribute $500,000 over five years to the CMI.[61] However, this grant was conditional upon additional funding coming not only from the university but from government. The Department of Canadian Heritage (PCH) had indicated it was prepared to give $620,000 to develop French-language modules for the CMI but, as the SSBFF directors were learning in their dealings with the federal bureaucracy, the process took a great deal of time. In March 2000, Poole wrote to Hubert Lussier, director-general of the department's arts program, asking for a progress report; with no encouraging news and a new fiscal year underway, the new president at Waterloo, David Johnston, wrote directly to the minister, Sheila Copps, "requesting an urgent resolution of this outstanding funding issue," and then followed up with phone calls to both minister and deputy minister.[62] Despite receiving no confirmation of upcoming money, the CCM proceeded to develop ten English-language Interactive Learning Modules and remained in hopeful contact with their counterparts at the HEC.

Another year of delays ensued, largely because of a federal election. A meeting was finally held in June 2001 between Poole, Hobday, François Colbert of the HEC, and several PCH officials; nothing was concluded but some indication was made that the government might be willing to make a greater contribution than $620,000.[63] Early in 2002, PCH announced it would grant $718,419 to the CMI to create twenty-two French-language modules. Poole and Colbert discussed their upcoming collaboration.[64] It was the spring of 2003 by the time the money was actually in the Poole's hands and the CCM could proceed to develop "'Expanded content and bilingual access' to build the French language version and complete the final English modules of this web-based distance education model" in partnership with HEC.[65]

The SSBFF continued to support the CMI throughout the five-year period even when this funding was not being matched as promised. Indeed, they did so despite being unhappy with the product. Technically, the website delivered what it was supposed to, but they felt its "visual look ... left much to be desired."[66] The directors were therefore in the curious position of having created something that was very successful and well-funded but which they did not particularly like. Although this situation left them disinclined to continue supporting the CCM as they wound the foundation down, it did not detract from the overall accomplishment of having systematically improved the training of cultural managers.

Arts Stabilization

For all the success of the CCM, the foundation was to make an equal if not greater impact on the arts through its arts stabilization initiative. The need for action was born of the 1990s recession, which sparked renewed concern for the survival of arts and cultural institutions. Although plenty of organizations were experiencing real financial difficulties, even facing extinction, the SSBFF did not wish merely to supplement existing funding and potentially create new dependencies. Instead, it looked for creative ways to insulate cultural institutions from ongoing political and economic change.

Hobday had been aware for some time of the growing arts stabilization movement in the United States. Concerned that weak management diminished the creative impact of its grants to arts organizations, the Ford Foundation had begun to work in the 1970s to improve fiscal management in the arts. In 1983, these efforts sparked the creation of National Arts Stabilization (NAS), an independent organization funded by the Ford, Rockefeller, and Mellon Foundations.[67] The NAS proved helpful to arts and cultural organizations, not by making core operating grants but by enabling them to develop good management practices that would sustain them even through difficult times. Hobday had what he called a "eureka" moment one day in 1993 while having a meal with someone who had been trying to adapt the NAS to Vancouver. Hobday was convinced that the SSBFF was the institution to spearhead the National Arts Stabilization Fund concept for all of Canada. "It wasn't a grants program," he realized, but rather "an interventionist program, designed firmly around organizational health, and it was going to require a lot of money, and the money was going to have to come from all three levels of government and the private sector."[68]

Hobday described arts stabilization as providing two types of assistance, technical and financial. The first of these consisted of "professional, experienced problem diagnosis and advice in those areas critical to success – planning, financial management, audience development, marketing, fundraising and organizational development – which is available to each organization as required, at low or no cost." The second took the form of grants, usually awarded over four years "based on a realistic plan for long-term financial stability, which is developed and supported by an organization's board, management, and artistic leadership." Such a plan would strive for "the liquidation of any existing operating deficit and the maintenance of a positive working capital position over the grant period. Grants are applied solely to aid in the elimination of accumulated deficits and in the building of working capital reserves."[69] Arts stabilization was a rigorous procedure, but it would provide an answer to a chronic problem – one that many groups were reluctant to admit they had; in that respect, Hobday likened it to Alcoholics Anonymous, where the first step was to acknowledge that the problem came from within.[70] Arts stabilization was also very much in the interest of funders, private and public, as in the long run it promised an end to constant pleas for financial bailouts.

In December 1993 Hobday brought the idea to the SSBFF board. The directors were enthusiastic, especially Peter Swann, who perhaps understood the issue best. They decided to allocate $60,000 to hire consultants to develop a proposal for a Canadian model.[71] Six months later, Peter

Brown and Diane Hoar presented a plan to create CASP (the Canadian Arts Stabilization Program) as a national organization. The SSBFF was willing to make an investment of $1 million over seven years to get the association started, with the proviso that CASP must line up another $3 million from other private sources; Hobday felt sure that $8 million or more could also be gleaned from the federal government, and promised to approach the Department of Canadian Heritage to discuss the matter.[72] By the end of the year, much progress had been made thanks to ongoing efforts by Brown and Hoar and of course Hobday. PCH was enthusiastic and promised $8.4 million at some point in the future. Several corporations pledged money to CASP, including the Chalmers Foundation, which promised $250,000 over four years. The Council for Business and the Arts in Canada (CBAC), an association of some seventy major corporate arts supporters, was approached as a potential partner; Hobday felt that CBAC would make an excellent body to take on CASP as a project, the unfortunate problem being that CBAC was rumoured to be running a deficit due to declining membership.[73]

The SSBFF also made contact with two regional arts stabilization organizations which were obvious partners for CASP: the recently founded Vancouver Arts Stabilization Program (VASP), and the Alberta Performing Arts Stabilization Fund (APASF) which was formally launched in January 1995 with participation from across the province. It was Brown and Hoar's impression that the APASF was unwilling to join CASP because of "regionalist sentiments" and because it did not feel it needed a national stabilization program, having plenty of resources of its own.[74] The APASF also had direct access to federal funding, as did its Vancouver counterpart; each program had received $1 million from PCH to get started.[75]

Brown and Hoar also reported that they had conducted a needs assessment study for Toronto, and were planning similar studies of Quebec, the Maritimes, and the Prairies for 1995. In Toronto, opposition to CASP had been advanced by some arts groups, who put forward arguments such as: "Adopting financial standards for funding will result in a compromise of artistic standards" or "This concept won't work here because it wasn't invented here" or "We know how to run our organizations and don't need help, just money." Even the Ontario Arts Council had argued that it was "wrong to imply to funders that arts organizations may need help with management and governance," lest funding be withdrawn. Brown and Hoar argued that in fact CASP was the only real answer to the problem of financial instability, citing the example of the Toronto Symphony which was prepared to borrow $15 million to invest and use the interest to gradually pay off its deficit, hoping the lenders would eventually forgive the loan in return for a tax receipt; by contrast, an investment of $18 million through CASP would stabilize as many as twenty at-risk Toronto organizations.[76]

Hobday felt that CASP was "the best shot we have to help arts organizations make the transition from the current high level of dependence on Governments to greater self-reliance."[77] To do this, of course, it needed government funding – but it was clearly in the government's best interest to pursue this course, as it was far more expensive having constantly to come to the rescue of floundering organizations. PCH agreed to host a stakeholders' meeting in Banff early in 1995, inviting representatives from the VASP, the APASF, the CBAC, and the SSBFF. Participants dedicated their time to working out the terms by which a national program would collaborate with regional ones; the agreement in principle was that CASP would provide 30 per cent of each region's funding as well as technical assistance to the regions and their associated community stabilization organizations.[78]

The process was compromised by regional disparities and provincial mistrust of federal programs. Provinces such as Alberta and Ontario were in a much better position to raise funds from the local private sector than were New Brunswick or Nova Scotia. In some regions there was more concern for gaining leverage with government funding programs than for building a common structure.[79] Suspicions were also voiced that CASP was essentially an inflated government program that would bring no real change, a shell game where existing money was simply reallocated to a new fund. Some feared that the success of a stabilization program might lead the government to cut or freeze funding for the cultural organizations in the future. Some suspected that the program's "national experts" would prove insensitive to local conditions and management systems.[80] Brown and Hoar concluded that the only way to ensure national cooperation was for PCH to "develop and articulate a comprehensive and cogent policy regarding arts stabilization," something they were beginning to fear would not happen.[81]

The SSBFF collaborated with PCH and other smaller foundations to fund a study of small and medium-sized arts institutions across the country to determine how well they could be served by arts stabilization. The study, carried out by Marion Paquet, Peter Brown, and François Colbert of the HEC, was completed by December 1995 and provided much crucial information.[82] The following May the SSBFF invited PCH's associate Deputy Minister Victor Rabinovitch and his junior colleague Hubert Lussier to a board meeting to discuss progress in creating a national stabilization program. Rabinovitch apologized for the delays, citing the ongoing challenge of convincing groups of the benefits of adopting a long-term solution when they really wanted a "quick fix."[83] This did not mean that federal support would not be given to regional and provincial stabilization projects, which the SSBFF had already begun to put together by approaching provincial governments and the local private sector. By the end of 1997 projects were underway in Nova Scotia, New Brunswick, Manitoba, and Saskatchewan – traditionally considered have-not provinces with limited resources for major initiatives – as well as in the "Bay Area" south of Toronto, with Hamilton (significantly, the minister of Canadian Heritage's own riding) at its centre.[84]

The federal government contributed to these efforts, but at lower rates than expected and with no apparent willingness to fund CASP. In a letter to Eileen Sarkar, who had replaced Victor Rabinovitch as associate deputy minister in December 1997, Hobday observed that the Nova Scotia initiative had requested $777,000 and received only $125,000. If PCH did not come through for Nova Scotia, "then it seems pointless to continue our efforts in New Brunswick, Quebec, Hamilton, Manitoba, [and] Saskatchewan."[85] Sarkar replied that she was "having difficulty in persuading her Minister, Sheila Copps that the Department … [should] contribute to the emerging programs which the SSBFF and the Department have been jointly encouraging over the last three years."[86] At their June 1998 board meeting, the SSBFF debated ways to put pressure on Copps to honour PCH's previous commitment to the program, such as writing an open letter to *The Globe and Mail* describing how arts stabilization would contribute to "cultural infrastructure," which the government was always claiming it supported.[87] In the end Hobday took the unusual step of engaging the services of a political advisor: Herb Metcalfe, whose extensive experience helping cultural organizations deal with government policy and regulations enabled him to keep abreast of developments within government circles in a way that no one within the SSBFF could hope to do. Hobday felt that this was the only way "to ensure that there were effective, ongoing and coordinated communications with the Minister, her staff and key members of the Parliamentary Committee on Culture and Communications."[88]

In an effort to advance the cause, the APASF hosted a two-day meeting in Calgary in September 1998 attended by over forty people, including representatives from arts organizations, private and public funding agencies, and art stabilization programs in both the United States and England.[89] The meeting ended in renewed optimism that the various parties would collaborate further, and as a result Copps made several public statements during the following months praising the benefits of arts stabilization.[90] Over the next year, the SSBFF continued to monitor the program's progress through regular reports from Metcalfe. Early in 1999 the foundation received word that a cabinet document was being prepared on the subject of arts stabilization, although the federal budget announced in February made no mention of the program.[91] Some weeks later PCH announced that the Nova Scotia arts stabilization program would receive an additional $175,000 "as a goodwill gesture" – presumably in anticipation of more.[92] Finally, in December 1999 the Social Policy Committee of the Liberal Party Caucus met to review a document entitled "Towards a National Arts Stabilization Program" which set out a plan for creating "a well-funded, comprehensive program over a five-year period."[93]

Confident that the minister was now "very anxious to move this forward," the SSBFF agreed that it would provide between $125,000 and $250,000 to each of the emerging programs, over a five-year period. "Amounts in this range should be sufficient so that each of the arts stabilization programs could make the most of our funding to lever other funds from governments and the private sector."[94] The foundation made grants to stabilization projects in Nova Scotia, Manitoba, and the Bay Area. In Quebec, the provincial Ministry of Cultural Affairs announced the creation of a *Fonds de consolidation* which seemed very similar to the notion of arts stabilization, deviating from the concept chiefly in that it was entirely funded by the government – an approach quite in keeping with the way programs tended to be run in Quebec.[95] Although this program had no overt links with its nascent federal counterpart, it had clearly been influenced by the SSBFF's efforts since 1993 and the feasibility study for Quebec City and Montreal conducted early in 1995. The only place in Canada that remained resistant to the concept of arts stabilization was Toronto, largely because its major arts organizations thought they were doing fine without this sort of assistance.[96]

The regional programs had to wait until after the next federal election to begin receiving the long-awaited funding. In May 2001, Sheila Copps, once again minister of Canadian Heritage, announced a government investment of $63 million over three years "in a national strategy to support modern management and greater financial stability in arts and heritage organizations."[97] The new program would go by the name of the Canadian Arts and Heritage Sustainability Program (CAHSP). After hearing of this development, the SSBFF directors knew that, despite all the delays, something significant had been accomplished: the federal government had endorsed the notion that better management was a key to creating financial stability in an arts organization. Furthermore, a policy had been established, a standard for arts stabilization that could be applied to all cases whatever the provincial and regional variables.[98] The directors proceeded to congratulate Hobday "for his hard work and commitment to the arts."[99]

With federal funding flowing, things moved quickly. A year later Hobday reported that the arts stabilization programs implemented by the SSBFF in Nova Scotia, Manitoba, and the Bay Area were now fully operational and that programs in Saskatchewan, New Brunswick, and PEI were underway.[100] Hobday was particularly enthusiastic about the Manitoba program, which enjoyed the greatest success in mobilizing

242 • SPIRITED COMMITMENT

resources to achieve effective arts stabilization.[101] No universal program could be implemented in Ontario because of lack of interest from the provincial government, but arts stabilization even came to reluctant Toronto: the Creative Trust, Working Capital for the Arts to assist medium-sized and smaller arts organizations.[102] As the SSBFF wound down its funding commitments in 2004 and 2005, it sent its last cheques to the New Brunswick Foundation, Arts Stabilization Fund Saskatchewan, and the Island Arts and Heritage Stabilization Program, bringing one of its most successful programs to a close.[103]

CONCLUSION

The SSBFF's cultural management program succeeded in creating two major institutions that achieved independence, one as part of the University of Waterloo and the other in connection with a major federal government program. The foundation provided generous funding to both, and in both cases worked hard to ensure success – and on the whole achieved it, even though they drew the line in the end at continuing to fund the Cultural Management Institute. Between them, these institutions provided crucial training for arts managers across Canada and equally crucial financial stability to arts organizations in every province, notably in the Atlantic region and the Prairies where very little public investment had been made up to that point in the arts. Almost certainly the efforts to help arts organizations function as businesses would have impressed Sam Bronfman.

TEN

HERITAGE: URBAN ISSUES

The destruction of urban environments was becoming a hot topic throughout North America by the early 1970s, and quickly caught the attention of the SSBFF. The impetus for its involvement came from Phyllis, who as an architect was deeply concerned by the post-war devastation of cities. The other directors were equally willing for the SSBFF to tackle the problems of architectural and urban heritage, and by 1975 this issue had become one of the SSBFF's five funding programs. Heritage provided support for such institutions as Heritage Montreal and Heritage Canada, which at different levels served to educate the urban population in the importance of architectural heritage. The goals of urban heritage were broader than keeping old buildings from demolition, however. For some years, critics of post-war planning pointed to the devastating social problems resulting from the destruction of inner-city neighbourhoods in the name of urban renewal. Activists called for the preservation not merely of old buildings but of whole urban areas, in the belief that design on a human scale was more conducive to social harmony than the visions of urban planners obsessed with renewal.

In an effort to address this larger question of the urban environment, the SSBFF created a new funding program in the early 1990s known as

Urban Issues. This program wrestled with the difficulty of how to provide community development in urban areas where local groups struggled against huge corporations, insensitive planners, and basic poverty. Moreover, the issue was how to do so in a way that would enable such groups to expand their reach and influence without making them dependent on the SSBFF. More than with any other program, Urban Issues succeeded in being a real agent for improving peoples' lives. It did so, however, without a specific national organization to oversee its progress, and required an even greater level of effort by SSBFF directors than usual to manage the granting process. The very real achievements of Urban Issues must be weighed against the obligation of SSBFF board and staff to commit time and energy to ensure its success.

THE HERITAGE MOVEMENT

Until the 1960s, the drive to preserve historic buildings in Canada, and especially in Quebec, came out of a search for national mythologies rather than an effort to improve the urban environment. The 1908 tercentenary of the founding of Quebec gave impetus to the movement to commemorate and preserve buildings and places that carried great significance for the country. Prior to the tercentenary, the Literary and Historical Society of Quebec – Canada's oldest heritage organization, founded in 1824 – convinced the federal government to purchase the Plains of Abraham just outside the city walls to keep it out of the hands of real estate developers. At the same time, the historically minded St Jean-Baptiste Society promoted converting the area into a commemorative park. As this was the site of the 1759 victory of the British over the French, this campaign had to be steered carefully through the political waters; promoters did not wish the result to appear to be a public relations victory for either British imperialists or Quebec nationalists. In March 1908, the federal government established the National Battlefields Commission to oversee the creation of the park. Composed of members from a variety of backgrounds and political positions, the commission proceeded to decide on the park's commemorative features, which included monuments to a wide variety of heroes to satisfy all objectors – or at any rate a sufficient number for the plan to be carried out.[1]

The success of the tercentenary and the recognition of the battlefield park as a historic site of national importance – however ambiguously that was defined – spurred the establishment of a national body to designate other such sites. The Historic Sites and Monuments Board of Canada was launched in September 1919 with a mandate to identify sites of historic significance and commemorate them in an appropriate manner. The mood of aggressive patriotism following the First World War resulted in a board that focused largely on battle sites; furthermore, despite some participation from French-Canadian historians, the notion of national significance often meant the achievements of the British at the expense of the French and native peoples.[2] Even apart from these limitations, the HSMBC played no role in actually preserving sites and monuments, jurisdiction over which was generally considered to lie with provincial governments as part of culture. Only in the wake of the Massey Report, which projected a stronger role for the federal government in this domain, was greater emphasis placed on preservation. Significantly, 1950s legislation enabled the HSMBC to recognize the urban landscape as worthy of designation and protection alongside buildings and sites.[3]

A parallel movement with parallel legislation emerged in Quebec, implicitly though not overtly nationalist in character, its focus being on religious heritage and buildings from the French regime.[4] The province's Historic or Artistic Monuments Act of 1922 sought to protect "monuments and objects of art, whose preservation is of national interest from an historic or artistic standpoint."[5] The act created a Historic Monuments Commission (HMC), which set out to classify buildings it deemed worthy of preservation, albeit without much in the way of legal power to prevent the destruction of classified buildings. Subsequent laws in 1935 and 1952 expanded the range of historic monuments to include spaces as well as buildings. One such heritage space or district was l'Île d'Orléans, downriver from Quebec City, whose historic character it was felt should not be marred by the construction of restaurants, gas stations, and billboards. It was only with the Quiet Revolution, and the 1961 creation of a provincial ministry of cultural affairs as part of the general shift of power from church to state, that the heritage preservation movement in Quebec would lose its emphasis on religious and French regime monuments – and acquire some teeth. In addition to classifying buildings, the Historic Monuments Act of 1963 authorized the HMC to zone certain urban areas designated as historic and to control building activity within such zones. It also prohibited the export of classified property without the permission of the HMC and gave authority to the government to help private individuals and organizations restore classified property in their possession.

The net effect was not stronger protection, however. The "urban renewal" that had been taking its toll on Montreal for several years would intensify over the course of the 1960s, resulting in much demolition of older buildings and neighbourhoods. Montrealers had greeted the seminal Place Ville Marie in 1962 with enthusiasm, partly because it was a bold new structure unlike anything they had seen in their city, but also because it filled what for decades had been a gaping hole in the middle of downtown caused by the opening of a railway tunnel.[6] Other dazzling modern skyscrapers rose across the city, and it was only as residents began to notice that historic buildings were being demolished to make way for them that concern began to grow. Buoyed by the success of Place Ville Marie, by the construction of a metro, and by the creation of whole new islands in the river as a site for the 1967 World's Fair, Montreal seemed to see itself as the city of the future, clearly at the expense of the past. In parts of town, entire blocks were bulldozed to make room for such vast projects as the CBC headquarters east of downtown and the sunken expressway cutting through the city centre; other areas such as Little Burgundy, cultural centre of the city's black community, were largely razed in anticipation of multi-storey social housing. Critics of the municipal government protested that the unchecked freedom given to developers would soon make Montreal resemble Detroit, the victim of urban renewal that had almost completely destroyed its downtown.[7]

The city did establish the Viger Commission (named after Montreal's first mayor) in 1962, a watchdog organization to advise the municipal government on heritage issues and with a special mandate to oversee the rehabilitation of Old Montreal. On the commission's suggestion, the city passed a bylaw forbidding any new parking lots in the old town, a move designed to eliminate the key motive for demolishing buildings. With the passing of the new Historic Monuments Act the following year, the commission recommended that the HMC designate the city's oldest quarter as a historic district, which it promptly did.[8] However, apart from restoring a few key buildings and laying out cobblestones on certain streets to attract tourists, the city did little to help make Old Montreal a living community. Efforts to rehabilitate the area as real urban space were undertaken almost entirely by the private sector. One such individual was journalist Eric McLean, who purchased the late eighteenth-century Papineau house and carefully restored it for use as his private residence; until that time, the house and most neighbouring buildings were seedy taverns or cheap boarding houses.[9]

Another individual who chose to live in Old Montreal was Phyllis Lambert. As an architect, Phyllis was already attuned to the problem of decaying inner cities and the need for sensitive architectural solutions. During the 1960s she had lived in Chicago and witnessed the wholesale destruction of neighbourhoods to make way for urban renewal. Her championing of modern architects such as Mies van der Rohe was matched by a great respect for more traditional buildings, and she spearheaded a number of intriguing projects in the United States. She and photographer Richard Pare, with Seagram funding, recruited twenty-four photographers to document the nation's historic county courthouses as part of the American Bicentennial celebrations. Phyllis also brought her own training to bear in Los Angeles, where she undertook the renovation of the 1921 Biltmore Hotel with her partner Gene Summers, hoping it would serve as a catalyst for efforts to revitalize the city's downtown.[10] Having returned to live in Montreal in 1973 after her father's death, she acquired a house in the old town, a building that had seen a variety of commercial uses since its erection in 1864 including that of a dried fruit factory. Classified in 1963 and refitted as a fashion house for the couturière Marie-Paule Nolin, the building was further restored by Phyllis and converted into a home and workspace. From this base she plunged into the world of Montreal's built heritage.[11]

Phyllis's involvement was as both researcher and activist. A major contribution to knowledge of the city's architectural history was in establishing the Groupe de recherche sur les bâtiments en pierre grise, which documented Montreal's greystone buildings between 1730 and 1920.[12] Phyllis also became intensely active in saving historic structures and communities from the wrecking ball and the bulldozer. At times, her activism challenged the plans of companies such as Cadillac Fairview, the real estate developer owned by her own family interests. Her initiatives drew the attention of the press and the admiration of thousands of Montrealers. Going out with her in public, where she wore her trademark overalls, was almost like walking the streets with "a rock star," according to a long-time associate.[13] Phyllis's very public presence in these years might not have surprised her father if he had lived longer, but it did not fit with his vision of what his daughter would do.

The fight over the Milton Park community focused many of Phyllis's ideas about the relationships between people and the urban built environment. This inner-city Montreal neighbourhood situated to the east of McGill University was made up of many limestone row houses dating from the late nineteenth and early twentieth centuries. Since the end of the Second World War, it had lost its middle-class base and attracted students, immigrants, and workers. Through the 1960s a development company, Concordia Estates Ltd., had quietly acquired most of the property in an area bounded by Sainte-Famille, Milton, and Hutchinson Streets and Pine Avenue.[14] The company announced in 1968 that it would undertake a three-phase, $200 million project to redevelop this twenty-five- acre section. In response, local residents organized the Milton Park Citizens' Committee to fight the project; when demolition began in 1972, committee members protested and occupied vacant buildings in an effort to stop the destruction.[15] The residents' cause was given additional fame and credence when Jane Jacobs, the American critic of urban renewal, visited the Milton Park area and raved about its architectural and human qualities.[16] Jacobs's involvement signalled the shift that had taken place in the heritage preservation movement over the previous decade, from an exclusive focus on historical significance to a holistic approach that emphasized the importance of streets and neighbourhood as antidotes to urban decay.

SAVING MONTREAL

In 1972, in an effort to address the demands of heritage preservationists, the Quebec government adopted the Cultural Property Act which replaced the 1963 act and expanded the regulatory powers of the provincial Ministère des Affaires culturelles. It created two classes of historic properties, "recognized" and "classified," the latter being the more binding when it came to a site's preservation. The ministry was also given power to create tax incentives to encourage the maintenance of historic patrimony, and the maximum fine for violating the law was raised from a mere $500 to a somewhat more intimidating $5,000.[17] There were hopes that this new policy would prevent the sort of wholesale demolition that had characterized Montreal for over a decade, but they would soon be dashed when persistent appeals to all levels of government failed to stop the destruction of the Van Horne house in the autumn of 1973. It was this action that pushed Montreal citizens into forming grassroots heritage organizations, beginning with Save Montreal, dedicated to preserving what was left of their city.

The Van Horne house on Sherbrooke Street was not only one of the few surviving mansions of the Golden Square Mile but a repository of art nouveau decorative elements unique in North America.[18] Hearing of its impending demolition, citizens launched a class action suit against the developer, arguing that the removal of the building would result in an unacceptable diminution in the quality of the neighbourhood.[19] At face value, this was a peculiar claim, given that several hotels and office buildings had already disrupted much of the street's charm, but it spoke to the notion that heritage preservation was about more than simply old buildings. While the case was in court, the city of Montreal withheld the demolition permit, but that was all it could do. The plaintiffs asked the provincial ministry to have the house classified and learned that the minister had apparently been about to do just that some months earlier, only to change his mind suddenly.[20] The National Historic Sites and Monuments Board had no power to prevent a building's demolition unless it was owned by the federal government. Phyllis suggested that CEMP purchase the mansion to use as its headquarters, but the developers refused to consider a bid.[21] In the end, the case was won by the developers, who immediately proceeded to demolish the house in the middle of the night.[22]

This incident prompted the formation of Save Montreal, a grassroots organization dedicated to the protection and improvement of Montreal's urban environment.[23] Phyllis joined this new organization and soon became one of its strongest champions. The SSBFF became involved in heritage preservation the following year when Save Montreal launched a campaign to raise $250,000 "for professional programmes proposing alternatives for the use of buildings and open spaces in danger of being destroyed." The foundation contributed $10,000 out of its Added Dimensions program.[24] Over the course of the next few years it also provided grants to other organizations wishing to restore buildings, including $10,000 in 1980–81 to the Centre culturel et sportif de l'est in Montreal to help renovate the magnificent building Le Marché de Maisonneuve. The directors declared themselves "very much in favour of support being given for the preservation of old buildings, and for their being recycled for new and viable community projects."[25]

Save Montreal proved a useful vehicle for protest, but it lacked the broader capacity to educate that the heritage movement needed in order to effect real change. In October 1975, along with various progressive members of the Montreal business community, Phyllis created Heritage Montreal with a more global focus and the capacity to raise funds. The letters patent for Heritage Montreal described its mandate as seeking "to promote and encourage the preservation of the historic, architectural, natural, and cultural heritage of communities."[26] The SSBFF took a special interest in developing this new organization; indeed, it was this interest that crystallized the SSBFF's decision to establish a new funding program for Heritage. In proposing the program, Swann asked for a budget of $50,000, but with Phyllis's encouragement the Board set it at an annual $75,000, raised to $104,500 within three years; of this, $15,000 went specifically to Heritage Montreal. Charles noted that Heritage Montreal had emerged as "a vibrant, energetic group, and should help solve some of the urban environmental problems in Montreal."[27]

A serious limitation facing the heritage movement was the relative toothlessness of the national Historic Sites and Monuments Commission, which could not physically protect buildings the government did not own. In an attempt to address this situation, the federal government created the Heritage Canada Foundation in 1973. Armed with a $12 million start-up grant, Heritage Canada was independent of the government, with a board consisting of representatives from across the country, and a full staff.[28] Although it was designed to become a kind of National Trust, modelled after the British institution, Heritage Canada had a more general mandate: to "encourage the preservation ... of the nationally significant historic, architectural, natural and scenic heritage of Canada with a view to stimulating and promoting the interest of the people of Canada in that heritage."[29] The last clause of the mandate had particular resonance for the SSBFF in its pursuit of programs with national significance. Apart from interest from its initial grant, Heritage Canada operated entirely through donations – many of them from the SSBFF. Appropriately, Phyllis was elected to the board of governors of Heritage Canada in 1977.[30]

When Hobday reviewed the SSBFF's Heritage Program in 1984 at the beginning of his term as executive director, he encouraged the SSBFF directors to curb their tendency to support a wide variety of disparate projects; instead, they should concentrate on building institutions that would create awareness of heritage issues and work to form policy. Heritage Canada clearly had the makings of a national organization with a wide reach; Hobday was particularly impressed with its Main Street projects, modelled after the program to revitalize downtown cores initiated in the 1970s in the United States by the National Trust for Historic Preservation. Heritage Montreal obviously had a more local focus, but it was well organized and had strong grassroots. Hobday suggested a modest increase in funding (to $130,000) for the Heritage program, and advocated providing core funding to both institutions: $15,000 for Heritage Canada and $25,000 for Heritage Montreal. He added the proviso that they submit regular progress reports of their activities.[31]

The SSBFF directors agreed to focus the program in this manner, including concentrating their efforts into larger-scale heritage projects. The SSBFF's principal heritage activity during the 1980s outside Heritage Montreal was the reconstruction of Ottawa's Rideau Street Convent Chapel inside the new National Gallery, which opened in the summer of 1988.[32]

HERITAGE MONTREAL

Heritage Montreal proved itself to be ambitious and innovative. Over the course of the 1970s and 80s it became an effective watchdog for architectural preservation in the city and provided vital consultancy on restoration projects. Under Phyllis's leadership, Heritage Montreal worked with the Milton Park Citizens' Committee and the cooperative housing movement that had arisen to counter the effects of urban renewal in that area. By 1976 half the original buildings had been lost, but in that year the committee succeeded in having the city pass a zoning bylaw prohibiting further high-rise construction in the area. Heritage Montreal then negotiated an agreement with the city whereby it would purchase the remaining properties and resell them to the cooperatives.[33] Over the next decade, some 600 dwelling units were acquired by twenty cooperatives and non-profit organizations and renovated with subsidies from all levels of government. Moreover, the benefits went far beyond creating comfortable and affordable inner-city housing. The Milton Park project set the standard for community activism in Montreal, militating for sane traffic regulations, citizen participation in municipal affairs, community support for low income residents and the elderly, and special facilities for the disabled. Community rules protected residents against eviction and avoided the problem of gentrification by ensuring that new tenants truly had need of low-income housing. Above all, Milton Park underscored the importance of grassroots involvement in the urban environment that was so central to Heritage Montreal's objectives.

The organization also sought more formal ways to impart its expertise. In the spring of 1984, Heritage Montreal approached the SSBFF with a proposal to create a summer full-credit course to be held at either the Université de Montréal or McGill University (each of which had schools of architecture) which would bring individuals from across the country to learn conservation and restoration techniques in both English and French. This course would form part of a regular university Heritage Studies program to be offered in collaboration with Montreal's universities and Heritage Canada. Heritage Montreal requested roughly $70,000 per year over the next three years to develop the course materials for the program and to put a coordinator in place. The SSBFF approved this plan and decided to concentrate more of their Heritage budget on Heritage Montreal with an eye to helping broaden its base of support and improve its administrative practices.[34]

Heritage Montreal held its first summer course in heritage conservation in May 1985. The program consisted of lectures by specialists in various fields (including Phyllis Lambert), hands-on demonstrations of restoration techniques, and visits to heritage sites around Montreal – which was home, the organizers noted, to "more heritage buildings than any other Canadian city."[35] After three successful summer sessions, Heritage Montreal and the Université de Montréal began work on developing a Master's Program in conservation, hoping for SSBFF support. A meeting between Phyllis and Liliane Stewart of the Macdonald-Stewart Foundation resulted in both foundations promising to provide matching grants. The new two-year Masters in Conservation was ready to accept graduate students in September 1987.[36]

In addition to these academic activities, Heritage Montreal offered a wide variety of public information programs: one-day seminars, lectures, and publications directed at citizens interested in renovating or restoring their homes. Acting as both advocate and consultant, Heritage Montreal also provided services to the city's municipal government on a contractual basis. In 1988, for example, the organization received $10,000 from the city to study the restoration of historic movie theatres for reuse as cultural facilities.[37]

More than ten years after its founding, Heritage Montreal had not lost the activist qualities that characterized its beginnings. A political battle emerged over a proposal to evict the residents and demolish the houses along Overdale Street, a neglected but historic stretch of grey-stone walkups in downtown Montreal, in order to erect a condominium and shopping complex. With additional funding from the SSBFF, Heritage Montreal commissioned a video that showed how tenants of the houses were working to prevent their eviction and the loss of the street.[38]

Heritage Montreal strove to engage the public in the city's downtown planning process. In 1988, the leaders of the organization pointed out that Montreal's new master plan was the first opportunity since 1672 for the public to articulate its vision of the city's future. The plan expounded a vision of Montreal that seemed in keeping with the one promoted by heritage activists, certainly much more so than any vision projected by previous civic administrations; it included the refurbishment of the city's waterfront and other open spaces as well as support for museums. Even so, many felt that despite some effort at public consultation, the city was not paying enough attention to criticism of many of the plan's details. Heritage Montreal determined that it needed to make a strategic shift and become a proactive "consultant" in the public policy process.[39] In effect, like other former grassroots and volunteer-driven organizations, Heritage Montreal now saw itself becoming an agent acting on behalf of its constituency.[40]

The SSBFF directors were generally pleased with the work Heritage Montreal was doing and willing to continue to provide core funding, but they also had an eye on the future. Heritage Montreal remained a grassroots organization, and as such needed to be member-driven and fiscally responsible to its membership. Concerned that the organization was not advancing sufficiently in this direction, the foundation directors asked Rose Potvin, an expert in the administration of not-for-profit organizations, to conduct a review of the organization's activities and suggest possible new directions.[41] Completed in the spring of 1986, Potvin's report emphasized the need for Heritage Montreal to expand its membership and create a network for gathering and disseminating information. It also expressed concern that Heritage Montreal was not paying enough attention to its financial health, and recommended that the SSBFF give additional funds to help its client forge better practices.[42]

The directors of Heritage Montreal and its executive director Mark London declared themselves willing to pursue these objectives as a condition for receiving further funding. By the autumn of 1986 they had put together an attractive membership recruitment campaign, including a brochure highlighting Montreal's fine architectural heritage and the work being done to preserve and restore it. The campaign was helped by the electoral victory of Mayor Jean Doré, who had declared himself enthusiastic about the heritage cause.[43] These efforts met with some success: by the end of 1988, the organization had 2,200 members.[44] The SSBFF was also encouraged to see a complete reorganization of Heritage Montreal's budgetary and accounting processes, enabling it to "exercise greater control"[45] over its finances. Unfortunately, Heritage Montreal failed to sustain the 1988 level of participation: attendance at meetings declined through 1989 and into 1990 as did membership renewals. By the spring of 1990, the organization could claim only a few more than 1,000 members.

For years the SSBFF had hoped that Heritage Montreal could become an outstanding example of what a conservation organization could do in a major Canadian city. This was the rationale for providing sustained annual funding to what was essentially a local group.[46] However, Hobday began to sense that Heritage Montreal was spending all its grant money on operations and none on developing a self-sustaining member base. He asked Gisele Rucker to undertake an evaluation. Rucker determined that while the leadership was committed to the cause of urban heritage conservation, it was not good at building a grassroots membership that would sustain the organization without the foundation's funding. She met with Dinu Bumbaru, the new executive director of Heritage Montreal, and two of its board members to try and develop a solid three-year plan for the organization.[47] Late in 1989 the directors of the SSBFF decided to phase out core funding for Heritage Montreal by 1991; after that, the foundation would consider only specific Heritage Montreal projects.[48]

The decision to withdraw funding proved wise in the end – and not because Heritage Montreal was a lost cause; far from it. Building on the profile it had acquired over the course of the city's master plan debates,

Heritage Montreal continued to engage the public in education and an appreciation for its built heritage, even as it sometimes irritated developers who no longer had quite the free hand they had enjoyed in the 1970s.[49] The year 1992 saw Montreal celebrate its 350th anniversary on a grand scale, and the SSBFF directors were happy to help support Heritage Montreal in its project to mark the numerous heritage buildings along Sherbrooke Street by commemorative plaques.[50] The organization's visibility during the course of the celebrations served to renew its sense of mission. Heritage Montreal also underwent a further internal readjustment, made possible by a one-time grant from the SSBFF to search for a new executive director; the hiring of Nancy Dunton in this capacity allowed Dinu Bumbaru to focus on education and outreach as director of programs.[51] Fifteen years later, Heritage Montreal continues as a very well-respected force for heritage issues in the city, and Bumbaru is an authoritative figure worldwide; in 1993 he was elected secretary-general of ICOMOS (International Council on Monuments and Sites).

ARCHITECTURE

As the 1980s began, Phyllis launched her most ambitious cultural project – the creation of the Canadian Centre for Architecture (CCA). Conceived as a library and archive, a museum, and a study centre for scholars of architecture and architectural history, the CCA was to be an institution like no other in the city – indeed, like few in the world. It began its intellectual life long before it had a permanent home, its offices and collections occupying space in various buildings in Montreal. Its archive contained vast numbers of photographs, plans, drawings, and models reflecting different ways people around the world have conceived and illustrated architecture. Its library contained rare books dating from as far back as the European Renaissance alongside a full range of architectural journals and monographs. Much of this material had been assembled by Phyllis herself over several decades. The completed centre would also host exhibitions, public lectures, films, conferences, and special activities for children pertaining to the world of architecture.

Determined to create a bold new structure but also showcase the benefits of heritage conservation, Phyllis decided to integrate the historic Shaughnessy house into the larger design. In 1974, following the destruction of the Van Horne house, Phyllis had purchased this Victorian mansion simply in order to save it.[52] The house was then restored to its original glory by restoration specialist Denis Saint-Louis, and a remarkable new building was planned, incorporating additional land donated by the city.[53] Conceived as a harmonious unity of old and new by architect Peter Rose in collaboration with Phyllis (as consulting architect) and Erol Argun (associate architect), the CCA would be a celebration of the ideals of both modern design and heritage preservation.[54]

While Phyllis provided the bulk of the resources needed for the $23 million building, her family and the SSBFF gave major contributions to the effort, beginning in 1981 with an annual grant of $25,000.[55] Funding was also received from private sector donors such as Alcan and Power Corporation. All levels of government promised support, as reflected in the presence at the May 1985 groundbreaking of Marcel Masse, federal minister of Communications; Clément Richard, Quebec minister of Cultural Affairs; Jean-Pierre Goyer, chairman of the Arts Council of the Montreal Urban Community; and Yvon Lamarre, chairman of the Executive Committee of the City of Montreal. At the event, these officials announced federal and provincial government grants of $4 million each to the project. For its part, the city of Montreal had consolidated the building site.[56] At the SSBFF meeting held soon after the groundbreaking, the directors confirmed their commitment to give $25,000 annually to the CCA for operating expenses; they also agreed to provide a $50,000 annual grant for the capital fund. These grants came out of the SSBFF's Plus program.[57]

The board's December 1988 meeting was held at the CCA, in advance of the official opening the following May. The next meeting was scheduled for 8 May 1989, to follow the official opening the day before. Over the next decade, the SSBFF continued to hold their meetings at the CCA, switching to the SSBFF office at Claridge on Peel Street only in the late 1990s when the next generation came to take charge of the foundation.[58]

To complement the work of the CCA, Phyllis urged McGill University to create a program in History and Theory in the School of Architecture. With support from the SSBFF in the form of an endowed chair in Saidye's name, the university launched its program in September 1987 under the direction of Professor Alberto Perez-Gomez. Nine full-time students enrolled in the first year, and ten the following year; most were Canadian but a couple came from the United States and one from France. The director of the School of Architecture, Bruce Anderson, stated that the program "continues to elicit considerable public interest, and to draw students of high calibre," although as a result there were strains on the program's resources, especially given that Perez-Gomez was the only full-time teacher.[59] Although the university provided "bridging funds" to hire a secretary and to appoint a number of thesis advisers and visiting critics, what was clearly needed was additional faculty. McGill's limited commitment frustrated the SSBFF Board and Phyllis particularly.[60]

When the program's third year attracted even more students with no relief for Perez-Gomez, Phyllis and Charles went to meet with the university president, David Johnston, to protest McGill's lack of financial and administrative support.[61] Although Johnston cited budget restraints, the complaint had obviously hit the mark, and the following September McGill appointed an additional full-time, tenure-track assistant professor. By this time there were thirty-five students in the graduate program, many of them commuting from the Université de Montréal.[62] The university also approved, "in principle," a Ph.D program in architecture, another development that Phyllis had been pressing for. The production of Ph.Ds within a few years became one of the program's greatest achievements; when Phyllis started the CCA "there wasn't a Ph.D around," but two decades later institutions could turn to a healthy supply of specialists trained in architectural history and theory.[63]

VISIONING URBAN HERITAGE

The decision to phase out core funding for Heritage Montreal left the foundation without a primary client in its Heritage program. In line with the work being done with seniors, learning disabilities, and cultural management, one might have expected that the SSBFF would look to support or create a new client with a pan-Canadian perspective. But the next step was not obvious.

In 1990 Gisele Rucker began planning the visioning conference for the SSBFF's Heritage program with an eye to redefining its scope and direction. She worked closely with Phyllis Lambert and Isabel Corral, an urban planner at the CCA.[64] "The Redefinition of the Needs of Heritage and Urban Patrimony: The Future of Our Past" conference took place in October 1990 at Hovey Manor in North Hatley, Quebec.[65] For this workshop, Phyllis and Gisele brought together an interesting group of participants reflecting a variety of perspectives on heritage issues. In addition to Phyllis herself, Dinu Bumbaru of Heritage Montreal, and Jacques Dalibard of Heritage Canada, there were academics, educators, conservationists, and business people from across the country, and representatives from New York and as far afield as Spain and Scandinavia.

As conference participants wrestled with the relationship between the urban past and the future, a number of themes emerged. The group was convinced that "a crisis of confidence in the political institutions of representative democracy" was leading to an expansion of citizen efforts "to take heritage and other matters of importance to the life of cities into their own hands." A rising concern for the multicultural nature of Canadian society would reshape perspectives on the heritage of the country. Increasingly people were looking for urban environments with a human scale and ecologically sustainable systems. At the same time, new technologies were reshaping the form and function of cities and would continue to do so in the future. Furthermore, a continued pattern of urbanization and depopulation in rural areas was likely to exacerbate the market pressures on downtown real estate, displacing lower income residents. To focus more closely on these patterns, the workshop broke into groups associated with specific issues. One addressed "Democracy/Ethnic Diversity/Community," while another looked at the environment; a third group focused on "Technology, In-Migration, and Market Forces."[66] "We all left there quite encouraged that heritage conservation was going to move away from the stuffy museum image," recalled one participant, Judy Oberlander, "and be more into the community."[67]

There were two obvious next steps: to produce a coherent statement of the North Hatley meetings, and to develop a new funding program that would reflect the workshop's conclusions. Isabel Corral was hired to take the conclusions of the workshop and create a publishable document; in February 1991, she convened an editorial team comprising workshop participants and set to work. The following month a steering committee was formed to create a framework for a new funding program focused on urban heritage. Preferring not to influence the process directly, the ssbff set up a secretariat for the project based at the Université de Montréal, and provided an initial grant with another sum awaiting the formation of a prospectus for the new program. From the foundation's point of view, the ideal outcome of this process would be the creation of a new client to implement the decisions reached at the conference.[68]

Herb Stovel, a professor in the Faculty of Urban Planning and the head of the Masters Program in Conservation and Restoration, agreed to direct the project. Stovel supervised Corral and contributed to the publication; he also sat on the steering committee (originally chaired by Phyllis) along with Kent Gerecke from the University of Manitoba and Judy Oberlander from Simon Fraser University. The publication was ready in May 1992, but the committee seemed to have made very little progress in developing a new program. After discussions with Stovel, Hobday recommended that the foundation needed to take back the lead for launching this initiative.[69] They did so, and as things turned out, retained direct control over the project for the duration.

As it was eventually defined, the new program strove to develop "places of prosperity, civility and full cultural richness" through "partnerships with individuals, grass roots neighbourhood associations, local governments and the private sector." The emphasis was on local initiative and local cooperation; while the end result would, ideally, be the preservation of urban spaces, the program aimed to "increase community awareness of the decision-making process" and "increase the citizenry's capability to develop and implement urban conservation policies which will result in the future well-being of their communities."[70] This focus on community suggested to the board that the program's title be changed from "Urban Heritage Redefinition Project" to "Community Heritage Program." At the board meeting in May 1992, Jean de Gunzburg pointed out that it was more "urban issues" than "heritage" per se. Phyllis agreed and the board adopted the new name.[71]

Urban Issues: The First Round

A call for proposals for the Urban Issues program went out in the autumn of 1992 and a deadline for applications set for 1 March 1993. An elaborate brochure highlighting the program's goals and vision was sent to nearly 3,000 potential applicants across the country. Despite this information, many of the proposals that came back reflected a failure to engage the visionary aspects of the program. "We had a lot of urban planning departments from cities writing us about roads to the airport or redoing infrastructure," recalled Rucker.[72] "We had very few applications from really grassroots organizations." Applications from particular constituencies were also disappointing. Universities offered proposals that were "quite academic" and did not "provide opportunities for students, researchers, and professors to interact with the community." "Main Street" projects tended to reinforce the status quo.[73] Of the 283 proposals received, only 32 reflected the spirit and intent of the new program.

To provide an overall assessment of the applications, the SSBFF decided to seek the help of a consultant who would provide expert advice without being required to run the program. Judy Oberlander, a participant in the North Hatley workshop and a member of the program steering committee, seemed a logical choice to continue to guide the foundation's heritage initiative. Oberlander's background and passion reflected the kind of deeply committed expertise that the SSBFF tapped for its consultants. Her mother, Cornelia Oberlander, was recognized as the most accomplished landscape architect in Canada. Her father, a professor in the School of Architecture at the University of British Columbia, was the founding director of the Centre for Human Settlements. Both were members of the Order of Canada. Judy had earned her master's degree in conservation at Columbia University in New York and went to work for Heritage Canada in 1981. She joined architect Harold Kalman and others in 1984 when they founded one of the first consulting practices in heritage conservation. Five years later she launched her own consultancy helping local governments to define their heritage conservation policies. She was also a lecturer in preservation planning at the University of Victoria.[74]

Together, Oberlander and the SSBFF staff divided the proposals into four rough categories: 1) community participation, education, and cooperation; 2) master plans and preservation planning; 3) main street or downtown revitalization projects; and 4) building restoration. Proposals in the first two areas attracted the most attention at the SSBFF, especially when they demonstrated strong grassroots or community participation.[75]

The SSBFF established a panel of outsiders to handle the next step, the first time it had done so. From the perspective of those critics of the foundation world who complain about the lack of an open selection process at many philanthropic organizations, the creation of an outside jury was an important step toward transparency. The panel consisted of Herb Stovel, Dinu Bumbaru, and Dimitri Roussopoulos. (The latter was the publisher of Black Rose Books and a community organizer in Milton Park where he lived; like the others he had been a participant in the workshop and a member of the editorial committee.) These three were given the thirty-two culled proposals and reduced them to eighteen which were deemed worthy of site visits and further review to ensure the efficacy of the candidates.[76]

Rucker and Oberlander set out to visit the potential grantees. The two spent four weeks on the road in the late spring and early summer of 1993 meeting applicants, interviewing references, and photographing sites. According to Oberlander, the trip offered "an incredible insight into Canada." In each community they interviewed people involved with the proposed project, as well as city officials or other informants who might have a perspective and eventually be called upon to help support the initiative. They asked themselves whether a particular organization was grounded in the community, or were they just pulling together partners to show that they had partners. Some of the most interesting projects had been developed by organizations with very few resources. "At that time, $30,000 was a lot of money," Oberlander recalled, "enough to pay a community development worker's salary. In some cases, it was larger than the budget for the organization and we worried about their capacity to carry out their plan."[77] As they travelled, Oberlander was struck by the uniqueness of their effort: "It was highly unusual for a foundation to be this thorough, not just checking a grantee out, but sending a scouting team essentially, for a grant of only $30,000."

When they returned to Montreal, Oberlander and Rucker submitted their reports to the jury for the final selection. For this stage, the jury included Phyllis herself, and Philip O'Brien of Devencore, Inc., a financial advisor from World Trade Centre Corporation in Montreal, whose expertise proved useful in determining whether any of the applicants were financial risks. On 9 July 1993, the panel chose seven projects for funding. It was an exciting meeting, charged with the energy that Phyllis enjoyed most, where sharp minds crossed paths with practical efforts by residents to preserve and enhance their own communities.[78]

The first projects ranged widely across Canada and they were marked by a great diversity of approaches to the problems of urban communities. In Vancouver, residents of the oldest neighbourhood in the city had come together to restore the porches on their aging Victorian homes. Led by historian and novelist Nora Kelly, the group hoped to conserve the historic character of the neighbourhood and connect residents by bringing them back outside.[79] "In the time before television," Kelly told a reporter, "the front porch was where people got most of their news, talking to their neighbours walking by, inviting them for coffee." With people sitting on their porches with eyes on the street, the Strathcona Residents Association also hoped to make the community safer. The project was exactly the kind of thing that Urban Issues was supposed to be about – the self-renewal of a neighbourhood from a community base, or as Gisele Rucker put it, "people taking control of their environment."[80]

In Edmonton, unemployment, crime, and low incomes threatened the quality of life of many of the residents of the Boyle Street/McCauley neighbourhood. Responding to a proposal developed by a community planner working for the neighbourhood, the SSBFF provided funds to make sure the plan received full access to competent, professional resources during its implementation. In Sudbury, the decline of the once-lucrative copper and nickel mining industries had left many neighbourhoods environmentally and economically devastated. Better Beginnings, Better Futures was an organization founded to improve the community by reclaiming the natural environment. With the Urban Issues grant, the group hired a naturalist to rehabilitate two derelict parks by organizing members of the community to landscape, erect playgrounds, install picnic tables, and plant butterfly bushes.[81] In Halifax, SSBFF funds would help sponsor a new certificate program in community develop-ment at the Henson College of Public Affairs and Continuing Education at Dalhousie University. The intent of this program was to strengthen grassroots organizations by providing a supply of trained community organizers. In Ottawa, the Transport 2000 project planned to use SSBFF funding to help promote its transit advocacy program. In Montreal, the Société de développement communautaire Milton Parc proposed to move beyond its initial efforts to create land trusts and housing cooper-atives to focus on innovative economic development. The organization planned to encourage investment and renovation in an environmentally sensitive way. One of the most innovative of the projects was the "Return of the Dummies," which staged multilingual theatrical per-formances in vacant urban storefronts to draw attention to the archi-tectural and social potential of such spaces.[82]

By the following spring, Rucker reported to the board that each of the projects had succeeded in putting the ideas formed in North Hatley into practice. Each had also met with considerable success: not only were urban spaces being improved, but the media were giving the projects welcome attention. In the case of the Edmonton project, the municipal government had been so impressed by the improvements so far that it decided to provide $8 million in infrastructure improvements. The board expressed delight at the news of the program's achievements.[83]

In addition to the seven site-specific programs funded by Urban Issues, the SSBFF also backed two national projects intended to foster commu-nication on urban issues nationwide. The first was an urban issues-themed show in the television series CBC Street Cents, a program aimed at teens and younger audiences that had previously received general support from the SSBFF. The foundation also provided aid to *City Magazine* to support research and reporting on the Urban Issues projects funded in the first round of grants. The magazine, targeted to the community of people interested in urban problems nationwide, would help ensure the broader dissemination of ideas coming out of the funded projects.[84]

These two communications efforts reflected an epiphany that Rucker and Oberlander had experienced during their travels. As important as each project was, the opportunity for dialogue and mutual support among the various grantees offered enormous potential for Canada's cities. As the program moved forward, the foundation made this dialogue possible.

A COLLEGE OF COLLABORATORS

Urban Issues represented not only a new venture in the field, but also a new approach for the SSBFF. From the visioning workshop to the peer review of proposals, the program had opened the foundation to greater participation in the grant-making process. Like the Seniors and Learning Disabilities programs, Urban Issues was a pan-Canadian initiative. Rucker, Hobday, and the board expected it to develop into a nationwide force or movement of some kind. But the path to that destination was not clear from the beginning. Unlike the Seniors or Learning Disabilities programs, there was no existing system of provincial organizations that could be brought together through a process of coalition-building. The recipients of Urban Issues grants themselves would have to provide this sort of cohesion.

It was part of the vision expressed at the North Hatley workshop that grantees of a new program would form a kind of college of collaborators, learning and sharing their experiences with one another to grow a body of effective knowledge. At Phyllis's urging, additional funds were set aside for Urban Issues to enable recipients of grants to attend the annual meetings of the grantees and to allow them to visit one another's projects; such funds also supported the development of a listserv in the early days of the World Wide Web, and eventually the creation of an internet site. A college of collaborators would provide the mutual support system for people across the country trying to improve their poverty-stricken neighbourhoods.

The annual meetings of grantees provided the main forum for developing that shared vision. The first was held in Montreal in the fall of 1993 just months after the recipients of the first cycle of grants were announced. Foundation staff and members of the selection panel listened to presentations by each of the grantees talking about their community and the problems their projects aimed to address. Although these sessions were enlightening, many participants felt the best moments of exchange were at mealtimes and coffee breaks where they could share experiences, offer advice to each other, and recommend books, contacts, methods, and tactics.[85] As they got to know one another and understand how the eclectic projects fit into the abstract vision of Urban Issues that had been articulated at North Hatley, participants also began to see the usefulness of forming a network. The foundation, in turn, gained a deeper appreciation for the challenges that grantees faced in Canada's inner cities.

The Urban Issues grantees held their second meeting in Sudbury in the autumn of 1994, hosted by the Better Beginnings, Better Futures Association. As well as hearing from one another about their respective projects and taking a tour of the Donovan-Flour Mill neighbourhoods with project coordinator Joan Kuyek, the Urban Issues grantees began to wrestle with fundamental questions. What were the things that they had in common? Would telling their stories help other neighbourhoods and other communities address their own problems of poverty and decline? Should the foundation be asked to help communicate their stories or network with people working on similar projects? Did they as grantees have a collective identity or sense of purpose that should be reflected in the evolution of the Urban Issues program? What feedback should they provide to the foundation to help it be more effective in working with grantees? It was not easy to reach consensus on answers to such questions; people tended to see their work from a narrow field of interest – their neighbourhood or city, or their discipline (landscaping, art, architecture).[86]

The third meeting, which took place in Halifax in June 1995, was organized by Anne Bishop, an author and social activist who had taught adult education and community leadership at Henson College, Dalhousie University since 1987. Bishop was recognized as a facilitator for community groups dealing with diversity and racism. Her book, *Becoming an Ally*, provided readers with ways to examine and undo patterns of oppression in their lives and their communities. With funding from the SSBFF, she had helped to launch the certificate program in community development to develop skills among leaders in low income neighbourhoods. As part of the program, an advisory and networking committee of graduates met on a monthly basis to share information, develop strategies, provide mutual support and constantly refresh the program with new knowledge from the front lines. It was this committee that hosted the June gathering, which included such innovative workshops as "Dealing with Racism in Community Organizations," "Housing the Homeless," and "Understanding Prostitution." The sessions were productive and enjoyable, although the issue of forming a network of grantees was not advanced.[87]

Coming out of the Halifax meetings, Rucker and the SSBFF found themselves addressing the familiar question of when to continue funding a project and when to stop. As the Urban Issues' three-year funding commitment drew to a close, the foundation anticipated advertising for a new round of projects. It had been their intention to award another series of grants to a different slate of recipients, but that would rule out former grantees continuing what seemed to be valuable work. Many of them might very well benefit from another round of funding. On the other hand, were there not some that should be cut loose? In the end, the foundation decided to allow existing grantees to apply for a second three-year round of funding and decide on an individual basis.[88]

In the autumn of 1995, the SSBFF staff went to work on the call for proposals for the second round of Urban Issues funding. The North Hatley concept, articulated in the booklet *Urban Issues: The Bold New Vision of Heritage* was updated to reflect the perspective developed by the first round of grants. The call for proposals went out across the country, and applications poured in – albeit in significantly smaller numbers than in 1993. Having fewer applicants suggested that the foundation could be doing a better job of publicizing the program, although it was also agreed that the revised brochure was more focused than the previous one and the proposals received were generally closer in spirit to the sorts of projects Urban Issues was intended to address. When Rucker and Oberlander hit the road a second time to evaluate applicants, they felt that the program had become better understood and was therefore able to make a real impact.[89]

After the second cycle of grants was awarded in the fall of 1996, the SSBFF board and staff began to take stock of their achievements to understand where the program was heading. On the ground in individual communities it was clear that a lot of exciting things were being accomplished. But at a program level, was there a need to create something larger and of more national significance? As Rucker expressed it, "It has always been our hope that the projects ... not remain isolated points of activity, but form a 'college' dedicated to attaining the goals and embodying the concept as outlined in the North Hatley statement."[90] The SSBFF hoped that the grantees' meeting held in Montreal at the end of October 1996 would bring this "college" closer to reality, but again the willingness to organize did not present itself.

In June 1997, Rucker came to the board with a proposal that promised to satisfy both the short-run needs of the grantees as well as the long-run goals of the program. From her perspective, since Urban Issues had chosen a bottom-up strategy focused on identifying innovative and entrepreneurial groups in cities all over Canada, then the next steps seemed to be to find a way to network these groups at the city level to develop synergies among them. She proposed hiring an experienced community organizer as an "animator" who would spend time in each city working with the Urban Issues projects and begin to look for a way to develop a larger network for dialogue. As Rucker put it, "The quintessential skill of a community development worker is the skill to create enthusiasm in others, because without enthusiasm, nothing will happen." Rucker suggested that the animator would bring key organizers together and promote dialogue, build leadership at the grassroots by fostering a good group dynamic, and "scout for future Urban Issues project applicants and look for cutting-edge projects." This person would work to transfer knowledge about best and worst practices in community organizing. Rucker suggested that the animator should spend two weeks a month in the field for a period of ten months. The foundation would ask the projects to evaluate the organizer so that the foundation would see whether the effort was useful or not.[91]

Rucker's candidate for this job was Joan Kuyek, who had done such sterling work in Sudbury with Better Beginnings, Better Futures. The board agreed with this strategy, making the proviso only that Kuyek understand that part of her responsibility would be to ensure that Urban Issues continue to grow as a program.[92] The directors also agreed that Kim Klein, a fundraiser for grassroots initiatives who had moderated the Montreal meeting, should be hired on contract to provide grantees with her expertise in finding ways to expand their own capacity. They also provided funding to SODEC-M (Société de développement communautaire de Montréal) to create a web site for the Urban Issues program with links to the North Hatley statement and information on each of the program's recipients.[93] As a result of Kuyek's networking and the development of the website and an electronic database, Rucker felt confident in suggesting that Urban Issues could easily fund twenty projects in its next round, scheduled for 1999.[94] True enough, the third call yielded a large number of applicants which the staff and jury were able to reduce to twenty viable projects.

Kuyek's efforts did not, however, bring Urban Issues any closer to creating a national network, although grantees and their communities continued to appreciate the shared wisdom and networking opportunities provided by the SSBFF. The yearly grantee meetings were uniformly successful, following the pattern set in Halifax of tackling critical focal issues. Rucker reflected that the major reason for convening the 1997 meeting in Vancouver ("Affordable Housing and the Gentrification of Communities") was "to provide an opportunity for ... active players in social, cultural and political change – people who are seeking to transform the world into a more just, more civil, more meaningful place, to know that they are *not* alone. There are others who aspire to achieve similar goals and who confront the same barriers and are seeking to dissolve these barriers."[95] The following year's event was entitled "Creating

Sustainable Urban Communities – Visions and Realities." In addition to representatives from the Urban Issues grantees, the conference included nine groups undertaking urban environmental projects funded by the North American Fund for Environmental Cooperation (NAFEC), which was run by the Commission for Environmental Cooperation (CEC), an institution formed as a complement to NAFTA.[96]

The ability of Urban Issues to effect change beyond the local level was evident – and yet there was still no real sense of where things were going. As Phyllis pointedly asked, "Where is the Urban Issues Program headed? How do we take it to the next level?"[97]

Taking Urban Issues to the Next Level

As it was becoming clear that Urban Issues was not going to generate a national network, Rucker began to explore ways to take the program in different directions. Her first thought was to identify a need or underlying problem that the foundation could address systematically, rather than respond to individual project proposals as it had been doing so far. She was inspired by the ongoing efforts of three different initiatives designed to strengthen community development in Canada, all of which had received funding through the SSBFF Futures program.

The first of these initiatives was the Community Development Skills Program sponsored by the Social Planning and Research Council (SPARC) of British Columbia, which had come to the SSBFF in 1991 seeking funds to help produce "A Citizen's Guide to Community Social Planning." SPARC intended to create a manual that would help the residents of a community set the agenda for their own future. The second initiative was the West Coast Community Leadership Training Society (WCCLTS); the SSBFF had given the society funds to sustain its annual "Mayor's Institute," which brought together the chief executives from smaller communities throughout British Columbia to enhance their skills, knowledge, and contacts. Finally, the foundation had provided funding to the Institute in Management and Community Development at the Centre for Continuing Education at Montreal's Concordia University to allow leaders from economically marginalized groups to attend the institute's summer program in community organizing and development.[98] All three of these initiatives had given the foundation staff a better understanding of current efforts in Canada to develop the manpower (or womanpower) necessary to lead the process of social change.

The work of the Concordia institute's summer program suggested to Rucker a path that the SSBFF could follow in order to expand Urban Issues beyond its current focus. Borrowing from the model established in the Cultural Management program, Rucker developed the idea that what was needed to facilitate the work being done in communities across the country was better training for community organizers. Rucker drew up three scenarios in which the SSBFF would go into partnership with either Concordia's Centre for Continuing Education or BC's Social Planning and Research Council to create a training program for community organizers, or else fund a series of lectures and public forums to provide such training. Indeed, the coordinator of the Institute in Management and Community Development, Lance Evoy, had recently submitted a proposal to the SSBFF to turn the Summer Institute program into a year-round course. After much consideration, the board decided against funding a year-round program for Concordia, and felt that going into partnership with any of these organizations would not advance the interests of Urban Issues or the communities the program was intended to serve.[99]

While Rucker continued to think about community development techniques, the board called for a detailed assessment of the Urban Issues program. Directors were feeling increasingly uneasy as they continued to fund large numbers of projects without getting much assurance that change was taking place in any measurable way. What was needed was a systematic method of evaluating the projects – always a difficult process to implement and particularly so with so many people and activities involved. Rucker turned to Joan Kuyek for a report of her findings. Kuyek had travelled to eleven different cities in Canada and talked to more than 250 people in the course of an eight-month contract; she had asked hundreds of questions related to the issues that community groups faced as they tried to invigorate the health and welfare of their neighbourhoods.

Kuyek's report outlined the array of challenges facing community organizations: a typical lack of charitable status which prevented them from securing donations; poor communication between boards and staff; community workers with insufficient training; and dependency on corporate funders with agendas that may not coincide with that of the funded organization. Too often, she wrote, "community organizations are totally dependent on whatever the current wave of government policy or foundation interests are to do their work, and each funder and program has its own buzz words, reporting requirements and outcomes to contend with." Kuyek then provided a list of areas on which, in her opinion, the program should focus, from tackling pollution to encouraging affordable housing to redesigning the suburbs. In particular, she suggested that the SSBFF promote awareness of ecologically sound renovation and building methods, encourage discussion of community development, and support the two community development institutes (at Concordia and SPARC).[100]

When presented with Kuyek's report and recommendations in June 1999, the directors were impressed with the descriptive detail in the evaluations, but were frustrated by the lack of analysis. They had anticipated receiving guidance as to how the projects they had funded so far were making a difference in the community, and whether the next round of grants should be conducted differently. Jean de Gunzburg felt that by this time the foundation should be able to synthesize lessons learned from the Urban Issues program. Stephen Bronfman suggested Rucker document the projects with a video camera so that the directors "could have a better feel for the activities and the people involved." Despite this frustration, the directors agreed to approve up to three years' funding to a maximum of $30,000 each for twenty urban issues projects across Canada: four in the Maritimes, six in Quebec, four in Ontario, three in the Prairies, and four in British Columbia.[101]

Rucker continued to explore ways to take Urban Issues to another level. In July 2000, she attended a national training session run by the Industrial Areas Foundation (IAF) in the United States and was impressed by the organization's depth of experience and the commitment of its people. The IAF had been launched in the 1950s by Saul Alinsky, one of the most famous community organizers in North American history, whose *Rules for Radicals* was now a bible in the field. Since Alinsky's death in 1972, the IAF had carried on his work, offering training to community and labour organizers throughout the United States. Rucker found it difficult, however, to imagine a way to bring this approach to Canada. She met with the Maytree Foundation in Toronto which was already providing leadership development training to individuals in the immigrant neighbourhoods, and discussed a possible collaboration between the two foundations for a demonstration project on "organizing practices." She continued to talk with people at Concordia's Institute in Management and Community Development and with the US-based Center for Community Change (CCC) which had been conducting collaborative research with the Concordia Institute. Unfortunately, there did not seem to be an obvious role for the SSBFF to play – other than to continue with the successful Urban Issues program.[102]

The foundation decided to let the program's grantees tackle the question of how effective Urban Issues was at making a systematic difference to social problems. The October 2000 annual meeting was held in Toronto, and saw nineteen projects represented. Participants were asked to evaluate their projects in terms of what Rucker described as a "four-axis model" based on her investigations into best practices. The questions were how well did each project (1) enhance local democracy, (2) create a sense of community, (3) improve the natural or built environment, and (4) contribute to economic strength and stability?[103] Two facilitators helped focus the discussion and to distill its conclusions. It was clear from the evaluations that certain projects had greater potential to effect long-term change than others: some organizations grew by reaching out to and incorporating the community and exercising leadership, whereas other grants were being "managed" to achieve some purpose without creating permanent capacity in the community for change. By the end of the second year in a funding cycle the foundation should be able to identify the successful, "empowering" organizations and invite them to apply for a second round of funding.[104] Rucker also suggested that a special effort be made in the next round to target cities that had never had a project supported by Urban Issues.[105]

The directors, ever eager to find ways to develop the program, expressed appreciation for these insights at their December 2000 meeting, but still felt that more could be done. They had not abandoned the idea that Urban Issues should take on a life outside the foundation, and instructed Rucker to continue to explore other avenues. Reflecting on her experience with the development of the CCA, Phyllis suggested that maybe a group of people should be assembled as a kind of advisory committee to help manage the program. In the meantime, a fourth round of funding should go ahead for 2002, although Jean requested that some procedural questions be addressed: was the process for getting new proposals the right one? Should the proposals be targeted only at certain key cities? Should they ask for an inquiry letter first instead of a full proposal? Was the period between the September call for proposals and the March deadline too long? Was it really necessary for the jury members to meet three times, and how could their task of reading so many proposals be eased? Did Rucker and Oberlander have to make all the site visits across Canada or could this process be simplified? It was time to consider fine-tuning the program as well as plan its future.[106]

A new plan was developed for the fourth call for proposals, involving a communications strategy and a new applications procedure. The call was announced on the new Urban Issues website which the board had approved in May 2001, as well as by means of press releases issued to non-profit groups and charitable networks across the country. A direct mail campaign was launched using a database developed from twenty-eight directories issued by all major Canadian cities. Face-to-face presentations were made in each new city by local scouts who were hired at fifty dollars an hour; Rucker worked to locate the "people who know everybody and what's going on in the city" who would then organize meetings with local community leaders. This method yielded the highest response rate of all the techniques. The total cost of the communications strategy was $35,000, a worthwhile investment given that the foundation planned to give away over $1.5 million in this funding cycle. Costs and time were saved on the review process: now applicants were to send a letter of intent by 30 November, and only those that passed the initial screening would be asked to submit a full proposal by the beginning of March; these would be discussed by the committee via conference call, and the finalists visited by Oberlander by the end of May. In order to be eligible for renewed funding, a project would need to "spawn a new institution within a community ... or produce a crossover effect, show efforts to build local leadership, [or have] plans to replace SSBFF funding."[107]

The SSBFF directors were pleased by this fresh approach to the funding process and confessed to being satisfied that Urban Issues would be most effective if left at the "non-institutional, grassroots level."[108] In July 2002, eighteen new projects were chosen, each of which had "the potential to create the 'synthesis' evoked in the North Hatley Statement," namely "a dynamic between the economy, environment, community and governance." The jury, which had met only once during the whole process, had received 473 letters of intent and then requested 60 full proposals. It had been the smoothest-run of all the Urban Issues rounds of funding.[109]

As the foundation contemplated winding down, consultant Bruce Fraser was called in to propose exit strategies for Urban Issues. Fraser warned that if the directors chose to end the program they should be careful how to convey this news to the grantees, who might find it demoralizing; as a result, the SSBFF's credibility might be undermined, which could "damage the ability of existing grantees to use the foundation's support to attract other funds." He advised against entrusting Urban Issues to another funding agency, given that times were hard for everyone and that another foundation would be "unlikely to adopt someone else's cast-off programs, however meritorious." The best path would be to find one or more organizations worthy of receiving continuing funding beyond the current cycle as part of a legacy program.[110] The directors felt they should continue to search for partners, although they were willing to consider the option of finding a successor from within the community. A decision needed to be made by the middle of 2004, at which point potential applicants would be anticipating a fifth round of funding.[111]

Rucker embarked upon a concerted effort to find partners and found some – all with merits but also plenty of drawbacks, including excessive bureaucracy. Eventually the board decided to hire a consultant who would put together a "consortium" of funders, community foundations, and community organizations to oversee the program. In this manner, they could create a "designated fund within locally based community foundations" wherein the Urban Issues program "can continue to be identified as a program of the" SSBFF.[112] The proposed title of this new program was "Placemaking in Canadian Cities," a name that had an "immediate resonance" with various potential partners.[113] The pursuit of "Placemaking" involved many exciting discussions on many levels, notably at a Key Stakeholders meeting held in Vancouver at the end of October 2004.[114] In the end, however, Rucker was not able to present the proposal as a distinct enough program to marshal a wide array of funding sources, government or private; many agencies and potential partners felt that other programs of this nature existed in different form, and were not prepared to invest in a new organization.[115] When the fourth cycle of Urban Issues came to an end in 2005, the program was discontinued. There did not seem to be any way to turn Urban Issues into a national program or to reshape it as a separate organization outside the control of the SSBFF.

CONCLUSION

The SSBFF's Heritage program, which began in the mid-1970s and was eventually recast as Urban Issues, was in many ways one of its most successful. It did not establish a client organization that could function at the national level, although its efforts to launch Heritage Canada did result in a body that answered many of the needs of heritage preservation, including the capacity to acquire properties, which the various historic monuments commissions could not. Heritage Montreal had always been local in its focus, even though it set the tone much more widely for heritage activism and education. Although the SSBFF stopped providing Heritage Montreal with core funding by the end of the 1980s, it did so only after encouraging the organization to devote energy to building a solid membership base and with the understanding that it would continue to fund occasional projects. As a result, Heritage Montreal was stimulated to find its way, and continues to be an effective voice for conservation in Canada.

Despite much effort to turn it into an independent national organization, Urban Issues remained an organ of the SSBFF. As such, it did not require the foundation to make difficult decisions about how much to fund and when to pull back. Not finding a way to take the program to the "next level" was frustrating for board and staff, as was the need for them to manage the program more directly than they did the others. At the same time, the experience of processing applications, making funding decisions and working with grantees proved unusually satisfying for Phyllis, Rucker, and Oberlander – as is often the case with institutional board members and executives who do not normally find themselves actively managing programs and projects. Furthermore, the pattern of proposals and negotiation and follow up was one to which Canadians eagerly responded, and most of the recipients of grants expressed satisfaction with the degree of collaboration and guidance offered by the SSBFF. Over a twelve-year period, dozens of projects across the country were carried out under the Urban Issues program, a great many of which resulted in considerable improvement within their communities. For that reason alone, Urban Issues clearly can be said to have made a difference.

ELEVEN

CRAFTS

The Saidye Bronfman Award for Excellence in Crafts was one of the foundation's most successful programs, not only because it was run smoothly and efficiently for a full thirty years but because it filled a real need in Canadian society that simply would not have been addressed without the SSBFF.[1] Despite widespread interest in craft, there was no official support for it in Canada as an art form. Until the success of the Bronfman award, mainstream museums and galleries rarely considered the display of crafts as part of their mandates, believing that to be the role of decorative arts museums or commercial exhibitions. The SSBFF's efforts brought a level of prestige to craft that enabled it to be ranked among other more established art forms within the context of museums and ultimately within the purview of the Canada Council. The award also brought much-needed financial support to select practitioners of crafts, whose careers were forever changed by being thus honoured.

THE SAIDYE BRONFMAN AWARD

The crafts had a long but ambivalent history in Canada. Unlike the so-called "fine" arts of painting and sculpture, crafts had always been considered the work of ordinary untrained people who did the work out of daily necessity. Pottery, furniture making, printing on fabric, and glassblowing were done by artisans – as was most manufacturing prior to the Industrial Revolution – who had to be skilled to be successful but were clearly not "artists." The work of native peoples may have held some anthropological value, and the craftsmanship of early North American settlers may have held some folkloric or antiquarian interest, but in general, with the advent of industrialization, the handmade was devalued compared to its mass-produced, machine-made counterpart. It was only as disenchantment with the industrial age and its monotony grew, first in Europe and then in North America, that traditional crafts began to be seen in a different, more creative light, at least in some circles. Moreover, as modern artists departed from tradition in many bewildering directions – notably in their creative use of new media – it became harder to make a clear distinction between what was "fine" and what was merely "decorative."

At the turn of the twentieth century, the Arts and Crafts movement caught hold, first in Britain and then in North America, prompting a renewed interested in what became known as "fine crafts." In 1905 two Montreal women, Alice Peck and May Phillips, leaders in the local branch of the Women's Art Association (affiliated with the Museum of Fine Arts), established the Canadian Handicrafts Guild, with a mandate to promote crafts across Canada. Over the next several decades, similar guilds were created in Cape Breton, Charlotte County (New Brunswick), North Lanark (Ontario), Victoria (BC), and Regina.[2] Even so, craft continued to rank low within the arts, at least until after the Second World War when various government reports began to note and criticize its weak status. In 1951, the Massey Commission acknowledged the importance of crafts to Canadian culture and their role in capturing the character of the Canadian people, but this observation was intended mainly to underscore the lack of respect crafts generally received.[3] Lack of respect and lack of quality seemed to go hand in hand. Hobday recalled how, as a newcomer to Canada in the 1950s, when "looking for quality Canadian gifts to send to relatives … there was practically nothing available."[4]

Saidye Bronfman was a promoter of decorative arts and crafts and a believer in their worth as part of the fine arts. Her family had always respected this devotion and shared it: "Craft is another way of connecting us with our history and uncovering new meanings in form, process, and use," Phyllis wrote in a preface to a commemorative volume.[5] By the 1970s, interest in fine, handmade items was reviving with the youth movement and a growing disenchantment with the consumer society that had dismissed them as outdated. The quantity and quality of objects produced was also improving as more people strove to make their living as practitioners of various crafts.[6] When Saidye's children began looking for a way to honour her upcoming eightieth birthday, it seemed logical to consider hosting or sponsoring some event or project pertaining to crafts.

Peter Swann suggested that the foundation fund an annual award in Saidye's name to recognize distinction in this field. It was Swann's hope that by establishing such an award the SSBFF would stimulate interest in crafts, inspire practitioners to excellence, and expand the audience and market for fine handmade Canadian products. It is true that cash awards to individual artists or craftspersons provide a curious leverage to granting agencies. On the one hand, because they are given to a single person or a small number of individuals, their impact on the development of a field seems limited. Furthermore, in any branch of the arts, selecting a winner can often seem extremely subjective. On the other hand, awards generate excitement and interest, and with a strong jury, they offer the opportunity to showcase excellence and capture the public's attention.[7]

Swann was attuned to the qualities of craftsmanship, having been a collector since his teenage years. He had a fine appreciation for craft as the expression of both individual artistry and cultural identity. Before he moved to Canada in the 1960s, he had patronized a crafts shop on Sloan Street in London and befriended the owner, Peter Weinrich, who was interested in Canadian crafts and sold them in his shop. Like Swann, Weinrich soon moved to Canada and in 1974 became executive director of the Canadian Crafts Council. He contacted Swann the following year, hoping the SSBFF would be willing to help the Council in its work.[8] Swann's suggestion was that the council should administer the foundation's annual Saidye Bronfman Award for Excellence in the Crafts.

The SSBFF's offer came at an opportune moment. Frustrated by the lack of financial support from the Canada Council for the Arts, Weinrich had begun to look for ways the Canadian Crafts Council could honour leaders in various disciplines and thereby increase respect for crafts. Weinrich had been working with the Massey Foundation to build a National Collection of Canadian Crafts and had a jury in place to make the selections.[9] All that was needed was the prize. In the fall of 1976 the SSBFF board approved the concept of a ten-year program for awards of $15,000 a year, of which $10,000 would be given to the craftsperson and $5,000 would support putting on a good show of the recipient's work.[10] The award ceremony would be held at Saidye's home, with Saidye presiding, after which she would host a dinner for the recipient along with directors of the SSBFF and other guests.

The first winner of the Saidye Bronfman Award proved an excellent choice, not least because his career and approach to crafts personified the movement to have them recognized on a par with other art forms. Robin Hopper had studied ceramics at art college in England where he learned to appreciate European, classical, and Asian aesthetics. Immigrating to Canada in 1968, he began to experiment with historical Chinese and Japanese techniques. As a teacher at Central Technical School in Toronto and then at Georgian College in Barrie, Ontario, he was respected for his skill as a communicator as well as a craftsman. He emphasized technical mastery in his courses, believing that aesthetics would develop independently. In books and public lectures, on juries, and among his peers on several craft councils, he promoted a sensitivity to history and tradition.[11]

The night of the first Bronfman Award ceremony was, unfortunately, "a disaster" because of a terrible storm that forced all flights and trains to be cancelled. Most guests were unable to attend, including Secretary of State John Roberts, who had been recruited to make the presentation. This bad beginning did not hurt the success of the award in the long term, however. The Bronfman prize quickly acquired the prestige that its creators had hoped for, and it gave its recipients much-needed boosts in their careers. The award also became a source of delight for Saidye herself. "It was so wonderful," her son Charles recalled. "She would get all nervous about it: what she was going to serve for cocktails, what hors d'oeuvres – it was fabulous. She'd meet the winner ... She got a great kick out of it."[12] The award proved an apposite, and long-lasting, birthday present.

MASTERS OF THE CRAFTS

The SSBFF had been granting the Saidye Bronfman Award for Excellence in the Crafts for six years when John Hobday became director of the foundation. In that time, the market for crafts of all kinds – ceramic, wood, leather, glass, and fibre – had grown and the Bronfman Award had become recognized as the most prestigious award in the field. Success, as often happens, encouraged both the Crafts Council and the foundation to do more. In the spring of 1983, Hobday put forth a multi-faceted proposal to accelerate the development of the role of the crafts in Canadian society. Following discussions with Peter Weinrich and the Crafts Council, he proposed creating a series of awards for crafts fairs and provincial exhibitions across the country, providing bursaries to students at major craft schools, upgrading the leading crafts publication – *Artisan* – and developing a series of special travelling exhibitions that would expose "the widest possible public" to the finest craftsmanship.

In some ways, the plan emerged in the classic Hobday fashion. He saw the country as a system needing integration. In other program areas he would try to link provincial activities to create a national network or organization. Here, he believed that since the foundation had done work with the national council, the next step was "a complementary effort at the *provincial* level."[13] The board liked the concepts developed by Hobday and the Canadian Crafts Council, but after considerable discussion they agreed to pass the $132,000 proposal to Seagram. Edgar felt that with growing public interest in crafts, the project offered an interesting option from a marketing standpoint. Nevertheless, the board affirmed its intent to continue funding the Saidye Bronfman Award.[14]

As the award's tenth anniversary approached, Weinrich and Hobday began to pursue the idea of mounting an exhibition featuring the work of the first ten winners. The ssbff directors were keen to mark the anniversary, although some concern was raised that the winners had already had exhibitions mounted thanks to the award, and that additional exhibitions would in many cases be redundant. Swann pointed out that the earlier exhibitions had often been small and there had been insufficient funds to enable them to travel about or produce a catalogue; a major exhibition would go much further to promote both the work and the award. Hobday suggested that an excellent venue for such an exhibition would be Canada's National Museum of Man, which had recently acquired the Massey collection of crafts and seemed interested in becoming a repository of other work of this sort.[15] The museum currently shared cramped quarters with the Museum of Natural Sciences in Ottawa (originally the National Museum), but was planning to move to an expansive new home across the river in Hull.

Hobday and Weinrich talked to Stephen Inglis, director of Research and Collections at the National Museum of Man. Inglis, passionate about crafts and keen to expand the collection, drew up a proposal for an exhibition honouring the Saidye Bronfman Award's first ten winners, to open at the museum's new facilities on 1 July 1988.[16] The new museum, to be renamed the Canadian Museum of Civilization, would contain a Fine Crafts Gallery which would be the site of the exhibition. The ssbff directors approved Inglis's proposal on the condition that the exhibition space conform to the highest museum standards, and that the Saidye Bronfman award exhibition be the first one held in the new gallery.[17] The foundation's contribution included the purchase of some works by the award winners, on the understanding that the museum would begin purchasing works by subsequent winners for display in the Fine Crafts Gallery, thereby obviating the need to hold a second exhibition after the award's twentieth anniversary.[18] Other works were purchased for the exhibition by private donors.[19] Eventually the museum's completion date was postponed to the summer of 1989, which gave the curators time to acquire additional objects for the exhibition – not an easy matter when much of the work in question was still in progress.[20]

In March 1988, the museum approached the foundation with the proposal to name the Fine Crafts Gallery after Saidye Bronfman, an honour that carried with it "a donation value of $500,000." When Hobday presented this proposal to the board, a number of important questions were raised. Should a national museum receive private funding for "bricks and mortar?" Would funding the gallery really assist the promotion of the crafts in Canada or help Canada's artisans? At the end of this discussion, the board concluded that their desire to promote Canadian crafts would be furthered by other uses of the foundation's resources.[21] They did, however, agree to provide an annual $20,000 towards the acquisition of works, provided that a matching amount be provided from the museum's own acquisitions budget and an additional $20,000 secured from outside sources.[22] The museum agreed to host the Saidye Bronfman Award presentation in future and to create a small exhibition focusing on each winner.[23] It also agreed to commission CBC television to create a thirty-second spot on each of the award recipients, both to promote each artist's work and to publicize the award itself.[24]

For Stephen Inglis, the development of the exhibit, Masters of the Crafts, offered interesting insight into the character of the SSBFF as a foundation. In a project closely associated with the family, John Hobday was very hands-on. He followed the progress of exhibition planning, attended meetings with the designer, and offered suggestions here and there. According to Inglis, however, "We always felt we were the authors." The SSBFF was very conscious of the professionalism of the staff at the museum. From his point of view, Inglis suspected that that respect reflected not only Hobday's approach, but the sensibility of the SSBFF's board as well.[25] Nevertheless, Hobday found the experience frustrating. The prestige of mounting an exhibition that inaugurated the new museum was countered by the headaches involved in completing a new building on time. Aside from the inevitable cost overruns, the construction schedule took on a "kind of lunacy" when "the Prime Minister ordered that [the museum] be opened by July 1st, Canada Day, and ... they brought in several hundred electricians from all over Quebec to finish it." The museum did open on schedule along with the crafts exhibition, and there was even time to prepare a high-quality catalogue.[26]

Masters of the Crafts underscored the continuing expression of craftsmanship in Canadian society. Its presence in the museum linked the work of contemporary craftspeople with ancient native people. The show included Robin Hopper's haunting landscape ceramics, Lois Etherington Betteridge's exquisite silver, Monique Cliche-Spénard's narrative quilts, the collaborative stoneware of Louise Doucet and Satoshi Sato, Joanna Staniszkis' large woven tapestries, Micheline Beauchemin's sculptural weavings, Wayne Ngan's glistening stoneware, William Hazzard's fine carvings of raptors and other birds, and Michael Wilcox's beautifully bound books.[27] It was an appropriate tribute to the SSBFF's work in the field of crafts, and served to promote both foundation and museum. Masters of the Crafts was extended at the Museum of Civilization until October 1990, and the following summer it went on tour to numerous museums and galleries across Canada. The SSBFF continued its support for the award by providing additional funding to create videos of the works of winning artists. The directors were hesitant to substantially increase their funding of the award, however, at least until after assessing the outcome of the visioning workshop.[28]

VISIONING CRAFTS

In April 1991, the SSBFF cooperated with the Canadian Crafts Council and the Woodlawn Arts Foundation to sponsor the final gathering in its visioning series, held at the Banff Centre for Continuing Education. The Woodlawn Arts Foundation was the creation of Joan Chalmers, daughter of Ontario philanthropists Floyd and Jean Chalmers and a vigorous patron of arts and crafts in her own right; she established the foundation in 1981 to support the performing and visual arts across Canada.[29] Woodlawn was an obvious partner for the SSBFF in its crafts program.

Entitled "Canadian Crafts in the Twenty-First Century," the Banff workshop brought together twenty-three participants ranging from craftspeople and designers to educators, curators and architects, as well as business agents and marketers.[30] The discussion reflected a critical transition taking place in the world of crafts. Throughout the 1980s, having successfully elevated crafts to be roughly on a par with fine art, the craftspeople had increasingly turned to private patronage and government support. As in other areas, however, declining government funding posed serious long-term problems, as did the increasing inability of the Canadian Crafts Council and the Ontario Crafts Council, the two largest organizations in the country, to respond to the situation. Participants at the workshop concluded that the best hope was to build better relationships at the community level.[31]

In May 1991 Hobday proposed to the SSBFF Board that it step in to fund and guide a strategic planning process at the Canadian Crafts Council. Despite the current downturn in its fortunes, the council had the potential to act as a national organization to raise the awareness of crafts across the country; at the same time, the process would enable the council to identify "new partners in sectors able to take the crafts into potentially profitable markets." He added: "The final outcome we seek is to allow the constituencies to drive a rejuvenated organization, thereby reshaping it to provide real benefits on their behalf."[32] Once more, in other words, the SSBFF would seek to guide an organization to financial independence sustained by national direct membership. Hobday proposed that the SSBFF work with Joan Chalmers' Woodlawn Arts Foundation and engage Salasan Associates to lead a series of focus groups around the country. The directors were not immediately enthusiastic about this proposal, however, unsure whether this pursuit would really advance the original objectives of the funding program. After much discussion they voted not to support the series of focus groups.[33]

The board began to devote more of its resources to promoting the Saidye Bronfman Award. A survey taken in the autumn of 1991 suggested that much work could be done to make the award better known within the crafts and museum communities, and for it to have a higher profile within the media.[34] Hobday proposed that the funds normally given to the Canadian Museum of Civilization to promote the award winner be redirected to the hiring of an independent communications and promotion agent to publicize the event; the board agreed, and the following year they engaged the services of a marketing consultant, Heather Hatch. From this point on, the award ceremony became a well-publicized and well-attended event accompanied by a brochure highlighting the award and the recipient.[35]

Twentieth and Thirtieth Anniversaries

Despite the earlier feeling that it would not be necessary, the SSBFF decided to mount a second retrospective exhibition to mark the award's twentieth anniversary as well as Saidye's 100 th birthday.[36] In collaboration with the Canadian Crafts Council and the Museum of Civilization, the exhibition took shape despite some apparent hesitation by the museum, which declared itself unable to provide $20,000 out of its acquisitions budget for 1995.[37] After some negotiation, the museum reversed its decision and matched the SSBFF's support for acquisition of crafts, but at the same time the Canadian Crafts Council was experiencing severe financial problems.[38] Hobday looked further afield for funding and encountered the same prejudices against crafts from some major institutions; the Art Gallery of Ontario proved particularly resistant. "They thought it was opening the doors to having macramé hung on their walls," he concluded. Although many institutions did appreciate the importance of crafts and agreed to participate in the exhibition, in the end the bulk of the funding came from Seagram – a rare occasion when the SSBFF and Seagram worked together on a project since the foundation's endowment in the 1980s.[39]

A successful exhibition, entitled "Tranformations," did open in May 1996 – alas, without Saidye, who died early in 1995 – and proceeded to tour not only Canada but New York City, where 42,000 people attended over a sixteen-week period and spent over $100,000 US on craft items.[40] The popularity of the exhibition was a clear indication of how far crafts had come, at least in the popular mind but also in most professional circles, over a mere quarter century.

The award's twentieth anniversary proved an occasion for taking stock. After a twenty-year run, the Saidye Bronfman Award had become very successful, but did the family want to continue funding it? Moreover, the Canadian Crafts Council had reached a crisis and had essentially ceased to operate and would be hard-pressed to continue the jurying process. The foundation had little interest in bringing the process in-house.[41] In the end, the administration of the award was turned over to a jury organized by the Canada Council. The board agreed that it would be a good idea for a representative from the SSBFF to sit on the jury, an offer that had originally been made by the Canadian Crafts Council but never taken up. The obvious candidate to represent the SSBFF was Peter Swann, whose efforts had started the Saidye Bronfman Award many years earlier.[42] Unfortunately, Swann did not live to serve on the jury as his health rapidly declined over the latter part of 1997 and he died in December.

The SSBFF continued to fund the Saidye Bronfman Award for excellence in crafts, tinkering occasionally with the way it was marketed and how the recipients were celebrated. When the board began to discuss winding down the work of the SSBFF in 2003, the craft award was still going strong, though clearly it could not be extended indefinitely without the foundation's backing. As a vehicle for commemorating Saidye's name, the Saidye Bronfman Centre seemed worthier of support, located as it was in Montreal and involving so many aspects of the arts. At the same time, there was no institution with a national focus bearing Saidye's name other than the award.[43] The board decided to extend its contract with the Canada Council and the Canadian Museum of Civilization until the award's thirtieth anniversary in 2006, and then bring the program to a close.[44]

As the thirtieth anniversary of the award approached, discussions continued as to whether there might be some way to continue the life of the program. Hobday wondered if it would be possible to transfer the award to the Canada Council as a Governor General's Award to complement the prizes given out in literature and media arts. The directors were intrigued with this proposal and called for further investigation.[45] Nancy Rosenfeld, by then the SSBFF's executive director, worked with Carol Bream of the Canada Council to develop the idea; there followed over a year of negotiations between the two organizations over the nature of the award. The SSBFF insisted that the award become one of the governor general's annual prizes, even though historically there had never been any recognition of crafts at this level.[46] In the end, the Canada Council agreed to accept the endowment on the SSBFF's terms: the Saidye Bronfman Award for excellence in crafts would be given as one of the Governor General's annual awards alongside those for painting, sculpture, dance, and other traditional fine arts. Furthermore, the winners would have their works displayed in Canada's National Gallery, in keeping with the tradition of the Governor General's awards; perhaps more than anything else, this distinction represented a victory for crafts-people over old and outdated notions of what was art.[47]

The SSBFF directors were keen that the award's thirtieth anniversary should be celebrated in style, and budgeted $134,000 toward the total cost of a third retrospective exhibition at the Canadian Museum of Civilization; the money was redirected from the foundation's acquisitions budget, which had not been touched for some years since the museum had slowed its purchase of the winners' works.[48] The exhibition, entitled "Unique: 30 Years of Outstanding Crafts," took place in October 2006. Its opening ceremonies were attended by over 1,200 people, one of the largest openings ever held at the museum.[49] Of the thirty past winners of the award, a full twenty-five were still working at their crafts and able to participate in the retrospective. The presence of these past winners on stage was a testament to the impact of the award and provided an emotional reflection for Phyllis, Charles, and Stephen, who attended the event.

Prior to this opening, the smaller presentation ceremonies took place honouring the thirtieth winner of the award, New Brunswick ceramics artist and sculptor Peter Powning. It was on this occasion that Robert Sirman, John Hobday's successor as director of the Canada Council, made the official announcement regarding the SSBFF's decision to provide a $1.5 million endowment to the council to fund and administer the Saidye Bronfman Award.[1] The following March, Governor General Michaëlle Jean presided over the presentation of the first Saidye Bronfman Award for Crafts given under the auspices of the Canada Council.

CONCLUSION

Over thirty years, the Saidye Bronfman Award had grown from a relatively modest prize to one of the nation's top artistic honours. Although the SSBFF had always provided the prize money, and while she was alive Saidye herself had always presented the award, the foundation had collaborated with an independent organization, the Canadian Crafts Council (and later the Canada Council), which administered the competition and selected the winners. In the end, finding a separate home for the award in the Canada Council's Governor General awards proved the greatest tribute to Saidye and the clearest indication that crafts had won their place at the table. From the SSBFF's point of view, the successful transfer of this long-standing project into an even more prestigious public arena serves as a positive example of keeping the foundation's vision alive after it ceases its operational involvement. The Saidye Bronfman Award is an example of perseverance, of starting a small project and continuing to build with dedication and confidence.

TWELVE
————

PASSING THE TORCH

On an evening in September 1997, Phyllis, Matthew, and Jean had dinner together at the Four Seasons restaurant, located in New York's Seagram building. Stephen was supposed to join them, but bad weather in Montreal prevented him from getting away. Peter Swann had also been invited, but he was entering the final stages of his battle with cancer and could not travel. Phyllis had asked for the meeting. She felt it was time to pass on the leadership of the SSBFF to the next generation.

Three possible courses of action emerged from this discussion: 1) maintain the SSBFF as an active Canadian foundation; 2) "wind it up, except for the commitment to institutions carrying the family name"; and 3) move the offices of the SSBFF to the United States. By the end of the dinner, however, Jean and Matthew declared their determination that the SSBFF should continue to function, and do so in Canada – "in great part because all three branches of the family have members who are Canadian citizens, and express a genuine interest for Canada." One option facing the family was to continue the SSBFF but gradually give it up to greater involvement by non-family members. This option was rejected. According to Jean, all three agreed "that it is essential that the foundation remains controlled by the family." The challenge they faced was "to find a way to operate the foundation with active involvement of the family (possibly including more family members than today)."[1]

With a quarter century of dedicated work behind them, the more senior members of the foundation were ready to pass the torch to the next generation. Having ascertained their enthusiasm and been reassured, Phyllis proceeded to shift the major responsibilities onto the shoulders of Jean, Matthew, Stephen, and others. The issue of non-family representation on the board remained a sensitive one, but much care was taken to keep the leadership of the foundation involved, informed, and supported. The last years of the twentieth century and the first of the next proved challenging to the SSBFF as the social and economic environments changed for philanthropic organizations, and as the Bronfman family members themselves continued to find their own interests and grow apart. Even so, the foundation found time to undertake a number of new projects – notably a study of the impact of art education on disadvantaged youth and the heritage preservation of Saidye Bronfman's home town – and find ways to leave a lasting legacy even as it wound up its grants program.

A FAMILY FOUNDATION

Phyllis was encouraged by the continuing participation of the next generation, even though Matthew had to come from New York and Jean from France in order to attend board meetings. Inevitably, the next generation also brought with it new attitudes and new approaches to running a foundation. Stephen's perspective on philanthropy became more complicated, particularly as he inherited the expectations of the Jewish community in Montreal for leadership, just as his father had inherited them from Sam Bronfman. When he joined the board in 1992, he was ambivalent. He sensed that new problems were taking centre stage in the world and he was not sure that the family's traditional philanthropies, including the SSBFF, were focused on the right things.[2] He was not alone among the foundation's directors in his desire to move in new directions.

At the board meeting in November 1997, Phyllis announced that that time had come "to pass the President's baton over to another family member."³ Jean, who had served on the board longer than anyone else of the third generation, was the natural choice. As a way of easing the transition, Phyllis suggested that each board member develop one particular area of programmatic interest and so lighten the potential weight on the president's shoulders. Her focus, she suggested, would be Urban Issues. Stephen noted that he was particularly interested in the Federation CJA, the Saidye Bronfman Award, and the Saidye Bronfman Centre. Matthew and Jean, the two who did not reside in Canada, demurred, asking for time to consider the suggestion.⁴

In June 1998, the leadership of the SSBFF passed to Sam and Saidye Bronfman's grandson, Jean de Gunzburg, who was formally elected to the office of president at a meeting of the directors held at the CCA. In keeping with the tradition that had begun with Saidye, Jean proposed that Phyllis be named honorary president, an idea that received unanimous approval.⁵ The title belied the level of managerial work Phyllis continued to have to do within the foundation, however; she was the only one of her siblings still living in Montreal, and apart from Stephen the only resident family member on the board. Although Jean kept in regular telephone communication with Hobday and the staff, his direct input was limited when so much of his time was spent away from Montreal. Moreover, Phyllis was passionate about the work of the SSBFF, and very particular about her vision of its purpose and mandate. Clearly, for her, passing the torch was not as simple as merely handing over a title.

The June 1998 meeting represented the passing of the guard in another way. Peter Swann had died in December, and his death left the board with a vacancy. It also raised the question of the role of non-family directors in the future. Up to that time, Swann had been the only board member not to be related to Sam and Saidye Bronfman, although outsiders such as Arnold Ludwick, Philip (and in recent years his son, Robert) Vineberg, and Robert Rabinovitch had served as secretaries and treasurers to the board. In a sense, even Swann did not represent a real precedent, as he was, in Jean's phrase, "one of the family."⁶ Nevertheless, Hobday suggested that the SSBFF might consider adding up to three new board members, and mentioned that he was already developing a preliminary list of names, including "generalists" (people with a broad view of Canadian society) and "specialists" (people with expertise in particular issues).[7] The board was at a crossroads again: it could strengthen its ranks and possibly become more effective, or remain essentially a family institution and run the risk of having members lose interest as they turned their attentions to other activities.

For his part, Jean approved of the idea of bringing in someone from outside the family – in principle. The other board members agreed that they should make a list of candidates and begin narrowing it down by September.[8] The September meeting did not materialize, however, and when a phone meeting was organized in December, the issue was not addressed. It was put back on the table only at the board meeting in February 1999. Phyllis had a candidate in mind: Nancy Neamtan, a member of the Working Group on the Social Economy and president of the *Chantier de l'économie sociale*. A discussion ensued, but once again the board decided to wait until a longer list of candidates could be considered.[9] When the board met again in June, Jean noted that only Phyllis had come forward with a candidate. He concluded that the directors were not eager to bring an outsider into the foundation's governance. Stephen and Phyllis agreed that there was "no rush."[10] The issue was not raised again.

The National Arts and Youth Demonstration Project

In 1998, the third generation of Sam and Saidye's family began to influence the foundation's agenda by pushing to find ways to improve the lives of disadvantaged youth. The staff responded by suggesting that the foundation commission an exploratory study to determine the extent to which community-based organizations could successfully engage young people in artistic endeavours and in the process help them develop important life skills. The foundation wanted to focus on community organizations rather than schools to avoid entanglements with the existing public education bureaucracies. Other funders, such as Los Angeles's

Getty museum, had made costly investments in trying to change the arts education curriculum without achieving their goals. The ssbff also wanted to provide another avenue of support for community-based groups working to empower themselves and their communities.[11]

As a way of exploring the potential for arts education for disadvantaged youth, the ssbff turned to Robin Wright, a professor at the McGill University School of Social Work. Wright agreed to conduct interviews and study the literature to determine the extent to which extracurricular art programs for children and youth were in operation in Canada, the United States, and Britain, and how effective they were at improving the life chances of disadvantaged children and youth; the study also hoped to identify the best practice models within the field.[12]

Wright's preliminary report suggested that the effectiveness of community-based art programs was generally anecdotal. The field needed a longitudinal intervention study to see if art programs could really make a difference in the lives of disadvantaged youth. Among practitioners, there was enthusiastic support for the foundation's interest in providing stable funding to the organizations that were already involved in this arena and for the development of effective evaluation tools. When the ssbff board met in December 1999, they discussed the findings of the study and agreed to fund a planning and development phase to determine the parameters of a potential program.[13]

Pushing forward on the concept, the staff of the ssbff assembled two roundtable discussions with key experts in policy, research, and the arts, as well as people who were running arts programs for children and youth. From these discussions, Robin Wright and the ssbff staff assembled a set of recommendations for a National Arts and Youth Demonstration Project. This project would determine what art strategies would work across the board for all children and verify whether arts education could promote the well-being of children and youth.

The project that Wright outlined to the board on 13 July 2000 would last three years and include a maximum of seven sites in Canada. Foundation staff wanted to make sure that it reflected geographic and cultural diversity, as well as a mix of rural and urban communities and different economic levels. Wright estimated it would take $2 million to fund this demonstration project. On behalf of McGill, she asked the foundation to commit $500,000 and promised to raise the remaining $1.5 million from other funders.[14] The directors agreed to commit to the $500,000 subject to McGill's ability to raise the remaining project funds by the middle of December. As was its practice, the foundation gave $75,000 up front to help the project get started.[15]

Six months proved to be ambitious. Hobday and Rucker opened doors to potential private and public funders where they could, and Robin Wright and her team at McGill had a strong expression of interest from the Mounted Police Foundation amounting to $100,000 over three years. The deputy minister for Canadian Heritage (PCH), Alex Himelfarb, assembled representatives from Health Canada, Justice Canada, the Youth Initiatives Branch of Human Resources Development Canada (HRDC), and the National Crime Prevention Centre to listen to the McGill proposal; the mayor of Toronto, Barbara Hall, also expressed strong support. As of the first week of December, however, no one had committed to the project.[16] At its December meeting, the SSBFF board agreed to extend the deadline to 31 March 2001.

The process of seeking major support from the government continued to slow the project down. To verify the integrity and methodology of the study, the government created an expert advisory group with representation from all the agencies that were considering funding. During the first half of 2001, Wright and her colleagues met with the expert group several times and refined the study's goals to meet the concerns of the federal officials. By May, three agencies had expressed strong interest in the project and outlined the level of funding they would provide. With potential contributions from PCH, the National Crime Prevention Centre, and the Youth Justice Program of the Department of Justice, the federal government seemed poised to contribute $1 million to the project. In addition, McGill's School of Social Work promised $250,000 from its own resources.[17]

Once again, the directors were asked to extend their deadline with the hope that the project could still be funded, but as Hobday noted, even if the federal government came through with $1 million, McGill still needed to raise another $412,000 based on its total budget. Given

this information, Hobday asked the directors in May 2001 whether they
wanted to think about moving ahead with interim funding, scaling back
the scope of the project, or waiting for more definite word on the government's commitment? After considering the situation, the board chose
to wait, withholding the foundation's funds until at least $1 million had
been funded by the government.[18]

Through the summer, Wright continued to push for final approval
from the federal government. By October, they were only waiting for a
final signature from the deputy minister of Canadian Heritage. With an
expected $1.75 million almost in hand, Wright wondered if this might
satisfy the SSBFF's conditions to award the project the balance of the
funding.[19] The foundation was still appropriately cautious, however.
Jean de Gunzburg proposed two options: downsize the project to fit
existing funds or keep waiting for the federal commitment before
releasing the foundation's funds. The board chose a combination of the
two, asking McGill to develop a new plan based on fewer dollars and
stipulating that it would continue to wait for confirmation from the
federal government at least until 31 March 2002. If the government
had not come through by that time, McGill could submit a new proposal to the foundation based on a lower overall project cost.[20]

A major reorganization at PCH delayed matters through the early part
of 2002. In the meantime, the project received a verbal commitment for
$500,000 from the National Crime Prevention Centre and Youth Justice.
With continuing verbal reassurances from PCH that the money was coming, Wright and her colleagues at McGill decided to risk launching the
project, and selected five community-based sites in Toronto, Tillsonburg
(Ontario), Vancouver, Montreal, and Winnipeg.

Though the groups and communities differed from site to site, Arts
Starts Neighbourhood Storefront Cultural Centre in Toronto typified the
kind of effort the project was looking at. Based in the former City of
York, Arts Starts functioned as a small gallery, offering a programming
space for children's workshops and a performing arts space for various
kinds of activities. The area had a high unemployment rate, and over
half the residents had been born outside of Canada, many in Somalia, the
Caribbean, Italy, Portugal, South America, and India. The project would

provide art programs to youth between ten and fifteen years old in this underserved community. Researchers from McGill would try to assess the impact these programs had on the students and the community over three years.[21]

The team at McGill had taken a risk in launching the project before the funding from the government was actually in hand. To fit a tighter budget, they scaled down the number of sites from seven to five and they began training research assistants and working with people in the field to develop curriculum. It was well into the summer of 2002, with recruitment already underway for the autumn, when the new deputy minister of PCH, Judith LaRocque, sent a letter to Hobday confirming that the department's $500,000 contribution to the project was actually on its way.[22]

By October, nearly 150 students in five cities were engaged in a variety of artistic activities. Wright's research assistants collected data, tabulating the results of questionnaires directed at children and their parents, and culling statistics from school forms and community mapping surveys. The data was compared to the National Longitudinal Survey of Children and Youth which had been conducted by HRDC and Statistics Canada. Rucker worked with the researchers to fine-tune the methodology so that the project's statistics would yield analyzable results. The intention was to see if the art programs had any effect on the children's self-esteem, communication skills, and academic performance.[23] Over the course of the following three years an impressive amount of data was generated, enough to suggest that art activities did have a positive impact on children's lives. The long-term outcome of such activities would obviously need to be followed over a more extensive period, work the SSBFF was not prepared to fund. The project's results were passed on to the federal Department of Justice, the Department of Canadian Heritage, and the National Crime Prevention Centre in order to help form policy.[24] Despite the limitations of the study, this report was quickly hailed as a touchstone document in the field; at conferences and seminars on youth at risk, Wright's study is generally assumed to be basic reading.[25]

The McGill team's work won them considerable praise: while the research was still continuing across Canada, they were offered a grant of $450,000 US to implement a similar program in Florida.[26] Considering the difficulties Wright experienced just two years before trying to put together a government funding package, this was remarkable – and testimony to how effective seed money can be if properly marketed. The SSBFF devoted the remainder of this project budget into funding a symposium on the results. Held in Montreal in September 2004, the "NAYDP Symposium: Research to Policy to Practice" attracted 150 participants from the field of cultural arts education. Acknowledging the SSBFF's contribution, Robin Wright wrote that the project "resulted in policy-makers and practitioners striving for higher standards of practice in art programs that enhance the well-being of children and youth." She also reported that PCH was considering expanding the program to other high-risk communities in Canada, and that the Department of Justice was exploring ways to adapt the NAYDP model to the needs of youth in conflict with the law.[27] The SSBFF had reason to agree with Stephen's comment that with the NAYDP they had "accomplished a lot." [28]

Plum Coulee

At some point in the discussions surrounding the upcoming centenary festivities for 2001, the townspeople of Plum Coulee, Manitoba, realized that Saidye Rosner had been born and raised there – the same Saidye Rosner who had married Sam Bronfman and whose children were now, among many other things, funding heritage projects. Saidye herself had died just a few years earlier but the centenary committee decided to contact her daughter, Phyllis Lambert, to see if the family might like to make a contribution to the project. The committee, a "small but dedicated group of residents" who shared "a vision for pathways in the community," had created a project known as "Pathways 2000" whose goal was to provide "recreational and heritage amenities" for Plum Coulee, a town of some 750 people.[29] Although not quite so culturally diverse as it had been in Saidye's day – the Jewish families had long since gone – the town still boasted a rich heritage, above all people of Mennonite and Ukrainian origin. More than anything else it was the pioneering spirit of hard-working prairie settlers that Plum Coulee stood for and wished to celebrate.

Phyllis was intrigued by the chance to explore this aspect of her mother's childhood and travelled out to attend the festivities in July 2001. The warmth of the people and the unpretentiousness of the town touched a chord with her: "Folksy – you just felt good about it," was the way Hobday later described his own reaction.[30] Phyllis met with the members of Pathways 2000 and told them that she had discussed their request with the other SSBFF directors, who had expressed great interest in contributing to the project if provided with sufficient details.[31] The project's leader, Avery Schulz, a local schoolteacher, was a dynamic individual who seemed more than ready to begin putting a detailed proposal together, but Phyllis felt they needed professional assistance. She spoke to colleagues and directors of architecture and planning schools in the region, and one name surfaced: Garry Hilderman, a Winnipeg landscape architect and planner. Hilderman was asked to develop a strategy and a budget for creating some sort of heritage park. "It sounded like a simple enough assignment at the time," he admitted.[32] He was soon bombarded with elaborate ideas from the surprisingly passionate people of Plum Coulee, and took some time preparing preliminary designs, which he presented to Phyllis and Hobday in October.[33]

In early November, Schulz organized a public meeting in Plum Coulee to discuss the proposals and decide whether or not to proceed. Over 200 people took part, including representatives from the media and the provincial government. Hilderman gave a slide presentation outlining the various projects that had been suggested and showing the plans and sketches he had designed for each one. He also gave very precise figures for how much each project would cost; the entire package would run to $3,657,791.67. Schulz conducted an informal poll to assess the popularity of individual projects, and discovered that the Agricore grain elevator ranked highest, followed by the proposals for the Heritage Square and the Main Avenue Streetscaping. There was a sense, however, that people liked the entire package and were willing to pursue even the less elaborate parts of the plan. [34]

The most expensive project by far (over $2 million) was the restoration and redevelopment of one of the two Agricore grain elevators standing unused next to the train tracks which now saw only occasional cargo traffic. One of the elevators had been earmarked for refurbishment as a private business, but the other would be transformed into a multi-level complex featuring a museum and interpretive centre, an arts and crafts studio, a restaurant and banquet hall, a daycare and seniors' centre, and the Wild Plum Café on the top floor with views over the surrounding prairie.[35]

Next in level of popularity and cost (at over $500,000) was the Heritage Square, to be built on the site of the disused CPR railway station. The square would "serve as a public gathering space, a farmers' market and a playground" and would include such features as a bandstand and speaker's corner, a sheltered seating area, a fountain, a bell tower, an arboretum (featuring the ubiquitous plum trees of the town's name), a play structure, and "historic plaques or artifacts." The latter were intended to honour "the special people and events in Plum Coulee's past while ensuring vibrant and meaningful uses for the present."[36] The Main Avenue Streetscaping project, to cost nearly $300,000, would involve the beautification of Main Street by widening the sidewalks, planting trees, installing ornamental lighting with hanging baskets, and positioning heritage interpretive panels. Smaller projects included laying out a pedestrian/bicycle/ski trail; turning the old swimming hole into a proper recreational beach with walkways, washrooms, and changing facilities; transforming the old reservoir site into a marshland with floating boardwalk for nature study; and building an amphitheatre, campgrounds, and bridges over weir and river.[37]

One might have assumed that the crowd was enthusiastic about the entire proposal because they expected that the SSBFF would pay the bill, but this was not the case. Hilderman had made it clear that the committee, and the townspeople in general, would need to work very hard to raise funds, including making appeals to government and other private sources. The prospect of a challenge seemed, if anything, to engage them; furthermore, it was Hobday's impression, once he too had visited Plum Coulee and toured its surrounding countryside, that there was local money to be tapped if only the prosperous farming population could be rallied.[38] Hilderman had also made it clear what the SSBFF was willing to provide: the services of a fundraising consultant, starting grants to develop the projects, the costs of all designs and plans, assistance in setting up a community foundation for Plum Coulee, and assistance in establishing a sustainable management strategy for the projects.[39] In practice, this meant that the SSBFF directors were willing to invest $50,000 in Plum Coulee to develop the project, and then to contribute $500,000 over five years to the capital campaign. Such sums would be conditional upon receiving evidence that the committee was engaged in fundraising through both the private and the public sectors; the foundation also called for a feasibility study to ensure that the project would be self-sustaining.[40]

The town's first step was to create the Plum Coulee Community Foundation (PCCF), which was incorporated in April 2002; the second was to establish the Plum Coulee Heritage and Recreation Development Corporation, incorporated the following June. The first of these was a charitable organization which would receive and process all donations to the project; the second was a non-profit organization which would function as "the operating arm for development in Plum Coulee, and may at some point have ownership of assets and be involved with the operation of some developmental business ventures."[41] By these means, the Plum Coulee project was able to function as an independent client of the SSBFF and other funders. Avery Schulz, who took a leave of absence from teaching, became the director of both organizations.

Schulz was already hard at work lining up partners and making deals. In May 2002, Agricore United signed a "Gift Arrangement and Agreement" with the town of Plum Coulee whereby the elevator was effectively donated in return for a tax receipt for $30,000; a team of volunteers was soon busy cleaning the building and repairing the roof. That same spring, a grant from Manitoba Hydro enabled 400 trees to be purchased and planted by volunteer labour along the banks of the stream running through Plum Coulee. The owners of North Border Auto Service, which was discovered to lie on the site of the original Rosner-Brownstone General Store, agreed to allow the west wall of their building to be used for "a mural depicting the original store and history of the site," to be painted by a southern Manitoba artist. The town also organized its first annual Plum Festival in August, attended by Phyllis, Hobday, and other distinguished guests, including politicians.[42]

Schulz had been working on politicians since the beginning of the project, with limited success. In the spring of 2002, Hilderman showed his designs to "a bevy of Federal and Provincial Government bureaucrats" who were impressed but not forthcoming. The provincial assistant deputy minister for Intergovernmental Affairs informed him that the current government was "more concerned with providing hospital beds than tree planting in rural towns." Despite his annoyance at such remarks, Hilderman remained convinced of "the need to go the political route to get any serious government participation."[43] Hobday realized that Plum Coulee was represented both federally and provincially by opposition political parties, not a good way to secure financial backing for a local project.[44] The provincial minister of Intergovernmental Affairs appeared to think differently, however, at least after the success of the Plum Festival; a meeting between him and Hobday, Hilderman, Schulz, and the mayor of Plum Coulee, Kim Porte, resulted in a change of heart on the part of the assistant deputy minister, who declared herself "extremely enthusiastic" about the project and offered her help in securing provincial funding.[45] Unfortunately, by the following April nothing had materialized on this front. Elmer Hildebrand, a "major Manitoba media baron" who was the guest speaker at the PCCF's first Annual General Meeting, told the crowd that if they expected funds to come from the government of Manitoba "not to hold their breath" but "to realize the bulk of funding would need to be raised from the resourceful citizens within [the] communities of southwestern Manitoba."[46]

For the time being, the bulk of the funding was coming from the SSBFF. Despite the lack of progress in government circles, the project was advancing thanks to the foundation's seed money and the efforts by Schulz, Hilderman, and dozens of volunteers. Indeed, Phyllis expressed some concern that Schulz was suffering a "burn-out" and needed an additional staff person to write grant proposals.[47] At the PCCF's general meeting in April 2003, very favourable reports were presented from the project's numerous committees (Main Avenue Streetscape, Elevator Redevelopment, Pathways and Bridges, Pond, Heritage Square, Reservoir Meeting Place, and Finance and Fundraising) which were sent on to the SSBFF. Impressed, the directors approved another $100,000 grant for the project and agreed that this amount should be repeated through 2006. They stipulated that payments would be made prior to 1 April each year (to take advantage of the spring construction season) providing there was sufficient evidence of ongoing fundraising efforts by the PCCF and the town. The SSBFF also offered to pay 50 per cent of the maintenance costs every year, providing the town and the PCCF paid the balance; a gradually increasing total sum was projected over several years to take into account deterioration over time.[48] The directors had learned the importance of maintenance costs after their headaches with the Saidye Bronfman Centre.

Plum Coulee acknowledged the foundation's generosity by declaring that the project should be named "The Saidye Rosner Bronfman Heritage and Recreation Park." The town also commissioned a plaque to honour the historic role played by Saidye's father, Samuel Rosner, who was designated as a "Community Builder of the Past." The plaque featured the inscription: "Samuel Rosner, Early settler, businessman, farmer, Councilor and Mayor, For his vision and dedication to his Community of Plum Coulee, With appreciation on behalf of all the citizens of Plum Coulee."[49] In December 2003, a CBC National News story was aired on Plum Coulee and its efforts to redefine itself; it featured an interview with Phyllis who described her family's roots in the town and what it meant to be able to encourage its rejuvenation.[50] Over the next three years, SSBFF grant money saw the Heritage Square through to completion, as well as many of the smaller projects and the feasibility study for the elevator.[51] It also paid for Hilderman's professional fees as well as Schulz's salary and that of a much-needed assistant.

The rest came through fundraising. One particularly effective tool was the production of an annual report for the PCCF, a glossy spiral-bound volume in full colour featuring historical and cultural background and a detailed account of the project's success so far, including a report from Hilderman. By the end of 2004, the PCCF had raised almost a quarter of a million dollars through local pledges.[52] On top of that, the Thomas Sill Foundation, a Manitoba-based organization dedicated to promoting local initiative, committed $50,000 toward the Amphitheatre and Nature Study area.[53] Elmer Hildebrand, head of Golden West Broadcasting, continued to show interest in the Plum Coulee project and agreed to help raise funds for the Prairie View Elevator, the largest piece of the project still to be completed by the time the SSBFF's five-year commitment came to an end in 2006. Hilderman estimated that the elevator would require an additional $2–$3 million, but declared he was optimistic of success given the tremendous results so far.[54]

The results were truly impressive, especially for a town of 750, and even given the interest and involvement of the Bronfman family. When Phyllis visited Plum Coulee in the summer of 2006 she was amazed by the achievements of such a small community.[55] What was particularly encouraging was that the project had embraced the larger ambitions of heritage preservation: not only was the town improved physically, but the social, cultural, and even economic life of the entire area had been enhanced. Several new families had moved to Plum Coulee, seeking a stimulating and attractive home environment even as they commuted to work in larger towns nearby. Schoolchildren were brought to Plum Coulee from as far away as Winnipeg to learn about prairie heritage, and especially to see "where the bread that they eat comes from" – as Nancy Rosenfeld reported when describing the agricultural exhibits already installed in the elevator.[56] Plum Coulee was becoming a tourist destination in its own right, a place that demanded a much longer visit than a town of its size normally warranted. When visitors came to the Saidye Rosner Bronfman Heritage and Recreation Park they were giving life to what had become one of the foundation's most successful projects – to say nothing of a lasting tribute to the Rosner family and the SSBFF's origins on the Canadian Prairies.

THE FUTURE OF THE FOUNDATION

The booming stock market through the 1990s helped extend the reach of the SSBFF endowment, but by the end of 1999 a downturn in the markets made the directors begin to worry that their funding commitments might soon be at risk. Andrew Parsons, a financial advisor at Claridge who became the SSBFF's treasurer after Robert Rabinovitch left to take up an appointment as president and CEO of the CBC/Radio Canada, suggested that the SSBFF reconsider its investment strategies. The directors agreed to this, and asked Hobday to freeze administrative expenditures for the coming year.[57] Some improvement in the foundation's financial situation ensued, but 2001 was not a good year overall and the market slump following 9/11 exacerbated the decline. This was offset somewhat by the sale of Saidye's house on Belvedere Road, which enabled $2.2 million to be injected into the SSBFF's endowment, but by November 2001 it looked as though that might soon have to be eaten into.[58]

The Bronfman family's sale of Seagram the year before had some repercussions for the SSBFF as well, notably for the shared costs agreement between the foundation and the company. Hobday's position as executive director of Seagram Corporate Donations was now terminated, but he expressed his wish to remain at the head of the SSBFF until his seventieth birthday in 2007. The board decided to assume the full-time costs of the director and his assistant without diminishing the program costs.[59] This was no small promise: as of May 2001, operating costs for the foundation increased by nearly $100,000 a year.[60] The SSBFF had also had an arrangement with Seagram regarding shared costs whereby the company would recover 100 per cent of the GST charged for financial services and the foundation (which as a charitable organization could recover only 50 per cent) would bill Seagram for the difference; the termination of this arrangement cost the SSBFF an additional $20,000 per year.[61]

By July 2002, given the SSBFF's financial condition and expectations for earnings, Jean suggested that it was time to make some hard decisions about the future. If the foundation chose to rebuild its capital by cutting spending and donations, its integrity as a charity would be compromised. The alternative was to let the foundation wind down. If they were to follow this course, he added, it made little sense to search for a successor to John Hobday, who was scheduled to retire in 2007.[62] Jean suggested that the directors reach a decision about the SSBFF's fate at their next meeting in early December – which, ironically, would fall almost exactly fifty years from the creation of the SSBFF and thirty years from the day of the seminal meeting when Swann was first hired.[63] To help with this decision, SSBFF assistant treasurer Michel Boucher prepared a long-range forecast which suggested that at the current rate of spending for operations and donations, and given projected returns on the invested capital, the foundation's assets would shrink from $62.6 million in 2002 to $32.6 million by the end of 2008. Without substantial cuts in operations and donations or a new infusion of capital, the foundation's funds would run out in 2016.[64]

A surprise development towards the end of 2002 was that Hobday was in serious contention for the position of director of the Canada Council. The current director, Shirley Thomson, was stepping down, and Prime Minister Jean Chrétien was expected to announce her replacement any day.[65] By the time of the SSBFF's 9 December board meeting there was no news – indeed, two days after the meeting an article appeared in *The Globe and Mail* highlighting the careers of the four contenders – so another meeting was called for 15 January 2003. Soon after, the choice was announced: John Hobday. While pleased that Hobday would have a new career challenge, the SSBFF directors were left having to replace him whether or not they decided to wind down the foundation.

In anticipation of his departure, Hobday drafted a series of scenarios for the foundation's future, with the help of Rucker and the financial advisors at Claridge. He began by summing up points that had been articulated at the meeting in December. Over the course of its history, the foundation had benefited Canadian society and enhanced the reputation of the founders. During this same period, however, the children and grand-children of the founders had either moved away from Montreal or created their own philanthropies. (The Stephen Bronfman Foundation was the latest of these.) The decline in earnings on the portfolio meant that the foundation would no longer be able to continue its fixed contribution of \$2.775 million to the Federation CJA and maintain the director's programs. [66]

Given these assumptions, Hobday outlined a plan to wind down the existing elements of the director's program by the middle of 2004, following one of two financial scenarios. The board faced a choice between prolonging the SSBFF's annual contribution to the Federation CJA and shortening that horizon by several years in order to provide an "enhanced legacy" to its major programs. Under the first scenario, the foundation would shut down all programs, sustaining donations only to the Saidye Bronfman Award, the Saidye Bronfman Centre, and the Federation CJA. Under the second scenario, the foundation would choose to accelerate the liquidation of its capital by providing a legacy contribution to Urban Issues and Cultural Management over ten years, as well as a sustaining contribution to Plum Coulee, and an increased annual contribution to the Saidye Bronfman Centre and the Saidye Bronfman Award. [67] The directors chose the second scenario. They also agreed with Hobday's schedule for ending financial commitments to the National Arts and Youth Demonstration Project and the remaining three Arts Stabilization initiatives.[68]

But who to replace Hobday during this brief period? After considerable discussion in camera at their January 2003 meeting, the directors asked Gisele Rucker to take on the position of acting executive director, on the understanding that she would serve only until July 2004 when the foundation's major business would be concluded. Partly because she had provided excellent program management over fifteen years, and partly because she was still heavily involved in Urban Issues, Rucker was an obvious choice. The directors also decided that any outstanding issues pertaining to the SSBFF after July 2004 would be handled by the Stephen Bronfman Foundation (also headquartered at Claridge) and its executive director Nancy Rosenfeld. In the meantime, it was agreed that the anticipated termination of the SSBFF should not reach the ears of the general public, especially not to cause anxiety to any of the current holders of grants. "Should anyone ask further questions," Jean suggested to his fellow directors, "we will say the future of the foundation is under discussion."[69]

By the end of the January 2003 meeting, emotions were mixed. Jean congratulated Hobday on his appointment as director of the Canada Council on behalf of the board and thanked him for his nearly twenty years of service to the foundation. The directors talked of honouring Hobday by funding a program in his name at the Centre for Cultural Management at the University of Waterloo. De Gunzburg also expressed his sincere feeling that board and staff had comprised a "fantastic" working group in the five years that he had served as president of the foundation. That evening, the foundation hosted a goodbye party for Hobday in Montreal and wished him well in his next career.[70]

LEGACIES

As matters turned out, the directors chose not to follow through with the proposed legacy contributions to the Saidye Bronfman Centre and the Cultural Management program, and were unable to do so with Urban Issues. The Saidye Bronfman Award had the happiest transition of any of the SSBFF programs, becoming one of the Governor General's awards owing to a collaborative plan developed by John Hobday and Nancy Rosenfeld.

The SSBFF directors did wish to make a special endowment in Hobday's name in recognition for his work at the foundation. Early in 2005, Rosenfeld approached the Canada Council once again to suggest that the two bodies collaborate to establish a commemorative award that would take effect when Hobday's term as director of the council came to an end in January 2006. The John Hobday Award in Arts Management would be an annual prize given to "senior managers in the artistic disciplines the Council supports (music, dance, theatre, visual arts, media arts, and writing & publishing)" so they could either study at some appropriate venue (National Arts Stabilization seminar, Getty Museum Institute seminar, Banff Centre programs, etc.) or act as a mentor to "an outstanding management protégé." The council proposed two funding alternatives: 1) an endowment of $1 million which would yield an approximate income of $35,000 a year in income for two awards, or 2) an annual donation of $100,000 for ten years for six annual awards. Both options included the possibility of having matching funds provided from the Department of Canadian Heritage.[71]

By this time the SSBFF, still in operation, was run by Nancy Rosenfeld with Stephen Bronfman as president. Because the board's commitment could not be assured over ten years, and because they had planned to make a legacy endowment in any event, the directors opted for the Canada Council's first funding scenario.[72] Rosenfeld began at once to negotiate the terms of the donation, a process that became delayed as the foundation also found itself making arrangements with the council over the Saidye Bronfman Award. Eventually all the contingencies were worked out and the SSBFF issued a press release announcing the new John Hobday Award, to be presented for the first time in 2007. The award was launched at a cocktail reception held at the Saidye Bronfman Centre on 20 June 2006, with Laurent Lapierre representing the Canada Council and Stephen Bronfman the SSBFF. Rosenfeld reminded the directors that Sam Bronfman once served proudly on the first board of the Canada Council, so "the connection goes back a long time."[73]

Conclusion

For more than fifty years, the SSBFF set out to make a difference in people's lives. This objective was pursued deliberately, if not always strategically. Sam Bronfman made most of his philanthropic decisions without adhering to a formal program, but he gave because he believed in a project and what it set out to accomplish. This approach was as true for single acts of giving as it was for an entire philanthropic philosophy. At no time did Sam – or Saidye or any of their descendants working with the SSBFF or the staff they employed – give for the sake of giving; philanthropy was not something undertaken to make the givers feel good about themselves. Sam and Saidye's motivations for engaging in charitable work may have been complex, but at the heart of their efforts was a desire to make better the society in which they lived. For Sam and his successors in the SSBFF, philanthropy was a way to effect change on a large or small scale. At this, they succeeded.

During the latter part of the SSBFF's existence, the efforts were more focused and the investments of money more substantial: a recent calculation pegged the total sum of grant money expended between 1969 and 2007 at approximately $125,099,400. Consequently, the results of such investment were more spectacular than they had been in the early years – but the philosophy of giving was the same. So was the effect on people's lives. The SSBFF's archives contain references to countless beneficiaries of Sam Bronfman's philanthropy and the thousands of recipients of foundation grants given under Peter Swann's direction and through the Added Dimensions, Special Initiatives, or Futures programs. Their number speaks (and requires) volumes. It is perhaps slightly easier to focus on the people who benefited from the SSBFF's more carefully constructed programs under Hobday, if only because we know more about the programs' objectives, the needs that inspired them, and the organizations that put them into play. Even so, one could not list them all: the children helped through Learning Disabilities and the researchers whose work was carried out thanks to the program, the graduates who have gone on to rewarding careers after training in the Cultural Management program at Waterloo, those who learned and profited from the agricultural research at the University of Manitoba and the architects and architectural historians trained at McGill, the recipients of craft awards, the seniors who were able to speak with one voice about their pensions, the citizens whose environments were improved through heritage preservation and community activism across the country from Halifax and St John's to Vancouver and Victoria, and the generations who enjoyed art courses and exhibitions and good theatre at the Saidye Bronfman Centre – indeed, when it comes to the arts and heritage one must step back and include the millions whose lives were made better for having seen or heard the works produced through SSBFF grants, and for having lived in streets that are livelier or safer or more beautiful as a result of exposure to these programs.

There were, of course, difficulties. The directors of the SSBFF were occasionally frustrated by grantees who did not deliver what was expected and by projects that, even after much patience and dedication, had to be terminated. Even so, there were dividends to be drawn from the investment: the foundation learned a great deal from the shortcomings of One Voice, and no doubt so did all the people involved with it. There are also different ways of measuring success: the directors often expressed regret that Urban Issues could not be taken to a broader level, and yet this was one of the SSBFF's most successful projects. For the most part, the SSBFF did not think merely in terms of results, but saw the impact of its grants in a wider light that also took in the obstacles faced, the kind of effort being made, and always the lessons learned. As such, the SSBFF served as a model for governments and other foundations. Significantly, unlike most other funding agencies, the SSBFF did not cut funds off abruptly when results were not being achieved, but continued to nurture and help find solutions to problems, and if necessary give advanced warning of termination, often as much as three years.

Indeed, the SSBFF was distinguished as a foundation by its willingness to work with its grantees, helping shape the proposals and advising on practical matters such as staffing and marketing; it was always very hands-on in its relationships. Building on the notion that it is better to teach people how to fish than simply to give them fish, the foundation spent time and money helping organizations learn how to do things with the money it was already giving them. Instead of giving more money to struggling organizations, the SSBFF typically paid for a consultant who would conduct an evaluation of their operations, or funded a marketing strategist, or even hired additional staff. In many cases, the skills and understanding acquired were worth as much to an organization as the funding itself; at the very least, grantees whose projects did not pan out would be all the wiser in subsequent endeavors.

This is the story of a foundation, an organization engaged in philanthropic activity over more than half a century, one of the major players in the realm of arts and heritage and social activism in twentieth-century Canada. The SSBFF was a very particular institution, with unusual origins for a body giving away several million dollars a year, and with strong-minded personalities on the board and on staff whose interests and skills took the foundation in very specific directions. Although it is widely known in funding circles, the Samuel and Saidye Bronfman Family Foundation and its achievements need to be better understood. Many people hear the name Bronfman and think Seagram. In a way, this is unsurprising, as there was much overlap: the SSBFF shared office space, financial resources, and executive directors with Seagram, and also did so to an extent with CEMP, Claridge, and other Bronfman companies and foundations. At the same time, not to appreciate the role played by the SSBFF in funding and nurturing a wide variety of projects is to overlook its basic mandate and think only in terms of corporate donations. The extent of the SSBFF's achievements should not be reduced to the mere impact of money, Seagram or Bronfman. It took an infinitely greater effort, and the application of patience and experience, over fifty years, to make a very significant and widely recognized difference.

APPENDICES

Appendix 1

SSBFF PROGRAMS AND THEIR BUDGETS, 1972–83

YEAR	PROGRAM 1	PROGRAM 2	PROGRAM 3
1973	Learning Disabilities $75,000	Culture $75,000	The North $75,000
1975			The North $70,000
1977			The North $100,000
1979	Learning Disabilities $82,500	Social Problems Concerned with the Elderly $82,500	The North $110,000

YEAR	PROGRAM 4	PROGRAM 5
1973	Educational & Community TV $75,000	Added Dimensions $50,000
1975	Heritage Montreal, Heritage Canada & related projects $75,000	Added Dimensions $225,000
1977	Heritage Montreal, Heritage Canada & related projects $95,000	Added Dimensions $250,000
1979	Heritage Montreal, Heritage Canada & related projects $110,000	Added Dimensions $275,000

Source: SSBFF Board Books, 19 November 1979, SSBFF Archives

SSBFF FUNDING OF MAJOR CLIENTS, 1983–2007

TIMELINE	LEARNING DISABILITIES	SENIORS	ARTS / CULTURAL MANAGEMENT	HERITAGE / URBAN ISSUES	CRAFTS
Before 1983	Various / McGill University Children's Learning Centre	Various under Social Problems Concerned with the Elderly	Various, 1973–79	Heritage Montreal / Heritage Canada	Canadian Crafts Council: Saidye Bronfman Award for Excellence in the Crafts
1983 "Towards Tomorrow"	McGill University Children's Learning Centre; Canadian Assoc. for Children with Learning Disabilities		Canadian Assoc. of Arts Admin. Educators CAAAE; Arts Management Training programs	Heritage Montreal / Heritage Canada	
1986	Learning Disabilities Assoc. of Canada LDAC	One Voice			

1988				Centre for Cultural Management, U. of Waterloo (CCM)	Heritage Montreal / Heritage Canada		
1990 / 91 Visioning Workshops	LDAC (Montebello, QC)	One Voice (Mont Ste-Marie, QC)	CCM (Elora, ON)			Various (North Hatley, QC)	Canadian Crafts Council (Banff, AB)
1991	LDAC	One Voice	CCM	Arts Stabilization		Urban Issues	Canadian Crafts Council: Saidye Bronfman Award
1993		(discontinued)					
1997	(discontinued)						
2005				(dis-continued)	(discontinued)		Canada Council: Saidye Bronfman Award

Appendix 3
Saidye Bronfman Award Winners, 1977–2008

2008 Chantal Gilbert, jeweller, Quebec, QC

2007 Paul Mathieu, ceramicist, Vancouver, BC

2006 Peter Powning, sculptor, Markhamville, NB

2005 Michael Hosaluk, wood turner, Saskatoon, SK

2004 Maurice Savoie, ceramicist, Longueuil, QC

2003 Walter Ostrom, ceramic artist, Indian Harbour, NS

2002 Kai Hung Chan, textile artist, Toronto, ON

2001 Léopold L. Foulem, ceramicist, Caraquet, NB & Montreal, QC

2000 Peter Fleming, furniture designer and maker, Toronto, ON

1999 Susan Low-Beer, ceramic artist, Toronto, ON

1998 Marcel Marois, tapestry artist, Quebec, QC

1997 William (Grit) Laskin, guitarmaker, Toronto, ON

1996 Steven Heinemann, ceramic artist, Richmond Hill, ON

1995 Louise Genest, bookbinder, Montreal, QC

1994 Daniel Crichton, glass artist, Toronto, ON

1993 Michael C. Fortune, furniture designer and maker, Lindsay, ON

1992 Walter Dexter, ceramicist-potter, Metchosin, BC

1991 Susan Warner Keene, fibre artist, Toronto, ON

1990 Dorothy Caldwell, textile artist, Hastings, ON

1989 Harlan House, potter, Marysville, ON

1988 Lutz Haufschild, glass artist, West Vancouver, BC

1987 Carole Sabiston, fibre artist, Victoria, BC

1986 Bill Reid, metalsmith and wood carver, Vancouver, BC

1985 Michael Wilcox, bookbinder, Woodview, ON

1984 William Hazzard, wood carver, Regina, SK

1983 Wayne Ngan, potter, Hornby Island, BC

1982 Micheline Beauchemin, fibre artist, Les Grondines, QC

1981 Joanna Staniszkis, fibre artist, Vancouver, BC

1980 Louise Doucet and Satoshi Saito, potters, Ayer's Cliff, QC

1999 Monique Cliche-Spénard, quilt maker, St-Joseph-de-Beauce, QC

1978 Lois Etherington Betteridge, metalsmith, Guelph, ON

1977 Robin Hopper, potter, Metchosin, BC

Source: Canada Council for the Arts, Endowments and Prizes

Notes

Introduction

1 Marrus, 461.
2 CEMP was named for Sam and Saidye's four children, Charles, Edgar, Minda, and Phyllis.
3 Interview with Nancy Rosenfeld, 27 June 2007.
4 See for example the conduct of the extended Kaplan family in Husock, "Family Foundation Governance at the J.M. Kaplan Fund."
5 This issue is discussed very effectively in Jeffrey Brison's *Rockefeller, Carnegie and Canada*.
6 Lagemann, "Foundations in History: New Possibilities for Scholarship and Practice," in Lagemann, *Philanthropic Foundations*, ix.

Chapter One

1 Johnson, *A History of the Jews*, 358–64.
2 Johnson, *A History of the Jews*, 365. Marrus, 29.
3 Tulchinsky, 119.
4 Tulchinsky, 120.
5 Marrus, 33.
6 Tulchinsky, 118.
7 Marrus, 35–9.
8 Marrus, 48.
9 Marrus, 49.

10 Marrus, 95.

11 Saidye Rosner Bronfman, *Recollections of My Life*, 36.

12 Plum Coulee Community Foundation, Annual Report, 2002, in SSBFF Board Books, 4 July 2002, SSBFF Archives.

13 Marrus, 93–4.

14 Saidye Rosner Bronfman, *Recollections of My Life*, 17 and *My Sam*, 7; Marrus, 93.

15 Heron, *Booze: A Distilled History*, 180–2.

16 Marrus, 104–5.

17 Kolber, 31; Marrus, 105.

18 Marrus, 109.

19 Marrus, 130.

20 Newman, 132.

21 Marrus, 173. Remillard and Merrett, 38.

22 Marrus, 195f.

23 Newman, 129–31.

24 King, *From the Ghetto to the Main*, 36.

25 King, *From the Ghetto to the Main*, 106.

26 Tulchinsky, *Taking Root*, 41.

27 First Annual Meeting of the Montreal Hebrew Philanthropic Society, printed in the *Occident and American Jewish Advocate*, vol. 6, no.7: October 1848.

28 King, *From the Ghetto to the Main*, 73.

29 For a full discussion of the development of Protestant social welfare in Canada, see Christie and Gauvreau.

30 Frisch, 29.

31 Frisch, 29, 74ff. Brinkmann, 181.

32 Brinkmann, 181.

33 Tulchinsky, *Branching Out*, 22.

34 Marrus, 111.

35 Tulchinsky, *Taking Root*, 138ff.

36 Tulchinsky, 137–8.

37 King, *From the Ghetto to the Main*, 141.

38 Kolber, 214.

39 King, *From the Ghetto to the Main*, 147.

40 Tulchinsky, 145.

41 King, *Fabled City*, 81.

42 King, *From the Ghetto to the Main*, 80, 146.

43 The FJP was renamed the Federation of Jewish Community Services in 1951, became the Allied Jewish Community Services (AJCS) in 1965, and finally the Federation/CJA (Combined Jewish Appeal) in 1997.

44 King, *From the Ghetto to the Main*, 335.

45 Quoted in King, *Fabled City*, 82.
46 King, *From the Ghetto to the Main*, 94, 114.
47 Saidye Rosner Bronfman, *Recollections of my Life*, 80.
48 Tulchinsky, 274.
49 King, *From the Ghetto to the Main* 144; Marrus, 175.
50 Abella and Troper, 12.
51 King, *From the Ghetto to the Main*, 154.
52 Marrus, 383.
53 Marrus, 166ff.
54 Adam, 16.
55 Marrus, 45–6, 90.
56 Marrus, 94.
57 King, *From the Ghetto to the Main*, 148, and *Fabled City*, 119–21.
58 King, *From the Ghetto to the Main*, 336.
59 Marrus, 175, 253.
60 Quoted in Saidye Rosner Bronfman, *Recollections of My Life*, 83–4.
61 King, *From the Ghetto to the Main*, 149.
62 King, *Fabled City*, 100.
63 King, *From the Ghetto to the Main*, 166.
64 Interview with Phyllis Lambert, 5 July 2004.
65 King, *Fabled City*, 104.
66 Saidye Rosner Bronfman, *My Sam*, 56.
67 King, *From the Ghetto to the Main*, 176.
68 Marrus, 256.; Abella and Troper, 10
69 Interview with Saul Hayes cited in Abella and Troper, 57.
70 Marrus, 264.
71 Abella and Troper, 57–8.
72 Abella and Troper, 54.
73 Marrus, 271.
74 Marrus, 281.
75 Marrus, 284–5.
76 Marrus, 286.
77 Saidye Rosner Bronfman, *Recollections of My Life*, 17.
78 Marrus, 313.
79 Marrus, 174–5.
80 Marrus, 281.
81 Marrus, 268.
82 King, *Fabled City*, 95.
83 Quoted in Kolber, 214–15.
84 Marrus, 298–9.
85 Kolber, 216.

86 Marrus, 298.
87 King, *From the Ghetto to the Main*, 281.
88 King, *Fabled City*, 84.
89 The Montreal Holocaust Memorial Centre: www.whmc.ca.
90 Saidye Rosner Bronfman, *My Sam*, 53.
91 Marrus, 337.
92 Marrus, 342.
93 Marrus, 429.
94 Interview with Edgar Bronfman, 23 June 2004.
95 Interview with Charles Bronfman, 23 June 2004.
96 Newman, 170.
97 Newman, 164–5.
98 Edgar Bronfman, *Good* Spirits, 65 & 138-9; Saidye Rosner Bronfman, *My Sam*, 1982, 101.
99 Newman, 186–8.
100 Marrus, 378.
101 Kolber, 31.
102 Marrus, 399–401.
103 Interview with Manuel G. Batshaw, 3 April 2004.
    Phyllis Lambert, note to author, 30 September 2005.

CHAPTER TWO

1 The SSBFF should not be confused with the Samuel Bronfman Foundation, established in New York in 1951 to provide funds for the Bronfman Chair in Democratic Business Enterprise at Columbia University. Over time, the Samuel Bronfman Foundation would become the agent through which the family's charitable donations in the United States were made. See Saidye Rosner Bronfman, *My Sam*, 92.
2 "Acts and Resolves Passed by the General Court of Massachusetts," 1874, quoted in Hall, *Inventing the Nonprofit Sector,* 38.
3 Whitaker, 42.
4 Brison, 21.
5 Hall, 44.
6 Brison, 22.
7 Whitaker, 41.
8 Brison, 19.
9 Sealander, "Curing Evils at Their Source," 218.
10 Hall, 45.
11 Sealander, "Curing Evils at Their Source," 218.
12 The YMCA was established in London in 1844 by a group of evangelical

Christians. The organization spread to Australia and then to North America. The first YMCA established in North America was organized in Montreal in November 1851 (archives3.concordia.ca/YMCA/default.html).

13 Galambos, "The Emerging Organizational Synthesis in Modern American History," 279–90. See also Galambos, "Technology, Political Economy, and Professionalization: Central Themes of the Organizational Synthesis," 471–93.

14 Sealander, 218.

15 Sealander, 224.

16 Ross, 482.

17 Brison, 44.

18 Macdonald left his tobacco company to the family of his business partner David Stewart, who continued to make donations to McGill and other institutions. In 1973 the Stewarts established the Macdonald-Stewart Foundation, now one of Canada's major philanthropies.

19 Tippett, 119.

20 Martin, 263.

21 Tippett, 120.

22 Semple, 340.

23 Fong, 518.

24 Martin, 263.

25 Whitaker, 42.

26 www.vancouverfoundation.bc.ca/about/history.htm.

27 Interview with Amelie Bourbeau, 29 November 2006. See Bourbeau thesis.

28 Tippett, 94.

29 Svanhuit, 8.

30 Blishen, 19.

31 Ostry, 28f.

32 Quoted in Tippett, 73.

33 Tippett, 95ff; Ostry, 37.

34 Tippett, 105.

35 Tippett, 104.

36 Tippett, 66f; Ostry, 32.

37 Tippett, 17, 24.

38 Tippett, 67.

39 Brison, 5, 44.

40 Brison, 100, 125.

41 Frost, 152; Brison, 159.

42 Brison, 70.

43 www.ccarts.ca/en/about/history/documents.

44 Tippett, 187.

45 *Report of the Royal Commission on National Development in the Arts, Letters and Sciences, 1949–1951.* Ottawa: Edmund Cloutier, 1951.

46 The money came from death taxes on the estates of two wealthy Canadians, Isaac Walton Killham of Royal Securities, and Sir James Dunn of Algoma Steel. Half of the money was invested in higher education; the other half created an endowment for the Canada Council. See Martin, 80.

47 Brison, 202.

48 Letters patent, Samuel and Saidye Bronfman Family Foundation, 29 November 1952, SSBFF Archives.

49 Interview with Arnold Ludwick, 4 April 2004.

50 SSBFF Minute Books, 29 January 1953, SSBFF Archives.

51 The accusation that McGill governor J.W. McConnell was largely responsible for denying Sam a seat on the McGill board appears to be based merely on circumstantial evidence, namely that this honour only came to Sam following McConnell's death in 1963. Clearly there was an ongoing rivalry between the two men, who were among Canada's most successful businessmen and philanthropists, as their competitive patronage of the School of Commerce indicates. See Marrus, 298, and Fong, 481.

52 Frost, 460.

53 Canada Council, "Opening Proceedings," May 1957.

54 The Montreal Museum of Fine Arts, "Proposition to revise the acquisition policy of the Saidye and Samuel Bronfman Collection of Contemporary Canadian Art," March 1981, in SSBFF Board Books, April 1981, SSBFF Archives. Matthew Ram, "Brief outline of the program and services of various organizations and associations supported in the past by the Bronfman Interests and B. Aaron," 28 July 1972, Acc.2126, Box 16, File: Report on Donations, Hagley Museum and Library.

55 Saidye Rosner Bronfman, *Recollections of My Life*, 95, 151.

56 In 1999, as part of a reorganization of its staff and offices, the Canadian Jewish Congress donated the Samuel Bronfman House to Concordia University to house the university's Institute for Jewish Studies. Concordia University Press Release, 14 September 1999. At the time of the transfer, Charles and Andrea Bronfman provided a $1 million donation to Concordia's Institute for Jewish Studies. See Arnold, "Concordia University takes over Bronfman House," *Canadian Jewish News*, 16 September 1999.

57 Marrus, 414, 416, 463.

58 John Hobday to Manuel G. Batshaw, 25 March 1988, AB3 File, SSBFF Archives.

59 Interview with Manuel G. Batshaw, 4 April 2004.

60 Kolber, 29.

61 Marrus, 437.

62 Tulchinsky, *Branching Out*, 294.

63 Interview with Manuel G. Batshaw, 3 April 2004. See also, Marrus, 447–8.

64 Tulchinsky, *Branching Out*, 301.

65 Edgar Bronfman, *The Making of a Jew*, 34.

66 Interview with Charles R. Bronfman, 23 June 2004.

67 Morgan, 238.

68 A.H.S. Gillson to Edgar Bronfman, 11 June 1953, Acc. 2126, Box 16, File: Rosner Chair in Agronomy at the University of Manitoba, Hagley Museum and Library.

69 R.B. Carleton to Charles R. Bronfman, 8 May 1970, Acc.2126, Box 16, File. Rosner Chair in Agronomy at the University of Manitoba, Hagley Museum and Library.

70 Hulse and Spurgeon, 72–80.

71 Hulse and Spurgeon, 72–80. See also E.N. Larter, "A Review of the Rosner Research Program – 1954–1972, University of Manitoba," Acc.2126, Box 16, File: Rosner Chair in Agronomy at the University of Manitoba, 1953–1974, Hagley Museum and Library.

72 Larter, "A Review of the Rosner Research Program – 1954-1972, University of Manitoba," Acc.2126, File: Rosner Chair in Agronomy at the University of Manitoba, 1953–1974, Hagley Museum and Library.

73 For Borlaug's award see nobelprize.org/peace/laureates/1970/borlaug-bio.html. Note also that in the fall of 1967 Jacob Javitz wrote to Charles Bronfman suggesting that the work on triticale at the University of Manitoba was worthy of a nomination to the Nobel Peace Prize Committee. Jacob K. Javits to Charles Bronfman, 12 September 1967, Acc.2126, Box 16, File: Rosner Chair in Agronomy at the University of Manitoba, 1953–1974, Seagram Archives, Hagley Museum and Library.

74 Hulse and Spurgeon, 72–80. Larter, "A Review of the Rosner Research Program – 1954–1972, University of Manitoba," and Plant Science Department, University of Manitoba, "Triticale: Current Situation Summary Report," 1 April 1968, Acc.2126, Box 16, File: Rosner Chair in Agronomy at the University of Manitoba, 1953–1974, Hagley Museum and Library.

75 SSBFF Minute Books, 19 April 1974, SSBFF Archives.

76 Executive director's report, in SSBFF Board Books, 19 November 1979, SSBFF Archives.

CHAPTER THREE

1 Ostry, 128–9.

2 Allemang, 32; Martin, 81.

3 Charles Bronfman to Robert Bourassa, n.d., "Final Draft," Acc. 2126, Box 14, File: Allied Jewish Community Services, Hagley Museum and Library.

4 Martin, 30.

5 Hall, 70.
6 Hall, 71.
7 Hall, 74.
8 Arlett, *A Canadian Directory to Foundations and Other Granting Agencies,* 22.
9 Arlett, "Where the money is: who's who in Canada's philanthropic organizations," n.d., clipping in Acc.2126, Box 16, File: SSBFF, Hagley Museum and Library. See also Arlett, ed., *A Canadian Directory to Foundations and Other Granting Agencies,* 3RD ed., 1973.
10 Arlett, "Where the money is," Acc.2126, Box 16, File: SSBFF, Hagley Museum and Library.
11 Council on Foundations, Inc., "Survey Shows Public Supports Tax Deduction For Charity and Looks Favorably on Foundations," 22 February 1973 in Acc.2126, Box 16, File: SSBFF, Hagley Museum & Library.
12 Hall, 74.
13 Frumkin, 72.
14 Hall, 76–7.
15 Philip Vineberg to Dr Peter Swann, 28 June 1974, AB3 File: "Documents re: charitable status," SSBFF Archives. Also Consumer and Corporate Affairs, Canada, "News Release," 14 June 1974.
16 Martin, 271.
17 Peter Swann to all directors, 19 July 1976, Box 08-L-391, Fonds Phyllis Lambert, Canadian Centre for Architecture.
18 Artlett, "Where the money is," Acc.2126, Box 16, File: SSBFF, Hagley Museum and Library.
19 Hodson, *The International Foundation Directory* (4th ed.), 35.
20 Interview with Phyllis Lambert, 5 July 2004.
21 Interview with Phyllis Lambert, 5 July 2004.
22 Interview with Charles R. Bronfman, 23 June 2004.
23 Interview with Charles R. Bronfman, 23 June 2004.
24 Interview with Phyllis Lambert, 5 July 2004.
25 For more on Matthew Ram (1919–1986), see Canadian Jewish Congress National Archives and Reference Center, Personal Collections, www.cjc.ca.
26 Leo Kolber to Charles Bronfman, 3 February 1972, Acc.2126, Box 16, File: "Report on Donations," Hagley Museum & Library.
27 Matthew Ram, "Brief outline of the program and services of various organizations and associations supported in the past by the Bronfman Interests and B. Aaron," 28 July 1972, Acc. 2126, Box 16, File: "Report on Donations," Hagley Museum and Library.
28 Matthew Ram, "Brief outline of the program and services of various organizations and associations supported in the past by the Bronfman Interests and

B. Aaron," 28 July 1972, Acc. 2126, Box 16, File: "Report on Donations," Hagley Museum and Library.

29 Peter Swann, "You Don't Know Me But..." unpublished autobiography, chapter 1, Fonds Phyllis Lambert, Canadian Centre for Architecture.

30 Pitman, "ROM has the wrong kind of trustees," *Toronto Star*, 9 June 1972, 9.

31 Brown, "Swann sits in gloom looking for a reason why he was sacked," *Toronto Star*, 2 June 1972, 4.

32 Interview with Charles Bronfman, 23 June 2004.

33 SSBFF Minute Books, 20 November 1972, SSBFF Archives.

34 Interview with John Hobday, 21 June 2004.

35 See the "Descriptive Directory" list in Arlett's Canadian Directory to Foundations. Of the ninety-seven family foundations listed about which sufficient information is given, seventy had boards of directors that included members of the donor's family. Some of the others may also fall into this category as it is difficult to tell just from the names that a person is *not* related to the donor. For more on the composition of foundation boards of trustees, see Andrews, 63ff. The composition of the board of the McConnell Foundation is described in Fong, 516–18.

36 SSBFF Minute Books, 20 November 1972, SSBFF Archives.

37 SSBFF Minute Books, 20 November 1972, SSBFF Archives.

38 Interview with Arnold Ludwick, 4 April 2004.

39 Interview with Arnold Ludwick, 4 April 2004.

40 See Background Financial Statements attached to Letter, John Hobday to Jean de Gunzburg, 10 August 1987, in SSBFF Board Books, August 1987, SSBFF Archives.

41 Interview with Phyllis Lambert, 5 July 2004.

42 SSBFF Minute Books, May 1973, SSBFF Archives.

43 Peter Swann to all directors, 22 February 1973, Acc.2126, Box 16, File: SSBFF, Hagley Museum and Library.

44 Charles R. Bronfman to Peter Swann, 26 January 1973, Acc.2126, Box 16, File SSBFF, Hagley Museum & Library.

45 See Arlett's "Descriptive Directory."

46 Fong, 544.

47 Peter Swann to all directors, 22 February 1973, Acc.2126, Box 16, File: SSBFF, Hagley Museum and Library.

48 Peter Swann to all directors, 22 February 1973, Acc.2126, Box 16, File: SSBFF, Hagley Museum and Library.

49 Minda de Gunzburg to Peter Swann, 6 March 1973, Acc.2126, Box 16, File: SSBFF, Hagley Museum and Library.

50 Phyllis Lambert to Peter Swann, 7 March 1973, Acc.2126, Box 16, File: SSBFF, Hagley Museum and Library.

51 SSBFF Minute Books, 4 May 1973, SSBFF Archives. See also Charles R. Bronfman to Peter Swann, 26 January 1973, Acc.2126, Box 16, File: SSBFF, Hagley Museum & Library.

52 Peter Swann to Charles R. Bronfman, 16 August 1973, Acc.2126, Box 16, File: SSBFF, Hagley Museum and Library.

53 Peter Swann to Charles R. Bronfman, 16 August 1973, Acc.2126, Box 16, File: SSBFF, Hagley Museum and Library.

54 SSBFF Minute Books, 21 September 1973, SSBFF Archives.

55 See for example the lists in the SSBFF Board Books, 19 November 1979, SSBFF Archives.

56 SSBFF Minute Books, 18 September 1974, SSBFF Archives.

57 SSBFF Minute Books, 19 April 1974, SSBFF Archives.

58 SSBFF Minute Books, 18 September 1974, SSBFF Archives.

59 SSBFF Minute Books, 21 September 1973 and 18 September 1974, SSBFF Archives.

60 SSBFF Minute Books, 19 November 1979, SSBFF Archives.

61 Royal Commission on Aboriginal Peoples, Canada, *People to People, Nation to Nation*, 11–17.

62 Finkel and Conrad, 538.

63 SSBFF Minute Books, 19 April 1974, SSBFF Archives.

64 Dickason, 405-6.

65 Canadian Association in Support of the Native Peoples, Annual Report, 1975, 1.

66 John Hobday, "Towards Tomorrow," 11, SSBFF Archives.

67 SSBFF Minute Books, 12 November 1975, SSBFF Archives.

68 SSBFF, Minute Books, 19 November 1980, SSBFF Archives.

69 Executive director's report, in SSBFF Board Books, 19 November 1981, SSBFF Archives.

70 Executive director's report, in SSBFF Board Books, 1982, SSBFF Archives.

71 Interview with John Hobday, 21 June 2004.

72 Hobday, "Towards Tomorrow," 11.

73 Hobday, "Towards Tomorrow," 12.

74 See John Hobday, "Towards Tomorrow," 11, SSBFF Archives.

75 Peter Swann to all directors, 1 April 1974, Acc.2126, Box 16, File: Rosner Chair in Agronomy at the University of Manitoba, 1953–1974, Hagley Museum & Library.

76 MMFA, Proposition to revise the acquisition policy of the Samuel and Saidye Bronfman collection of contemporary Canadian art, March 1981, in SSBFF Board Books, 19 November 1981, SSBFF Archives.

77 SSBFF Minute Books, 19 November 1981, SSBFF Archives.

78 SSBFF Minute Books, 4 June 1985, SSBFF Archives.

79 Allied Jewish Community Services, "Budget Requests for 1977/78 – Prelimi-

nary Local Summary," Acc.2126, Box 14, File: Allied Jewish Community Services (1974–75), Hagley Museum and Library.

80 John Hobday, "Notes for a Meeting with Phyllis Lambert, President of the Saidye Bronfman Family Foundation," 13 June 1986, Box 08-L-259, Fonds Phyllis Lambert, Canadian Centre for Architecture.

81 Interview with Phyllis Lambert, 5 July 2004.

82 Arlett, Canadian Directory to Foundations, 5th ed, xiv.

83 Peter C. Swann to Charles R. Bronfman, 28 November 1979, "Foundation Staffing and Other Matters," Acc.2126, Box 16, File: SSBFF, Hagley Museum and Library.

84 Executive director's report, in SSBFF Board Books, 1982, SSBFF Archives.

CHAPTER FOUR

1 Peter C. Swann to Charles R. Bronfman, 28 November 1979, "Foundation Staffing and Other Matters," Acc.2126, Box 16, File: SSBFF, Hagley Museum and Library.

2 Interview with Charles R. Bronfman, 23 June 2004.

3 University of Waterloo, Archives and Rare Books, "Introduction to the Seagram Museum Collection," www.lib.uwaterloo.ca/discipline/SpecColl/archives/seagram .html. Unfortunately, the Seagram Museum was closed in 1997 and the archival material dispersed, the historical materials to the University of Waterloo, the company and family records to the Hagley Museum and Library, Delaware. See interview with Charles Bronfman, 23 June 2004.

4 SSBFF Minute Books, 18 May 1983, SSBFF Archives.

5 Interview with John Hobday, 21 June 2004.

6 Interview with John Hobday, 21 July 2004.

7 Interview with John Hobday, 21 July 2004.

8 Charles R. Bronfman, "Corporations and the Community," 7 April 1981, Box 08-L-310, Fonds Phyllis Lambert, Canadian Centre for Architecture.

9 Charles R. Bronfman, "Corporations and the Community," 7 April 1981, Box 08-L-310, Fonds Phyllis Lambert, Canadian Centre for Architecture.

10 John Hobday to Arnold Ludwick, "The Proposed New Chairman's Fund," 27 September 1983, Box 08-L-350, Fonds Phyllis Lambert, Canadian Centre for Architecture. Allemang, 32.

11 John Hobday to Arnold Ludwick, "The Proposed New Chairman's Fund," 27 September 1983, Box 08-L-350, Fonds, Phyllis Lambert, Canadian Centre for Architecture.

12 John Hobday to Arnold Ludwick, "The Proposed New Chairman's Fund," 27 September 1983, Box 08-L-350, Fonds Phyllis Lambert, Canadian Centre for Architecture.

13 Allemang, 32

14 John Hobday to Arnold Ludwick, "The Proposed New Chairman's Fund," 27 September 1983, Box 08-L-350, Fonds Phyllis Lambert, Canadian Centre for Architecture.

15 N.A., "Relocation from Tupper Street: aide-mémoire," 12 May 1983, SSBFF Archives.

16 SSBFF Board Books, 3 December 1985, SSBFF Archives.

17 Executive director's report, in SSBFF Board Books, 19 November 1981, SSBFF Archives.

18 Interview with Ivan Hale, 14 October 2005. See also www.nrtee-trnee.ca/eng/programs/ArchivedPrograms/Climate_change/climatechange.

19 Hobday, "Towards Tomorrow," 1983, SSBFF Archives.

20 Historians J. Craig Jenkins and Abigail Halcli argue that the Ford Foundation "almost single-handedly, launched a set of new advocacy organizations, such as the National Council of La Raza to serve as the 'NAACP for Mexican-Americans.'" See Jenkins and Halcli, 232. In a related essay, Susan A. Ostrander characterizes the Rosenwald Fund (established in 1917) as an early practitioner of social movement philanthropy. Rosenwald played a key role in funding the National Association for the Advancement of Colored People (NAACP) and the National Urban League as well as the Highland Center, a training center for union organizers in the South established in the 1930s. See Ostrander, 264–5.

21 Hobday, "Towards Tomorrow," 20.

22 Hobday, "Towards Tomorrow," 23.

23 'Possible Future Directions," SSBFF Board Books, 20 November 1984, SSBFF Archives.

24 SSBFF Minute Books, 1 November 1983. SSBFF Archives.

25 For example, at the November 1984 meeting Charles refers to "Recent family decisions which had been taken" in which there was "still some uncertainty regarding the special transfer of additional funds from CEMP to meet the family's obligations to the Canadian Jewish Appeal." SSBFF Minute Books, 20 November 1984.

26 Interview with Edgar Bronfman, 23 June 2004.

27 Canadian Directory of Foundations, 1985, 15.

28 Interview with Arnold Ludwick, 8 April 2004.

29 King, *From the Ghetto to the Main*, 282.

30 Interview with Phyllis Lambert, 5 July 2004.

31 SSBFF Minute Books, 4 June 1985, SSBFF Archives.

32 SSBFF Minute Books, 4 December 1986 and 30 November 1989, SSBFF Archives.

33 Charles Bronfman to Minda de Gunzburg, 18 June 1984, SSBFF Board Books, 12 August 1987, SSBFF Archives.

34 SSBFF Minute Books, 30 November 1989, SSBFF Archives.

35 Charles Bronfman to Minda de Gunzburg, 18 June 1984, SSBFF Board Books, 12 August 1987, SSBFF Archives.
36 Financial Statements attached to Memo, John Hobday to Jean de Gunzburg, 10 August 1987, SSBFF Board Books, August 1987, SSBFF Archives.
37 Kolber, 77.
38 "De Gunzburg Family Increases Support for Center for European Studies," Harvard University *Gazette*, 22 May 1997 (www.news.harvard.edu/gazette/1997/05.22/DeGunzburgFamil.html).
39 SSBFF Minute Books, 4 December 1986, SSBFF Archives.
40 Interview with Matthew Bronfman, 30 June 2004.
41 Interview with Edgar Bronfman, 23 June 2004.
42 Bronfman, Edgar, *Good Spirits*, 176.
43 SSBFF Minute Books, November 1987, SSBFF Archives.
44 Interview with Matthew Bronfman, 30 June 2004.
45 Kolber, 57.
46 Kolber, 57.
47 Executive director's report, SSBFF Board Books, May 1993, SSBFF Archives.
48 Interview with Arnold Ludwick, 4 April 2004.
49 Kolber, 103–9.
50 Kolber, 110–11.
51 Financial Statements attached to Memo, John Hobday to Jean de Gunzburg, 10 August 1987, SSBFF Board Books, August 1987, SSBFF Archives.
52 Financial Statements attached to Memo, John Hobday to Jean de Gunzburg, 10 August 1987, SSBFF Board Books, August 1987, SSBFF Archives.
53 SSBFF Board Books, 12 August 1987, SSBFF Archives.
54 Charles R. Bronfman to E. Leo Kolber and P.F. Vineberg, 12 August 1987, Box 08-L-349, Fonds Phyllis Lambert, Canadian Centre for Architecture.
55 Charles R. Bronfman to Sam Bronfman II, Edgar Bronfman, Jr; Matthew Bronfman, 5 October 1987, Box 08-L-349, Fonds Phyllis Lambert, Canadian Centre for Architecture.
56 "Report of the Investment Committee," in SSBFF Board Books, 7 April 1988, SSBFF Archives.
57 Job Descriptions attached to letter, John Hobday to Arnold Ludwick, 6 June 1986, "Draft notes for memo re: administrative operations of JES Donations and the Foundation," Box 08-L-259, Fonds Phyllis Lambert, Canadian Centre for Architecture.
58 John Hobday to Arnold Ludwick, 6 June 1986, "Draft notes for memo re: administrative operations of JES Donations and the Foundation," Box 08-L-259, Fonds Phyllis Lambert, Canadian Centre for Architecture.
59 SSBFF Investment Committee, 24 November 1987 and 9 December 1987, in SSBFF Board Books, 7 April 1988, SSBFF Archives.

60 "Report of the Investment Committee," n.d. in SSBFF Board Books, Meeting, 7 April 1988, SSBFF Archives.

61 John Hobday to Phyllis Lambert, 16 December 1987, Box 08-L-349, Fonds Phyllis Lambert, Canadian Centre for Architecture.

62 Financial Statements, in SSBFF Board Books, 8 April 1988, SSBFF Archives.

63 Interview with Matthew Bronfman, 30 June 2004.

64 Phyllis Lambert to Ellen Bronfman, 19 August 1991, Box 08-L-259, Fonds Phyllis Lambert, Canadian Centre for Architecture.

65 SSBFF Minute Books, December 1992, SSBFF Archives.

66 Interview with Stephen Bronfman, 15 June 2004.

67 SSBFF, Minute Books, 7 April 1988, SSBFF Archives.

68 Interview with Phyllis Lambert, 5 July 2004.

69 SSBFF, Minute Books, 15 December 1988, 26 June 1989, and 21 May 1991, SSBFF Archives.

70 SSBFF Minute Books, June 1985, SSBFF Archives.

CHAPTER FIVE

1 Interview with Lon Dubinsky, 17 June 2004.

2 Hobday, "Proposed Program Focus – 1988 to 1991," in SSBFF Board Books, 7 April 1988, SSBFF Archives.

3 Hobday, "Proposed Program Focus – 1988 to 1991," in SSBFF Board Books, 7 April 1988, SSBFF Archives.

4 Hobday, "Proposed Program Focus – 1988 to 1991," in SSBFF Board Books, 7 April 1988, SSBFF Archives.

5 Hobday and Rucker, "Preparing for the Nineties," November 1988 in SSBFF Board Books, 15 December 1988, SSBFF Archives.

6 Dubinsky, "Philanthropic Choices and Strategies," SSBFF Archives.

7 Arlett and Von Rotterdam, "The Power of Giving," *The Financial Post*, 9 March 1987.

8 Dubinsky, "Philanthropic Choices and Strategies," SSBFF Archives.

9 Dubinsky, "Philanthropic Choices and Strategies," SSBFF Archives.

10 Dubinsky, "Philanthropic Choices and Strategies," SSBFF Archives.

11 Dubinsky, "Philanthropic Choices and Strategies," SSBFF Archives.

12 Executive director's report, in SSBFF Board Books, 4 December 1986, SSBFF Archives.

13 Executive director's report, in SSBFF Board Books, November 1990, SSBFF Archives.

14 Hobday and Rucker, "Preparing for the Nineties," November 1988, SSBFF Board Books, 15 December 1988, SSBFF Archives.

15 Executive director's report, in SSBFF Board Books, 26 June 1989, SSBFF Archives.
16 Hobday, "Proposed Program Focus – 1988 to 1991," in SSBFF Board Books, 7 April 1988, SSBFF Archives.
17 Executive director's report, in SSBFF Board Books, 4 December 1986, SSBFF Archives.
18 Gisele Rucker to Judith McCullough, 19 May 1992, SSBFF Board Books, 15 December 1988, SSBFF Archives.
19 Interview with Gisele Rucker, 28 June 2004.
20 Interview with Gisele Rucker, 28 June 2004.
21 Hobday and Rucker, "Preparing for the Nineties," November 1988, SSBFF Board Books, 15 December 1988, SSBFF Archives.
22 Hobday and Rucker, "Preparing for the Nineties," November 1988, SSBFF Board Books, 15 December 1988, SSBFF Archives.
23 Interview with Gisele Rucker, 28 June 2004.
24 SSBFF Minute Books, 15 December 1988, SSBFF Archives.
25 Executive director's report, in SSBFF Board Books, 4 December 1986, SSBFF Archives.
26 Hobday and Rucker, "Preparing for the Nineties," November 1988, SSBFF Board Books, 15 December 1988, SSBFF Archives.
27 Executive director's report, in SSBFF Board Books, 26 June 1989, SSBFF Archives.
28 Executive director's report, in SSBFF Board Books, May 1993, SSBFF Archives.
29 Steve Smith to John Hobday, 16 April 1990 in SSBFF Board Books, 8 May 1990, SSBFF Archives.
30 Steve Smith to John Hobday, 16 April 1990 in SSBFF Board Books, 8 May 1990, SSBFF Archives.
31 SSBFF Minute Books, 8 May 1990, SSBFF Archives.
32 SSBFF Minute Books, 8 May 1990, SSBFF Archives; executive director's report, in SSBFF Board Books, 8 May 1990, SSBFF Archives.
33 Ziegler, 1.
34 Interview with Gisele Rucker, 28 June 2004.
35 On the leadership opportunity, see executive director's report, SSBFF Board Books, 29 November 1990, SSBFF Archives.
36 Executive director's report, in SSBFF Board Books, 29 November 1990, SSBFF Archives.
37 Executive director's report, in SSBFF Board Books, 29 November 1990, SSBFF Archives.
38 Executive director's report, in SSBFF Board Books, 8 May 1990, SSBFF Archives.
39 Interview with Gisele Rucker, 28 June 2004.

40 Executive director's report, in SSBFF Board Books, 29 December 1990, SSBFF Archives.
41 Executive director's report, in SSBFF Board Books, 8 May 1990 and 29 November 1990, SSBFF Archives.
42 Executive director's report, in SSBFF Board Books, 29 November 1990, SSBFF Archives.
43 Executive director's report, in SSBFF Board Books, 30 May 1991, SSBFF Archives.
44 SSBFF Minute Books, 1 December 1993, SSBFF Archives.
45 John Hobday to all directors, Inter-Office Memo, "Foundation Update," 12 April 1985 in SSBFF Board Books, 4 June 1985, SSBFF Archives.
46 Executive director's report, in SSBFF Board Books, 8 May 1990, SSBFF Archives.
47 McClintock, 12.
48 Executive director's report, SSBFF Board Books, May 1991, SSBFF Archives.
49 Alistair Gamble to John Hobday, 25 February 1991, in SSBFF Board Books, 21 May 1991, SSBFF Archives. Also, Gisele Rucker, "Mutual Concerns- Mutual Benefits: Why a Canadian Private Foundation Supports the Community Foundations of Canada, 21 May 1992, Box 14, File: CFC Second National Conference, SSBFF Archives.
50 SSBFF Minute Books, 21 May 1991, SSBFF Archives. Also, "New National Organization for Community Foundations," Press Release, 23 May 1992, Box 14, File: CFC Second National Conference, SSBFF Archives.
51 Le Group Léger & Léger, "Attitudes and Behaviour of the Québec Population Regarding Philanthropy," sponsored by the Canadian Centre for Philanthropy and CEPAQ, September 1993, Box 08-L-259, Fonds Phyllis Lambert, Canadian Centre for Architecture.
52 Executive director's report, in SSBFF Board Books, December 1993, SSBFF Archives.
53 "Samuel and Saidye Bronfman Family Foundation – Long Range Forecast," 16 March 1993, SSBFF Board Books, May 1993, SSBFF Archives.

CHAPTER SIX

1 Gold, 15. Gold's history of the theatre at the SBC has, however, almost nothing to do with the Bronfmans or their mother.
2 See Gold, 203.
3 Interview with Charles Bronfman, 23 June 2004.
4 Interview with Phyllis Lambert, 5 July 2004.
5 Interview with Charles Bronfman, 23 June 2004; Charles R. Bronfman to Irving Riddell, "Draft No. 3," Acc. 2126, Box 165, Hagley Museum & Library.

6 Harvey Golden to Saul H. Levine and Moe Levitt, 26 March 1963, Box 22, File: Saidye Bronfman Centre, SSBFF Archives.
7 "Memorandum of Agreement" between CEMP Investments, Ltd. and the Young Men's and Young Women's Hebrew Association of Montreal, 10 September 1964, Box 22, File: Saidye Bronfman Centre, SSBFF Archives.
8 "Memorandum of Agreement," Box 22, File: Saidye Bronfman Centre, SSBFF Archives.
9 Phyllis Lambert, Curriculum Vitae, August, 1980, File 3, Fonds Phyllis Lambert, Canadian Centre for Architecture.
10 Weintraub, 243.
11 Tippett, 4.
12 Weintraub, 241. Gold, 45.
13 Trépanier, 26.
14 www.mmfa.qc.ca/en/musee/historique.html.
15 "Saidye Bronfman Centre Dedicated to Public," Beacon, 45:9 (October, 1967).
16 Rucker, quoting Minutes of a Meeting of the Officers of the Saidye Bronfman Centre, 13 February 1969, in her Report: "Outlines of a New Mission Statement," June 1986, in SSBFF Board Books, 19 June 1986, SSBFF Archives.
17 Rucker, quoting Minutes of a Meeting of the Officers of the Saidye Bronfman Centre, 13 February 1969, in her Report: "Outlines of a New Mission Statement," June 1986, in SSBFF Board Books, 19 June 1986, SSBFF Archives.
18 "Saidye Bronfman Centre", Canadian Theatre Encyclopedia, www.canadian theatre.com, updated 5 October 2006. Interview with Phyllis Lambert, 5 July 2004.
19 "Muriel Gold," Canadian Theatre Encyclopedia, www.canadiantheatre.com, updated 25 October 2006.
20 "Muriel Gold," Canadian Theatre Encyclopedia, www.canadiantheatre.com, updated 25 October 2006.
21 List of contributions made to the Saidye Bronfman Centre by the SSBFF and the SBF, 1969–86, in SSBFF Board Books, 4 December 1986, SSBFF Archives.
22 SSBFF Minute Books, 12 November 1975, SSBFF Archives.
23 SSBFF Minute Books, 15 November 1977, SSBFF Archives.
24 Interview with John Hobday, 13 June 2007.
25 Peter C. Swann to Charles R. Bronfman, 29 November 1979, Acc.2126, Box 16, File: Saidye Bronfman Gift to YMHA, Hagley Museum and Library.
26 Manuel G. Batshaw to Charles R. Bronfman and Phyllis Lambert, 22 December 1986, Box 08-L-349, Fonds Phyllis Lambert, Canadian Centre for Architecture.
27 SSBFF Minutes, 19 November 1979, SSBFF Archives.
28 SSBFF Minutes, 19 November 1979, SSBFF Archives.

29 List of contributions made to the Saidye Bronfman Centre by the SSBFF and the SBF, 1969-86, in SSBFF Board Books, 4 December 1986, SSBFF Archives.

30 Interview with John Hobday, 13 June 2007.

31 Ackerman, "There's magic in the air at new Bronfman theatre," *The Montreal Gazette*, 6 September 1986.

32 Ackerman, "There's magic in the air at new Bronfman theatre," *The Montreal Gazette*, 6 September 1986.

33 Interview with John Hobday, 21 June 2004.

34 M.G. Batshaw, "Saidye Bronfman Centre Funding by SSBFF & SBF," in SSBFF Board Books, 4 December 1986, SSBFF Archives.

35 John Hobday to Jean de Gunzburg, 10 August 1987, in SSBFF Board Books, 12 August 1987, SSBFF Archives.

36 "Report of the Y-SBC Relationship Committee," n.d., attached to Edward Spiegel to John Hobday, 11 December 1984, Box 08-L-349, Fonds Phyllis Lambert, Canadian Centre for Architecture.

37 SSBFF Minutes, 15 June 1984, SSBFF Archives.

38 "Report of the Y-SBC Relationship Committee," n.d., attached to Edward Spiegel to John Hobday, 11 December 1984, Box 08-L-349, Fonds Phyllis Lambert, Canadian Centre for Architecture.

39 Ackerman, "There's magic in the air at new Bronfman theatre," *The Gazette*, 6 September 1986.

40 Hobday, Progress Report, 1 January 1985 to 31 March 1985, in SSBFF Board Books, 3 December 1985.

41 SSBFF Minutes, 20 November 1984.

42 M.G. Batshaw, "Saidye Bronfman Centre Funding by SSBFF & SBF," in SSBFF Board Books, 4 December 1986, SSBFF Archives.

43 Manuel G. Batshaw to Charles R. Bronfman and Phyllis Lambert, 22 December 1986, Box 08-L-349, Fonds Phyllis Lambert, Canadian Centre for Architecture.

44 Ackerman, "There's magic in the air at new Bronfman theatre," *The Gazette*, 6 September 1986.

45 Interview with Gisele Rucker, 28 June 2004.

46 Harry Gulkin to John Hobday, 6 June 1986, in SSBFF Board Books, 19 June 1986, SSBFF Archives.

47 Gisele Rucker, "Outlines of a New Mission Statement," June 1986, in SSBFF Board Books, 19 June 1986, SSBFF Archives.

48 Harry Gulkin, "Aims and Objectives: Saidye Bronfman Centre Discussion Paper, Draft #2", June 1986, in SSBFF Board Books, 19 June 1986, SSBFF Archives.

49 Marcel Masse to Harry Gulkin, 21 March 1985, in SSBFF Board Books, 4 June 1985, SSBFF Archives.

50 SSBFF Minutes, 4 June 1985, SSBFF Archives.

51 SSBFF Minutes, 19 June 1986, SSBFF Archives.

52 SSBFF Minutes, 3 December 1985, SSBFF Archives.

53 M.G. Batshaw, "Saidye Bronfman Centre Funding by SSBFF & SBF," in SSBFF Board Books, 4 December 1986, SSBFF Archives.

54 Interview with John Hobday, 21 June 2004.

55 Interview with Gisele Rucker, 28 June 2004.

56 Jane Needles to John Hobday, 29 May 1986, in SSBFF Board Books, 19 June 1986, SSBFF Archives.

57 Jane Needles to John Hobday, 29 May 1986, in SSBFF Board Books, 19 June 1986, SSBFF Archives.

58 Executive director's report, in SSBFF Board Books, 19 June 1986, SSBFF Archives.

59 Lucinda Chodan, "Full roster at Bronfman Centre," *The Montreal Gazette*, 6 September 1986.

60 Ackerman, "Stage is set for a promising theatre season in Montreal," *The Montreal Gazette*, n.d.

61 Interview with Gisele Rucker, 28 June 2004.

62 Executive director's report, in SSBFF Board Books, 4 December 1986, SSBFF Archives.

63 Manuel G. Batshaw to Charles R. Bronfman and Phyllis Lambert, 22 December 1986, Box 08-L-349, Fonds Phyllis Lambert, Canadian Centre for Architecture.

64 Executive director's report, in SSBFF Board Books, 19 June 1986 and 4 December 1986, SSBFF Archives.

65 Report from Ed Spiegel, 28 November 1986, in SSBFF Board Books, 4 December 1986, SSBFF Archives.

66 Brochure, "Arts Showcase 1986-87" in SSBFF Board Books, 4 December 1986, SSBFF Archives. See also Trépanier, *Jewish Painters and Modernity*.

67 Interview with John Hobday, 21 June 2004, and with Phyllis Lambert, 5 July 2004.

68 Executive director's report, in Board Books, 12 August 1987, SSBFF Archives.

69 Charles Bronfman to the YM-YWHA and NHS of Montreal, 23 June 1987, in SSBFF Board Books, 12 August 1987, SSBFF Archives.

70 Executive director's report, in SSBFF Board Books, 15 December 1988, SSBFF Archives; Saidye Bronfman Centre Annual Report, 1988-9, in SSBFF Board Books, 30 November 1989, SSBFF Archives.

71 Gold, 157. See also www.friends.ca/News/Friends_News/archives/articles 10199901.asp.

72 Interview with John Hobday, 21 June 2004.

73 Interview with John Hobday, 21 June 2004.

74 John Hobday to Charles R. Bronfman and Stephen R. Bronfman, 19 February 1992, Box 22, File: Saidye Bronfman Centre, SSBFF Archives.

75 Cecil Rabinovitch to Charles Bronfman, 21 November 1991, in SSBFF Board Books, 26 November 1991, SSBFF Archives.

76 Cecil Rabinovitch to Charles Bronfman, 21 November 1991, in SSBFF Board Books, 26 November 1991, SSBFF Archives.

77 SSBFF Minutes, 26 November 1991, SSBFF Archives.

78 Executive director's report, SSBFF Board Books, 19 May 1992, SSBFF Archives. Harvey Wolfe to Stephen Bronfman, 20 April 1992, in SSBFF Board Books, 19 May 1992, SSBFF Archives.

79 Cecil Rabinovitch to Charles Bronfman, 21 November 1991, in SSBFF Board Books, 26 November 1991, SSBFF Archives. Executive director's report, SSBFF Board Books, 1 December 1992, SSBFF Archives.

80 Interview with John Hobday, 21 June 2004.

81 Cecil Rabinovitch to Stephen Bronfman, (n.d.) April 1992, in SSBFF Board Books, 19 May 1992, SSBFF Archives. SSBFF Minute Books, 19 May 1992, SSBFF Archives.

82 Interim Report, the Saidye Bronfman Centre, Winter 1992 – Spring 1993, in SSBFF Board Books, 5 May 1993, SSBFF Archives.

83 Executive director's report, in SSBFF Board Books, 1 December 1993, SSBFF Archives.

84 Executive director's report, in SSBFF Board Books, 1 December 1993, SSBFF Archives. Barry Silverman to John Hobday, 24 November 1993, in SSBFF Board Books, 1 December 1993, SSBFF Archives.

85 SSBFF Minutes, 5 May 1993, SSBFF Archives.

86 Alain Dancyger to John Hobday, 3 May 1994 in SSBFF Board Books, 31 May 1994, SSBFF Archives. SSBFF Minute Books, 31 May 1994, SSBFF Archives.

87 Alain Dancyger to John Hobday, 3 May 1994 in SSBFF Board Books, 31 May 1994, SSBFF Archives. SSBFF Minute Books, 31 May 1994, SSBFF Archives.

88 SSBFF Minute Books, 4 May 1995, SSBFF Archives. Alain Dancyger to John Hobday, 26 April 1995, in SSBFF Board Books, 4 May 1995, SSBFF Archives.

89 Eisenthal, Bram, "Saidye Bronfman, Matriarch of Canadian Jewry, dies at 98," *Jewish Telegraphic Agency* (www.jewishf.com/content/2-0-/module/displaystory/story_id/21091/format/html/ edition_id/22/displaystory.html).

90 Interview with Stephen Bronfman, 15 June 2004.

91 Executive director's report, SSBFF Board Books, 14 December 1995 and 28 May 1996, SSBFF Archives. SSBFF Minute Books, 14 December 1995, SSBFF Archives.

92 Executive director's report, in SSBFF Board Books, 11 December 1996, SSBFF Archives.

93 Executive director's report, in SSBFF Board Books, 14 December 1995, SSBFF Archives.

94 Interview with John Hobday, 21 June 2004.
95 Interview with Stephen Bronfman, 15 June 2004.
96 David Moss, Progress Report, 18 May 1998, in SSBFF Board Books, 10 June 1998, SSBFF Archives. Progress Report, 2 November 1998, in SSBFF Board Books, 17 December 1998, SSBFF Archives.
97 Alain Dancyger to John Hobday, 3 May 1994, in SSBFF Board Books, 31 May 1994, SSBFF Archives.
98 Executive director's report, in SSBFF Board Books, 28 May 1996, SSBFF Archives.
99 David Moss, Progress Report, 18 May 1998, in SSBFF Board Books, 10 June 1998, SSBFF Archives.
100 David Moss, Progress Report, 2 November 1998, in SSBFF Board Books, 17 December 1998, SSBFF Archives.
101 Policies and Guidelines of the Properties Committee, Saidye Bronfman Centre for the Arts, 12 February 1997, in SSBFF Board Books, 17 June 1997, SSBFF Archives.
102 Interview with Stephen Bronfman, 15 June 2004.
103 SSBFF Minute Books, 17 February 1999, SSBFF Archives.
104 Executive director's report, in SSBFF Board Books, 10 June 1999, SSBFF Archives.
105 David Moss to John Hobday, 6 December 1999, in SSBFF Board Books, 13 December 1999, SSBFF Archives.
106 David Moss, Progress Report, 15 November 1999, in SSBFF Board Books, 13 December 1999, SSBFF Archives.
107 SSBFF Minute Books, 15 November 2001, SSBFF Archives.
108 David Moss, Progress Report, June 2002, in SSBFF Board Books, 4 July 2002, SSBFF Archives.
109 SSBFF Minute Books, 9 December 2002, SSBFF Archives.
110 SSBFF Minute Books, 14 December 2000, SSBFF Archives.
111 SSBFF Minute Books, 15 January 2003, SSBFF Archives.
112 Draft of Contribution Agreement between the SSBFF and the YM-YWHA, 7 May 2003, in SSBFF Board Books, 27 May 2003, SSBFF Archives.
113 Interview with Phyllis Lambert, 5 July 2004.
114 Email, Phyllis Lambert to Jean de Gunzburg et al., 2 June 2003, inserted in SSBFF Minute Books, 27 May 2003, SSBFF Archives.
115 Interview with Gisele Rucker, 22 July 2005.
116 Vianney Bélanger, Report to the SSBFF, 18 November 2003, in SSBFF Board Books, 9 December 2003, SSBFF Archives.
117 SSBFF Minute Books, 9 December 2003, SSBFF Archives.
118 Executive director's report, in SSBFF Board Books, 8 June 2004, SSBFF Archives.
119 SSBFF Minute Books, 8 June 2004, SSBFF Archives.

120 Interview with Charles Bronfman, 23 June 2004.
121 SSBFF Minute Books, 23 November 2004, SSBFF Archives.
122 SSBFF Minute Books, 21 June 2005 and 29 November 2005, SSBFF Archives.
123 Interview with John Hobday, 13 June 2007; SSBFF Minute Books, 12 June 2006, SSBFF Archives.
124 SSBFF Minute Books, 1 December 2006, SSBFF Archives.
125 Joel Goldenberg, "From Saidye to Segal," *The Suburban*, 6 June 2007.
126 Gil Troy, "A Saidye Reborn of Hope and Vision," *The Suburban*, 21 February 2007.
127 Joel Goldenberg, "From Saidye to Segal," *The Suburban*, 6 June 2007.
128 Interview with John Hobday, 13 June 2007.
129 Interviews with Charles Bronfman, 23 June 2004, and Phyllis Lambert, 5 July 2004.
130 Interview with Stephen Bronfman, 15 June 2004.

CHAPTER SEVEN

1 Alan King to Charles R. Bronfman, 22 October 1971, Acc.2126, Box 16, File: SSBFF, Hagley Museum and Library.
2 Alan Edwards to Charles R. Bronfman, 23 November 1971, Acc.2126, Box 16, File: SSBFF, Hagley Museum and Library.
3 Charles R. Bronfman to Peter Swann, 26 January 1973, Acc.2126, Box 16, File: SSBFF, Hagley Museum and Library.
4 Hobday, "Towards Tomorrow," 6, SSBFF Archives. Weinstein,136.
5 This is not the Dr Samuel Rabinovitch whose hiring by the Notre Dame Hospital in 1934 resulted in a staff strike. See chapter 1 above.
6 Weinstein, 135–6
7 Hobday, "Towards Tomorrow," 6, SSBFF Archives.
8 Brochure: "Pathway to Learning: The McGill-Montreal Children's Hospital Learning Centre" in SSBFF Board Books, 19 June 1986, SSBFF Archives.
9 Peter Swann to Charles R. Bronfman, 16 August 1973, Acc.2126, Box 16, File: SSBFF, Hagley Museum & Library.
10 SSBFF Minute Books, 21 September 1973, SSBFF Archives.
11 Executive director's report, in SSBFF Board Books, 19 November 1982, SSBFF Archives.
12 SSBFF Minute Books, 15 June 1984, SSBFF Archives.
13 Executive director's report, in SSBFF Board Books, May 1984, SSBFF Archives.
14 Executive director's report, in SSBFF Board Books, 12 August 1987, SSBFF Archives.
15 William J. Smith: "Interim Report of the 1988–89 Activities of the Learning Centre," 16 June 1989, in SSBFF Board Books, 26 June 1989, SSBFF Archives.

16 *The Montreal Gazette*, 28 March 1988.
17 The McGill-Montreal Children's Hospital Learning Centre Proposal, 12 October 1988, in SSBFF Board Books, 15 December 1988, SSBFF Archives.
18 Alan Edwards to John Hobday, 28 October 1988, in SSBFF Board Books, 15 December 1988, SSBFF Archives.
19 Executive director's report, in SSBFF Board Books, 26 June 1989, SSBFF Archives.
20 William J. Smith, "Interim Report of the 1988-89 Activities of the Learning Centre," 16 June 1989, in executive director's report, SSBFF Board Books, SSBFF Archives.
21 SSBFF, Minute Books, 26 June 1989, SSBFF Archives.
22 William J. Smith to John Hobday, 15 November 1989 in SSBFF Board Books, 30 November 1989, SSBFF Archives; SSBFF Minute Books, 30 November 1989, SSBFF Archives.
23 SSBFF Minute Books, 8 May 1990, SSBFF Archives.
24 SSBFF Minute Books, 8 May 1990, SSBFF Archives.
25 William J. Smith, "Towards a New Beginning: The Restructuring of the McGill-Montreal Children's Hospital Learning Centre," 11 April 1990, in SSBFF Board Books, May 1990, SSBFF Archives.
26 SSBFF Minute Books, 21 May 1991, SSBFF Archives.
27 Pink donation cards, SSBFF Archives.
28 Hobday, "Towards Tomorrow," 7, SSBFF Archives.
29 John Hobday to all directors, "The Samuel and Saidye Bronfman Family Foundation – Progress Report," 12 March 1984, in SSBFF Board Books, 23 May 1984, SSBFF Archives.
30 Hobday, "Towards Tomorrow," 9, SSBFF Archives.
31 www.ldac-taac.ca/index-e.asp.
32 John Hobday to all directors, "The Samuel and Saidye Bronfman Family Foundation – Progress Report," 12 March 1984, in SSBFF Board Books, 23 May 1984, SSBFF Archives.
33 John Hobday to all directors, "The Samuel and Saidye Bronfman Family Foundation – Progress Report," 12 March 1984, in SSBFF Board Books, 23 May 1984, SSBFF Archives.
34 Letter, June Bourgeau to John Hobday, 18 April 1984, in SSBFF Board Books, 15 June 1984, SSBFF Archives.
35 Executive director's report, in SSBFF Board Books, May 1984, SSBFF Archives; SSBFF Minute Books, 4 December 1986, SSBFF Archives.
36 SSBFF Minute Books, 4 December 1986, SSBFF Archives.
37 Executive director's report, in SSBFF Board Books, 4 December 1986, SSBFF Archives.
38 Hobday, "Proposed Program Focus – 1988 to 1991," in SSBFF Board Books, 7 April 1988, SSBFF Archives.

39 Executive director's report, in SSBFF Board Books, 26 June 1989, SSBFF Archives.
40 SSBFF Minute Books, 26 June 1989, SSBFF Archives.
41 Executive director's report: The Visioning Series, in SSBFF Board Books, 29 November 1990, SSBFF Archives.
42 "Report of the Visioning Workshop," 1 November 1990, in File: LDAC National – 1990, SSBFF Archives.
43 Executive director's report, in SSBFF Board Books, 29 November 1990, SSBFF Archives.
44 SSBFF Minute Books, 29 November 1990, SSBFF Archives.
45 Executive director's report, in SSBFF Board Books, May 1991, SSBFF Archives.
46 LDAC Progress Report, 19 March 1993, in SSBFF Board Books, 5 May 1993, SSBFF Archives.
47 Executive director's report, in SSBFF Board Books, 5 May 1991, SSBFF Archives.
48 SSBFF Minute Books, 26 November 1991, SSBFF Archives.
49 SSBFF Minute Books, 19 May 1992, SSBFF Archives.
50 SSBFF Minute Books, 5 May 1993, SSBFF Archives.
51 Executive director's report, in SSBFF Board Books, 1 December 1993, SSBFF Archives.
52 Executive director's report, in SSBFF Board Books, May 1993, SSBFF Archives.

CHAPTER EIGHT

1 Lockhart, 127.
2 McKay Task Force Report cited in Baum, *The Final Plateau*, xiv.
3 Kane, 13.
4 Hobday, "Towards Tomorrow," 1, SSBFF Archives.
5 St Thomas University and the New Brunswick Senior Citizens' Federation, Joint Proposal, "A National Consultation on Networking for Seniors in Canada," May 1984, in SSBFF Board Books, 15 June 1984, SSBFF Archives.
6 SSBFF Minute Books, 19 November 1979, SSBFF Archives.
7 Hobday, "Towards Tomorrow," 2, SSBFF Archives.
8 John Hobday to all directors, "The Samuel and Saidye Bronfman Family Foundation – Progress Report," 12 March 1984, in SSBFF Board Books, 23 May 1984, SSBFF Archives.
9 Peter Swann to Mrs Samuel Bronfman and all directors, in SSBFF Board Books, 19 November 1981, SSBFF Archives.
10 SSBFF Minute Books, 19 November 1980, 1, SSBFF Archives.
11 Hobday, "Towards Tomorrow," 3, SSBFF Archives.

12 St Thomas University and the New Brunswick Senior Citizens' Federation, Joint Proposal, "A National Consultation on Networking for Seniors in Canada," May 1984 in SSBFF Board Books, 15 June 1984, SSBFF Archives.

13 St Thomas University and the New Brunswick Senior Citizens' Federation, Joint Proposal, "A National Consultation on Networking for Seniors in Canada," May 1984 in SSBFF Board Books, 15 June 1984, SSBFF Archives.

14 Executive director's report, May 1984 in SSBFF Board Books, 15 June 1984, SSBFF Archives; SSBFF Minute Books, 15 June 1984, SSBFF Archives.

15 Executive director's report, September 1984, in SSBFF Board Books, 20 November 1984, SSBFF Archives.

16 Executive director's report, in SSBFF Board Books, 19 June 1986, SSBFF Archives.

17 Executive director's report, in SSBFF Board Books, 3 December 1985, SSBFF Archives.

18 Gifford, 111–13.

19 Executive director's report, in SSBFF Board Books, 4 December 1986, SSBFF Archives.

20 www.aarp.org/Articles/a2003-01-13-aarphistory/tools/printable.

21 Executive director's report, in SSBFF Board Books, 4 December 1986, SSBFF Archives.

22 Gifford, 111–13.

23 Executive director's report, SSBFF Board Books, 4 December 1986, SSBFF Archives.

24 Weaver, 610–19.

25 www.hrsdc.gc.ca/en/isp/horizons/pub/nhbrochure-en.pdf.

26 Drabek, "The Greying of the Electorate," *The Globe and Mail*, 12 September 1988, A7.

27 Thelma Scambler to John Hobday, 23 October 1988 in SSBFF Board Books, 15 December 1988, SSBFF Archives.

28 Executive director's report, in SSBFF Board Books, 26 June 1989, SSBFF Archives.

29 John Hobday, "Proposed Program Focus – 1988 to 1991," in SSBFF Board Books, 7 April 1988, SSBFF Archives.

30 SSBFF Minute Books, 7 April 1988, SSBFF Archives.

31 Executive director's report, in SSBFF Board Books, 15 December 1988, SSBFF Archives.

32 Executive director's report, in SSBFF Board Books, 26 June 1989, SSBFF Archives.

33 Executive director's report, in SSBFF Board Books, 8 May 1990, SSBFF Archives.

34 Thelma Scambler to John Hobday, 23 October 1988, in SSBFF Board Books, 15 December 1988, SSBFF Archives.

35 SSBFF Minute Books, 15 December 1988, SSBFF Archives.

36 "Workshop Participants à l'Atelier," 13-16 September 1990, in SSBFF Board Books, 29 November 1990, SSBFF Archives. See also: The Visioning Series: Seniors: Report-Follow-Up, Box 9, SSBFF Archives.

37 Executive director's report, in SSBFF Board Books, 29 November 1990, SSBFF Archives.

38 Jean Woodsworth to John Hobday, 11 April 1991, in SSBFF Board Books, 21 May 1991, SSBFF Archives.

39 Executive director's report, in SSBFF Board Books, 21 May 1991, SSBFF Archives.

40 Jean Woodsworth to John Hobday, 11 April 1991, in SSBFF Board Books, 21 May 1991, SSBFF Archives.

41 Executive director's report, in SSBFF Board Books, May 1993, SSBFF Archives.

42 One Voice Activity Report to 10 April 1991, in SSBFF Board Books, 21 May 1991, SSBFF Archives.

43 Executive director's report, in SSBFF Board Books, 1 December 1992, SSBFF Archives.

44 ARA Consulting Group, Inc., "One Voice – The Canadian Seniors Network: External Assessment," November 1997, 1, in Fonds Phyllis Lambert, Box 08-L-259, Canadian Centre for Architecture.

45 Executive director's report – Summary of External Team's Assessments and Recommendations, in SSBFF Board Books, 1 December 1992, SSBFF Archives.

46 Executive director's report – Summary of External Team's Assessments and Recommendations, in SSBFF Board Books, 1 December 1992, SSBFF Archives.

47 Interview with Ivan Hale, 14 October 2005.

48 Executive director's report, in SSBFF Board Books, May 1993, SSBFF Archives.

49 Executive director's report, in SSBFF Board Books, December 1993, SSBFF Archives.

50 One Voice: The Canadian Seniors' Network, "No More Cuts: Fair Taxation for Deficit Reduction," March 1993, in SSBFF Board Books, 5 May 1993, SSBFF Archives.

51 SSBFF Minute Books, 5 May 1993, SSBFF Archives.

52 SSBFF Minute Books, 1 December 1993, SSBFF Archives.

53 Executive director's report, in SSBFF Board Books, 31 May 1994, SSBFF Archives.

54 SSBFF Minute Books, 31 May 1994, SSBFF Archives.

55 SSBFF Minute Books, 31 May 1994, SSBFF Archives.

56 Inverview with John Hobday, 13 June 2007.

57 Program Report: Transitions, in SSBFF Board Books, 14 December 1995 and SSBFF Board Books, 28 May 1996, SSBFF Archives.

58 Program Report: Transitions, in SSBFF Board Books, 28 May 1996, SSBFF Archives.

59 One Voice, "Measuring Our Progress: A Report to the Samuel & Saidye Bronfman Family Foundation," November 1996, in SSBFF Board Books, 11 December 1996, SSBFF Archives.

60 SSBFF Minute Books, 11 December 1996, SSBFF Archives.

61 SSBFF Minute Books, 17 June 1997, SSBFF Archives.

62 John Hobday to Phyllis Lambert, 8 September 1997, in Fonds Phyllis Lambert, Box 08-L-259, Canadian Centre for Architecture.

63 John Hobday to Phyllis Bentley, 10 September 1997 – draft attached to John Hobday to Phyllis Lambert, 8 September 1997, in Fonds Phyllis Lambert, Box 08-L-259, Canadian Centre for Architecture.

64 John Hobday to Phyllis Bentley, 10 September 1997 –draft attached to John Hobday to Phyllis Lambert, 8 September 1997, in Fonds Phyllis Lambert, Box 08-L-259, Canadian Centre for Architecture.

65 ARA Consulting Group, Inc., "One Voice: the Canadian Seniors Network, External Assessment," November 1997, in SSBFF Board Books, November 1997, SSBFF Archives.

66 ARA Consulting Group, Inc., "One Voice: the Canadian Seniors Network, External Assessment," November 1997, in SSBFF Board Books, November 1997, SSBFF Archives.

67 SSBFF Minute Books, 17 November 1997, SSBFF Archives.

68 Interview with Ivan Hale, 14 October 2005.

69 Interview with Ivan Hale, 14 October 2005.

70 Interview with Jean de Gunzburg, 28 June 2004.

CHAPTER NINE

1 Interview with John Hobday, 21 July 2004.

2 Interview with John Hobday, 21 July 2004.

3 "New Program Trains Managers for the Arts," photocopy in SSBFF Board Books, 15 December 1988, SSBFF Archives.

4 David S.R. Leighton, "Canada's Cultural Resources: Where Are the Managers?" Unreferenced article in Box 08-L-349, Fonds Phyllis Lambert, Canadian Centre for Architecture.

5 Interview with John Hobday, 21 June 2004.

6 Canadian Association of Arts Administration Educators, "The CAAAE Story," in SSBFF Board Books, 15 December 1988, SSBFF Archives.

7 SSBFF Minute Books, 19 November 1980 SSBFF Archives.
8 "SSBFF Proposed Support of Arts Management Training Opportunities," May 1984, Box 21, File: Trustee Handbook: proposal (1986), SSBFF Archives.
9 Interview with John Hobday, 13 June 2007.
10 "Proposed Support of Arts Management Training Opportunities," May 1984 in SSBFF Board Books, 15 June 1984, SSBFF Archives.
11 Canadian Association of Arts Administration Educators, "The CAAAE Story," in SSBFF Board Books, 15 December 1988 and "SSBFF Proposed Support of Arts Management Training Opportunities," May 1984, Box 21, File: Trustee Handbook: proposal (1986), SSBFF Archives.
12 Telephone interview with Marion Paquet, 10 May 2004.
13 Interview with John Hobday, 21 June 2004.
14 Interview with John Hobday, 21 June 2004.
15 Interview with William Poole, 21 May 2004
16 SSBFF, "Centre for Cultural Management at the University of Waterloo and its relationship to the Foundation," 29 September 1992, AB3 file, SSBFF Archives. See also interview with William D. Poole, 21 May 2004.
17 "Meeting Package," Cultural Board Development in Canada, National Meeting, Winnipeg, October 23–24, 1990, Box 21, File: Board Development 1990, SSBFF Archives.
18 Phyllis Lambert to Peter Swann, 20 May 1986, Fonds Phyllis Lambert, Canadian Centre for Architecture
19 www.arts.uwaterloo.ca/ccm/documents/cmls_docs/cmls1.html.
20 www.hec.ca/artsmanagement/mca/foreword.html. See interview with William D. Poole, 21 May 2004.
21 "Arts Administration and Cultural Management at the University of Waterloo," in SSBFF Board Books, 7 April 1988, SSBFF Archives.
22 Interview with John Hobday, 13 June 2007.
23 Executive director's report, in SSBFF Board Books, 4 May 1995, SSBFF Archives.
24 Interview with John Hobday, 13 June 2007.
25 The National Museums of Canada were a group of federally funded and directed institutions that collaborated in such areas as collection, conservation, publication, and, to an extent, administration; all were located in the National Capital Region, and represented the nation's major collections. They were the National Gallery, the National Museum of Man (later the Canadian Museum of Civilization), the Museum of Natural Sciences, and the National Museum of Science and Technology.
26 Phyllis Lambert to Peter Swann, 20 May 1986, Fonds Phyllis Lambert, Canadian Centre for Architecture.
27 The Samuel and Saidye Bronfman Family Foundation, "Proposed Support of

Arts Management Training Opportunities," May 1984 in SSBFF Board Books, 15 June 1984, SSBFF Archives.

28 Interview with John Hobday, 21 June 2004.
29 Interview with John Hobday, 21 June 2004.
30 "New Program Trains Managers for the Arts," photocopy in SSBFF Board Books, 15 December 1988, SSBFF Archives.
31 "Arts Administration and Cultural Management at the University of Waterloo," in SSBFF Board Books, 7 April 1988, SSBFF Archives.
32 SSBFF Minute Books, 15 December 1988, SSBFF Archives.
33 Hobday, "Proposed Program Focus – 1988 to 1991," in SSBFF Board Books, 7 April 1988, SSBFF Archives.
34 SSBFF, "Centre for Cultural Management at the University of Waterloo and its relationship to the Foundation," 29 September 1992, in AB3 file, SSBFF Archives.
35 SSBFF Board Books, executive director's report, 29 November 1990, SSBFF Archives.
36 "Arts Administration and Cultural Management at the University of Waterloo," in SSBFF Board Books, 7 April 1988, SSBFF Archives.
37 Executive director's report, in SSBFF Board Books, 26 June 1989, SSBFF Archives.
38 "New Program Trains Managers for the Arts," photocopy in SSBFF Board Books, 15 December 1988, SSBFF Archives.
39 SSBFF Minute Books, 30 November 1989, SSBFF Archives.
40 SSBFF Minute Books, 29 November 1990 and 21 May 1991, SSBFF Archives.
41 SSBFF Minute Books, 26 June 1989, SSBFF Archives.
42 Interview with William D. Poole, 24 May 2004.
43 Interview with William D. Poole, 24 May 2004.
44 Executive director's report, SSBFF Board Books, 29 November 1990, SSBFF Archives.
45 Centre for Cultural Management, "Strategic Perspectives – 1993," March 1993 (Draft), in SSBFF Board Books, May 1993, SSBFF Archives.
46 Centre for Cultural Management, "Report to the Samuel and Saidye Bronfman Family Foundation," 8 April 1993, in SSBFF Board Books, May 1993, SSBFF Archives.
47 SSBFF Minute Books, 11 December 1996, SSBFF Archives.
48 "Summary of External Team's Assessments and Recommendations, Centre for Cultural Management, in SSBFF Board Books, 1 December 1992.
49 James Downey, president of the University of Waterloo, to John Hobday, 22 April 1994 in SSBFF Board Books, 31 May 1994, SSBFF Archives.
50 SSBFF Minute Books, 31 May 1994, SSBFF Archives.
51 SSBFF Minute Books, 5 May 1995 and 14 December 1995, SSBFF Archives.

52 SSBFF Minute Books, 14 December 1995, SSBFF Archives.

53 Bill Poole to John Hobday, 11 February 1999, in SSBFF Board Books, 17 February 1999, SSBFF Archives.

54 SSBFF Minute Books, 17 November 1997 and 10 June 1998, SSBFF Archives.

55 SSBFF Minute Books, 17 December 1998 and 17 February 1999, SSBFF Archives.

56 Executive director's report, in SSBFF Board Books, 17 February 1999, SSBFF Archives.

57 Bill Poole to John Hobday, 11 February 1999, in SSBFF Board Books, 17 February 1999, SSBFF Archives.

58 SSBFF Minute Books, 17 February 1999, SSBFF Archives.

59 SSBFF Minute Books, 10 June 1999, SSBFF Archives.

60 William D. Poole & David W. Barr, "Online Professional Development for Cultural Managers," paper presented at the Fifth International Conference on Arts and Cultural Management, 13-17 June 1999, Helsinki, Finland, in SSBFF Board Books, 10 June 1999, SSBFF Archives.

61 SSBFF Minute Books, 13 December 1999, SSBFF Archives.

62 CCM Report to the SSBFF, Executive Summary, June 2000, in SSBFF Board Books, 13 July 2000, SSBFF Archives.

63 Executive director's report, in SSBFF Board Books, 30 May 2001 and 15 November 2001, SSBFF Archives.

64 CCM Report to the SSBFF, Executive Summary, June 2002, in SSBFF Board Books, 4 July 2002, SSBFF Archives.

65 Executive director's report, in SSBFF Board Books, 27 May 2003, SSBFF Archives.

66 SSBFF Minute Books, 9 December 2003, SSBFF Archives.

67 www.fordfound.org/news/more/05042000arts/index.cfm.

68 Interview with John Hobday, 21 June 2004.

69 John Hobday, "Arts Stabilization in Canada: An Update," April 1996, in SSBFF Board Books, 28 May 1996, SSBFF Archives.

70 Interview with John Hobday, 13 June 2007.

71 SSBFF Minute Books, 1 December 1993, SSBFF Archives.

72 SSBFF Minute Books, 31 May 1994, SSBFF Archives.

73 Peter Brown and Diane Hoar to John Hobday, 17 November 1994, in SSBFF Board Books, 7 December 1994, SSBFF Archives.

74 Peter Brown and Diane Hoar to John Hobday, 17 November 1994, in SSBFF Board Books, 7 December 1994, SSBFF Archives.

75 Executive director's report, in SSBFF Board Books, 10 June 1998, SSBFF Archives.

76 Peter Brown and Diane Hoar to John Hobday, 17 November 1994, in SSBFF Board Books, 7 December 1994, SSBFF Archives.

77 SSBFF Minute Books, 7 December 1994, SSBFF Archives.
78 "Québec Stabilization Fund – Feasibility Study," in SSBFF Board Books, 4 May 1995, SSBFF Archives.
79 Peter Brown and Diane Hoar to Phyllis Lambert, 17 April 1995, in SSBFF Board Books, 4 May 1995, SSBFF Archives.
80 "Québec Stabilization Fund – Feasibility Study," in SSBFF Board Books, 4 May 1995, SSBFF Archives.
81 Peter Brown and Diane Hoar to Phyllis Lambert, 17 April 1995, in SSBFF Board Books, 4 May 1995, SSBFF Archives.
82 Executive director's report, in SSBFF Board Books, 4 December 1995, SSBFF Archives.
83 SSBFF Minute Books, 28 May 1996, SSBFF Archives.
84 SSBFF Minute Books, 17 June 1997 and 17 November 1997, SSBFF Archives.
85 John Hobday to Eileen Sarkar, 23 April 1998, in SSBFF Board Books, 10 June 1998, SSBFF Archives.
86 Executive director's report, in SSBFF Board Books, 10 June 1998, SSBFF Archives.
87 SSBFF Minutes, 10 June 1998, SSBFF Archives.
88 Executive director's report, in SSBFF Board Books, 17 December 1998, SSBFF Archives.
89 Executive director's report, in SSBFF Board Books, 17 December 1998, SSBFF Archives.
90 Executive director's report, in SSBFF Board Books, 17 December 1998, SSBFF Archives.
91 Executive director's report, in SSBFF Board Books, 17 February 1999, SSBFF Archives; SSBFF Minute Books, 17 February 1999, SSBFF Archives.
92 SSBFF Minute Books, 10 June 1999, SSBFF Archives.
93 "Towards a National Arts Stabilization Program," in SSBFF Board Books, 13 December 1999, SSBFF Archives.
94 SSBFF Minute Books, 13 December 1999, SSBFF Archives.
95 Executive director's report, in SSBFF Board Books, 10 June 1999 and 13 December 1999, SSBFF Archives.
96 Interview with John Hobday, 13 June 2007.
97 PCH, "Tomorrow Starts Today," Fact Sheet, 2 May 2001, in SSBFF Board Books, 30 May 2001, SSBFF Archives.
98 Interview with John Hobday, 13 June 2007.
99 SSBFF Minute Books, 30 May 2001, SSBFF Archives.
100 Executive director's report, in SSBFF Board Books, 4 July 2002, SSBFF Archives.
101 Interview with John Hobday, 13 June 2007.
102 Executive director's report, in SSBFF Board Books, 8 June 2004, SSBFF Archives.

103 Executive director's report, in SSBFF Board Books, 23 November 2004, SSBFF Archives.

CHAPTER TEN

1 Nelles, 50, 75, 95.
2 Gordon, 64.
3 Historic Sites and Monuments Board of Canada, www.pc.gc.ca/clmhc-hsmbc/clmhc-hsmbc/clmhc-hsmbc1_e.asp.
4 Handler, "On Having a Culture," 199.
5 Handler, "On Having a Culture," 195.
6 Gabeline et al., 48.
7 Gabeline et al., 9.
8 Wilson and McLean, 18–19.
9 Gabeline et al., 128.
10 Newman, 168.
11 Centre historique de Montréal: le Vieux-Montréal: www.vieux.montreal.qc.ca/inventaire/fiches/fiche_pers.php?id=373.
12 Lambert and Lemire, *Inventaire des bâtiments du Vieux Montréal.*
13 Interview with Pierre-André Themens, 20 July 2005.
14 Marsan, 386.
15 "Area dodged wrecking ball for 10 years," *Montreal Star*, 29 August 1979, n.p. See also: Goliger, 2.
16 Gabeline, 65.
17 Handler, "On Having a Culture," 197.
18 Gabeline, 27.
19 Gabeline, 23.
20 Gabeline, 24.
21 Gabeline, 29.
22 Gabeline, 20, 29.
23 Bumbaru, 1.
24 SSBFF Minute Books, 21 September 1973 and 18 September 1974, SSBFF Archives. See also Charles R. Bronfman to Nathanael V. Davis, 15 November 1974, Acc.2126, Box 16, File: Save Montreal/Green Spaces Campaign, 1974–1975, Hagley Museum & Library.
25 SSBFF, Minute Books, 18 September 1974, SSBFF Archives.
26 *IIT Catalyst*, Summer 2001 and *Canadian Heritage*, June 1980, Box 08-L-499, File: Heritage Montreal, Fonds Phyllis Lambert, Canadian Centre for Architecture.
27 SSBFF Minute Books, 12 November 1975, SSBFF Archives; executive director's report, in SSBFF Board Books, 19 November 1979, SSBFF Archives.

28 Gabeline, 162.

29 www.heritagecanada.org/eng/about/who.html.

30 "Canadian Architectural Records Survey," Box 08-L-471, File: CARS Funding/Grants, Fonds Phyllis Lambert, Canadian Centre for Architecture.

31 Hobday, "Towards Tomorrow," 15ff, SSBFF Archives.

32 Agnes M Benidickson to John Hobday, 22 September 1988, in executive director's report, SSBFF Board Books, 15 December 1988, SSBFF Archives.

33 Goliger, 4.

34 Executive director's report, May 1984, and Heritage Montreal, Program of Heritage Studies proposal, 2 April 1984, in SSBFF, Board Books, 15 June 1984, SSBFF Archives; SSBFF Minute Books, 15 June 1984, 19 June 1986, SSBFF Archives.

35 Heritage Montreal, Program of Heritage Studies Progress Report, 30 October 1984, and University Summer School Preliminary Program for 13-31 May 1985, in SSBFF Board Books, 20 November 1984, SSBFF Archives.

36 Heritage Montreal, Annual Report for 1986, and Masters in Conservation brochure, in executive director's report, SSBFF Board Books, 12 August 1987, SSBFF Archives.

37 Heritage Montreal, Annual Report for 1988, in SSBFF Board Books, 15 December 1988, SSBFF Archives.

38 Heritage Montreal, Annual Report for 1988, in SSBFF Board Books, 15 December 1988, SSBFF Archives.

39 Heritage Montreal, Annual Report for 1988, in SSBFF Board Books, 15 December 1988, SSBFF Archives.

40 This transition on the part of many non-profit organizations between the 1960s and the 1990s is described in Putnam, Bowling Alone.

41 SSBFF Minute Books, 4 December 1986, SSBFF Archives.

42 Rose Potvin, "Heritage Montreal Study," 27 May 1986, in executive director's report, May 1986, SSBFF Board Books, 19 June 1986, SSBFF Archives.

43 Rose Potvin, "Heritage Montreal's Initiatives: Interim Report," 14 November 1986, and John Hobday to Mark London, 11 November 1986, and "Join Heritage Montreal" brochure and Heritage Montreal Bulletin, Vol.1, No.2, November 1986, in SSBFF Board Books, 4 December 1986, SSBFF Archives.

44 Heritage Montreal, "Annual Report for 1988," in SSBFF Board Books, 15 December 1988, SSBFF Archives.

45 Executive director's report, in SSBFF Board Books, 12 August 1987, SSBFF Archives.

46 Executive director's report, in SSBFF Board Books, 26 June 1989, SSBFF Archives.

47 Executive director's report, in SSBFF Board Books, 8 May 1990, SSBFF Archives.

48 SSBFF Minute Books, 8 May 1990, SSBFF Archives.

49 Bell, "Heritage Montreal reaches crossroads in its evolution," *The Montreal Gazette*, 3 April 1993.

50 SSBFF Minute Books, 1 December 1992, SSBFF Archives.

51 Executive director's report, and Heritage Montreal: Interim Report of Activities 1993, in SSBFF Board Books, 5 May 1993, SSBFF Archives.

52 Gabeline et al., *Montreal at the Crossroads*, 151.

53 SSBFF Minute Books, 18 May 1983, SSBFF Archives.

54 *Centre canadien d'architecture: les débuts, 1979–1984*, Montreal: Centre canadien d'architecture, 1988.

55 SSBFF, Minute Books, 19 November 1981, SSBFF Archives.

56 *Centre canadien d'architecture: les débuts*, 111. CCA Press Release, 13 May 1985.

57 SSBFF Minute Books, 4 June 1985; Donations lists, SSBFF Board Books, 15 December 1988, SSBFF Archives.

58 SSBFF Minute Books, 15 December 1988; executive director's report, 8 May 1989 and ff, SSBFF Archives.

59 Bruce Anderson to Gisele Rucker, 28 September 1988 in Board Books, 15 December 1988, SSBFF Archives.

60 Executive director's report, in SSBFF Board Books, 15 December 1988, SSBFF Archives.

61 SSBFF, Minute Books, 30 November 1989 and May, 1990, SSBFF Archives.

62 S.O. Freedman to John Hobday, 17 September 1990, SSBFF Board Books, 29 November 1990, SSBFF Archives.

63 Interview with Phyllis Lambert, 5 July 2004.

64 Executive director's report, in SSBFF Board Books, 19 May 1992, SSBFF Archives.

65 "The Visioning Series: The Redefinition of Heritage and Urban Patrimony," Workshop Agenda, in File: Phase I-SSBFF/CCA Visioning Workshop, Workshop Information, Box 3, SSBFF Archives.

66 The Visioning Series: The Redefinition of Heritage and Urban Patrimony, "Draft Summary of the Discussions at Hovey Manor, North Hatley, Quebec, October 18–21, 1990," in SSBFF Board Books, 29 November 1990, SSBFF Archives.

67 Interview with Judy Oberlander, 10 January 2005.

68 Executive director's report, SSBFF Board Books, 21 May 1991, SSBFF Archives.

69 Executive director's report, in SSBFF Board Books, 19 May 1992, SSBFF Archives.

70 Urban Issues Program Brochure, in SSBFF Board Books, 1 December 1992, SSBFF Archives.

71 SSBFF Minute Books, 1 December 1992, SSBFF Archives.

72 Interview with Gisele Rucker, 22 July 2005.

73 Judy Oberlander Preservation Consultants, Inc., "The Urban Issues Program: Developing a Framework for the Adjudication of Applications," April 1993, in SSBFF Board Books, May 1993, SSBFF Archives.

74 Interview with Judy Oberlander, 10 January 2005.

75 Judy Oberlander Preservation Consultants, Inc., "The Urban Issues Program: Developing a Framework for the Adjudication of Applications," April 1993, in SSBFF Board Books, May 1993, SSBFF Archives.

76 Executive director's report, SSBFF Board Books, 5 May 1993, SSBFF Archives.

77 Interview with Judy Oberlander, 10 January 2005.

78 Executive director's report, in SSBFF Board Books, 1 December 1993, SSBFF Archives; Interview with Phyllis Lambert, 5 July 2004.

79 Executive director's report, in SSBFF Board Books, 1 December 1993, SSBFF Archives

80 Sarti, "Foundation takes steps to fix up sagging porches," *Vancouver Sun*, 1 October 1993.

81 Joan Kuyek, "Reweaving the Fabric of Community," *Canada's Children: Children's Mental Health* (Winter 1996), Child & Family Canada.

82 Executive director's report, in SSBFF Board Books, 1 December 1993, SSBFF Archives.

83 SSBFF Minute Books, 31 May 1994, SSBFF Archives.

84 Executive director's report, SSBFF Board Books, 1 December 1993, SSBFF Archives.

85 Executive director's report, SSBFF Board Books, 1 December 1993, SSBFF Archives.

86 Interview with Gisele Rucker, 22 July 2005.

87 Anne Bishop to Gisele Rucker, 20 April 1995, in SSBFF Board Books, 4 May 1995, SSBFF Archives.

88 SSBFF Minute Books, 5 May 1995 and 14 December 1995, SSBFF Archives.

89 SSBFF Minute Books, 28 May 1996, SSBFF Archives.

90 Gisele Rucker, "Animator for College Dedicated to Urban Issues," n.d., in SSBFF Board Books, 17 June 1997, SSBFF Archives.

91 Gisele Rucker, "Animator for College Dedicated to Urban Issues," n.d., in SSBFF Directors Books, 17 June 1997, SSBFF Archives.

92 SSBFF Minute Books, 17 June 1997, SSBFF Archives.

93 Executive director's report, SSBFF Board Books, 17 June 1997, SSBFF Archives

94 Executive director's report, SSBFF Board Books, 10 June 1998, SSBFF Archives.

95 Executive director's report, SSBFF Board Books, 17 November 1997, SSBFF Archives.

96 Gisele Rucker, "Urban Issues: Program Report," 30 May 1998, in SSBFF Board Books, 10 June 1998, SSBFF Archives.

97 SSBFF Minute Books, 14 December 2000, SSBFF Archives.

98 Executive director's report, SSBFF Board Books, 31 May 1994, SSBFF Archives.
99 Executive director's report, SSBFF Board Books, 10 June 1998; Minute Books, 10 June 1998, SSBFF Archives.
100 Joan Kuyek, "Evaluation of Projects Funded through Urban Issues to 1999," in SSBFF Board Books, 10 June 1999, SSBFF Archives.
101 SSBFF Minute Books, 10 June 1999, SSBFF Archives.
102 Gisele Rucker, "Urban Issues Management Report," Fall 2000, in SSBFF Board Books, 14 December 2000, SSBFF Archives.
103 Registration Package, Urban Issues Conference: Toronto, 12-15 October 2000 in SSBFF Board Books, 14 December 2000, SSBFF Archives.
104 Gisele Rucker, "Urban Issues Management Report," Fall 2000, in SSBFF Board Books, 14 December 2000, SSBFF Archives.
105 Program Report – Current Program for 2000, in SSBFF Board Books, 14 December 2000, SSBFF Archives.
106 SSBFF Minute Books, 14 December 2000 and 30 May 2001, SSBFF Archives.
107 Executive director's report, in SSBFF Board Books, 15 November 2001, SSBFF Archives.
108 SSBFF Minute Books, 15 November 2001, SSBFF Archives.
109 SSBFF Minute Books, 4 July 2002, SSBFF Archives.
110 Bruce Fraser, "The Future of the Urban Issues Program: A Framework for Decision," in SSBFF Board Books, 9 December 2002, SSBFF Archives.
111 SSBFF Minute Books, 9 December 2002, SSBFF Archives.
112 Gisele Rucker, Search for a successor for the Urban Issues Program: Executive Summary, in SSBFF Board Books, 9 Dec 2003, SSBFF Archives.
113 SSBFF Minute Books, 9 December 2003, SSBFF Archives; Executive director's report, in SSBFF Board Books, 8 June 2004, SSBFF Archives.
114 SSBFF Minute Books, 23 November 2004, SSBFF Archives; Placemaking in Canadian Cities Interim Report, 18 May 2005, in SSBFF Board Books, 21 June 2005, SSBFF Archives.
115 Interview with Nancy Rosenfeld, 27 June 2007.

CHAPTER ELEVEN

1 Interview with John Hobday, 13 June 2007.
2 McLeod, 3. Weinrich, "A Very Short History of Craft," 9–13.
3 Flood, "Canadian Craft: Change and Continuity," 9.
4 Interview with John Hobday, 21 June 2004.
5 Lambert, preface to Transformation: Prix Saidye Bronfman Award 1977–1996, 9.
6 Massey, introduction to The Craftsman's Way: Canadian Expressions, 3–19.
7 Interview with John Hobday, 21 June 2004.

8 Interview with Peter Weinrich, 11 May 2004.
9 Peter Weinrich to Peter Swann, 14 October 1976, Acc.2126, Box 16, File: Saidye Bronfman Foundation, Hagley Museum and Library.
10 Peter Swann to Minda de Gunzburg et al., 29 October 1976, Acc.2126, Box 16, File: Saidye Bronfman Foundation, Hagley Museum and Library.
11 Inglis and Rothschild, "Masters of the Crafts," 29–30.
12 Interview with Charles Bronfman, 23 June 2004.
13 John Hobday to Charles R. Bronfman, 11 May 1983, "The Crafts in Canada – Some Proposed New Initiatives," in SSBFF Board Books, 18 May 1983, SSBFF Archives.
14 SSBFF Minute Books, 18 May 1983, SSBFF Archives.
15 SSBFF Minute Books, 1 November 1983, SSBFF Archives.
16 SSBFF Minute Books, 15 June 1984, SSBFF Archives.
17 SSBFF Minute Books, 20 November 1984, SSBFF Archives.
18 SSBFF Minute Books, 19 June 1986, SSBFF Archives.
19 Executive director's report in SSBFF Board Books, 4 December 1986, SSBFF Archives.
20 Bronfman Award Recipients Exhibition Status report, 28 January 1988, in SSBFF Board Books, 7 April 1988, SSBFF Archives.
21 Brian V. Arthur to John Hobday, 25 March 1988, in SSBFF Board Books, 7 April 1988, SSBFF Archives; SSBFF Minute Books, 7 April 1988, SSBFF Archives.
22 SSBFF Minute Books, 15 December 1988, SSBFF Archives.
23 Peter Weinrich to John Hobday, 6 September 1988, in SSBFF Board Books, 15 December 1988, SSBFF Archives.
24 Interview with John Hobday, 13 June 2007.
25 Interview with Stephen Inglis, 10 May 2004.
26 Interview with John Hobday, 22 June 2004.
27 Canadian Museum of Civilization, *Master of the Crafts: Recipients of the Saidye Bronfman Award for Excellence in the Crafts, 1977–1986.*
28 Executive director's report, SSBFF Board Books, 29 November 1990, SSBFF Archives; SSBFF Miinute Books, 29 November 1990, SSBFF Archives.
29 Betty Ann Jordan, "Joan Chalmers: In the Service of Art," Canada Council for the Arts, www.canadacouncil.ca/prizes/ggavma/xh127240204281875000.htm?subsiteurl=%2Fcanadacouncil%2Farchives%2Fprizes%2Fggvma%2F2001%2F2001-07-e.asp.
30 "Canadian Crafts in the Twenty-First Century," revised draft, Box 31, File: Crafts Policy Review, SSBFF Archives; executive director's report, in SSBFF Board Books, 30 May 1991, SSBFF Archives.
31 Executive director's report, SSBFF Board Books, 30 May 1991, SSBFF Archives.
32 Executive director's report, in SSBFF Board Books, 30 May 1991, SSBFF Archives.

33 SSBFF Minute Books, 21 May 1991, SSBFF Archives.
34 Executive director's report, SSBFF Board Books, 26 November 1991, SSBFF Archives.
35 SSBFF Minute Books, 26 November 1991, 1 December 1992, 5 May 1993, SSBFF Archives.
36 SSBFF Minute Books, 5 May 1993, SSBFF Archives.
37 SSBFF Minute Books, 7 December 1994, SSBFF Archives.
38 SSBFF Minute Books, 14 December 1995, SSBFF Archives.
39 Interview with John Hobday, 22 June 2004.
40 SSBFF Minute Books, 17 February 1999, SSBFF Archives.
41 Hobday, "Program Report: Saidye Bronfman Award," in SSBFF Board Books, May 1996, SSBFF Archives.
42 SSBFF Minute Books, 17 June 1997, SSBFF Archives.
43 Interview with Nancy Rosenfeld, 27 June 2007.
44 SSBFF Minute Books, 9 December 2003, SSBFF Archives.
45 SSBFF Minute Books, 21 June 2005, SSBFF Archives.
46 Interview with Nancy Rosenfeld, 27 June 2007.
47 Interview with Nancy Rosenfeld, 27 June 2007.
48 SSBFF Minute Books, 8 June 2004, 23 November 2004, SSBFF Archives.
49 SSBFF Minute Books, 1 December 2006, SSBFF Archives.
50 Interview with Nancy Rosenfeld, 27 June 2007.

CHAPTER TWELVE

1 Jean de Gunzburg to Phyllis Lambert, 27 October 1997, Fonds Phyllis Lambert, Box 08-L-259, Canadian Centre for Architecture.
2 Interview with Stephen R. Bronfman, 15 June 2004.
3 SSBFF Minute Books, 17 November 1997, SSBFF Archives.
4 SSBFF Minute Books, 17 November 1997, SSBFF Archives.
5 SSBFF Minute Books, 10 June 1998, SSBFF Archives.
6 SSBFF Minute Books, 10 June 1999, SSBFF Archives.
7 SSBFF Minute Books, 10 June 1998, SSBFF Archives.
8 SSBFF Minute Books, 10 June 1998, SSBFF Archives.
9 SSBFF Minute Books, 17 February 1999, SSBFF Archives.
10 SSBFF Minute Books, 10 June 1999, SSBFF Archives.
11 Program Report, Futures, in SSBFF Board Books, 13 July 2000, SSBFF Archives.
12 Executive director's report, in SSBFF Board Books, 13 December 1999, SSBFF Archives.
13 Program Report, Futures, in SSBFF Board Books, 13 July 2000, SSBFF Archives.

14 Program Report, Futures, in SSBFF Board Books, 13 July 2000, SSBFF Archives.
15 Wright's presentation represented another first in the history of the foundation: she was the first consultant or grantee to speak to the board directly. Andrea Barile, who took notes for the meeting, remembered that Wright's presence brought a human connection between the directors and the project. Conversation with Andrea Barile, 5 December 2005.
16 Robin Wright to John Hobday, 4 December 2000 in SSBFF Board Books, 14 December 2000, SSBFF Archives.
17 Program Report – Program Update and Plans for Remainder of 2001 – Futures: Arts & Youth Development, in SSBFF Board Books, 20 May 2001, SSBFF Archives; Robin Wright to John Hobday, 11 May 2001 and Jan Michaels to Robin Wright, 7 May 2001, in SSBFF Board Books, 20 May 2001, SSBFF Archives.
18 SSBFF Minutes, 30 May 2001, SSBFF Archives.
19 Robin Wright to John Hobday, 22 October 2001 attached to Program Report – Current Programs for 2001, in SSBFF Board Books, 15 November 2001, SSBFF Archives.
20 SSBFF Minute Books, 15 November 2001, SSBFF Archives.
21 Robin Wright to John Hobday, 29 April 2002, and Dr Robin Wright and Dr Lindsay John, "National Arts & Youth Demonstration Project, Quarterly Report, 28 January – 31 March 2002," May 2002 attached to Program Report – Program Update and Plans for Remainder of FY 2002, in SSBFF Board Books, 4 July 2002, SSBFF Archives.
22 Judith A. LaRocque to John Hobday, 26 June 2002 in SSBFF Board Books, 4 July 2002, SSBFF Archives.
23 SSBFF Minute Books, 9 December 2002, SSBFF Archives.
24 SSBFF Minute Books, 15 January 2003, SSBFF Archives.
25 Interview with John Hobday, 13 June 2007.
26 SSBFF Minute Books, 27 May 2003, SSBFF Archives.
27 Robin Wright to Nancy Rosenfeld, 11 November 2004, in SSBFF Board Books, 23 November 2004, SSBFF Archives.
28 SSBFF Minute Books, 23 November 2004, SSBFF Archives.
29 Plum Coulee Community Foundation, Annual Report 2002, in SSBFF Board Books, 27 May 2003, SSBFF Archives.
30 Interview with John Hobday, 22 June 2004.
31 SSBFF Minute Books, 30 May 2001, SSBFF Archives.
32 Planning Consultant's Report, Plum Coulee Community Foundation Annual Report, in SSBFF Board Books, 27 May 2003, SSBFF Archives.
33 Executive director's report in SSBFF Board Books, 15 November 2001, SSBFF Archives.

34 Garry Hilderman to John Hobday, 9 November 2001, in SSBFF Board Books, 15 November 2001, SSBFF Archives.

35 Garry Hilderman to John Hobday, 9 November 2001, in SSBFF Board Books, 15 November 2001, SSBFF Archives; Plum Coulee Community Foundation Annual Report, 2002, in SSBFF Board Books, 4 July 2002, SSBFF Archives.

36 Garry Hilderman to John Hobday, 9 November 2001, in SSBFF Board Books, 15 November 2001, SSBFF Archives; Plum Coulee Community Foundation Annual Report, 2002, in SSBFF Board Books, 4 July 2002, SSBFF Archives.

37 Garry Hilderman to John Hobday, 9 November 2001, in SSBFF Board Books, 15 November 2001, SSBFF Archives.

38 Interview with John Hobday, 13 June 2007.

39 Garry Hilderman to John Hobday, 9 November 2001, in SSBFF Board Books, 15 November 2001, SSBFF Archives.

40 SSBFF Minute Books, 15 November 2001, SSBFF Archives.

41 Garry Hilderman to John Hobday, 14 June 2002, and Gary Gilmour to the Plum Coulee Community Foundation, 31 May 2002, both in SSBFF Board Books, 4 July 2002, SSBFF Archives.

42 Garry Hilderman to John Hobday, 14 June 2002, in SSBFF Board Books, 4 July 2002, SSBFF Archives; Garry Hilderman, Plum Coulee Heritage Recreation Project, Summary of Activities to 22 November 2002, in SSBFF Board Books, 9 December 2002, SSBFF Archives.

43 Garry Hilderman to John Hobday, 14 June 2002, in SSBFF Board Books, 4 July 2002, SSBFF Archives.

44 SSBFF Minute Books, 4 July 2002, SSBFF Archives.

45 Garry Hilderman, Plum Coulee Heritage Recreation Project, Summary of Activities to 22 November 2002, in SSBFF Board Books, 9 December 2002, SSBFF Archives.

46 Executive director's report, in SSBFF Board Books, 27 May 2003, SSBFF Archives; SSBFF Minute Books, 12 June 2006, SSBFF Archives.

47 SSBFF Minute Books, 9 December 2002, SSBFF Archives.

48 Executive director's report, in SSBFF Board Books, 27 May 2003, SSBFF Archives.

49 SSBFF Minute Books, 27 May 2003, SSBFF Archives.

50 Executive director's report, in SSBFF Board Books, 8 June 2004, SSBFF Archives.

51 SSBFF Minutes, 29 November 2005, SSBFF Archives.

52 Executive director's report, in SSBFF Board Books, 23 November 2004, SSBFFArchives.

53 Executive director's report, in SSBFF Board Books, 8 June 2004, SSBFF Archives.

54 SSBFF Minute Books, 29 November 2005 and 12 June 2006, SSBFF Archives.

55 SSBFF Minute Books, 1 December 2006, SSBFF Archives.

56 SSBFF Minute Books, 29 November 2005, SSBFF Archives.

57 SSBFF Minute Books, 13 December 1999, SSBFF Archives.

58 SSBFF Minute Books, 30 May 2001 and 15 November 2001, SSBFF Archives.

59 SSBFF Minute Books, 30 May 2001, SSBFF Archives.

60 Samuel and Saidye Bronfman Family Foundation, Planning and Administration Summary 2001/2002, 22 November 2002, in SSBFF Board Books, 9 December 2002, SSBFF Archives.

61 SSBFF Minute Books, 15 November 2001, SSBFF Archives

62 SSBFF Minute Books, 4 July 2002, SSBFF Archives

63 SSBFF Minute Books, 9 December 2002, SSBFF Archives.

64 Samuel and Saidye Bronfman Family Foundation, "Long Range Forecast," in SSBFF Board Books, 9 December 2002, SSBFF Archives.

65 Martin, "A Tireless Champion of the Arts," *The Globe and Mail*, 11 December 2002.

66 Samuel and Saidye Bronfman Family Foundation, Long Range Forecasts, Scenario F & G "Enhanced Legacy Program," in SSBFF Board Books, 15 January 2003, SSBFF Archives.

67 Samuel and Saidye Bronfman Family Foundation, Long Range Forecasts, Scenario F & G "Enhanced Legacy Program," in SSBFF Board Books, 15 January 2003, SSBFF Archives.

68 SSBFF Minute Books, 15 January 2003, SSBFF Archives.

69 SSBFF Minute Books, 15 January 2003, SSBFF Archives.

70 SSBFF Minute Books, 15 January 2003, SSBFF Archives.

71 Canada Council Proposal, 16 March 2005, in SSBFF Board Books, 21 June 2005, SSBFF Archives.

72 SSBFF Minute Books, 21 June 2005, SSBFF Archives.

73 SSBFF Minute Books, 12 June 2006, SSBFF Archives.

BIBLIOGRAPHY

Interviews

Andrea Barile, 5 December 2005
Manuel G. Batshaw, 3 April 2004
Charles R. Bronfman, 23 June 2004
Edgar M. Bronfman, 23 June 2004
Stephen R. Bronfman, 15 June 2004
Lon Dubinsky, 17 June 2004
Jean de Gunzburg, 28 June 2004
Ivan Hale, 14 October 2005
John Hobday, 21 June 2004, 13 June 2007
Stephen Inglis, 10 May 2004
Phyllis Lambert, 5 July 2004
Arnold Ludwick, 4 April 2004
Judy Oberlander, 10 January 2005
Marion Paquet, 10 May 2004
William Poole, 21 May 2004
Nancy Rosenfeld, 27 June 2007
Gisele Rucker, 28 June 2004, 22 July 2005
Pierre-André Themens, 20 July 2005

ARCHIVAL SOURCES

Canadian Centre for Architecture, Montreal
Fonds Phyllis Lambert: Boxes 8-L-259, 8-L-310, 08-L-349, 08-L-350,
  08-L-353, and 08-L-499
Fonds Phyllis Lambert: Peter Swann, "You Don't Know Me But …," unpublished autobiography, chapter 1.

Hagley Museum and Library, Wilmington, Delaware
Acc. 2126: Records of the Seagram Company Ltd: Record Group 1, Subseries
  E, Philanthropy and Jewish Affairs, Boxes 14–17.
Acc. 2126: Records of the Seagram Company Ltd: Record Group 2, Series I,
  Boxes 165 and 167.
Acc. 2173: Seagram Museum Collection, 1682-1997: Series 3, Boxes 67, 68,
  and 83.

Samuel and Saidye Bronfman Family Foundation Archives, Montreal
Lon Dubinsky, "Philanthropic Choices and Strategies for The CRB Founda-
  tion, the Samuel and Saidye Bronfman Family Foundation, The Joseph E.
  Seagram Company, Seagram Company Limited, and Claridge Investments,"
  21 June 1988.
John Hobday, "Towards Tomorrow," October 1983
Letters patent, Samuel and Saidye Bronfman Family Foundation, 29 Novem-
  ber 1952.
Samuel and Saidye Bronfman Family Foundation, Board of Directors, Board
  Books, 1975–2006
Samuel and Saidye Bronfman Family Foundation, Board of Directors, Minute
  Books, 1953–2006
Samuel and Saidye Bronfman Family Foundation Files, Storage, Boxes 3, 9,
  14, 21, 22, 31, and AB3 File.
Samuel and Saidye Bronfman Family Foundation Pink Donation Cards.

PUBLISHED SOURCES

Abella, Irving, and Harold Troper. *None Is Too Many: Canada and the Jews
  of Europe, 1933–1948.* Toronto: Key Porter Books, 3rd edition, 2000.
Ackerman, Marianne. "There's magic in the air at new Bronfman theatre."
  The Montreal Gazette, 6 September 1986.
Ackerman, Marianne. "Stage is set for a promising theatre season in Mon-
  treal." *The Montreal Gazette,* n.d.
Adam, Thomas, editor. *Philanthropy, Patronage and Civil Society: Experi-*

ences from Germany, Great Britain and North America. Bloomington, IN: Indiana University Press, 2004.

Allemang, John. "Standing Up for Arts Support." *En Route*, September 1982.

Andrews, F. Emerson. *Philanthropic Foundations.* New York: Russell Sage Foundation, 1956.

Arlett, Allan, editor. *A Canadian Directory to Foundations and Other Granting Agencies*, 3rd ed. Ottawa: Association of Universities and Colleges of Canada, 1973.

Arlett, Allan, and Ingrid Von Rotterdam. "The Power of Giving." *The Financial Post*, 9 March 1987.

Arnold, Janice. "Concordia University takes over Bronfman House." *Canadian Jewish News*, 16 September 1999.

Baader, Maria Benjamin. "Rabbinic Study, Self-Improvement, and Philanthropy: Gender and the Refashioning of Jewish Voluntary Associations in Germany, 1750-1870." In *Philanthropy, Patronage and Civil Society: Experiences from Germany, Great Britain and North America*, edited by Thomas Adams. Bloomington, IN: Indiana University Press, 2004.

Baum, Daniel Jay. *The Final Plateau: The Betrayal of Our Older Citizens.* Toronto: Burns & MacEachern Limited, 1974.

Bell, Celina. "Heritage Montreal reaches crossroads in its evolution." *The Montreal Gazette*, 3 April 1993

Blishen, Bernard R. "A Sociological Study of Three Philanthropic Financial Campaigns in Montreal." MA diss., McGill University, 1950.

Booth, Philip. "The Montreal Repertory Theatre, 1930–1961: A History and Handlist of Productions." MA diss., McGill University, 1989.

Bourbeau, Amélie. "La réorganisation de l'assistance chez les catholiques Montréalais: La Fédération des Oeuvres de charité canadiennes-françaises et la Federation of Catholic Charities, 1928–1974." Ph.D. diss., Université de Québec à Montréal, 2008.

Bovey, Edmund, and Joan Chalmers. *Funding of the Arts in Canada to the Year 2000.* Report of the Task Force. Ottawa, Supply and Services, 1986.

Brinkmann, Tobias. "Ethnic Difference and Civic Unity: A Comparison of Jewish Communal Philanthropy in Nineteenth-Century German and US Cities." In *Philanthropy, Patronage and Civil Society: Experiences from Germany, Great Britain and North America*, edited by Thomas Adams. Bloomington, IN: Indiana University Press, 2004.

Brison, Jeffrey D. *Rockefeller, Carnegie and Canada: American Philanthropy and the Arts and Letters in Canada.* Montreal & Kingston: McGill-Queen's University Press, 2005.

Bronfman, Edgar. *Good Spirits.* New York: G.P. Putnam's Sons, 1998.

Bronfman, Edgar. *The Making of a Jew.* New York: G.P. Putnam's Sons, 1996.

Bronfman, Saidye Rosner. *Recollections of My Life.* Printed privately, 1986.

Bronfman, Saidye Rosner. *My Sam.* Printed privately, 1982.

Brown, Jeremy. "Swann sits in gloom looking for a reason why he was sacked." *Toronto Star,* 2 June 1972.

Bumbaru, Dinu. "Heritage Montreal: Already in its Fifteenth Year, Yet Still Plenty to Do." *Bulletin of Heritage Montreal Foundation,* 4:4, Fall 1990.

"The Business of Giving." *The Economist,* 378:8466, 25 February 2006.

Canada Council for the Arts. "Bronfman Family Foundation endows John Hobday Awards in Arts Management." News Release, Ottawa, 23 May 2006.

Canada Council for the Arts. "The Evolution of the Canada Council's Support of the Arts." August 2007, www.canadacouncil.ca/canadacouncil.

Canada Council for the Arts. "Opening Proceedings." May 1957. Library of the Canada Council, 1957.

Canada Council for the Arts. "Saidye Bronfman Award to Become Part of the Governor General's Awards in Visual and Media Arts." News Release, Ottawa, 26 October 2006.

Canadian Association in Support of the Native Peoples. *Annual Report,* 1975.

Canadian Museum of Civilization. *Masters of the Crafts: Recipients of the Saidye Bronfman Award for Excellence in the Crafts, 1977–1986.* Hull, QC: Canadian Museum of Civilization, 1989.

Centre canadien d'architecture: Les débuts, 1979–1984 / Canadian Centre for Architecture: The First Five Years. Montreal: Centre canadien d'architecture/ Canadian Centre for Architecture, 1988.

Christie, Nancy and Michael Gauvreau. *A Full-Orbed Christianity: The Protestant Churches and Social Welfare in Canada, 1900–1940.* Montreal & Kingston: McGill-Queen's University Press, 1996.

Chodan, Lucinda. "Full roster at Bronfman Centre." *The Montreal Gazette,* 6 September 1986.

Cliche, D. "Status of the Artist or of Arts Organizations: A Brief Discussion on the Canadian Status of the Artist Act." *Canadian Journal of Communication* [on-line], 21 (2) 1996, cjc-online.ca.

Consumer and Corporate Affairs, Canada. "News Release," 14 June 1974.

Demchinsky, Brian, editor. Grassroots, *Greystones and Glass Towers: Montreal Urban Issues and Architecture.* Montreal: Véhicule Press, 1989.

Dickason, Olive Patricia. *Canada's First Nations: A History of Founding Peoples from Earliest Times.* Toronto: McClelland & Stewart, 1992.

Drabek, Jan. "The Greying of the Electorate." *The Globe and Mail,* 12 September 1988.

Drouin, Martin. Le combat du patrimoine à Montréal, 1973–2003. Quebec: Presses de l'Université du Québec, 2005.

Eisenthal, Bram D. "Saidye Bronfman, matriarch of Canadian Jewry, dies at ninety-eight." *Jewish Telegraphic Agency*, 1995.

Finkel, Alvin, and Margaret Conrad. *A History of the Canadian Peoples: 1867 to the Present*. Toronto: Copp Clark Pitman, Ltd., 1993.

First Annual Meeting of the Montreal Hebrew Philanthropic Society, printed in the *Occident and American Jewish Advocate*, vol.6, no.7, October 1848.

Flood, Sandra. "Canadian Craft: Change and Continuity." In Canadian Museum of Civilization, *Transformation: Prix Saidye Bronfman Award, 1977–1996*. Ottawa: Canadian Museum of Civilization, 1998.

Fong, William. *J.W. McConnell: Financier, Philanthropist, Patriot*. Montreal and Kingston: McGill-Queen's University Press, 2008.

Frisch, Ephraim. *An Historical Survey of Jewish Philanthropy from the Earliest Times to the Nineteenth Century*. New York: Macmillan and Co., 1924.

Frost, Stanley Brice. *McGill University: For the Advancement of Learning, Vol. II*. Montreal and Kingston: McGill-Queen's University Press, 1984.

Frumkin, Peter. *On Being Non-Profit: A Conceptual and Policy Primer*. Cambridge, Mass: Harvard University Press, 2002.

Frumkin, Peter. "Private Foundations as Public Institutions: Regulation, Professionalization, and the Redefinition of Organized Philanthropy." In *Philanthropic Foundations: New Scholarship, New Possibilities*, edited by Ellen Condliffe Lagemann. Bloomington, IN: Indiana University Press, 1999.

Frumkin, Peter. *Strategic Giving: The Art and Science of Philanthropy*. Chicago: University of Chicago Press, 2006.

Frumkin, Peter and Jonathan B. Imber, editors. *In Search of the Non-Profit Sector*. New Brunswick, NJ: Transaction Publishers, 2004.

Gabeline, Donna, Dane Lanken, and Gordon Pape. *Montreal at the Crossroads*. Montreal: Harvest House, 1975.

Galambos, Louis. "The Emerging Organizational Synthesis in Modern American History." *Business History Review* 45:3, Autumn 1970.

Galambos, Louis. "Technology, Political Economy, and Professionalization: Central Themes of the Organizational Synthesis." *Business History Review* 57, Winter 1983.

Gifford, C.E. *Canada's Fighting Seniors*. Toronto: James Lorimer & Co., 1990.

Gold, Muriel. *A Gift for Their Mother: The Saidye Bronfman Centre Theatre*. Westmount, Quebec: Miri Productions, 2007.

Goldenberg, Joel. "From Saidye to Segal." *The Suburban*, 6 June 2007.

Goldstein, Judith. *Crossing Lines: Histories of Jews and Gentiles in Three Communities*. New York: Morrow, 1992.

Goliger, Gabriella. "How the People of Milton-Parc Saved Their Neighborhood." *Habitat* 25:3, 1982.

Gordon, Alan. *Making Public Pasts: The Contested Terrain of Montreal's Public Memories, 1891–1930*. Montreal and Kingston: McGill-Queen's University Press, 2001.

Hall, Peter Dobkin. *Inventing the Nonprofit Sector*. Baltimore: Johns Hopkins University, 1992.

Handler, Richard. "On Having a Culture: Nationalism and the Preservation of Quebec's *Patrimonie*." In *Objects and Others: Essays on Museums and Material Culture*, edited by George W. Stocking Jr. Madison, WI: University of Wisconsin Press, 1985.

Handler, Richard. *Nationalism and the Politics of Culture in Quebec*. Madison, WI: University of Wisconsin Press, 1988.

Heron, Craig. *Booze: A Distilled History*. Toronto: Between the Lines, 2003.

Hodson, H.V., editor. *The International Foundation Directory*. Detroit: Gale Research Company, 4th edition, 1986.

Hulse, Joseph H, and David Spurgeon. "Triticale." *Scientific American* 231:2 (August 1974), 72–80.

Husock, Howard. "Family Foundation Governance at the J.M. Kaplan Fund." Kennedy School of Government Case Program, C14-99-1551.0, 1999.

Inglis, Stephen, and Kristin Rothschild. "Masters of the Crafts." In Canadian Museum of Civilization, *Masters of the Crafts: Recipients of the Saidye Bronfman Award for Excellence in the Crafts, 1977–1986*. Hull, QC: Canadian Museum of Civilization, 1989.

Jenkins, J. Craig, and Abigail Halcli. "Grassrooting the System?: The Development and Impact of Social Movement Philanthropy, 1953–1990." *Philanthropic Foundations: New Scholarship, New Possibilities*, edited by Ellen Condliffe Lagemann. Bloomington, IN: Indiana University Press, 1999.

Johnson, Paul. *A History of the Jews*. London: Weidenfeld & Nicolson, 1987.

Kane, Robert L. *A Will and a Way: What the United States Can Learn From Canada About Caring for the Elderly*. New York: Columbia University Press, 1985.

Kiger, Joseph C. *Philanthropists and Foundation Globalization*. New Brunswick (US) and London (UK): Transaction Publishers, 2008.

King, Joe. *From the Ghetto to the Main: The Story of the Jews of Montreal*. Montreal: Jewish Publications Society, 2001.

King, Joe. *Fabled City: The Jews of Montreal*. Montreal: Price-Patterson, 2009.

Kolber, Leo with L. Ian MacDonald. *Leo: A Life*. Montreal and Kingston: McGill-Queen's University Press, 2003.

Kuyek, Joan. "Reweaving the Fabric of Community." *Canada's Children*, Vol.3: No.1, Winter 1996: Children's Mental Health.

Lambert, Phyllis. Preface to *Transformation: Prix Saidye Bronfman Award 1977–1996*. Ottawa: Canadian Museum of Civilization, 1998.

Lambert, Phyllis and Robert Lemire. *Inventaire des bâtiments du Vieux Montréal: Du quartier Saint-Antoine et de la Ville de Maisonneuve construits entre 1880 et 1915*. Quebec: Centre de documentation, Service de l'inventaire des biens culturels, 1977.

Lockhart, Charles. *Protecting the Elderly: How Culture Shapes Social Policy*. University Park, PA: Pennsylvania State University Press, 2001.

Loewenberg, Frank M. *From Charity to Social Justice: The Emergence of Communal Institutions for the Support of the Poor in Ancient Judaism*. New Brunswick, NJ: Transaction Publishers, 2001.

Marcus, George E., editor. *Elites: Ethnographic Issues*. Albuquerque: University of New Mexico Press, 1983.

Marcus, George E. with Peter Dobkin Hall. *Lives in Trust: The Fortunes of Dynastic Families in Late Twentieth-Century America*. Boulder, San Francisco, Oxford: Westview Press, 1992.

Marrus, Michael Robert. *Mr Sam: The Life and Times of Samuel Bronfman*. Toronto: Viking Press, 1991.

Marsan, Jean-Claude. *Montreal in Evolution*. Montreal and Kingston: McGill-Queen's University Press, 1981.

Martin, Samuel A. *An Essential Grace*. Toronto: McClelland and Stewart, 1985.

Martin, Sandra. "A Tireless Champion of the Arts." *The Globe and Mail*, 11 December 2002.

Massey, Hart. Introduction to *The Craftsman's Way: Canadian Expressions*. Toronto: University of Toronto Press, 1981.

McClintock, Norah. "Canada's First Virtual Foundation." *Front & Centre*, January 1995.

McLeod, Ellen Easton. *In Good Hands: The Women of the Canadian Handicrafts Guild*. Montreal and Kingston: McGill-Queen's University Press, 1999.

Miller, John J. *A Gift of Freedom: How the John M. Olin Foundation Changed America*. San Francisco: Encounter Books, 2006.

Morgan, Dan. *Merchants of Grain*. New York: Viking Press, 1979.

Nelles, H.V. *The Art of Nation Building: Pageantry and Spectacle at Quebec's Tercentenary*. Toronto: University of Toronto Press, 1999.

Newman, Peter C. *Bronfman Dynasty: The Rothschilds of the New World*. Toronto: McClelland and Stewart, 1978.

Odendahl, Teresa. *Charity Begins at Home: Generosity and Self-Interest among the Philanthropic Elite*. New York: Basic Books, 1990.

Ostrander, Susan A. "When Grantees Become Grantors." In *Philanthropic*

Foundations: New Scholarship, New Possibilities, edited by Ellen Condliffe Lagemann. Bloomington, IN: Indiana University Press, 1999.

Ostry, Bernard. *The Cultural Connection: An Essay on Culture and Government Policy in Canada*. Toronto: McClelland and Stewart, 1978.

Paquet, Marion A., *A Handbook for Cultural Trustees: A Guide to the Role, Responsibilities and Functions of Boards of Trustees of Cultural Organizations in Canada*. University of Waterloo Press, 1987.

Penslar, Derek J. "The Origins of Modern Jewish Philanthropy." In *Philanthropy in the World's Traditions,* edited by Warren F. Ilchman, Stanley N. Katz, and Edward L. Queen II. Bloomington, IN: Indiana University Press, 1998.

Pitman, Walter. "ROM has the wrong kind of trustees." *Toronto Star*, 9 June 1972.

Putnam, Robert. *Bowling Alone: The Collapse and Revival of American Community*. New York: Simon & Schuster, 2000.

Rémillard, François, and Brian Merrett. *Mansions of the Golden Square Mile, Montreal, 1850–1930*. Montreal, Meridian Press, 1987.

Rogow, Faith. *Gone to Another Meeting: The National Council of Jewish Women, 1893–1993*. Tuscaloosa: University of Alabama Press, 1993.

Rosenberg, Louis. *Chronology of Canadian Jewish History*, National Bicentenary Committee of the Canadian Jewish Congress, 1959.

Ross, Aileen D. "Organized Philanthropy in an Urban Community." *Canadian Journal of Economics and Political Science*, 18:4, November, 1952.

Royal Commission on Aboriginal Peoples, Canada. *People to People, Nation to Nation: Highlights from the Report of the Royal Commission on Aboriginal Peoples*. Ottawa: Minister of Supply and Services Canada, 1996.

"Saidye Bronfman Centre Dedicated to Public." *Beacon*, 45:9, October, 1967.

Sarti, Robert. "Foundation takes steps to fix up sagging porches." *Vancouver Sun*, 1 October 1993.

Sealander, Judith. "Curing Evils at Their Source." In *Charity, Philanthropy, and Civility in American History,* edited by Lawrence J. Friedman and Mark D. McGarvie. Cambridge, UK: Cambridge University Press, 2003.

Semple, Neil. *The Lord's Dominion: The History of Canadian Methodism*. Montreal and Kingston: McGill-Queen's University Press, 1996.

Solomon, Jeffrey R. "Reinventing North American Jewish Communal Structures: The Crisis of Normality." *Journal of Jewish Communal Service*, Spring/Summer 2001.

Svanhuit, Gordon and Josie Svanhuit. *Charitable Donations in Canada*. Ottawa, 1949.

Taylor, C.J. *Negotiating the Past: The Making of Canada's National Historic Parks and Sites*. Montreal and Kingston: McGill-Queen's University Press, 1990.

Tippett, Maria. Making Culture: English-Canadian Institutions and the Arts before the Massey Commission. Toronto, Buffalo, London: University of Toronto Press, 1990.

Trépanier, Esther. *Jewish Painters and Modernity, Montreal 1930–1945*. Montreal: Saidye Bronfman Centre, 1987.

Troy, Gil. "A Saidye Reborn of Hope and Vision," *The Suburban*, 21 February 2007.

Tulchinsky, Gerald. *Taking Root: The Origins of the Canadian Jewish Community*. Toronto: Lester Publishing, 1992.

Tulchinsky, Gerald. *Branching Out: The Transformation of the Canadian Jewish Community*. Toronto: Lester Publishing, 1998.

Weaver, Jerry. "The Elderly as a Political Community: The Case of National Health Policy." *The Western Political Quarterly* 29:4, December 1976.

Weinrich, Peter. "A Very Short History of Craft." In Canadian Museum of Civilization, *Masters of the Crafts: Recipients of the Saidye Bronfman Award for Excellence in the Crafts, 1977–1986*. Hull, QC: Canadian Museum of Civilization, 1989.

Weinstein, Rhona S. "Reflections on Becoming a Community Psychiatrist." In *Six Community Psychologists Tell Their Stories: History, Contexts and Narrative,* edited by James G. Kelly and Anna V. Song. New York: Routledge, 2004.

Weintraub, William. *City Unique: Montreal Days and Nights in the 1940s and 50s*. Toronto: McClelland and Stewart Inc., 1996.

Whitaker, Ben. *The Foundations: An Anatomy of Philanthropy and Society*. London: Eyre Methuen, 1974.

Wilson, R.D. and Eric McLean. *The Living Past of Montreal*. Montreal and Kingston: McGill-Queen's University Press, 1976.

Wright, Robin and Lindsay John. *National Arts and Youth Demonstration Project*. McGill University: School of Social Work, 2004.

Ziegler, Warren. *Enspirited Envisioning: A Guidebook to the Enspiriting Approach to the Future*. Denver: Enspiriting Press, LLC., 1996.

INDEX

for, 6, 13, 56–60, 221, 223–4;
graphic arts, 87; performing arts, 87;
private foundations and, 78, 102,
123; Gisele Rucker and, 127; SSBFF
programs for, 7–9, 61, 86–90, 105,
121, 190, 221, 313. *See also* arts administration, arts stabilization,
Canada Council, crafts, cultural
management, National Arts, Saidye
Bronfman Centre, and Youth
Demonstration Project
arts administration and the Association of Cultural Executives, 223; at
the Banff School of Fine Arts, 223–4;
and the Bovey-Chalmers Report,
224–6; and the Canada Council 223,
226; at Confederation College, 227;
and Donner Canadian Foundation,
78; at the Ecole des hautes études
commerciales, 227, 229, 233; learning on the job, 222–3; as an MBA
program, 227; national organization
for, 223; and Peter Swann, 87, 90,
99, 225; at the University of California, 222; at the University of Waterloo, 225, 227–35; at York
University, 223. *See also* Canadian
Association of Arts Administration
Educators, cultural management
Arts Administrator Distance Learning
Project (AADLP), 229, 232–3
arts stabilization: and the Alberta Performing Arts Stabilization Fund,
237–8, 240; in the Atlantic
Provinces, 237–9, 241–2; in the Bay
Area, 239, 241; and Peter Brown,
236–9; and the Canadian Arts and
Heritage Sustainability Program,
241; and the Canadian Arts Stabi-
lization Program (CASP), 237–8; and
Canadian Heritage (Department of),

237–41; and the Chalmers Foundation, 237; and François Colbert,
239; and Sheila Copps, 239–41; and
the Council for Business and the Arts
in Canada, 237–8; and Cultural Affairs (Ministry of), 241; and the
Ecole des hautes études commerciales, 239; and Diane Hoar, 237–9;
and John Hobday, 235–42; impact
on the arts, 235; and Hubert Lussier,
239; and Herb Metcalfe, 240; national program for, 237; and the Ontario Arts Council, 238; opposition
to, 237–8, 241–2; and Marion Paquet, 239; on the Prairies, 237, 239,
241–2; purpose of, 236; in Quebec,
237, 239, 241; and Victor Rabinovitch, 239; and Eileen Sarkar, 239;
SSBFF program, 15, 221, 235–42,
308; and Peter Swann, 236; in
Toronto, 237–8, 241–2; and the
Vancouver Arts Stabilization Program, 237–8. *See also* National Arts
Stabilization Fund
Art Stabilization Fund Saskatchewan,
242
Association of Canadian Universities
for Northern Studies, 93
Association of Cultural Executives,
223
L'association de soutien et de diffusion
d'art, 42, 108
A View from the Bridge, 184
awards: art, 57; drama, 57–8; Gover-
nor General, 58, 288–90, 309; im-
pact of, 280; John Hobday award,
309–10; literary, 58; music, 57; for
Dora Wasserman, 182; Yechiel and
Mindel Bronfman Scholarship, 63.
See also Saidye Bronfman Award for
Excellence in the Crafts

non-family board members, 294;
reasons for participating in SSBFF, 4,
115, 291–3; recollections of grandparents, 117; replaces Charles on
SSBFF board, 117; and the Saidye
Bronfman Award for Excellence in
the Crafts, 289; and the Saidye
Bronfman Centre, 177–8, 180–2,
185, 189; as SSBFF president, 310;
and the Stephen Bronfman Foundation, 307–8; and Urban Issues, 272
Bronfmans, third generation: leadership of the SSBFF, 291–3; reasons
for participating in SSBFF, 4, 15,
291–3
Bronfman, Yechiel, 19–21, 32
Bronfman Guest Lecture Series, University of Toronto, 130
Bronfman family and business world,
4; and CEMP, 3, 112–13, 161–2;
fame of, 4, 7; as immigrants from
Russia, 18–19; name, 109, 160, 166,
168, 174–5, 185–6, 189, 284; and
philanthropy, 7, 23; social class of,
17, 30–31; support for the SSBFF,
14–15, 114–17, 121; wealth of, 7.
See also Montreal Jewish Community, Saidye Bronfman Centre
Brown, Peter, 237–9
Bumbaru, Dinu, 255–6, 259, 262

Cadillac Fairview Corporation and
Matthew Bronfman, 112; and Phyllis Lambert, 248; sale of, 113, 117
Canada: constitutional issues, 136–7;
first foundation in, 53; heritage
preservation in, 244–5; immigration
policy, 18, 30; wealth, 51–2
Canada Business Corporations Act,
77–8
Canada Council: and arts administration, 224, 226; and Samuel Bronfman, 61; and crafts, 278, 281, 287–
90; creation of, 59; grants to artists,
71–2, 221; and John Hobday, 226,
289, 306–9; and Cecil Rabinovitch,
176; and Nancy Rosenfeld, 309–10;
and Gisele Rucker, 127; and Saidye
Bronfman Award, 15, 278, 287–8,
310; and the Saidye Bronfman
Centre, 174; and Robert Sirman,
289; and A.W. Trueman, 164
Canada Mortgage and Housing
Corporation, 209
Canada's Atlantic Provinces: and arts
stabilization, 237–9, 240–2; and
learning disabilities, 197; and seniors,
204; study for McGill University
Children's Learning Centre, 192–3;
submit few proposals to SSBFF, 136;
Urban Issues projects in, 272
Canada's centenary: and Expo 67, 162;
as occasion for public building, 72
Canada's native peoples (First Nations):
and Canadian Arctic Resources
Committee (CARC), 90; and Canadian Association in Support of the
Native Peoples, 91–2; and crafts,
279; and Donner Canadian Foundation, 78; government policy toward,
90–1; and historic sites, 245; land
claims, 71, 92; marginalized position
of, 71, 92; SSBFF programs for, 7,
71, 86–8, 90–3, 95, 105, 121
Canadian Arctic Resources Committee
(CARC), 91
Canadian Arts and Heritage Sustainability Program (CAHSP), 240–2
Canadian Arts Council, 59. See also
Canadian Conference of the Arts
Canadian Arts Stabilization Program,
237–40
Canadian Association for Arts Administration Educators (CAAAE), 221,

Canadian Heritage (Department of PCH): and arts stabilization, 237–41; creation of, 136–7; and the Cultural Management Institute, 234–5; and Alex Himmelfarb, 296; and the John Hobday Award, 310; and Judith Laroque 298; and Hubert Lussier, 234, 239; and the National Arts and Youth Demonstration Project, 296–8; and Victor Rabinovitch, 239; and Eileen Sarkar, 239

Canadian identity: Britishness, 71; desire for, 88; and Expo 67, 162; and Quebec nationalism, 136–7. *See also* Canadian Understanding

Canadian International Development Agency, 66

Canadian Jewish Committee for Refugees (CJCR), 37

Canadian Jewish Congress and Canadian identity, 38; Samuel Bronfman president of, 36, 61–2; headquarters, 63, 72, 114, 159; the JIAS, 30; and origins, 30; Matthew Ram, 81; and the war effort, 37; and Zionism, 30, 32, 36–7, 41

Canadian Museum of Civilization and the fine crafts gallery, 283; and Stephen Inglis, 283–4; and Masters of the Crafts, 284–5; new location in Hull, Quebec, 283. *See also* Saidye Bronfman Award for Excellence in the Crafts

Canadian Museums Committee, 58

Canadian North and Canadian Arctic Resources Committee, 91; problems of, 71, 86, 91; SSBFF program for, 87–8, 90–3, 105

Canadian Pensioners Concerned, 205

Canadian philanthropy: literature on, 6; political challenges, 73; rise of,

51–9; and scientific research, 65; theory of, 6

Canadian prairies: arts stabilization project for, 237–42; Bronfmans origins on, 13, 17–19, 32, 67, 305; Jewish colonies on, 18–19; landscape, 301, 305; Rosners origins on, 19–21, 300, 305; Urban Issues project for, 272

Canadian Social Science Research Council, 58–9

Canadian society: defining needs of, 4, 14, 70, 80, 82, 86, 121–2, 202; diversity of, 71, 88, 259; francophone, 71, 136; "mosaic," 71, 90, 162; postwar, 70–71; priorities of, 76; social change within, 4, 8, 10, 17, 70, 124, 203; SSBFF and, 4, 10, 13, 79, 115, 294, 307

Canadian Technion Society, 109

Canadian Understanding (SSBFF program), 106–7

Canadian Welfare Council, 37

Cardinal, Donna: and the Handbook for Cultural Trustees, 225; and visioning workshops, 131

Carnegie, Andrew: and education, 49; foundation, 48–50; motivations for philanthropy, 48; and wealth, 49, 52

Carnegie Corporation: history of 47–50; and social movement philanthropy, 105; support for Canadian culture, 58–9

CEMP: and Bronfman family, 3, 112; creation of, 44; dissolution of, 112–13; and the Saidye Bronfman Centre, 161–2, 170; and SSBFF, 103, 313; success of, 88, 113; and the Van Horne house, 250

Centraide, 211

Centre for Cultural Management

(CCM): and the Arts Administrator Distance Learning Project, 229–30, 232–3; and David Barr, 234; and Canadian Heritage, 234–5; and François Colbert, 234; and the Cultural Management Institute, 232–5; and James Downey, 233; evaluation of, 230, 232; and the Floyd S. Chalmers Foundation, 229; French program in, 233–5; and Hautes études commerciales, 233–5; and Imperial Oil, 229; and David Johnston, 234; and the McConnell Family Foundation, 229–30; and the McLean Foundation, 229; and Michael McDonald, 228; and Mobil Canada, 229; and Mavor Moore, 227; and Marion Paquet, 229–30; and William Poole, 132, 230–5; and the Richard Ivey Foundation, 229; SSBFF client, 125, 132, 221, 227–35; and John Stubbs, 227, 230; at the University of Waterloo, 228–30; and Douglas Wright, 227; and the visioning workshops (Elora), 231. *See also* arts administration, Canadian Association of Arts Administration Educators, cultural management, John Hobday Award

Centre for the Great Lakes, 129

Centres Offering Independent Lifestyles, 195

Centro Internacional de Mejoramiento de Maiz y Trigo (CIMMYT), 65–6

Chalifoux, Thelma, 219

Chalmers, Floyd and Jean, 285

Chalmers, Joan: and the Bovey-Chalmers Report, 225–6; and Woodlawn Arts Foundation, 285–6

Chantier de l'économie sociale, 294

Charlottetown: art school in, 57;

learning disabilities workshop in, 196. *See also* Confederation Centre

Charity: Catholic attitudes towards, 25; from individuals, 55; Jewish attitudes towards, 25–6, 28, 31; Protestant attitudes towards, 25, 48–9; and public welfare, 25, 28, 34–5; role of women in, 29; social aspect of, 25. *See also* philanthropy

Charles R. Bronfman Foundation: and Canadianism, 108; creation of, 108; and Lon Dubinsky's study, 122, 124; headquarters, 112–13; and Jewish people, 108

Chicago: and the Illinois Institute of Technology, 162; and Phyllis Lambert, 42–3, 69, 79, 247; urban renewal in, 247

Children at Risk, 196

Children for Peace: Youth Nuclear Disarmament Tour, 129–30

Children's Learning Centre. *See also* McGill University Children's Learning Centre

Chrétien, Jean, 136–7, 181, 307

City Magazine, 265

Claridge Inc: art collection, 178; creation of, 112; donation program, 124; headquarters, 112–13; and SSBFF, 112–13, 122, 257, 306–7, 313; and Stephen Bronfman Foundation, 308

Cliche-Spénard, Monique, 285

Cohen, Ari, 181

Cohen, Maxwell, 91

Colbert, François, 234–5, 239

Combined Jewish Appeal: and Charles Bronfman, 79–80; Samuel Bronfman and, 39–40, 62; and Israel, 41, 64; origins, 39–40; and refugees, 40–41; SSBFF donation to, 8–9, 13, 41,

John Hobday, 221–4, 227–30, 232–4; international conference in Helsinki, 234; as a legacy program, 308; national organization for, 223–6; as a profession, 222–3; SSBFF program, 15, 57, 90, 105–6, 131–2, 135, 221–2, 224–35, 242, 258–9, 271, 309, 312; and Peter Swann, 221, 223–5; and visioning workshops (Elora), 231–2. *See also* arts administration, Centre for Cultural Management

Cultural Management Institute: distance learning, 232–5, 242; French-language component, 233–5

Cultural Property Act (Quebec), 249

Dalhousie University, Halifax, 264, 267

Dalibard, Jacques, 259

Dancyger, Alain: and Les Grands Ballets Canadiens, 183; and the Saidye Bronfman Centre, 179–80, 183

Davis, Mortimer Barnett, 28, 30

de Gunzburg, Alain, 42

de Gunzburg, Charles, 42, 111, 181

de Gunzburg, Jean, 42: advises against supporting medical research, 131; education, 111; Investment Committee, 115; joins the SSBFF board, 107, 111, 119; and One Voice, 219–20; reasons for participating in SSBFF, 4; and the Saidye Bronfman Centre, 186; as SSBFF president, 293–4, 297, 309; and Urban Issues, 261, 272, 274

de Gunzburg, Minda: and the *Association de soutien et de diffusion d'art* (ASDA), 42, 62, 108; at Samuel Bronfman's eightieth birthday, 69; and CEMP, 44; death of, 110, 112; determining the SSBFF's focus, 79–

80, 85; education of, 31, 42; at formation of SSBFF, 60; and the Jewish community, 9, 86, 95; letter to, 110, 113; marriage to Alain de Gunzburg, 42; in Paris, 42, 107–8; reasons for participating in SSBFF, 4, 79–80; relationship with Saidye Bronfman, 62; and the Saidye Bronfman Centre, 160; selecting SSBFF programs, 86–7, 90

Depression of the 1930s: and the arts, 58; Bronfmans' activities during, 17, 34–5, 46; and charitable giving, 50; and the Jewish community, 34–5, 170–1; and labour movement, 34; and McConnell Foundation, 54; and public welfare, 28, 56

Development of the Arts and Culture in Canada (SSBFF program), 105–6

Distillers Corporation Limited. *See also* Seagram

Dominion Drama Festival: Governor General's Literary Awards, 58; and the Massey Foundation, 53; Negro Theatre Guild wins prize at, 163

Donnellan, Kevin, 210

Donner Canadian Foundation, 78

Dora Wasserman Endowment for Jewish Culture, 182

Doré, Jean, 255

Doucet, Louise, 285

Downey, James, 233

Dubinsky, Lon, 120, 122–5

Dufferin, Earl of, 57

Dunn, James, 60n46

Dunton, Nancy, 256

Ecole des Beaux Arts, Montreal, 164

Ecole des hautes études commerciales (HEC), Montreal: and arts management, 227, 229, 233–5; and arts

Hobday, John: approach to philanthropy, 97, 103–4, 119, 120–2, 137,
312; and arts programs, 105, 221–2;
and arts stabilization, 235–41;
award, 309–10; background, 99–
100; and the Canadian Conference
of the Arts, 99–100, 105, 222; and
the CBC, 100; and the Charlottetown
Confederation Centre, 100; and
community foundations, 138; and
crafts, 279, 282–4, 286–9; and cultural management, 223, 226–30,
232–4; as gatekeeper to the board,
128; as head of the Canada Council,
307, 309; and Heritage Canada,
251–2; and Heritage Montreal, 251–
2, 255; hired as executive director,
14, 99, 103; and learning disabilities, 105, 196, 199–200; and the
McGill Children's Learning Centre,
193–5; and the National Arts and
Youth Demonstration Project, 296–
8; and native peoples, 93, 105; and
the Neptune Theatre, 100; and One
Voice, 206–8, 211, 214–9; and Plum
Coulee, 300, 302–3; and Preparing
for the Nineties, 128–9; promotes
national advocacy organizations, 5,
10, 14, 97, 105, 121, 136; promotes
new SSBFF programs, 105–6, 122–6,
129; and the Saidye Bronfman Centre, 168, 170–2, 174–80, 182, 184,
186–7; and Seagram, 99–103, 116,
306; and seniors, 105, 204–8; and
the theatre, 99–100; and Toward Tomorrow, 106–7, 168, 193, 204, 224;
and Urban Issues, 260, 265; and the
visioning workshops, 132, 134; and
winding down the SSBFF, 306–9. *See
also* arts stabilization, cultural management, learning disabilities, One
Voice, Saidye Bronfman Award for
Excellence in Crafts, Saidye Bronfman Centre, Urban Issues
Holland, Gerry, 206–8
l'hôpital Sainte-Justine, Montreal, 195
Hopper, Robin, 282, 285
Hull, Quebec, 206
Humanities Research Council of
Canada, 59
Human Resources Development
Canada (HRDC), 215, 296, 298

Illinois Institute of Technology,
Chicago, 162
Imperial Oil, 229
Income Tax Act of 1930, 55
Income Tax Act of 1976, 78
Indian History Film Project, University
of Regina, 93
Industrial Areas Foundation (IAF),
272
International Council on Monuments
and Sites (ICOMOS), 256
International Development Research
Centre, Ottawa, 66
International Federation on Ageing,
211, 214–15, 218
Island Arts and Heritage Stabilization
Program, 242
Israel: Bronfmans' support for, 13,
40–1, 47, 63–4, 110; and Charles
Bronfman, 117; and charitable
groups, 50; and Guardian's Dinner,
63; and Hebrew University, 63; Jew-
ish Institute for the Blind, 63; Manu-
facturers Association, 63; Maritime
League, 63; Museum, 64; Negev
Dinner, 63; and United Israel Appeal,
64; and United Palestine Appeal,
40–41
Israel Museum, 64, 109

National Film Board, 59, 164

National Gallery of Canada: creation of, 57; and Phyllis Lambert, 227; and the Massey Foundation, 53; and Ottawa's Rideau Street Convent Chapel, 252.

National Museum of Canada, 57, 167, 283. *See also* Canadian Museum of Civilization

National Museum of Man. *See* Canadian Museum of Civilization

National Museums: criticisms of, 227; Task Force, 225

National Longitudinal Survey of Children and Youth, 298

national organizations: for arts stabilization, 236–40; for children, 196–7; for crafts, 282, 286; for cultural management, 131, 224; difficulties creating, 58; government encourages, 58, 73, 136; for heritage preservation, 245, 251; Hobday promotes, 5, 10, 104–5, 120–1, 136, 193, 282, 286; for learning disabilities, 131, 196–7; for seniors, 15, 131, 204–6, 218; SSBFF's clients as, 120, 130–1, 204; and Urban Issues, 244, 268–70, 276–7

National Retired Teachers Association (NRTA), 206–7

National Transportation Agency, 208

National Trust for Historic Preservation (USA), 251

native peoples. *See* Canada's native peoples

Neamtan, Nancy, 294

Needles, Jane, 172–3

Negro Theatre Guild, Montreal, 163

Neptune Theatre, Halifax, 100

Neumann, Ernst, 164

New Brunswick: and arts stabilization, 238–9, 241–2; Foundation, 242; Senior Citizens' Federation, 204–5, 211

New Democratic Party, 208

Newman, Peter C., 7

New York: Edgar Bronfman in, 43–4, 69, 79, 107; Matthew Bronfman in, 111, 292; as immigrant destination, 24; Jewish community of, 79, 169; Seagram offices in, 23, 42–3, 112, 291

Ngan, Wayne, 285

Nolin, Marie-Paule, 247

non-profit organizations: in the arts and heritage, 225–6; and Canadian law, 73, 78; changes to, 138; in hard times, 104, 211; for housing, 252; national character of, 136; rise of, 74; Saidye Bronfman Centre as, 169; seeking funding, 105–6

North American Fund for Environmental Cooperation (NAFEC), 270

North Hatley (Quebec), 259–60, 264–9, 275

Nova Scotia and arts stabilization, 238–9, 241

"Oaklands": Bronfman family home, 30–1, 178; Saidye Bronfman as hostess, 33; and philanthropic activity, 31, 33, 35, 40, 42; sale of, 306; SSBFF meetings held at, 84

Oberlander, Cornelia, 261

Oberlander, Judy: background, 261–2; as consultant for Urban Issues, 261–3, 265, 268, 274; on Urban Issues steering committee, 260; at visioning workshop, 259

O'Brien, Philip, 263

63; built for Canada's centenary, 72; and the McConnell Foundation, 87

Peck, Alice, 279

Peres, Shimon, 41

Philanthropy: in Canada, 6, 13, 51–9; and education, 49, 52; Jewish traditions of, 25, 48; political challenges to, 73, 103; Protestant traditions of, 25, 48–9, postwar decline, 72; purpose of, 3–4, 10, 48; in Quebec, 138; and self-improvement, 48–9; and social change, 4, 10; socially driven, 35, 117; tax incentives for, 48, 51, 55; in the United States, 13, 46–51; versus charity, 48, 50, 81–2; women and, 57, 61–2. *See also* charity, corporate philanthropy, foundations, SSBFF

Phillips, Lazarus, 44

Phillips, May, 279

Pillar, Heinar, 100

Placemaking in Canadian Cities, 276

Plum Coulee: and the Agricore grain elevator, viii, 300–2, 304–5; centenary committee, 299; Community Foundation, 302; cultural diversity of, 20, 299–300; Heritage and Recreation Development Corporation, 302; and the Heritage Square, 300–1, 304; and Elmer Hildebrand, 303, 305; festivities, 20; and Gary Hilderman, 300–5; and John Hobday, 300, 302–3; and Phyllis Lambert, 299–300, 303, 305; and Main Avenue Streetscaping, 301, 304; and the Manitoba government, 300, 303; media coverage, 304–5; and Pathways 2000, 299–300; Plum Festival, 303; and Kim Porte, 303; public square, 20; and Nancy Rosenfeld, 305; Rosner family in, 20–21, 32,

299, 303–5; and the Saidye Rosner Bronfman Heritage and Recreation Park, 304–5; and Avery Schulz, 300, 302–4; SSBFF project, 15–16, 292, 300–5, 308; swimming facilities in, 21, 301, 304; and the Thomas Sill Foundation, 305; and the Wild Plum Café, 301

Plus (SSBFF program), 95, 110

Poole, William, 132; and the Centre for Cultural Management, 230–5

Porte, Kim, 303

Potvin, Rose, 254

poverty: and Catholic Church, 55; relief of, 25–6, 28, 35, 40, 54

Powning, Peter, 289

Preparing for the Nineties, 128–9

Prince Edward Island and arts stabilization, 241–2

private sector: in Canada, 6, 72; funding for the arts, 72, 120; versus public, 46, 137

Prohibition, 21–2

Project Focus, 130–1. *See also* Vision 2020

Protestant school system in Quebec: and Jews, 27–8, 126; and the Learning Centre, 192; and W.C. Macdonald, 52

Quebec: and arts stabilization, 237, 239, 241; and heritage preservation, 244–6; Urban Issues projects in, 272

Quebec Association for Children with Learning Disabilities, 190, 197

Quebec City: and Ile d'Orléans, 245; tercentenary celebrations, 244–5;

Quebec government: and the CCA, 257; and culture, 73; and education, 72; and the French language, 73; and heritage preservation, 245–6;